Nuer Dilemmas

Nuer Dilemmas

Coping with Money, War, and the State

SHARON E. HUTCHINSON

University of California Press

BERKELEY LOS ANGELES LONDON

University of California Press
Berkeley and Los Angeles, California

University of California Press, Ltd.
London, England

Parts of this book were published in earlier versions.
Prologue: "War through the Eyes of the Dispossessed: Three Stories of Survival," *Disasters* 15, no. 2 (1992): 166–71. Reprinted by permission of Blackwell Publishers.
Chapter 3: "The Cattle of Money and the Cattle of Girls among the Nuer, 1930–83," *American Ethnologist* 19, no. 2 (1992): 294–316. Reprinted by permission of the American Anthropological Association. Not for sale or further reproduction.
Chapter 4: "Rising Divorce among the Nuer, 1936–1983," *Man* 25 (1990): 393–411. Reprinted by permission of the Royal Anthropological Institute of Great Britain and Ireland.
" 'Dangerous to Eat': Rethinking Pollution States among the Nuer of Sudan," *Africa* 62, no. 4 (1992): 490–504. Reprinted by permission of the International African Institute.
Chapter 5: "Changing Concepts of Incest among the Nuer," *American Ethnologist* 12, no. 4 (1985): 625–41. Reprinted by permission of the American Anthropological Association. Not for sale or further reproduction.
The translation of "Strutting with My Rifle" is reprinted from Terese Svoboda, *Cleaned the Crocodile's Teeth: Nuer Song* (New York: Greenfield Press, 1985), by permission of Terese Svoboda.

Library of Congress Cataloging-in-Publication Data

Hutchinson, Sharon Elaine, 1952–
    Nuer dilemmas : coping with money, war, and the state / Sharon E. Hutchinson.
       p.   cm.
    "A Centennial book"—
    Includes bibliographical references (p.   ) and index.
    ISBN 0-520-08869-7 (acid-free paper). — ISBN 0-520-20284-8 (pbk. : acid-free paper)
    1. Nuer (African people)—Social conditions.   2. Nuer (African people)—Economic conditions.   3. Nuer (African people)—Politics and government.   4. Sudan—Ethnic relations.   5. Sudan—Politics and government.   I. Title.
DT155.2.N85H88   1996
962.4'004965—dc20   95-1248
                                                                  CIP
Printed in the United States of America
9 8 7 6 5 4 3

To all "black peoples" of Sudan: May your continuing struggles for justice and equality unite and strengthen you.

The publisher gratefully acknowledges the generous contribution provided by the General Endowment Fund of the Associates of the University of California Press.

Contents

Illustrations

Photographs

Maps

Figures

Acknowledgments

While I alone am responsible for whatever errors or intellectual weaknesses this book demonstrates, I cannot take full credit for the book's strengths. This book owes a great deal to many, many other people, whose generous offers of advice, assistance, hospitality, and friendship have sustained both me and this research project over the past fourteen years. I am deeply grateful to them all, but in particular I would like to thank the following for their encouragement, comments, kindnesses, and inspirations: Lila Abu-Lughod, Abdel Ghaffar M. Ahmed, David Deng Athorbei, Mark Auslander, Edward Ayom Bol, Thomas Beidelman, James Goanar Chol, Jean and John Comaroff, Michael Wal Duany, Francis Mading Deng, Steven Feierman, James Ferguson, James Mabor Gatkuoth, the late Peter Gatkuoth Gual, Gabriel Giet Jal, John Ruac Jal Wang, the late Paul P. Howell, Wendy James, Douglas Johnson, Ivan Karp, Maria Lepowsky, the late Godfrey Lienhardt, Riäk Machar Teny, Bona Malwal, Andrew Mawson, John Middleton, David Kek Moinydet, the late Kelual Nyinyar Rik and his extended family, Gabriel Gai Riam, John Ryle, the late Paul Riesman, Harold Scheffler, Norman and Bethany Singer, Raymond Smith, Marilyn Strathern, Angelina Teny, Sarah Nyadak Toang, Terence Turner, Richard and Pnina Werbner, Philip Winters, and Stephen Abraham Yar. I also gratefully acknowledge the many loving ways in which my late father, David Hutchinson, my sister, Nancy Hutchinson, and her husband, Bob Dunn, have supported me throughout the lengthy gestation period of this book.

Financial support for this project was initially provided by a generous grant from the Social Science Research Council and the American Council of Learned Societies through their International Dissertation Fellowship Program (1980–83). The vast majority of field and archival research contained in this book was carried out during this period. Two additional months of field research carried out during early 1990 were made possible by a grant from the Yale Center for International and Area Studies, supplemented by smaller grants from the Social Science Faculty Research Fund and A. Whitney Griswold Fund, both of Yale University. I also gratefully acknowledge the institutional support of Save the Children (UK), the National Endowment for the Humanities (Summer Stipend Program), and the Graduate School of the University of Wisconsin-Madison for having made my 1992 research trip into the southern war zone possible. I am also deeply thankful to the Department of Social Anthropology at the University of Manchester and the Royal Anthropological Institute for having awarded me the 1992–93 Leach/RAI Fellowship, which—in combination with a Senior Fellowship from the American Council of Learned Societies—enabled me to complete the writing of this book in the company of an exceptionally stimulating and congenial group of friends and scholars at the University of Manchester.

But above all, I am indebted to the many hundreds of rural Nuer men, women, and children who so graciously welcomed me into their homes and lives: May this book stand as an enduring tribute of the profound respect and esteem I hold for them. Last, I wish to thank my lovely children, Jasmine and Teddy (alias Nyajal and Lunyjɔk), for their boundless affection, energy, cheerfulness, and patience. They have kept me both human and in good humor throughout the writing process of this book.

A Note on the
Nuer Language

As a native English speaker, I find the seeming airy lightness and rich melodic qualities of the Nuer language to be attractive. The language contains few "hard" consonants—and those that do exist are often softened or silenced at the ends of words. A terminal 'k', for instance, often slides into a breathy 'gh' sound (represented by the ɣ) or a lighter 'h' sound or is suppressed entirely. This is especially true of the western dialect. Similarly, the letter 'c' in Nuer is never pronounced like the English 'c' in "cat" but, rather, as a soft 'ch' sound that often softens to either a 'sh' (ç) or an 'i' sound when serving as the terminal consonant of various words and stems. Another softening feature of the Nuer language—as perceived, of course, by a native English speaker—is the existence of four different 'n'-like consonants: an interdental 'n' (written as 'nh'), a standard English or alveolar 'n', a palatal 'ny', and a guttural 'ng' (also written as ŋ). The appealing "airiness" of the language stems from the fact that many Nuer vowels are heavily aspirated—that is, they are released with an audible bit of breath as in the English 'hi' and 'hea' in "behind" and "ahead." Indeed, one of the earliest obstacles I faced in trying to learn the language was to hear and to control the voice's "breathiness" or "nonbreathiness" in the pronunciation of various Nuer vowels. The pronounced and fluctuating intonation patterns of the language also presented hidden challenges: Nuer is "tonal" in that the relative musical pitches of words and particles can bear both lexical and grammatical significance.[1] Add to these linguistic subtleties regional complexities of dialect—and, most problematic of all, the lack of any standardized orthography for the Nuer vowel system—and one can begin to imagine, I think, some of the difficult decisions I have faced in

1. Two other features of the Nuer language may be of interest to English speakers. There are no gendered pronouns corresponding to "he," "she," and "it," only the single form jɛn. There are three distinct forms of "we": a dual inclusive form (I and you singular, kɔɔn), a plural inclusive form (I and you plural, kɔɔn); and a plural exclusive form (I and he or they, kɔn). Although these first two pronouns appear identical when standing alone, they are clearly distinguished in their possessive and verbally conjugated forms.

attempting to transfer my aural and oral knowledge of the language onto the printed page. The fact that Crazzolara's *Outline of a Nuer Grammar* (1933) identifies eleven distinctive vowels (without indicating aspiration) while the Nuer translation of the New Testament specifies seventeen (indicating aspiration) and Kiggen's *Nuer-English Dictionary* (1948) only seven (without indicating aspiration) has not helped matters. Moreover, these problems are only compounded when one begins to grapple with the numerous diphthongs and triphthongs characterizing the Nuer language. All of this is to say that there is no standardly accepted "right way" to spell many of the Nuer words contained in this book. Nevertheless, I have taken considerable care to indicate as best I could the relative length and aspiration values of various Nuer vowels. I have made no attempt, however, to indicate tones—the one exception being that I have added the symbol '/' to indicate the very high tone used to differentiate the negative particles of present-tense verbs (/ci, /caa, translated here as "not") from the identically spelled, lower-tone particles marking the positive past tense (ci, caa). To reduce strain on the reader, I have preserved commonly used English spellings for many Nuer personal names (particularly those belonging to the educated elite) and regional groupings in the main body of the text. However, I have also provided more accurate Nuer transliterations of these names—when notably different from Anglicized spellings—upon their first appearance in the text.

What follows, then, is a brief pronunciation guide for the orthography adopted. The Nuer consonants (and their English equivalents) are: 'b', 'c' (as in "chin"), 'd', 'dh' (as in "this"), 'g', 'ɣ' (a sounded velar fricative sometimes represented as 'gh') 'h', 'j', 'k', 'l', 'm', 'n', 'nh' (the interdental 'n'), 'ny' (the palatal 'n', pronounced like the French 'gn' in "Boulogne"), 'ŋ' (the guttural 'n', also written as 'ng' and pronounced as in "sing"), 'p' (which sometimes relaxes into a 'pf' sound), 'r' (trilled or rolled), 't', 'th' (as in "thin"), 'w', and 'y'. The basic vowels (which will be doubled to indicate greater length) are listed below.

i is nonaspirated and sounds like the English 'e' in "see"
i̱ is the aspirated or breathy version of 'i'
e is nonaspirated and sounds like the English 'e' in "bell"
e̱ is the aspirated version of 'e'
ë lies between 'i' and 'e', is aspirated and sounds like the French 'é' in *été*
ɛ is nonaspirated and sounds like the English 'e' in pet
ɛ̱ is the aspirated version of 'ɛ'

ä is always aspirated and sounds like the English 'u' in "luck"

a is nonaspirated and sounds like the English 'a' in "father" or "far"

a̠ is the aspirated version of 'a'

ɔ is nonaspirated and sounds like the English 'aw' in "law"

ɔ̠ is the aspirated version of 'ɔ'

o is nonaspirated and sounds like the English 'oa' in "boat"

o̠ is the aspirated version of 'o'

ö is always aspirated and sounds like the English 'u' in "put"

u is always aspirated and sounds like the English 'oo' in "fool"

(Two other vowels that are sometimes differentiated in written Nuer are ɛ̈, which sounds like the English 'a' in "bat" and is represented here as ɛa, and 'ï', which is a more centralized 'i' sound and is ignored.)

For the transliteration of italicized Arabic terms I have followed Hans Wehr's *A Dictionary of Modern Written Arabic* (edited by J. Milton Conwan, 1976). More common English equivalents for Arabic personal and geographic names, however, have been used in the main body of the text. For example, I write of ex-President Nimeiri (not Numayri) and of the river Bahr-el-Jebel (not Bahr-al-Jabal).

Finally, if I could choose one Nuer word for immediate, widespread adoption into the English language, I would propose the exclamation *wah!*—an exclamation that expresses simultaneous feelings of surprise and disappointment. When uttered with the proper "rising tone" of amused indignation, this exclamation, I find, can be quite effective with English speakers—especially, children. Why not try it and see?

Prologue

It is good that you are leaving before the rains begin," remarked Gatnyinyar, my long-standing host and "head chief" of the western Leek Nuer, as we walked together with his policemen to auction off several head of cattle confiscated in lieu of uncollected taxes. "When the rains come things will get worse." I had no reason to doubt his prediction: All indications on the eve of my departure from Gatnyinyar's village in late February 1983 were that Nuerland (*rool Nuärä*), along with the rest of southern Sudan, was rapidly plunging into full-scale civil war with the north. Armed attacks by incipient bands of southern resistance fighters had escalated sharply within the immediate area. Local "bush shops" stood silent, boarded up in anticipation. More ominous was the recent shuttling of hundreds of government paratroopers southwards into nearby Bentiu, the district headquarters of oil-rich western Nuerland.

Moreover, that morning the blue heron appeared again at Tharlual, Gatnyinyar's village—this time to stalk the perimeter of Nyapuka's home, silent and stately, its long neck curling above the underbrush. Two days earlier it settled near the footpath leading up to Cuol's cattle byre at the opposite end of the ridge, where it stood motionless for hours—its round eyes peering back at all passersby. Nyaroa, the aged matriarch, and the other women of the community had been discussing its every movement since its first appearance six days earlier. All were convinced that its unnatural behavior heralded disaster.

At that time it did not take much to alarm the women of Tharlual: Rumors of impending attacks by the *karɛŋni* (northern "Arabs")[1] or, alternately, by the *jidɔɔr* ("bush people/southern rebels") had sent them fleeing at dusk to outlying hamlets twice that month, dragging their startled children and belongings with them. But with this, the fourth appearance of

---

1. Although many northerners claim Arab descent, they have a deep African heritage as well—hence the quotation marks.

the mysterious bird, Nyarɔa decided to act. Penetrating into the men's circle beneath the great sausage tree where Gatnyinyar sat consulting with his policemen, Nyarɔa took advantage of a lull in the men's talk to warn her son: "The blue heron is back; it is 'divinity.' We must sacrifice for it. The 'Arabs' are surely coming."[2]

Engrossed in the more urgent matter of tax collection, Gatnyinyar did not react at first to his mother's words. He had just received word of the desertion of yet another subchief, the third thus far. Feeling trapped between the death threats of local "bush rebels" and the cattle-confiscation threats of their head chief, many lower-ranking "tax collectors" had begun disappearing quietly, together with their families and herds. Although Gatnyinyar immediately appointed substitutes, it was clear that his administration was fast collapsing. "Perhaps the heron brings us good fortune," I ventured in a futile attempt to calm Nyarɔa. This idea was utterly foreign to her: What good could come from the intrusion of creatures of the wild into the world of human beings? Her son, however, laughed and seconded my words: Nuer men are expected to belittle women's fears and, indeed, all fear. Nyarɔa spun around and left.

The general state of alarm in the village could not be so easily dismissed. During the initial scare—when rumors of rebel-slain headmen, captured cattle, and stolen wives criss-crossed from all directions—a truckload of government soldiers appeared suddenly at Tharlual, only to be withdrawn the following morning, leaving villagers feeling even more alarmed and vulnerable. After that, Gatnyinyar and his men were left to their own devices: "We write letters to the government asking for protection, but the government doesn't listen." Having failed to convince his remaining subchiefs to settle with him until the security situation stabilized, Gatnyinyar began appealing to distant relatives. Two half brothers, a sister's son, and a paternal cousin, together with their extended households, moved in from across the river Naam (Bahr-el-Ghazal). "In bad times, relatives stick together," one of them affirmed. Guns were cleaned and scouts sent out; and from that time on the men of Tharlual slept only in shifts. Clustered around dung fires in the midst of their cattle, they passed each night "laughing and joking away death," their most powerful of war amulets tied hidden just above their right elbows (see plate 1).

The general security situation in the south—though especially acute

---

2. In conformity with Lienhardt (1961) I will not be capitalizing "divinity"/"divinities" (*kuɔth*; gen. *kuɔdh*; pl., *kuuth*) except when referring to that single, overarching, distant, creator God—or "Divinity of the sky," *kuɔth nhial*.

Plate 1. The sweet smell of dung fires, an eastern Nuer cattle camp.

during my final weeks in Tharlual—had deteriorated steadily throughout the twenty-one months I lived in Nuer villages between December 1980 and February 1983. During this period, it became increasingly clear that the Nuer, along with all other southern Sudanese, were poised on the brink of a historical precipice.

During my initial eleven months of research among the eastern Jikany Nuer between late 1980 and early 1982, southern Sudan was rocked by four explosive political events. First, the national government in Khartoum sought (unsuccessfully) to modify the administrative boundary between northern and southern Sudan so as to extend northern control over mineral-rich regions of the Western Upper Nile and Bahr-el-Ghazal Provinces in the south.[3] Second, government security forces in Khartoum launched a campaign to arrest and evict thousands of southern Sudanese labor migrants from the nation's capital on the grounds that they had failed to obtain newly required identification cards and permits to work. Third, Gaafar Nimeiri, then president of Sudan, decided independently to switch the

3. This administrative boundary was originally established by British colonial agents of the Anglo-Egyptian Condominium Government of Sudan at the beginning of the twentieth century.

construction site of a Chevron-proposed oil refinery from the southern town of Bentiu—where 970 million barrels of proven oil reserves exist—to Kosti in the north. Fourth, and most controversial of all, the national government proposed to redivide the south into three autonomous regions. Having recently fought a major civil war (1955–72) in order to win "regional autonomy" for a "united south," the Nuer (and most other southern Sudanese) were not about to accept "redivision."[4]

These highly provocative government moves inflamed long-standing political tensions between a majority population in the north, identifying itself as "Arab" and "Muslim," and a minority population in the south, identifying itself as "black" and "African." Although both northern and southern Sudan contained numerous ethnic and linguistic groups that crosscut these regional identifications, the fact remained that, ever since Sudan declared independence from Britain and Egypt in 1956, "southerners" as a group had been marginalized by a national state government dominated by "Arab" and "Muslim" interests. The result was a dramatic surge in southern violence—most notably, in Nuer regions of the Upper Nile Province.[5]

In June 1981 I witnessed a spectacular nighttime rebel raid on the small town of Ulang, my principal field site among the eastern Jikany Nuer. With a terrifying burst of flares and machine gun fire, a small group of Nuer "bush rebels" swept through the town, capturing some 350–400 head of cattle that were being driven to export markets in the provincial capital, Malakal. These cattle were owned by a group of northern Arab merchants operating in the district headquarters at Nasir. The only fatality—a slow-moving ox—remained behind as a testimony to the rebels' organizational efficiency as well as to the unwillingness of the local police force to engage with them.

During 1982–83, political tensions, especially with regard to the issue of "redivision," rapidly approached boiling point. Although the Khartoum government was eventually forced by southern protest to abandon

---

4. The negotiated peace settlement that ended that war—known as the Addis Ababa Agreement of 1972—stipulated that no modifications in the political organization of the newly created Southern Regional Administration could be made without the support of two-thirds of southern voters in a regional-wide referendum.

5. Indeed, many contemporary Nuer men and women now look back on the chaotic years leading up to the full-scale renewal of civil war in 1983 with a profound sense of ethnic pride. "This war really began," they argue, "in our territories!" "It was we, Nuer, who first took up arms against the government."

its Kosti refinery proposal, its substitute proposal—the construction of a 1,455-kilometer pipeline to carry the crude directly from Bentiu to Port Sudan in the far north—did little to assuage southern fears of economic exploitation.[6] These fears were aggravated by simmering southern hostilities over the government's 1978 decision to construct a massive 360-kilometer canal in order to drain the water-rich heartlands of the southern Upper Nile and Jonglei Provinces for the benefit of irrigation projects in northern Sudan and Egypt.[7]

Nevertheless, it was not until after my departure from Nuerland in late February 1983 that President Gaafar Nimeiri's decisions to impose redivision on the south and Islamic shari'a law on the nation provoked the renewal of full-scale civil war in the south. By late 1984 I had learned that my principal field sites in both eastern and western Nuerland had been destroyed. Tharlual had been overrun and razed by a band of northern Baggara (Misseriya) Arabs that had been armed with automatic weapons and ammunition by the government and instructed to clear the oil-rich lands of the Western Upper Nile of its Nilotic inhabitants. Ulang and surrounding communities had fallen victim to a devastating series of government "retaliatory" raids. These traumas were soon compounded by massive air bombardments, extensive slave and cattle raids, encroaching rinderpest epidemics, and, ultimately, unprecedented famine.

Throughout the critical years leading up to the popular overthrow of President Gaafar Nimeiri in 1985 the U.S. government remained Sudan's staunchest political and military ally. This alliance was rooted in part on a shared cold war animosity toward the governments of Libya and Ethiopia. In fact, Sudan was the third-largest recipient of U.S. foreign aid in the world (after the governments of Israel and Egypt) during much of this period. A considerable proportion of this aid, moreover, was procured by the Sudanese government in the form of advanced military training, weaponry, and ammunition. Although acquired for the alleged purpose of deterring a possible invasion by Libyan forces, the bulk of these military supplies were subsequently unleashed against the civilian populations of the south.

By the time I returned to Sudan six years later in January 1990 the United Nations estimated that more than 500,000 southern Sudanese had

6. For an excellent analysis of the political and economic issues involved see Peter Nyot Kok (1992).

7. If completed, the "Jonglei Canal Project" will have enormous repercussion on the environmental base and immediate livelihood of many hundreds of southern Sudanese communities (cf. Howell, Lock, & Cobb 1988).

lost their lives as a direct consequence of war-provoked confrontations, famine, and disease. An additional three to four million southerners had been driven from their homes by escalating confrontations between the national government and its principal southern opponents, the Sudanese People's Liberation Army (SPLA)—as well as between the SPLA and other independent rebel factions loosely united under the title of the Anyanya II. These latter confrontations were fueled by fundamentally opposed southern visions of the future. Whereas the declared military objective of the SPLA was the creation of a "united, democratic, secular Sudan," Anyanya II forces advocated complete political independence for the south.[8] Although both the SPLA and the Anyanya II were supported by large numbers of Nuer, the leadership of the Anyanya II was dominated by them. Consequently, much of the heaviest fighting during the early years of this war took place in Nuer territories. In March 1984 and July 1985 two prominent Nuer leaders of the Anyanya II were slain. After these events one of their most respected surviving commanders, Gordon Kɔang (Gordon Kɔaŋ), defected to the SPLA on 1 January 1986, bringing with him the bulk of the Anyanya II army. This union was followed by rapid SPLA advances against the national army. By late 1990, the SPLA had gained military control of nearly two-thirds of the south, with only the Bahr-el-Ghazal and the towns of Juba, Malakal, Wau, Aweil, and Bentiu eluding its grasp.

The numbers of southern casualties and refugees, however, continued to rise unabated. By 1990 some 370,000 southern civilians had followed the growing "trail of [human] bones" eastwards in order to seek sanctuary in southwestern Ethiopia. An additional 1,800,000 southerners had braved the gauntlet of Arab militias northwards to reach Khartoum. There they settled into refuse dumps and other uninhabited stretches of bush to form a loose chain of densely packed squatter camps ringing the outskirts of the city. Barred from obtaining identity cards due to their lack of a registerable address, these displaced southerners were subject to arbitrary arrests, floggings, and forced conscription into the national army. Their settlements were also in the process of being systematically bulldozed as part of the national government's plan to "relocate" displaced southerners to "productive agricultural zones" far from the nation's capital or, alternatively, to "facilitate" their return to the south (see plate 2). Through a series

---

8. By taking the name Anyanya II, these forces were identifying with earlier southern secessionist forces—also known as the Anyanya—that had dominated the first Sudanese civil war (1955–72).

Plate 2. Displaced Nuer living on the outskirts of Khartoum. This photograph was taken just moments before government police forced everyone from this spontaneous settlement to move to a distant "relocation" camp.

of extended visits to these camps during January and February 1990 I reestablished contact with many Nuer whom I had known in the south, gathered a series of personal testimonies of the war, and investigated firsthand the conditions in which these people were struggling to survive.

By that time the military regime that had seized the national government in a coup d'etat on 30 June 1989 had fully revealed its Islamic fundamentalist objectives.[9] Determined to mold Sudan into an "Islamic state," it reinstated the government's "right" to flog, amputate, stone, crucify, hang, or otherwise punish Muslim and non-Muslim transgressors of its version of Islamic shari'a law.[10] "Apostasy" was declared a capital offense and the war in the south a holy *jihad*. The independent press was muzzled and all political parties, professional organizations, and trade unions suppressed. Sweeping purges of the military, the police, the universities, the judiciary, and all other branches of the government followed. Hundreds of suspected government opponents were also rounded up, tortured, and often slain in a secret network of "ghost houses" scattered throughout the capital.[11]

After consolidating its control of the national government, this self-declared National Salvation Revolutionary Command Council launched a major dry-season offensive against SPLA forces in the south during the early months of 1992. Aided by Iranian military advisers and by the arrival of $300 million worth of advanced weaponry purchased from China, it succeeded in winning back vast tracts of eastern Equatoria and the northern Upper Nile. By that time the SPLA had been severely weakened. The SPLA had lost its strategic supply lines and bases inside southwestern Ethiopia immediately following the fall of Mengistu's Dergue Government in May 1991.[12] The SPLA had also suffered from intensifying leadership

9. This coup was headed by General Omar Hassan Ahmed al-Bashir. Tragically, it took place just days before the elected government of Sadiq al-Mahdi it ousted was scheduled to begin extensive peace negotiations with the SPLA.

10. Although Islamic shari'a law was originally introduced in September 1983, these punishments had laid in abeyance ever since the popular overthrow of President Gaai in May 1985.

11. By 1993, this unrelenting campaign of terror had earned the current Sudanese government of Omar al-Bashir a well-documented reputation for being one of the most repressive governments in the world (see especially the extended report published by Africa Watch [1990] entitled *Denying the Honor of Living. Sudan: A Human Rights Disaster*).

12. This event also precipitated the mass evacuation/expulsion of the approximately 400,000 southern Sudanese refugees in southwestern Ethiopia. This sudden influx of returnees into, primarily, eastern Nuer regions put severe strains on the SPLA administration of that region—and, eventually, provoked the estab-

struggles over the question of whether the movement should abandon its aim of creating a "united, democratic, secular Sudan" in favor of "self-determination" or "national independence" for the south. These struggles culminated in August 1991 in a tragic split between the "Torit" and "Nasir" factions of the SPLA, under the leadership of John Garang and Riäk Machar Teny (Riäk Macar Tɛny) respectively.[13] This split ushered in a period of increasingly anarchic violence that has since destroyed scores of Dinka and Nuer communities along the upper White Nile (Bahr-el-Jebel) in the southern Jonglei Province.

In the wake of these events I returned again to Sudan in June 1992 under the auspices of Save the Children (UK). My mission was to document the current conditions and immediate needs of eastern Nuer communities deep within the war zone itself. Traveling throughout the Sobat and Baro river valleys, I visited numerous Nuer cattle camps and villages I had known during the early 1980s.

I found a people who were physically and emotionally exhausted but undefeated.[14] Although nothing would have improved their lives more than an immediate cease-fire between the Khartoum government and rival SPLA forces, a truce without hope of equality was unacceptable to them: "The peace of the slave is not worth it!" As one determined Nuer fighter explained, "We fought for seventeen years without even knowing of the true wealth of our lands. Now that we know the oil is there, we will fight much longer, if necessary!" The cultural resilience, collective determination, and sheer physical strength that had sustained Nuer men and women throughout the first civil war (1955–72) and other tumultuous periods remained both strong and evident. Powerful prophets, bearing messages of hope and self-reliance, had emerged throughout the region. Clusters of cattle contin-

---

lishment of a UN-based relief center at Nasir. Before this period, there was very little food relief flowing into Nuer regions of the Upper Nile. As will be explained in chapter 7, the introduction of this food aid played a major role in intensifying intra- and interethnic conflict in this region.

13. The "Nasir" faction subsequently adopted the official title of SPLA-United. This was later abandoned in favor of the more politically explicit title of the Southern Sudan Independence Army (SSIA)—by which they are currently known.

14. These were a people who desperately needed not only seeds to plant and medicines to cure but also schools and teachers for their children. For everyone had come to realize by that time that, without adequate educational facilities, there was little hope that future generations of Nuer would be able to help forge a genuinely responsive, democratic government attuned to the rectification of past discriminatory practices.

ued to graze the riverbanks, and fresh fields of sorghum shoots encircled many of the eastern Nuer villages I visited.

Nevertheless, the scars of war ran deep. Hundreds of Nuer families could be seen wandering the banks of the upper Sobat in search of food to eat and seeds to plant. Entire communities of unaccompanied children faced each day not knowing whether they would live to be reunited with their families.[15] Moreover, the sparkling humor, optimism, and openness that had so characterized Nuer social life during the early 1980s were far less evident.

It is difficult to fathom the depth of human suffering this war has caused since it began in 1983. Mounting reports of thousands of displaced southerners being banished from Khartoum to uninhabited desert sites without adequate supplies of water and food—or, alternately, of renewed waves of southern civilians being driven from their homes by escalating confrontations between SPLA forces deep within the south—can convey only so much (see map 1). Nor can I hope to fill this immense experiential gap with the personal testimonies, presented here, of a thirteen-year-old boy, a forty-year-old man, and a fifty-year-old woman.[16] However, they at least reveal something of the human face of this war—and as such bear witness to the immediate historical circumstances of the people to whom this book is devoted.

TESTIMONY 1: THE FLIGHT OF GATCAAR BILIU

At eleven years of age Gatcaar Biliu was overwhelmed by his mother's murder and his sister's kidnapping. He set out alone from his home in the Western Upper Nile in search of sanctuary from the war. Here he describes his

15. Armed only with sharpened sticks, many of these young boys struggled to supplement their rapidly diminishing UN relief supplies with fishing expeditions to distant pools.

16. These testimonies were among those I gathered from "displaced" Nuer camped on the outskirts of Khartoum during January 1990. Their living situation was becoming even more precarious at that time. Because they remained within the national boundaries of Sudan, they were officially not defined as "refugees." Consequently, the United Nations High Commission for Refugees could not intervene on their behalf. At the time, the Khartoum government severely restricted the activities of other international humanitarian organizations seeking to work among the "displaced." Indeed, the gravity of their situation was such that, during 1991–93, large numbers of "displaced" southerners returned to their southern homelands, where they hoped the conditions of life would be better than those they had experienced in Khartoum.

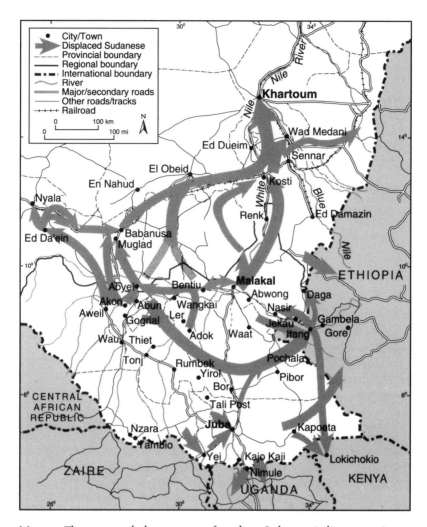

Map 1.   The war-provoked movements of southern Sudanese civilians, ca. 1984–92.

perilous flight northwards and subsequent survival as a street boy in Khartoum (see map 2).[17]

◊ I ran away from the war's destruction. The Arabs had killed my mother. She had gone to sell milk in Bentiu. When she came back with several other women she and the others were seized by

17. I have used pseudonyms in this section in order to protect my informants from the possibility of intensified government harassment.

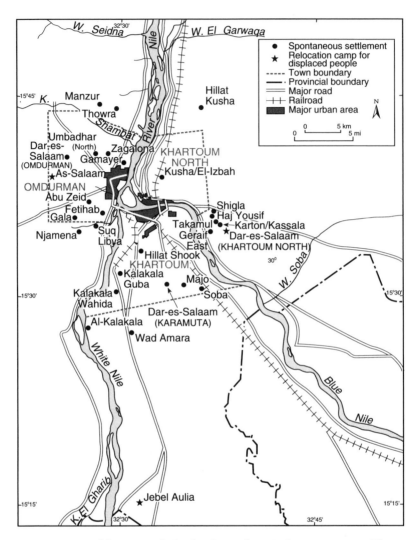

Map 2.   Principal locations of "displaced" southern Sudanese in greater Khartoum (ca. Jan. 1990). Many of the spontaneous settlements indicated here were subsequently bulldozed by the central government.

Arab soldiers. "Where are you going and where are you coming from?" the soldiers demanded. Without mercy, they forced them all to sit down. And then the soldiers said they were going to make them their women/wives [that is, rape them]. The other women realized that these soldiers were very serious. So they were saved. But my mother refused. The soldiers were many—eight in all. They tied up my mother and beat her. When they finished beating her she was kept behind while the other women [who had submitted] were let go. Soon after, the women heard a gun shot—and then they knew the Arab soldiers had killed my mother. These women were our neighbors, our kin. They came and told us what had happened. Then all of us—my sister, my brother, and people of other households—cried and cried. My father was very old, over sixty years. Five months later my sister was kidnapped by the Anyanya II. They also stole fifteen cattle. A month later my sister's husband was killed in the cross fire between SPLA and army troops. After that my sister's husband's people demanded their bridewealth cattle back, . . . and so fifteen cows went back to them. The world grew worse and worse. By then I was the oldest child [left]. My heart went bad [an expression of utter despair]. I dreaded the thought of going to Bentiu, but there was nothing left for me at home. So, finally, I left my home and family because I didn't know what else to do. My head was spinning: There was no good place for me.

In town the Arab soldiers found me and said that they were going to make me "their boy." I didn't want to but I agreed. They gave me food but I couldn't bear to eat it. I said I was too tired to eat—my heart just couldn't face the food. For two weeks I washed their clothes and was ordered around—and then at night they even wanted to make me their wife!! When I refused they got very angry. They swore at me calling me "dog" and "slave." While I was going through all of these hardships a man called Michael Tut, an administrative officer, arrived [in Bentiu]. He began to help people get places on the back of army trucks going to Kadugli. I got on.

From there we traveled through many regions—Parieng, Negobaya, Abith. . . . But all along the way, the Arabs [Misseriya militias] forced people down off the trucks. And they attacked us at night. Sometimes they grabbed you [off the truck] and stole all of your money. Anyone they wanted, they just took and carried away—such as boys they wanted to put to work and girls they wanted to make their women/wives. As for the men, they beat them and cut off their ears and threw them to the dogs to eat. Or they cut off their penises and shoved them into the men's mouths. And they did evil things with the women, too. They would rape a woman right in front of her husband—or they would catch her in the anus. This went on all the way to Kadugli. We survived, but our numbers dropped from 128 to 94 people. In Kadugli, the church people helped us with food, clothes, and other things. But because I had no other way to get money to go to Khartoum, I had to work as an "ass boy" for two weeks. Finally, in December 1988, I arrived in Khartoum.

At first I was amazed by everywhere I went. Then I saw black children, the children of southerners—there were Nuer, Dinka, Shilluk, Nuba, Baggara—and even Fur and Fellata. All kinds of people live in this cattle camp! As for my father, I don't know if he is alive or dead—nor do I know what's happened to my younger sister and brother. Right now I'm trying to save money so that some day I'll be able to stop begging and work as a shoe shiner. So far I have saved 91 pounds [roughly $8 at the time].

My best friends here in Khartoum are a Nuba boy named K. and a Dinka boy named Y. We also have a leader—a Nuer boy from Fangak named T. He's strong but weak in the mind. . . . We never store food: What little we find we eat right away. We get food from the trash bins of restaurants. Or sometimes we pay a restaurant owner less than the normal price and he fills our sack [with food]. We get money for food by begging in the streets. But whatever food we find, we always share because we love each other.

Benzine and glue we buy. Or sometimes a big boy will steal it if he is too old to beg [for money]—and then we buy it from him. We drink benzine to forget all the badness of our lives. Because when you drink benzine you become like a crazy boy. You become very brave and shameless—and you sleep well, too. Right now, I'm not sick. But what we suffer a lot from here is sores.[18] At night we sleep together in different places—behind a shop or a mosque or under a car or near a cinema. It's not one place that we go to. We walk together, we eat together, we sleep together—we do

18. While many of these "sores" undoubtedly stemmed from infected wounds, some street children were also suffering from kala-azar or visceral leishmaniasis. Spread by the bite of a sandfly, visceral leishmaniasis is invariably fatal if left untreated by a month-long series of extremely expensive injections. It initially manifests itself in the form of open sores. In later stages it is associated with a bloated stomach, fever, and wasted limbs. Due to the extended incubation period and development course of this disease, many southerners only discovered that they were infected upon reaching Khartoum. This kala-azar epidemic began devastating primarily Nuer and Dinka populations in the Western Upper Nile Region during the mid-1980s. By the early 1990s, this epidemic had reportedly wiped out 70 percent of the population in some areas of western Nuerland, according to representatives of Doctors without Borders—Holland (personal communication). When one considers the fact that this fatality rate was occurring within an open-air population, it could be argued that the raging kala-azar epidemic in the Western Upper Nile constituted one of the most virulent in the world during the latter 1980s and early 1990s.

everything together! We even get arrested together—and we play together, too. The government doesn't help us with any of our needs. But when the world becomes good again, I will get what I need.

TESTIMONY 2: THE RIVER ESCAPE OF RIÄK KAI

Unlike Gatcaar, Riäk Kai was a highly respected man of thirty-eight when he fled his war- and drought-engulfed home near Adok (Western Upper Nile) in June 1988. Moreover, he did not leave unaccompanied: He organized and courageously led a mass exodus of 117 people on a fleet of matted grass rafts. Both his parents and one of his children died of illness on the way to Malakal. Eventually, Riäk Kai reached Khartoum, where he settled in with some 35,000 other displaced southerners at Hillat Shook, a peripheral industrial waste site. In October 1990 Hillat Shook was burned and razed by government security forces and thousands of its residents forcefully removed to Jebel Aulia, a parched, treeless, clay plain some 25 miles south of Khartoum.

◊ We came to Ler (Western Upper Nile) from Adok, the place where I was born, because the world was full of war. We left our homes. Everyone bolted, leaving only the very old and small children. For if you stayed you were either forced to become a government spy or you were killed. War . . . that is not something that can be described! That is what brings everything that exhausts people: hunger, death, dying cattle, sickness, disease, kala-azar, schistosomiasis, typhoid, malaria, and people die from guns, too. Women are raped and children die of malnutrition.

Our home area was in drought. There was no water; nothing grew. The birds, locusts, and worms ate our crops. And people were not prepared for the coming of the Arabs. They burned the homes of our people in Leek Nuer country in late 1983. They wanted to take our lands from us. The [Misseriya] Arabs came because their lands were dry. There was no grass for their cattle. Soon we realized that they were really intent on taking our lands and that only the strong and brave [among us] would survive. It was then that all of western Nuerland united in opposition to the Arabs. The Arab militias razed the border region of Tharlual, Parieng, and many other villages. There was terrible illness, too, and great hunger. There was no grain. If you had a cow or a goat you sold it to get grain. The famine was so great that some people were left unburied. These were terrible days; death was everywhere. People and cattle and all living things were dying. Moreover, there were animals that ate people. The lions became very brave, even attacking people by day. Death was everywhere—from both war and disease. It exceeded all that people could bear. So, I abandoned my home in June 1988 with my wife and other people of my community who wanted to come with us to Khartoum. We were 117 in all. I told everyone who wanted to come with me to construct a grass raftlike boat. Our homes were destroyed; we could not live there anymore. Some of our people went to the bush [to join the SPLA]. Others of us are now here in Khartoum.

Coming to Khartoum was not easy, because when the Arabs learned that we had made rafts, they began to attack us from the river banks. They would open fire on us. Sometimes, they would put on long, white civilian robes so that we would not know that they were government troops [until it was too late]. It was a lie, an untruth! So, we intensified our efforts. During the journey, we were eaten alive by mosquitoes. There were also crocodiles and hippos and all the [dangerous] animals of the river. Whenever we met an army boat, it would fire on us. We would try to escape into the tall river grasses and papyrus. It took us 27 days to reach Malakal, and many, many people died. Of the original 117, only 87 people reached Malakal. None of us had any money when we arrived. There we were assisted by our people, the people of Dok. But there was no place for us to sleep or to put our possessions. Some of us had brought a few things, such as a mosquito net, a wooden head-rest, a sleeping mat, a calabash bowl, and limited supplies of grain, fish, and wild fruits. These we kept with us until we came one by one to Khartoum.

Life in Malakal was a bit better at first; it was not as bad as Ler. Those with kala-azar still died in Malakal. But a person with a light disease might be treated by a doctor at the Malakal hospital. But the evil ways of the Arabs were still there. If you tried to sell things like charcoal or firewood, the Arab soldiers would just come and seize them. Gradually, I began to see the evil way of life I had known in Ler appear again in Malakal.

It was then that I began to think about attempting to reach Khartoum by steamer. [Having worked as a day laborer in the Khartoum construction industry in 1978,] I knew Khartoum. Some of the others chose to stay in Malakal. But after three months I boarded a steamer—because a person can't just sit down in a place and wait for death; a person can't just let himself die when there is still a possibility of escape.[19]

On the boat many people were locked inside the storage compart-

19. Literally, Riäk said: "a person can't die when he sees the head of his father's tree." This is an allusion to a well-known folk tale in which a monkey succeeds in escaping from the jaws of an ungrateful lion by scurrying up a tree.

ments. None of these survived—they all suffocated to death. There
were two large storage compartments, and a total of 213 people died
inside them. When we discovered what had happened, the Arabs on
the boat realized that we, the black people, were going to report
them to the authorities as soon as we arrived. So the soldiers threw
the [dead] people into the river for the fish to eat. And then, when
the SPLA attacked our boat in the Zarzur forest, the Arab soldiers
aboard began shooting at the people on the boat [as well as the
SPLA]! This went on all the way until we reached Kosti. The people
were finished. The children that survived—and there were many—
were taken away by the soldiers. The government didn't question
the soldiers about them. I have since heard the children were sold
and transported to Kuwait. There they will be put to work.

When we reached Khartoum, we were given food and clothing
by people here at Hillat Shook as well as by the Islamic Call [*Daʿwa
Islāmiya*], the church, and Sudan Aid. Here at Hillat Shook, the government blocks the churches' attempts to help us so that the Daʿwa
will end up taking all the people. For you must be a Muslim or
accept Islam in order to get help from the Islamic Call. A family
of four gets one sack of sorghum for two months—or a tin of
grain per person per week. The Daʿwa is doing this so that people
will convert to Islam. Like when they started the school here, they
gave all the children Arab names and instructed them in Arabic,
in the Islamic religion, and in all the things having to do with Islam. Now our children's ways are changing; they are becoming different.

TESTIMONY 3: THE STRUGGLES OF NYAKƆAŊ PUOH

After the loss of three married daughters and a married son during the early
years of the war, Nyakɔaŋ Puoh, a widow of fifty, took responsibility for
raising four of her seven orphaned grandchildren. She left Bentiu in April
1988 for Khartoum, where she and her grandchildren currently survive by
brewing beer and selling peanuts. She sent her only remaining son, a youth
of twenty, to Kassala in an effort to reduce the risk of his being forcibly conscripted into the government army. Nyakɔaŋ's Khartoum settlement was
also razed by government security forces in October 1990.

◊ This is not the first time I have seen terrible destruction. I am
old and the first [civil] war [1955–72] was there as well. This one
began in 1983. Everything horrible you can imagine was done. Bentiu town was full of gun-toters. The Arabs lacked nothing: whatever
they wanted from the people, they seized. They would beat you,
steal your cattle, and then [try to] marry your daughter with cattle

stolen from you! If you refused, they would just take her! So, we were left with nothing because the soldiers took by force. If your son had a wife, they would just fall on her [and rape her] without a word—even in her husband's presence! Living conditions grew worse and worse until 1985. That's when our young men became strong and went to the bush to unite with the SPLA. They were fed up with being beaten! If you're a man, you can't just die, you must fight! A man can't die like a woman. The people [of Bentiu] were greatly diminished by this exodus. Only old men and old women, like myself, were left behind together with the small children. Government spies and prostitutes also stayed. Those of us who remained were forced to cut down surrounding trees and shrubs so that the army could see [any SPLA approaches]. We were forced to work in very dangerous places. And if you were bitten by a snake, there was no help for you either.

In 1986 the army became even worse. They would put on civilian clothes and go around shooting people and burning houses—after taking from them whatever they wanted. Or they would wrongly accuse you of being SPLA. People would have to lie, saying "No, I'm part of the 'friendly forces' " in order to save their lives. It was at this time that Mahmoud Diengthou became the administrative officer at Bentiu. He openly criticized the army's treatment of civilians. So the soldiers plotted to kill him and did so. And then the army turned its guns on the citizens of the town. Everyone bolted. We all ran to the place of Major Riäk Machar Tɛny [the SPLA zonal commander of the Western Upper Nile at that time] and Major Paul Dor Lampuar—where people treated each other well. But when the war between the SPLA and the army intensified, that's when the [kala-azar] epidemics began. Suddenly, people were caught by "cough" [tuberculosis], "swollen stomach" [kala-azar], *kuany* [an unidentified wasting disease], and "sudden death." Your stomach would swell badly, you would eat a lot, and there would be fever as well. Whole families were dying—and the cattle too. At times a whole village would have only one survivor. And then, when that person's relatives tried to help him [by taking him in], he carried the disease to them.

Afraid of kala-azar, I went back to Bentiu in 1988 to endure its hardships once again. What evil ways of the army and "friendly forces" I saw! They even fought in town. Death divided into two— [guns and disease]! Two of my daughters died in Bentiu for lack of a doctor. My third died during childbirth; she, too, was ill. Finally, I escaped on 15 April 1988 with my one remaining child, a son, to Khartoum via Muglad. We were two weeks on the road. On the way to Kadugli we were attacked by the "bush Arabs" [local militias] despite the presence of army soldiers. The soldiers, in fact, conspired with them against us. The Arabs took all the money I had saved—a total of 1,500 pounds! They ordered four men down from the truck. The Arabs beat them, saying "Why are you so fat/healthy? You're SPLA!" And then they killed them, right there, before our eyes! The wives and relatives of these men were ordered not to weep or mourn on pain of death. The Arabs also raped women and carried off boys they wanted to put to work and girls they wanted to make their women/wives. Many, many people were thus lost along the way. We were a caravan of 20 trucks—and of the original 270 passengers, only 165 reached Kadugli. There the church people helped us with food, clothing, and a place to sleep, until we came to Khartoum.

Living conditions here in Khartoum are extremely difficult. My son's wife and I brew beer. Together we are trying to raise the orphans. My granddaughters peddle peanuts and watermelon seeds; my grandson sells cigarettes and snuff. But all of us are continually harassed by the police. If you don't give the police money on demand, they confiscate your beer, tea, peanuts, tobacco, and the like. These they either sell or consume themselves. If you object, the police arrest you—and lash you too![20] All we have to eat is dry sorghum porridge—there is nothing else.

Moreover, people's ways of living here in Khartoum are profoundly distorted. If you manage to get on a bus, the northerners will refuse to let you sit next to them. They call you "dirty" or insult you in ways they think you won't understand. The Nuer, Dinka, Shilluk, and Nuba in the camps fight each other because there is no strong administration here. It is beer and tribalism that brings all the trouble. Just the other day a man was murdered with a big knife, but the government hasn't arrested anyone. But that's the way life is here. The Arabs have appointed [tribal] chiefs in order to divide us—that's what they really want. And the chiefs themselves benefit from all this fighting: That's how they eat [by imposing court fines for violence]. But what I hate most is when black

---

20. There was no government license that hawkers could acquire to legitimate their trade. Furthermore, the central government was in the process of vigorously suppressing the informal sector of the economy during the early 1990s. I witnessed scores of men, women, and children, who had been caught selling tea, brewing beer, peddling firewood, cigarettes, and the like, being publicly lashed and fined by security forces on a daily basis in the main market square of Khartoum. The poorest Sudanese citizens were the most likely to suffer these indignities, because they were unable to satisfy standard police demands for a bribe.

people are grabbed off the streets, inducted into the army, and then sent to fight their brothers in the south.[21] But that's how things are in Khartoum. My heart's gone bad with the north, I want to go south!

◊ ◊ ◊

This book describes the changing circumstances of, primarily, those Nuer men, women, and children who have remained within their rural homelands. The transformative impact of the first decade of the ongoing Sudanese civil war is explored in various ways. Nevertheless, the book's primary focus is on the half-century period leading up to the renewal of full-scale civil war in 1983. This loose temporal framework has been predetermined in part by the unresolved state of the present war and in part by the fact that this book builds directly on the path-breaking field studies carried out among the Nuer by Evans-Pritchard during the early 1930s.

Although the immediate realities of rural Nuer social life are swiftly becoming something other than those described here, it is important, I think, to place the revolutionary consequences of the current Sudanese civil war in a broader historical perspective. For in so doing, it becomes possible to show how past and present generations of Nuer women and men have actively intervened in the broader historical forces shaping their everyday lives. All in all, it is hoped that this book will not only provide a fresh image of the generative dynamics of Nuer culture and social life but also contribute, within the limits of a case study, to our understanding of the myriad ways "global" and "local" forms of power and knowledge are empirically entwined in the world today.

Although there is little reason to hope, at present, that the immediate plight of Nuer and other southern Sudanese communities will be relieved in the foreseeable future, this book bears witness to their extraordinary survival skills. I thus dedicate it to them and to all "black peoples" (*nei ti caar*) of Sudan: May their continuing struggles for justice and equality unite and strengthen them.

21. Because the government would not grant identity cards to displaced southerners living in unplanned settlements, these people were subject to arbitrary arrests and forced conscription at any time. Without access to an identity card, moreover, they were totally excluded from all government food rationing systems. Consequently, they were always the first to suffer from critical food shortages.

1 Orientations

This is a historical ethnography about one of anthropology's most celebrated peoples. The enduring disciplinary fame of "the Nuer" of southern Sudan derives directly from the intellectual virtuosity of their original ethnographer, Sir Edward E. Evans-Pritchard (1902–73). On the basis of some eleven months of field research carried out during the early 1930s, Evans-Pritchard went on to produce what is, arguably, the most comprehensive and detailed ethnographic portrait of any people in the whole of the anthropological literature. His three principal studies—*The Nuer: A Description of the Modes of Livelihood and Political Institutions of a Nilotic People* (1940a), *Kinship and Marriage among the Nuer* (1951b), and *Nuer Religion* (1956)—have been widely acclaimed by generations of anthropologists both as extraordinarily rich, well-crafted ethnographies in their own right and as exemplary models of inquiry and analysis for the entire field. Nearly all the great disciplinary debates that have emerged in recent decades have drawn at one time or another on the Nuer ethnographic corpus of Evans-Pritchard. Indeed, with the possible exception of the "Trobriand Islanders" made famous by Malinowski, "the Nuer" have been more widely cited, discussed, analyzed, and theorized about than any other "imagined community" within the anthropological discourse. The cumulative effect of decades of secondary reanalyses of Evans-Pritchard's materials, however, has fostered the illusion that Nuer culture and social life are somehow above history and beyond change.[1] This book seeks to shatter that illusion.

When Evans-Pritchard first pitched his tent in Nuerland (*rool Nuära*) in 1930 the Anglo-Egyptian Condominium Government of Sudan (1898–1955) was just beginning to consolidate its conquest of the region, thrusting forth its first roads and establishing rudimentary administrative centers. Although many Nuer were embittered by the massive military campaigns that led up to their definitive defeat by British colonial forces

1. I wish to thank James Ferguson and John Galaty for their stimulating comments on an earlier draft of this book and, in particular, for their suggestions to expand its opening and closing chapters. I am particularly grateful for the theoretical vision demonstrated by James Ferguson during a four-hour-long conversation in which he offered, literally, scores of excellent ideas for broadening and reshaping some of the book's main themes.

Plate 3. A wet-season hamlet surrounded by ripening sorghum fields, standing cattle, and grazing area.

in 1929, they could do little else but recognize the military superiority of their foreign invaders and accommodate themselves to the new administrative policies imposed. (Their hopes for a future government withdrawal, however, never died.)

At that time, the Nuer were thought to number around 200,000 and were fully engaged in a mixed agro-pastoralist economy centered on sorghum and cattle raising. Their economy necessitated semiannual migrations between relatively permanent, wet-season settlements—scattered across an unbroken territory of more than 25,000 square miles of marsh-laden savannah land—and more condensed, temporary, dry-season cattle and fishing camps running along major tributaries of the upper White Nile (see plates 3 and 4). There were no indigenous "chiefs" or "kings" among them. Rather, the Nuer were a profoundly egalitarian people, whose acephalous political organization was based on a combination of kinship and residency affiliations and was loosely divided into eleven major, named, territorial groupings (known as the Bul, Leek [Leeɣ], western Jikany [Jikäny ciëŋ], Nyuong [Nyuɔŋ], Dok [Dɔk], Jagei [Jagɛi], Gaawär [Gaawäär], Thiäng [Thiäŋ], Lak [Laak], Lou [Lɔu], and eastern Jikany Nuer [Jikäny dɔɔr]; see map 3). Although a few "government chiefs" were appointed by 1930, neither their effectiveness as local leaders nor their loyalty as government agents inspired British confidence. Consequently, whatever

Plate 4. Cattle on the move: Cattle are being driven to dry-season camps as outlying brushlands are burned.

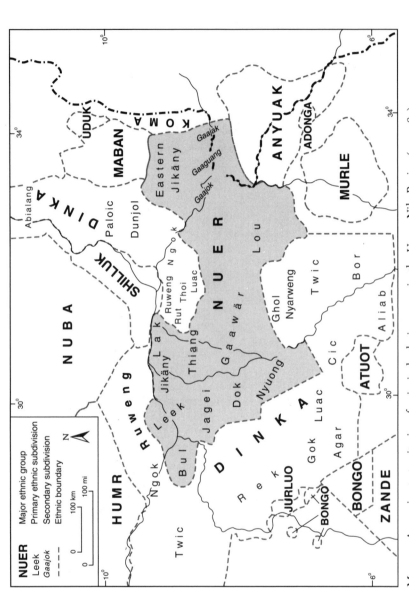

Map 3. Approximate territories of principal ethnic groups in the Upper Nile Region (ca. 1983).

semblance of a wider political order existed was based more on shifting patterns of intercommunity alliance and feuding than on the isolated efforts of a few roving British district commissioners.

A few northern "Arab" merchants had entered the region by that time, offering fishing hooks, beads, hoes, and metallic spearheads for hides, grain, and goats. Their impact on the region's economy, however, appeared negligible (Evans-Pritchard 1940a:87). As yet, Nuer women and men were unfamiliar with the concept of currency or the principles of market exchange. They apparently viewed their occasional interactions with "Arab" merchants not as impersonal transactions but, rather, as mutual relations of "gift giving" or "sacrifice" (kɔk) in which the idea of "price" played no direct part (Evans-Pritchard 1956:223–224).

Indeed, Evans-Pritchard argued that trade in general was a "very unimportant social process among Nuer" during the early 1930s (1940a:87–88). There was little diversity in the distribution of raw materials or in the production of local goods. Moreover, relations between Nuer and neighboring ethnic communities were seldom peaceful enough to permit more than sporadic exchange. But by far the most important factor inhibiting the development of extended trade networks in this region was, in Evans-Pritchard's opinion, "the dominant interest of the Nuer in their herds":

> Nuer have nothing to trade except their cattle and have no inclination to dispose of these; all they greatly desire are more cattle, and, apart from the difficulty that they have nothing to offer in exchange for them, herds are more easily and pleasantly increased by raiding the Dinka. . . . This narrow focus of interest causes them to be inattentive to the products of other people, for which, indeed, they feel no need and often enough show contempt. (Evans-Pritchard 1940a:88)[2]

In contrast, by the time I began my own field studies in this region some fifty years later, the Nuer were no longer the isolated, independent, cattle-minded warriors immortalized by Evans-Pritchard. They had been drawn from an indigenous society allegedly devoid of institutionalized rulers into a bewildering spiral of local government authorities, district councils, party bureaucracies, regional assemblies, and national parlia-

---

2. Although Evans-Pritchard underestimated the regional importance of intercommunity exchanges of cattle and grain in times of shortage as well as of the gun/ivory/cattle trade then developing along the Ethiopian (Abyssinian) frontier, his interpretation of the relationship between Nuer interest in their herds and the relative dearth of trade among them was perceptive and convincing. For a valuable history of the early emergence of the gun/ivory/cattle trade in this region, see Johnson (1986c).

ments—all of which were constantly being reshuffled, reorganized, and disbanded. Once-fluid patterns of community alliance likewise had given way to rickety tribal hierarchies of elected government chiefs, responsible for the suppression of feuding, the collection of taxes, and the enforcement of a now "standardized" body of Nuer customary law. Official estimates of their overall population, moreover, had crept up from some 450,000 during the mid-1950s to anywhere between 800,000 and well over a million by the early 1980s—figures that suggest that Evans-Pritchard's earlier population estimates were probably far too low.

Although the daily lives of the vast majority of Nuer men and women continued to revolve during the early 1980s around the care, protection, and exchange of their cherished cattle, small market centers had burgeoned throughout the region, together with a budding class of Nuer merchants. Some of the more successful of these merchants had penetrated the long-distance cattle-export and grain-import trade formerly monopolized by their northern "Arab" counterparts. Young bachelors in search of independent wealth and a quicker road to marriage were also journeying to northern cities on a massive scale. Generally employed as day laborers in the Khartoum construction industry, many youths returned home after four to eighteen months of intermittent employment laden with colorful clothing, mosquito nets, plastic shoes, blankets, mattresses, sun glasses, and other highly valued economic goods and courting paraphernalia. Indeed, failure to obtain these imported display items left young Nuer men in the east vulnerable to the coordinated insult and rejection of marriageable girls. "If he comes back from the north and his dog recognizes him, don't converse with him!" runs the legendary dictum of Nyabuoth Nguany Thoan (Nyabuɔth Ŋuany Thoan), an influential Lou girl leader. Among western Nuer communities, in contrast, a fat stately ox was still more likely to catch a girl's eye during the 1980s than were the flamboyantly colored dance leggings so avidly adopted by young men in the east (see plate 20, p. 211). Consequently, most western Nuer migrants preferred to invest their wages in bridewealth cattle—the "cattle of money" being considered less vulnerable to the claims of extended kinsmen than cattle acquired through marriage or inheritance. In fact, the cattle/money equation was by then so well accepted that it was not unusual for a "generous" father-in-law to accept cash in place of a bridewealth cow or two.

Moreover, owing to a dramatic surge in Christian conversion among Nuer after the first civil war, belief in the efficacy of cattle sacrifice was on the wane. "Cattle," people told me unambiguously, "are no longer as important as they once were." And, indeed, though major intercommunity feuds and fights continued to erupt among Nuer throughout the 1980s and early 1990s, cattle were rarely identified as the focus of such hostilities. Rather, the tactics and weaponry of local warfare were themselves changing rapidly. In many areas, guns were fast replacing spears, and national political issues, "tribal" conflicts. Having recently fought a grueling, seventeen-year civil war (1955–72), the Nuer men and women I came to know were a highly politicized people, deeply conscious of the vast, untapped oil wealth of their lands and of their tenuous integration into the national-state structure of Sudan.

Clearly, these developments suggest a very different people and social world from those described by Evans-Pritchard. My principal objective in this book is to convey an understanding of how Nuer men and women have variously experienced these last six decades of turbulent history and have incorporated that experience into their contemporary culture and social life. Drawing on twenty-four months of intensive field research (conducted during 1980–83, 1990, and 1992), on four months of English and Arabic archival study, and on Evans-Pritchard's earlier ethnographic accounts, the book traces Nuer struggles to comprehend and to come to terms with the massive social and economic transformations wrought by more than twenty-five years of British colonial rule (1929–55), by eleven years of "southern regional autonomy" (1972–83), and by two major civil wars (1955–72 and 1983–present). The analytic emphasis is on those values, concepts, and practices that contemporary Nuer women and men perceived as changing and were in the process of collectively defining and evaluating during the 1980s and early 1990s.

More specifically, this study shows how Nuer men and women have been actively reassessing local forms of power and sociality in their efforts to understand and keep pace with the oscillating expansion and contraction of state and market structures between, roughly, 1930 and 1992. Much of the analysis revolves around the ways Nuer have reinterpreted the symbolic and material forces of three key media of interpersonal bonding—*riɛm* (blood), *yɔk* (cattle), and *nyuak* ("commensality," or the sharing of *mieth* [food])—in light of their experience of powerful new media emanating from outside their immediate social world, most notably, those of *yiou* (money), *maai* (guns), and *waragak* (paper). Through a historical analysis of these and other complex dimensions of evolving Nuer concepts of personhood and sociality, this book seeks to identify the specific conditions and practices that led contemporary Nuer men and women to "problematize" fundamental aspects of who they were and what they did. Why did certain sociocultural patterns and practices fade and change, seemingly unnoticed by these people, while the alteration of others was accompanied by explicit debate and value struggle?

In the process this book raises a number of theoretical and ethnographic issues that Evans-Pritchard's earlier Nuer studies did not, namely: How can we move beyond static structural models rooted in presuppositions of cultural "boundedness," "homogeneity," and "order" so as to appreciate Nuer social life in a more historical and dynamic framework? How were changing Nuer patterns of social relations and cultural practices bound up over the generations with wider forces of economic transformation, civil war, colonial and postcolonial rule, and Christian and Islamic proselytism? How did differently situated Nuer view the social transformations they were experiencing, and what was at stake in their contestations and struggles over various concepts, conventions, and practices?[3]

Whereas Evans-Pritchard, like many of his contemporaries, was preoccupied during the 1930s and 1940s with issues of "unity," "equilibrium," and "order," viewing culture as something shared and ethnography as the compilation of those shared elements, this book concentrates on evolving points of confusion and conflict among Nuer—and thus on what was not fully shared by them. This study also views the dynamic social and cultural systems in which these people continued to live and work over the generations as inherently unfinished, open-ended, and riddled with uncertainties. These systems are also presumed to be essentially unbounded. For in a world where people, products, and ideas increasingly refuse to stay put, who is to say for certain where one sociocultural matrix begins and another ends?

This study thus supports a growing trend within the social sciences toward viewing culture and social conventions, more generally, as being "up for grabs." Rather than seek a homogenized image of what people hold in common, anthropologists and social historians have concentrated more and more on how conflicts of interest, perspective, and power among various age, gender, wealth, and status groups are continuously being renegotiated and worked out "on the ground." What earlier generations of anthropologists tended to view as "the logic" of a particular social system has thus often appeared, on closer inspection, to be merely the logic of some segment of it. As a result, our very notions of culture and society have begun to fracture and dissolve.

3. I wish to thank James Ferguson for his input in this formulation of my research objectives.

Accordingly, one of my principal objectives in this study is to call into question the very idea of "the Nuer" as a unified ethnic identity by drawing attention to striking regional variations of culture and history and to marked contrasts in the life orientations and experiences of Nuer men and women. In fact, one of the book's more general aims is to round out the excessively viricentric accounts of Evans-Pritchard in which the point of view of Nuer women was rarely considered or even inquired about.

All in all, this book is directed toward a processual, actor-oriented account of the ways global historical factors of ever-increasing scale and complexity are subtly registered within regionally specific social and cultural fields.[4] Through its emphasis on locally held perceptions and experiences of change, this book strives to deepen our understanding of the dynamic interplay between the "said" and the "unsaid," the "discursive" and the "nondiscursive," in the creation, perpetuation, and transformation of power differentials across the generations. It stands as an example of how systematic investigations of "other" peoples' perceptions and experience of change can help to dramatize and reveal the encounter between local forms of understanding and broader historical forces of social and economic transformation.[5]

Last, this book is unusual, I suspect, in the degree to which it was composed in active collaboration with Nuer not only as informants but as critical commentators. While in the field I discussed many of the book's main themes with numerous Nuer men and women living deep within the countryside (*rɛi ciëŋ*). All six core chapters were also read by a diverse group of university-educated Nuer located in Sudan, England, and the United States.[6] Thanks to their cooperation and assistance, I am confident that the

---

4. The term *global* is here meant to suggest broader historical processes connected with the expansion of cattle and labor markets, the creation of government administrative networks, the introduction of literacy and government schools, the proselytizing forces of both Christianity and Islam as well as all the complex social and political factors underlying two extended civil wars.

5. I wish to acknowledge John Galaty's intellectual input here.

6. Unlike many peoples of the world, contemporary Nuer images of themselves and their social life did not appear to have been heavily colored by the anthropological discourse. Only one of my university-trained Nuer readers had read any of Evans-Pritchard's monographs—although they had all heard about them. This low readership also appeared to be the norm among members of the Nuer educated elite I encountered in southern Sudan and elsewhere. And as for the 98 percent or more of the contemporary Nuer population that had no access to books (other than, perhaps, a Nuer version of the New Testament), Evans-Pritchard's work appeared to be completely unknown.

ethnographic materials presented here are not only sufficiently nuanced and accurate but, more important, successful in conveying an experientially resonant interpretation of the historical themes examined.

THE EXPERIENCE OF FIELDWORK

Often during the early stages of field research, as I struggled to listen in on heated court cases or to unravel the tangled names and connections of the immediate community, I would think back on the neat diagrams and sense of completeness that exuded from Evans-Pritchard's earlier Nuer accounts and would despair. I remember comparing my modest stack of field notes at month 11 with what I imagined his must have been when he left Nuerland for good. How could he have managed to observe and record so much in so little time—and to infuse it all with such a sense of order? Nowhere did I find in his writings evidence of the bewilderment that plagued me—only the occasional "apology" to the reader for his not quite having had time enough to observe the full social order.

Fortunately, these anxiety pangs were tempered by a deepening awareness of all that had been left out of Evans-Pritchard's accounts. Long before I embarked on my own field study, I realized that the image of a balanced social harmony he projected was not simply the product of a keen eye and a brilliant mind but also an illusion fostered by the dominant theories guiding anthropological research at that time. Although Evans-Pritchard was profoundly aware of "the colonial encounter" and was, in fact, part of it, he nevertheless played down its transformative effects in his Nuer corpus in an effort to reveal the autonomous inner workings, as it were, of a "traditional" African society. Consequently, we hear very little from Evans-Pritchard about the radical administrative measures imposed by the Anglo-Egyptian Condominium Government as part of the "Nuer Settlement of 1929–30" (Johnson 1979, 1980, 1994). Nor did he detail the extent to which Nuer were suffering during the early 1930s from drought and recurrent rinderpest epidemics (Johnson 1979). His principal research task—having been determined by the Anglo-Egyptian administration—was to discover the enduring principles underlying Nuer territorial groupings (Ahmed 1973). And thus, the brief references he made to the governmental suppression of cattle raiding, the machine-gunning of cattle camps, the demarcation of "tribal" borders, the collection of tribute, the appointment of government chiefs, and the creation of courts going on at that time tend to be lost within extended discussions of the historical amnesia structured into the "segmentary lineage organization" of Nuer community groupings.[7]

Regional variations of culture and history are likewise played down in favor of a generalized image of a timeless social order. More striking is the absence of alternative voices—particularly feminine voices—in his portrayal of Nuer social experience. The wry, dry, unflappable narrator of Evans-Pritchard's writings identifies, as I soon discovered, not simply with Nuer men as a group but, more specifically, with senior members of "aristocratic" lines.[8] Indeed, Evans-Pritchard's vision of Nuer social life appears at times so unified as to preclude the possibility of ideological struggle among groups within it.

Nevertheless, the thoroughness of Evans-Pritchard's ethnographic descriptions never ceased to amaze me. Indeed, it was this richness, coupled with the fact that he often noted regional variations of culture and history in passing, that first stimulated me—and scores of others—to venture an armchair reinterpretation of aspects of his materials. Sahlins (1961), Gough (1971), Newcomer (1972, 1973), Glickman (1972, 1974, 1977), Riches (1973), Southall (1976), Sacks (1979), and Kelly (1985) all strove to reinfuse his analyses with a much-needed sense of historical dynamism by focusing on the dramatic nineteenth-century expansion of Nuer communities eastwards across the White Nile into Dinka- and Anyuak-occupied lands. Most participants in these discussions sought to isolate the critical differences between "the Nuer" and "the Dinka" that could account for the consistent military superiority of the former throughout the nine-

---

7. Although Evans-Pritchard's Nuer research was largely synchronic, a note in the archives suggests that he would have supported a study of the Nuer emphasizing historical change. In a letter to the civil secretary dated 12 Feb. 1932, Governor Pawson wrote:

> I have discussed the position of functional experts with Dr. Evans-Pritchard and if he had returned [this year], he had intended to study the Nuer from the angle of their present development and customs with a view to showing the effect that recent contact with civilization and with the Government has had on their tribal organisation. An enquiry on these lines would have been a departure from the normal anthropological enquiry which tries to get back to the tribe in its most primitive stages and treats more modern developments as of little interest (Civsec 1/43/113).

Although Evans-Pritchard never realized this aim in his post-1932 Nuer research, he advocated the fundamental inseparability of anthropology and history in his later career.

8. Evans-Pritchard refers to the patrilineal descendants of the first Nuer settlers of a particular area as members of "aristocratic" or "dominant" lineages.

teenth century. Hypotheses ranged from those based primarily on alleged contrasts of culture (Southall 1976), social structure (Sahlins 1961, Newcomer 1972, 1973), and bridewealth expectations (Kelly 1985) to those based primarily on ecological variations (Glickman 1972, Riches 1973) or on the selective impact of Arab slave raiders (Sacks 1979).

Gough (1971), in contrast, probed these issues from the perspective of the expanding eastern Nuer "tribes." She suggested probable transformations in local group composition, leadership patterns, and gender relations resulting from the massive absorption of Dinka and Anyuak lands, cattle, and people. Her analysis, which is of special relevance to this study, called into question Evans-Pritchard's tendency to view agnation—and intermale relations more generally—as the universal and unchallenged principle of Nuer community organization.

Other social analysts searching for a rich data base through which to pursue their own theoretical concerns also turned to Evans-Pritchard's detailed Nuer materials. Beidelman (1966, 1968, 1971) plumbed ambiguities of power and of gender symbolism in Nuer culture. Gluckman (1955) puzzled through lacunae in Evans-Pritchard's accounts of local patterns of feud and alliance. Lewis (1951), Evans (1978), and Greuel (1971) challenged aspects of his interpretations of Nuer leadership; Burton (1974, 1981b, 1987) and Hayley (1968) questioned details of his analysis of Nuer religion—and I (1980) attempted to balance out his portrayal of relations between the sexes.

Thus locked in the museum case of Evans-Pritchard's analyses, "the Nuer" have provided a reassuringly secure reference point for a discipline that has been struggling in many ways to maintain a coherent sense of direction and purpose. Very little was known about what had become of these people since their 1930s encounters with Evans-Pritchard, and it was my deepening curiosity about this issue that eventually prompted me to consider undertaking full-scale field research among them. While attending a twelve-month program in intensive Arabic at the American University of Cairo in 1978–79, I took off six weeks in order to travel to southern Sudan. Riding on the backs of merchant lorries crowded with young Nuer migrants returning from Khartoum, I visited about a dozen small market centers and cattle camps among the Lou, Gaawär, and eastern Jikany Nuer.

My first reaction was one of amazement. Apart from some clothing, mosquito nets, and the occasional dead radio, there was remarkably little tangible evidence in Nuer cattle camps and villages to betray the passage of some fifty years of war-scarred history. The endless, flat, grass-covered plains stretching forth in all directions; the thick cotton soils, grayed and cracked by the harsh dry-season sun; the muddied pools and crocodile-infested swamps; the drifting rivers adorned with brightly colored birds; the gracefully curving cattle byres; the drifting odor of dung ash and the rhythmic clanging of cattle bells; the insatiable mosquitoes and the dazzling night skies—these were all as I had imagined them from Evans-Pritchard's evocative descriptions.

The small administrative centers I passed through during that trip were different: They, at least, bore traces of a half century of British colonial rule (1898–1956)—if, sometimes, only in the form of an isolated row of trees or a collapsed brick building. The devastating impact of seventeen years of civil war was also readily apparent in the gutted-out carcasses of former school buildings, in the bullet-riddled doors of market stalls, and in the deep ruts tracing the course of formerly raised and banked dirt roads. Yet there were still no permanent docks, no hard-topped roads, no senior secondary schools, no doctors, no well-supplied medical facilities, and no scheduled transportation of any kind in all of Nuerland at that time (see plate 5). Nor have these been established since. Rather, most of the small market centers I visited during that and subsequent research trips consisted of little more than a row of depressingly understocked market stalls flanked at one end by a small mud-and-thatch police post and, at the other, by a haphazard collection of "beer parlors."

Unlike Evans-Pritchard, however, I did not find "cows and oxen, heifers and steers, rams and sheep, he-goats and she-goats, calves and lambs and kids" (1940a:19) an incessant topic of conversation among Nuer men and women. Although my ability to converse with people was still limited during that initial journey to Arabic and English, I often inquired successfully into the subject of discussions going on around me.[9] And much to my initial surprise, many of these discussions revolved around national political issues, cabinet shake-ups, regional troop movements, and the Jonglei Canal scheme. Moreover, many women and men complained bitterly about the government's failure to address their urgent needs for more schools, roads, medical facilities, veterinary services, and the like. Whereas Evans-Pritchard was apparently impressed by the "outward harmony" of Nuer family life, stating that he never once saw a man strike his wife or heard of a serious quarrel between spouses (1951b:133), I stumbled across three

---

9. My knowledge of classical and colloquial Arabic was based at that time on two years of classes attended at the University of Chicago plus eight months of a year-long course at the American University in Cairo. I completed the latter course and an additional year of Arabic at the University of Chicago before embarking in October 1980 on full-time archival and field research in Sudan.

Plate 5. During eight months of the year, the only way to enter or leave Nuer territories is aboard privately owned and unscheduled river barges such as the one shown.

instances of wife-beating and several drunken brawls during my six-week tour. Furthermore, consensus on such cultural fundamentals as the importance of male initiation rites and the efficacy of cattle sacrifice was clearly lacking.

In brief, the social world I first encountered in 1979 appeared by no means as culturally unified or socially harmonious as that portrayed by Evans-Pritchard. Nevertheless, I could not help but wonder to what extent the cultural fluidity and social tensions I came to see as such a pervasive aspect of contemporary Nuer social life had existed at the time of Evans-Pritchard's field study. Could it simply have eluded Evans-Pritchard's gaze? Perhaps he noted major value controversies but dismissed them as distracting from his primary research goal: the construction of a precolonial contact model of Nuer society.

These initial impressions were elaborated and confirmed during two extended periods of intensive field research carried out between December 1980 and February 1983 and supplemented by additional trips to Sudan during 1990 and 1992. The first phase of research, totaling some eleven months, was spent among the Jikäny dɔɔr (literally, the "bush"/"outer"

Jikany), or the eastern Jikany Nuer—principally among the eastern Gaajok (Gaajiok) of *ciëŋ* ("the community of," hereafter spelled "cieng") Laang (see maps 3 and 4). After a two-month hiking tour of eastern Nuer villages and cattle camps running along the Baro and Sobat Rivers, I settled into Ulang, a small market center located some 23 miles downstream from Nasir on the Sobat River. Although situated in the thickly populated—by Nuer standards—region of cieng Laang, Ulang was somewhat isolated from the main dry-season truck route stretching between Malakal, the provincial capital to its northwest, and the district headquarters of eastern Nuerland at Nasir to its southeast.[10] Its resident population fluctuated during 1980 and 1981 between some 150 at the height of the dry season (mid-December to late April) and 65 during the height of the wet season (early June to late November). Besides a shady market street lined with eight brick stalls (two of which were owned by resident northern Sudanese), Ulang contained a mud-and-thatch police post, a brick primary school, an empty and nonoperating medical dispensary, a small freshly thatched (Presbyterian) church, and several enormous trees, beneath which meetings for two separate government chiefs' courts were held. A motley assortment of conical houses—many of which occasionally doubled as beer parlors—spread out in several directions. Beyond these stretched miles and miles of scattered Nuer hamlets.

The people of Ulang and its surrounding communities initially attracted me for two reasons. First, they had a well-founded reputation for effectively initiating and carrying out local "development" projects. Shortly before my arrival they erected a solid zinc and brick veterinary office with cattle contributions from the extended community. Much to their disappointment, however, this office was never opened, owing to the government's failure to furnish promised supplies and personnel. They had also recently cleared a second linkage with the main Malakal-Nasir dirt track in an effort to entice greater numbers of merchant lorries into Ulang during their west-east travels. Second, the people of cieng Laang were renowned for having staunchly resisted government army incursions during the first civil war. Their reputation for truculence and independence was such that, despite their construction of a second extension road, most northern truck owners continued to avoid their territories whenever possible during the early 1980s. Ulang and its surrounding settlements thus struck me as a particularly appropriate place to begin investigating current

10. In any event, this road was passable only a few months of the year—roughly, January through April.

Map 4. Principal town centers of the Upper Nile Region (ca. 1983).

tensions and developments in Nuer engagements with the wider political economy of Sudan.

My second period of intensive research, totaling over ten months, was conducted among the western Nuer, or *ji kuë ciëŋ/ciëŋ naadh* (literally, "homeland Nuer"), during 1982–83. After a one-month tour of the extended region, I settled into the village of Tharlual among the Leek Nuer of (cieng) Padang. The core community of Tharlual consisted of forty-one households—nineteen of which were strung along a central ridge and the rest scattered atop isolated patches of raised ground. My principal hosts were Kelual Nyinyar ("Gatnyinyar") Rik, a renowned "earth priest" (sing., *kuäär muɔn;* pl., *kuar muɔn*) and "head chief" of the Leek Nuer, and his eight resident wives. Thanks to their unswerving support, my months in Tharlual were especially enjoyable and productive. News from all over western Nuerland flowed into our compound daily. And major court cases and appeals were held just a few yards from my front door.

By that time I was also fluent in Nuer. My determination to carry out my research without aid of an interpreter or any other type of field assistant had finally paid off. Whereas the eastern Jikany had often tested my linguistic skills with spontaneous vocabulary quizzes, I was encouraged to note that my western Nuer acquaintances swiftly abandoned these in favor of rapidly delivered *märmääri*, or "riddles." Although it took me several weeks to adjust to the western Nuer dialect, I eventually opened an informal "school" in which I endeavored to teach a fluctuating group of between six and twenty-five village children how to read and write their own language. Open literacy classes were held two hours a day, four or five times a week, over a six-month period.[11] This experience further sharpened my skills in both written and spoken Nuer.

My decision to pursue twin field studies at the opposite geographical poles of Nuerland was initially motivated by the desire to avoid overly distorted generalizations about "Nuer culture" and to develop some of the intriguing contrasts between the "eastern" and "western" Nuer first noted by Evans-Pritchard. This approach ultimately yielded an abundance of insights into regional complexities of language, culture, history, social organization, ecology, and the like. Although Nuer images of themselves as a distinctive "people" (*nei ti naadh/nei ti Nuär*) with a unique "language" (*thok*) and "culture" (*ciaŋ;* pl., *ciɛŋ*) appeared to have grown stronger under the influence of British colonial rule and subsequent political upheavals, I soon discovered that contemporary "easterners" characterized themselves as more adaptable—more willing to "jump into" new social situations—than their "western" cousins. The latter, in contrast, prided themselves on being the "true" Nuer whose language and culture were not "all mixed up with Dinka ways." These regional stereotypes, significant in themselves, helped to draw my attention to the fact that historical circumstances had long favored the development of great cultural "flexibility" among the eastern Jikany Nuer. During their nineteenth-century advance across the White Nile, the forefathers of contemporary easterners had assimilated massive numbers of Dinka and Anyuak captives and immigrants. This "python-like" absorption of thousands of Dinka and Anyuak had a profound effect on everything from speech patterns to religious practices and from marriage rites to dance forms.

Moreover, events during the colonial and postcolonial eras continued to

11. A loyal core of six school-age children eventually became proficient enough to read and write extended letters.

nurture a certain social and cultural adaptability among easterners. In general their incorporation into the wider political economy of Sudan was more rapid and traumatic than that of Nuer communities living west of the White Nile. The creation of government chiefs, courts, roads, markets, schools, and medical facilities—to the extent that these were established at all—also proceeded somewhat earlier among the eastern Jikany and Lou Nuer. Furthermore, the eastern Jikany were especially hard hit by the first civil war. As confrontations between the newly independent Sudanese government and growing southern secessionist forces escalated sharply between 1963 and 1972, an estimated 40,000 easterners were eventually forced to flee across the Ethiopian frontier. During this same period many western Nuer communities were mercifully spared the full brunt of the war by massive flooding (1963–72), which made difficult the infiltration of southern secessionist forces across the White Nile. Consequently, when that war ended and the floods subsided, westerners were generally able to reestablish their communities more quickly, easily, and completely than their eastern cousins. Whereas the eastern Jikany Nuer, for instance, were swept up by a powerful wave of Christian conversion after the first civil war, as late as 1983 the western Leek Nuer showed absolutely no signs of following suit. Dependence on imported grain—generally obtained through the sale of cattle—was likewise greater among easterners during the early 1980s.

Regional contrasts of this nature will be developed in the historical analyses that follow. Here I only wish to stress two points. First, however valid Evans-Pritchard's generalizations about Nuer culture and social life may or may not have been during the 1930s, comparable assertions about "the Nuer" of the 1980s and early 1990s are exceedingly difficult for me to make. Second, the contemporary western Leek Nuer were, in my experience, far closer in culture and social outlook to the people described by Evans-Pritchard than were the contemporary eastern Jikany Nuer. Consequently, all of the historical interpretations advanced in this book are enriched and complicated by an appreciation of east/west variations of contemporary Nuer culture and history.[12]

---

12. My knowledge of the central Lak, Thiäng, Gaawär, and, to a lesser extent, Lou Nuer is very limited—being derived primarily from discussions with individual representatives of these sections outside their home territories. For this reason, all references to east-west variations in Nuer history and culture in this book refer primarily to the eastern Jikany Nuer (Jikääny dɔɔr, subdivided into the eastern Gaajok, Gaaguang, and Gaajak sections) and to the western Leek Nuer, among whom I carried out most of my research. Nevertheless, it was my impression that

As my knowledge of regional dialects and lifeways deepened, I also began to realize the extent to which contemporary Nuer men and women were reassessing the scope and meaning of various forms of interpersonal bonds in their efforts to cope with their rapidly expanding social universe. By the early 1980s everyone had realized that the governmental suppression of local fighting and the creation of regional courts and markets had opened up the option of "living alone"—and with it, the possibility of greater "individuality" in the definition of social values and practices. In the words of Deng Gatluak (Dɛŋ Gatluäy), a middle-aged eastern Gaajok man and sometimes driver of a government skiff: "Before everyone used to hoe together, eat together, and go to war together. But now that's all over: today, everyone wants to get ahead." "But can't people get ahead as a group?" I queried. "That may be," Deng responded, "but today everyone seems to want to get ahead by him/herself."

Other people pointed to the vast proliferation of governmental authorities as especially divisive: "We no longer speak with one voice." Rather, local government chiefs, police officers, elected parliamentarians, administrative officials, council members, and party bureaucrats all vied with one other to assert their independence and authority. Growing social disparities in people's engagements with the educational system, local government bureaucracies, and the Christian church had likewise intensified intergenerational conflicts. Or, at least, such was the opinion expressed by scores of parents who, for one reason or another, were frustrated by their children's "refusal to listen."

Significantly, the Nuer equivalent for the English verb "to change" (*gɛɛr rɔ*) is based on the idea of a "splitting away from" or a "moving apart from" that which went before. The transitive verb *gɛɛrɛ rɔ* ("to separate, to pull apart") requires the reflexive particle (*rɔ*), however, to convey this meaning. For example, the commonly invoked expression *Ciaŋ naadh cɛ rɔ gɛɛr* means, literally, "People's 'character/behavior/way of being' [*ciaŋ;* pl., *ciɛŋ*] has become separated from itself"—which is to say, it "has changed." It is as though change were invariably perceived as an internally motivated process of increased social separation. The influence of external forces—such as those of "education/literacy" (*gɔar*), the "government" (*kume*), and "Christianity" (*jiluäk kuɔth*)—only manifest them-

---

the contemporary culture and social outlook of the Lou Nuer (among whom Evans-Pritchard carried out much of his research) were very similar to those of the eastern Jikany, just as those of the western Jikany, Dok, Nyuong, and Bul Nuer evinced considerable similarities with contemporary Leek Nuer.

selves indirectly, as it were, through the actions and decisions of people themselves. In other words, this metaphor implies the existence of a continuing value struggle within Nuer communities—and, not uncommonly, within extended families—between individuals who seek to maintain certain values and practices associated with the past and others who, for one reason or another, advocated the modification or abandonment of such practices. A fully grown man, for example, could legitimately reject the rite of scarification during the 1980s on the grounds that he was "literate/educated": ε *yän gɔar, /caa yä bi gaar.* Similarly, a Christian convert could refuse to participate in a sacrificial event organized by his non-Christian relatives as a matter of religious principle. The expression *Ciaŋ naadh cε rɔ gεεr* encompassed these and many other points of social division generated by forces of "change" that people perceived as having grown too strong to stop. In essence, this expression was a lament that things are not the way they used to be.

Perhaps for this reason, contemporary Nuer men and women tend to invoke a different metaphor for changes that they perceive and evaluate positively. The principal metaphor used in such cases is that of "arrival," or *cop*—as in *ci nath cop*, meaning "people have arrived/caught up [with the foreigners, or *turuɔk*]." Whereas this metaphor stresses people's inherent abilities to change their surroundings by "moving ahead" (*wä nhiam*) or by becoming "knowledgeable" (*ŋac ŋɔani*), it also implies that people's efforts in this regard are directed toward a specific destination. And this destination was identified explicitly during the 1980s with the local establishment of schools, roads, courts, churches, medical facilities, and the like. In brief, Nuer concepts of "arrival" mirror English concepts of "development" or "progress."

But whenever the negativity of change is foremost in people's minds, images of increased social separation dominate. One of the most powerful of these metaphors is *ci rool day* ("the world has split apart, asunder"). When used with reference to a "marriage" (*kuen*) or other types of "relationship" (*maar*), the verb *däkε* (*däyε*) signifies a permanent rupture—which is to say, a "divorce" (*dak kuen*) or a definitive "severing of kinship" (*day maarä*). As a noun, *daay* means "boundary"; and as a transitive verb, it is the act of "dividing up" or "apportioning something" (*däyε ŋuuli*).[13]

The prevalence of these metaphors of social division did not surprise

---

13. The concepts of "shame" (*pöc;* verb, *puɔcε*) and "fear/respect" (*dual*) also play prominent roles in Nuer images of their changing social world. Patterns of behavior people consider to be both "new" (*payε tuɔy*) and "negative" (*jiäkε*) are often attributed to a "loss of shame"—or to a shift from "shame" to "fear" as the primary

me. I had expected that some twenty-five years of British colonial rule and seventeen years of civil war would have jostled these people's confidence in the "comprehensibility" of life and in the inherent superiority of their social values and practices. I anticipated finding, in other words, evidence of increased "heterodoxy" among them and also of a certain "disenchantment with the world"—to use two key phrases of Bourdieu (1977, 1979) and Weber. I was not disappointed.

Although many contemporary women and men spoke with great pride of themselves and their country (*rool Nuärä*), others appeared burdened by feelings of inherent inferiority, especially with respect to the people I represented, the *nei ti boor* ("white people"). I could not help but smile, for instance, when Macaar Turuk—a highly resourceful, self-educated Gaajok man who had once worked in Saudi Arabia, reasoned as follows:

> Nuerland is a very good place. Haven't you seen, Nyarial?[14] The Arabs came here. The British came here, too, . . . and now, the Americans. But have you ever heard of a Nuer going off to live in one of those places? Of course not. Nuerland is a very good place.

Majok Makuac, a western Leek youth who had never wandered far from his herd, was much less certain:

> Way back when the world was created by Divinity, we Nuer were thrown down in the grass with nothing. But you white people were lowered down gently. You have guns and you know how to write. But we know nothing. Old men, young men, women, and girls—all are ignorant. There is nothing that we know. Now we are saying, "Let's jump in and try it." Now we wear clothes but we are still ignorant.

---

force governing human interpersonal relations. Many people remarked, for instance, that the creation of chiefs' courts had the effect of undercutting the sense of shame formerly associated with acts of theft (*kuël*), incest (*ruaal*), adultery (*dhöm*), and other serious errors (*dueri*). To paraphrase an eastern Gaajok man:

> Way back, it was considered "scandalous" (*ɛ buaar*) for a person to steal something or, say, for a man to sleep with his mother-in-law. If you did something really bad and this became known, you would feel immediately ashamed. There was no time to run around the village trying to justify your action— the sense of shame was immediate. A person might even leave and go to the land of the foreigners (*turuɔk*) and stay there. But now, these are punishable offenses. A person who does wrong will be taken to court. There he will try to explain his action, to justify it—or to deny it. Perhaps he will be jailed or fined in cattle. And for this reason, shame is being replaced by fear.

14. Nyarial, or "daughter of the black and white splashed cow," was the name conferred on me and by which I became known throughout the region.

This all-too-commonly expressed self-image of Nuer as "an ignorant people who know nothing" (*thilɛ me ŋackɔ; kuiy nath ŋɔani*) was far less pronounced, I should stress, in contemporary self-comparisons with "northern Arabs" (*jalabni/karɛŋni*). On the contrary, the Arabs were characterized as a relatively weak people whose physical strength and endurance could not compare with those of Nuer. Furthermore, the political powers and knowledge currently wielded by northern Arabs were seen to derive directly from those of the *nei ti boor*. "It's just the Arabs' guns that are bigger," explained Nyapuoc, a western Leek woman, "and they get those from the white people!" In retrospect, the rule of the white people appeared mild compared to the heavy-handed military tactics adopted by northern Arabs during the first and second civil wars.

More important for my purposes, I found that many contemporary Nuer men and women were debating such fundamental issues as: What are the differences between cattle and money as everyday media of exchange and as potential means of creating and affirming social bonds? Do cattle purchased in the marketplace differ from those acquired through bridewealth or inheritance—and if so, how? What is the true basis and scope of "incest prohibitions" (*ruaal*)? Why should Divinity allow the Arabs to marry their relatives and bring forth living, healthy children but not ourselves? Is it because the Arabs marry with money instead of cattle, or is it because their blood (*riɛm*) is different? Do homicides carried out with guns have the same spiritual and social consequences as those carried out with spears? Can a death occur without the direct intervention of Divinity? How effective is cattle sacrifice in the curing of illness? Should Christians eat the meat of cattle sacrificed by non-Christians? Is manhood something that must be proven to self and others through the ordeal of scarification at initiation? Or is scarification merely a means of "tribal" identification, which is itself no longer necessary? What is it that distinguishes the Nuer as a people, indeed as "the people of the people" (*nei ti naadh*)?

Doubtless my sensitivity to the transient nature of all I observed was heightened during the early phases of field research by strong premonitions of an impending civil war with the north—premonitions that were broadly shared by Nuer themselves. However, it is difficult to determine how much of the fluidity in values I perceived among Nuer was the product of more than fifty years of tumultuous history and how much was the product of shifting rhetorical styles and theoretical interests within the discipline of anthropology as a whole. Fabian (1983), Asad (1986), Rosaldo (1986), Clifford (1986, 1988), Marcus and Fischer (1986), and other critics of "ethnography" have all expressed profound reservations about the ways cultures were defined and described by Evans-Pritchard, Malinowski, Mead, Geertz, and other key figures within the discipline. They have been especially critical of the ways many of these authors tended to mask the inherently reflexive, historical nature of field research with a rhetorical aura of timeless objectivity.

Interestingly, Paul Howell (1954), who began investigating Nuer "customary law" just six years after the completion of Evans-Pritchard's field study, found ample evidence of disparities of value and practice among Nuer. As the principal British officer responsible for the promotion of greater "standardization" in the laws enforced by government chiefs' courts, Howell uncovered numerous areas of social and ideological controversy, some tied to regional variations and others omnipresent. Moreover, most of his relevant publications (1945b, 1947, 1948a, 1952, 1953a), including *A Manual of Nuer Law* (1954), grapple directly with issues of historical change—and, in particular, with the impact of colonial rule on "traditional" Nuer practices of marriage, divorce, inheritance, homicide, adultery, cattle ownership, bloodwealth compensation, and the like. The very nature of his research task required him to be especially attentive to regional variations of value, history, and social form.

For me, this uncertainty flowed into the far more basic problem of adequately defining and documenting historical change. Evans-Pritchard's earlier monographs, in conjunction with subsequent historical accounts by Howell (1954) and Johnson (1980, 1994), certainly provided me with a richly detailed and provocative written image of the dynamics of Nuer social life during the 1930s and, to some extent, through the mid-1940s.[15] It thus seemed at least plausible to construct a hypothetical ("ideal-typical") model of the evolving bases of Nuer social life during the 1930s and then to cross-check this model with Nuer oral accounts and with archival records in order to isolate major historical trends. I therefore devoted four additional months of research to the reading of relevant Arabic and English archives located in the Sudan Collection of Durham University (UK), in the National Records Office and University Library in Khartoum, and in the government offices of Nasir and Bentiu in the Upper Nile Province. The historical interpretations advanced in this book thus rest firmly on an appreciation of the written record, and particularly on the lucid eth-

15. For a fuller listing of the many relevant publications of these two authors, see the bibliography.

nographic accounts of Evans-Pritchard and Howell. While I cannot claim absolute validity for the historicized model of Nuer social life I eventually developed, it did prove illuminating when used in close conjunction with Nuer understandings of their own changing social world.

ON BECOMING HUMAN IN NUER EYES:
METHODS OF INFORMATION GATHERING

My efforts to obtain a broad and internally diversified image of Nuer experiences of change permeated every aspect of my field research. Although I eventually carried out several extensive household and marital surveys, attended scores of court cases, interviewed numerous chiefs, merchants, and other unique groups, my principal research approach was nondirective. I tried to ask questions about events and practices that people were already discussing or directly engaged in at the time. Moreover, I took the attitude that I had something to gain from an hour's conversation with literally anyone—be they a seven-year-old boy or an elderly grandmother. I had no "key" informants but, rather, circulated widely, interacting with as many people of as many rural communities as I possibly could. Whenever I encountered a novel linguistic phrase or an intriguing explanatory comment or observation, I would take a moment to jot it down, word for word in Nuer, in the presence of the person who had offered it. Reading back what I had written, I would then ask that person if what I had written was accurate and if there was anything else he or she would like to add. I found this method of "open note taking" to be not only efficient but also a highly effective way of inviting individual acquaintances to participate directly in my research project—a project that I explained in the following terms:

> I've come here to live with you because, where I come from, very few people have heard about "the people of the people." So, I've come to learn your language and your ways of living together so that some day I will be able to write a book that will carry your reputation all the way to America.

In short, I appealed to people's collective sense of pride. I also paid very close attention to the types of questions Nuer asked me about how people lived and acted where I came from. For I realized that their questions suggested aspects of their own social world that they could conceive of as being "different" elsewhere.

Although Evans-Pritchard and I both engaged in what is commonly known as "participant-observation," I suspect that our modes of interacting with people were quite different. Consider the following passage from

Evans-Pritchard's famous essay entitled "Some Reminiscences and Reflections on Fieldwork":

> This brings me to what anthropologists sometimes speak of as participant-observation. By this they mean that in so far as it is possible and convenient they live the life of the people among whom they are doing research. This is a somewhat complicated matter and I shall only touch on the material side of it. I found it useful if I wanted to understand how and why Africans are doing certain things to do them myself: I had a hut and a byre like theirs; I went hunting with them with spear and bow and arrow; I learnt to make pots; I consulted oracles; and so forth. But clearly one has to recognize that there is a certain pretence in such attempts at participation, and people do not always appreciate them. One enters into another culture and withdraws from it at the same time. One cannot really become a Zande or a Nuer or a Bedouin Arab, and the best compliment one can pay them is to remain apart from them in essentials. In any case one always remains oneself, inwardly a member of one's own society and a sojourner in a strange land. Perhaps it would be better to say that one lives in two different worlds of thought at the same time, in categories and concepts and values which often cannot easily be reconciled. One becomes, at least temporarily, a sort of double marginal man, alienated from both worlds. (1976:243)

Although Evans-Pritchard's memories of fieldwork among the Nuer (and other peoples) capture beautifully the sense of cultural limbo that anthropologists so often have, I was surprised to find so little evidence in his writings of the active social interaction and direct intellectual engagement that was for me the most rewarding aspect of field research, both personally and "data-wise." Whereas Evans-Pritchard stressed the importance of remaining reserved in essentials—if there is disbelief, one should not let it show; if there are value conflicts, one should not bring them out—I found, to the contrary, that it was often helpful to express my uncertainties, curiosities, and experiences of "culture shock" openly with others and to take the conversation from there. "Observation" is, of course, extremely important—especially in the sense of being in the right place at the right time. But I more often thought of fieldwork as "perfecting the art of conversation." And for a rewarding conversation, one needs thoughts and opinions for other people to engage with.

Therefore, whenever people directly asked me for my opinion about some matter or my reaction to some event, I tried to answer their questions as openly and honestly as I could. Fortunately for me, many Nuer women and men were equally candid and open with me. What's more, I found that most of my Nuer friends and acquaintances had a splendid sense of humor.

There was plenty of cross-sex teasing, wit, and jokes woven into the give-and-take of daily life. Consequently, it was often possible for me to defuse delicate situations by giving them a witty twist. This was especially important in breaking through Nuer gender stereotypes as well as in rapidly establishing myself as fellow "human being" (*raan*; gen., *naadh*; pl., *nath/ nei*). And thus, as the months passed and I gradually became known as an entertaining conversationalist (*guạn muɔ̈ŋä*), many people began to volunteer observations on all kinds of subjects simply because they thought that they too "should be written down." In these and other ways I attempted to encourage Nuer to share as freely as possible their understanding of their own changing social world.

Being a woman—or rather, an awkward cross between a woman and a girl—was a definite advantage, for I experienced no difficulty whatsoever in moving at will between gatherings of men and of women, both young and old.[16] However, I did not find that people viewed me as an asexual being. Although I was married at the time I began field research, once it became obvious that my husband would not be joining me and, more important, that I was not pregnant, I often found it impossible to convince people that I was "married" at all. Insist as I might, my claims to "womanhood"—and hence "adulthood"—were inherently weak because I had not yet borne a child. I recall one humorous incident in which I was immediately approached upon arriving at a distant cattle camp by a group of curious girls who wanted to know whether I was a "woman" or a "girl." No sooner had I sought to lay some claim on the former category based on my marital status than our conversation was interrupted by an old woman. Stretching out her right hand to shake mine, she simultaneously reached out with her left, squeezed one of my breasts, turned, and announced: "It's a lie. She's a girl—she has never suckled a child!" How could I possibly counter such arguments? So I eventually settled into the social category of "school girl" (*nyaa duël gɔạrä*), knowing full well that this category gave me a certain degree of independence vis-à-vis "my father" and natal family (see plate 6).

Similarly, Nuer men were constantly reminding me that, in their eyes,

16. My femininity also helped to distance me from governmental powers: as a girl/woman, I was someone to be protected and cared for. I had no independent food supplies or household. Whatever luxuries I managed to obtain during my occasional trips to Malakal or more distant market centers—luxuries such as sacks of sugar, lentils and rice, decorative beads, soap, clothing, and the like—were immediately dispersed upon arrival among the various families with whom I ate.

I was an eminently marriageable "girl." Because Nuer men were required by rules of exogamy to marry persons classified as "non-kin" or "strangers," it was not at all uncommon for them to try to strike up a conversation with me—or any other mature, unrelated "girl" for that matter—with statements such as: "Hello, I'm going to marry you" or "Hello, I'm going to 'steal' you." The first dozen or so times I was confronted in this way by some swaggering young man or group of men that I had never before encountered, my immediate reaction was to *pöc* (that is, to show "embarrassment/shame"). I would look away and fall silent. I soon realized, however, that this was the worst reaction because it was immediately interpreted as evidence that I really was a "girl" and, therefore, could possibly be "interested." The next stage was for me to try to counter such greetings by asserting that I was already married—an argument that invariably fell on deaf ears: "We'll steal you anyway." Eventually, I discovered that the best way to derail such conversations was through humor. I tried to take advantage of the "cultural gap" that both these men and I knew existed. I would say things such as "Well, that's fine with me. But if I were you I'd think twice. My milking skills are weak, my cooking poor. If you married me, you would probably starve within the month!" This response was not all that effective because it could easily be countered by some version of: "Oh, that's not a problem. I'll get someone else to do the cooking and housework, all you have to do is bear the children." Alternatively, I would say: "Sure, you can marry me. But I should warn you that my father has no desire for more cattle. However, if you could find him a live buffalo, a live lion, a live crocodile [and I would go on to name five or six of the most dangerous animals I could think of] . . . then I'm sure he would agree." This response invariably provoked a good deal of laughter and usually spun off into playful musing such as "Hmm, I think I could get your father a lion cub and a cobra but—a wild buffalo? That could prove difficult." From there, the conversation was usually free sailing: I could open up just about any topic I liked. Sometimes if I had already parried several such greetings that day, I would fall back on a more direct "culture shock" approach: "Don't you men have any other way to strike up a conversation with a girl other than 'Hello, I'm going to marry you!'?" This response was one of the most effective: "Aye, Rial, that girl! What will she come up with next?" In brief, I found humor one of the most effective ways not only of "breaking the ice" but also of becoming a full-fledged person (*raan*) in people's eyes.

Throughout the fieldwork phases of my research, my contact with the

Plate 6.   The anthropologist, alias "Nyarial."

Nuer literate elite was minimal—being confined to brief encounters during occasional mail runs to the district headquarters of Nasir or Bentiu. It was only after I had formulated my research findings in written form and had returned with them to Khartoum in 1990 that I actively began to solicit the reactions of willing Nuer readers—several of whom openly acknowledged, after reading what I had written, that my awareness of regional variations of culture and history, in some cases, exceeded their own.[17]

By allowing Nuer to guide my research interests in these and many other ways, I hoped to avoid imposing on them my own notions of culture, history, and society. Moreover, I soon realized that many of the social and moral "dilemmas" contemporary Nuer perceived in their immediate social lives were not strictly "local." But neither could their historical emergence be equated with the progressive intrusion of "global" forces of social and economic change. In attempting to understand how Nuer women and men had experienced these past six decades of turbulent history, there were no master narratives of "nation-building," "modernization," or "development" to which I could appeal. It would have been impossible to frame their story with such terms.

Rather, contemporary Nuer perceptions and evaluations of change appeared to cross-cut—in often novel and fascinating ways—many of the same dilemmas that social scientists have faced in attempting to analyze the historical ramifications of broader processes of economic commodification, regional warfare, secularization, labor recruitment, arms dissemination, political subjugation, racism, ethnic identification, kinship contraction, resource extraction, religious conversion, literacy, and the continuing breakdown of the nation-state in many postcolonial states of Africa and beyond. Much of this book is thus devoted to an implicit—if not always explicit—elaboration of intriguing points of interconnection I perceived between Nuer understandings of their rapidly changing life circumstances and more abstract visions of the encounter between "global" and "local" forces of transformation gleaned from the social scientific discourse.

In brief, this book is the result of a conscious struggle on my part to preserve Nuer perceptions and understandings of their own social world

---

17. I have consciously refrained from emphasizing the extremely difficult field conditions in which I worked. Suffice it to say that in terms of general security, health hazards, food shortages, transport, and institutional support, the general situation in the Upper Nile had not improved—and in some ways had seriously deteriorated—since Evans-Pritchard worked among Nuer during the 1930s.

without abandoning my own perspective as a deeply concerned and informed outsider. That this book could have been written at all reflects, I think, the fact that many of the intellectual interests and historical concerns I brought with me to the field were shared to some extent by contemporary Nuer men and women. They too were actively trying to figure out the broader historical forces shaping their everyday lives. They too were constantly developing interpretations of the social changes they perceived and experienced. And these interpretations were in turn being reshaped and reevaluated in light of people's evolving aspirations for and apprehensions about the future. I saw myself, in other words, as one knowledge creator among many. Accordingly, this book represents only one of many possible perspectives on the diverse theoretical and historical issues explored. And yet, it is an ethnography that also makes serious claims at historical "explanation."

◊ ◊ ◊

All six core chapters of this book thus revolve around social or moral dilemmas that rural Nuer women and men perceived in their daily lives and were actively grappling with throughout the 1980s and early 1990s. Concentrating on socioeconomic processes connected with the spread of colonialism and of regional cattle and labor markets, chapter 2 explores the historical roots of contemporary Nuer debates over the "interchangeability" of cattle and money as everyday media of exchange. Specifically, it describes the unique system of hybrid wealth categories that Nuer gradually devised in order to facilitate movements of cattle and money between "market" and "nonmarket" spheres of exchange while simultaneously affirming the existence of an axiological boundary between these spheres. Money, I argue, did not develop into a generalized medium of exchange among Nuer. Nor did its introduction precipitate the emergence of a "unicentric economy." Rather, Nuer incorporated money into a weighted exchange system in which cattle remained the dominant metaphor of value. Money's powers of effacement were largely checked, I show, by an ideological elaboration of the unique "blood" bonds uniting cattle and people.

Although increasing recourse to monetary exchange between the 1930s and the early 1990s did not sunder people's bonds of identification with their cattle, it did foster a significant contraction of Nuer concepts of selfhood and sociality. Before the introduction of currency and markets, the sense of self people cultivated through their relations with cattle invariably implied the support of a broader collectivity of persons, including ancestors and divinities as well as numerous contemporaries. The role of cattle in creating and maintaining this socially augmented sense of self was subsequently weakened, however, by emerging market opportunities for the individual acquisition of cattle wealth. Consequently, relations of autonomy and dependence between men and women and between senior and junior men began to shift as individual and collective opportunities for the exercise of power through controls over cattle wealth declined.

My analysis shifts in chapter 3 from a focus on the creation and affirmation of enduring bonds of *maar* ("kinship")—a word that implies mutual harmony and peace—to relationships of permanent hostility, feuding, and warfare. I show how people's interpretations of the spiritual and social consequences of acts of inter-Nuer homicide were progressively narrowed and weakened by the secularizing thrust of expanding governmental powers, by the increasing availability of guns, and by the experience of two extended civil wars. The ethics and tactics of warfare, I argue, were radically different in a world where the power of guns and of the government increasingly displaced those of divinity as the primary creators and destroyers of the social and moral universe. Furthermore, as guns burned deeper and deeper into local forms of fighting, many men and women openly began to wonder whether the long-term spiritual and social consequences of gun slayings were identical to those perpetrated by spears. Unlike an individually crafted spear, a bullet's source was often difficult to trace in the heat of battle. Consequently, the idea that relations of feud emanated outwards from a mysterious blood bond forged between slayer and slain at the moment of death became increasingly difficult for people to maintain in those areas where gun warfare predominated.

Furthermore, ever since the consolidation of British colonial rule, Nuer men and women had been pressured into accepting the idea that acts of intraethnic homicide carried out in the name of "the government" were completely devoid of the spiritual dangers and long-term social consequences of homicides generated by interpersonal or intercommunity violence. Indeed, people's acceptance of this distinction, I argue, was tantamount to their acceptance of the "legitimacy" of the specific governmental regime in power. Consequently, as more and more Nuer men were incorporated into the national army, regional police force, and other branches of the government, many were forced to contemplate the possibility—if not actuality—of killing fellow Nuer "in the line of duty." These developments provoked profound moral dilemmas among Nuer—dilemmas that were progressively generalized to the population as a whole during the course of the first and second civil wars.

Chapter 4 analyzes the shifting bases of power and authority between Nuer men and women, young and old, with particular reference to the impact of government chiefs' courts on local patterns of courtship, marriage, and divorce. In many ways it constitutes the analytic heart of this book. For it shows how broadening court definitions of the procreative and sexual obligations of wives toward their husbands and affines progressively undermined women's possibilities for autonomy within marriage. At the same time they leveled—if not reversed—former asymmetries between wife-givers and wife-takers. Women's possibilities for autonomy outside of marriage, in contrast, were significantly strengthened by the introduction of regional courts. These court-related developments also reduced the importance of cattle exchange in Nuer definitions of the transgenerational scope and hierarchical structure of various types of enduring social bonds. As such, these trends contributed to a new dispersion of social powers previously concentrated in the hands of senior, cattle-wealthy men.

Another notable phenomenon during the 1980s and 1990s was the contracting scope of incest prohibitions and exogamic limits, a process that was proceeding more rapidly among eastern Nuer communities. This striking social development was stimulated in part by growing Nuer awareness of northern Arab marital practices and in part by spreading of Christian doctrines. By the early 1980s many Nuer were openly wondering whether the binding power of human blood extended beyond that of shared cattle rights in determining the limits of exogamy and incest prohibitions. Moreover, people were not only questioning the transgenerational scope of specific prohibitions but were grappling with the logic and meaning of incest itself. Chapter 5 explores this public rethinking of incest and exogamic prohibitions with respect to apparent changes in Nuer definitions of the transgenerational reach of various kinship connections. More specifically, it shows how evolving Nuer opinions in these regards had concentrated on certain categories of kin while simultaneously ignoring several crucial power axes of intercommunity and intrafamilial bonds.

A further field of contemporary debate among Nuer concerned the ultimate significance of male initiation rites, the historical conditions that gave rise to these rites, and their current sociopolitical relevance. This controversy, which developed among the western Nuer a full generation before it spread east, was everywhere associated with the emergence of a small but growing class of educated Nuer youths who had rejected the rite of initiation entirely. Although sexually mature, and thus equated in some respects with other "bulls of the herd," these uninitiated adults nevertheless straddled the categories of "boyhood" and "manhood." The appearance of this new breed of "bull-boys" provoked a society-wide reassessment and clarification of the role of initiation in the transfer of *mut* (agnatic spear-calls), *ric* (named age-sets), and collective cattle rights across the generations. Chapter 6 traces the development of this debate from the late 1940s, when the first bull-boys appeared, through a highly controversial proclamation issued by an SPLA commander in 1988 outlawing initiation for western Nuer youth. That chapter also shows how "paper"—and the hidden powers of literacy it conveys—became an increasingly important point of contention and cooperation between the emerging educated elite and the vast majority of Nuer men and women, who remained as yet totally uninitiated in the practices of reading and writing.

Finally, chapter 7 shows how the sacrificial role of cattle in Nuer social life—along with the social powers senior men derived from their exclusive control of it—was steadily being undermined during the 1980s and early 1990s by a wide variety of exogenous and endogenous factors. Among the most important of these were: changing Nuer assessments of the causes of illness and death, stimulated in part by their growing confidence in the efficacy of Western medicines and related etiologies of disease; increased Nuer acceptance of the nonsacrificial slaughtering of domestic animals for purposes of meat consumption, generated in part by a more open identification between cattle and cash and in part by evolving practices and principles of hospitality; and, most important of all, the rapid spread of Christian doctrines advocating the total rejection of cattle as objects of spiritual dedication and sacrifice. As a result of these trends, the conceptual separation formerly lying at the heart of Nuer sacrificial practices between the blood and food dimensions of human/cattle relations was weakened and blurred—as was the former centrality of age and gender distinctions in Nuer interactions with both cattle and divinity.

Chapter 7 further shows how orthodox forms of evangelical Protestantism contributed to the secularization of vast areas of contemporary Nuer social and moral life. Because Christianity, as locally practiced and interpreted, addressed a far narrower range of life crises and human misfortunes than those associated with cattle sacrifice, many converts were at a loss how to interpret and respond to experiences of infant mortality, severe illness, and many other hardships. Instead of confronting this "human power vacuum" directly, however, many leading Nuer pastors and evangelists were taking a tougher line during the 1980s in their condemnations of cattle sacrifice without offering much in the way of Christian alternatives. The result was that, by the mid-1980s, several Nuer prophets were beginning to step into this spiritual void in an effort both to "resacralize" a war-blighted world and to blunt sharpening ideological divisions between Christian and non-Christian Nuer. By far the most powerful of these was a contemporary Lak Nuer prophet by the name of Wutnyang Gatakɛk (Wutnyaŋ Gatäkɛk), whose spiritual and military activities form the final subject of chapter 7.

These six core chapters also form part of a more general analysis of changing relations of autonomy and dependence rooted in fundamental social distinctions of age, gender, wealth, and descent. On the assumption that "imagined communities" of whatever scale or scope may be approached, in part, as a set of mediated relationships that combine complex symbolic and material concerns, I have concentrated on the primary metaphors and social media Nuer have used over the years in developing interpersonal relations among themselves as well as with the broader social world of which they formed part. I argue that evolving Nuer concepts and practices of sociality were intimately bound up over the past sixty years with the symbolics of *riɛm* ("blood"), *yɔk* ("cattle"), and *mieth* ("food") as complementary means of creating and affirming enduring social bonds. Nevertheless, the relative prominence of these three media of "relationship," I suggest, gradually shifted as more and more Nuer began to appreciate how "new" media of exchange originating outside their immediate social world—*yiou* ("money"), *maai* ("guns"), and *waragak* ("paper") being the most important of these—were also capable of both binding and dividing their social world. More specifically, I show how metaphors of blood gained increasing prominence over those of cattle in Nuer perceptions and experiences of their rapidly expanding social universe. I argue that, prior to the consolidation of British colonial rule and the introduction of government courts, cattle markets, and wage labor opportunities, most Nuer operated under the premise that the social circulation of cattle should take precedence over that of human blood in the creation and affirmation of enduring bonds of descent and alliance. However, due to growing disparities in Nuer engagements with the wider political economy of Sudan, the principle by which cattle linkages were valued more than blood linkages became the subject of increasing controversy and challenge in a wide variety of social contexts. By exploring how Nuer variously understood and responded to these and other social transformations wrought by decades of British colonial rule and by two extended periods of civil war, it becomes possible to show how they were drawing creatively on implicit meanings and tensions in their culture in their efforts to make sense of an increasingly senseless world.

2   Blood, Cattle, and Cash
The Commodification of Nuer Values

I was once asked by a highly intelligent and unusually well-traveled eastern Gaajak youth, who had ventured at one point as far as Iraq in search of profitable employment, whether I knew the ultimate source of money (*yiou;* sg., *yieth*). After remarking spontaneously to the effect that he realized different countries used different currencies, Peter Pal Jola went on to say:

> But there's something I still don't understand about money. Money's not like the cow because the cow has blood and breath and, like people, gives birth. But money does not. So, tell me, do you know whether God or man creates money?

Peter's question took me by surprise—and, though I answered it as best I could, I am not at all sure my discussion of government mints and international currency markets satisfied him. Nor do I know how many other Nuer men and women shared his curiosity in this regard.

Yet, however widespread uncertainties of this nature may have been during the early 1980s, in no way did they prevent Nuer from appreciating and using money as an everyday medium of exchange. Indeed, individual musings about the ultimate source of money were in many ways extraneous to the immediate feel of those various bits of metal and paper ever passing through their hands. It was not the mystery of money's generative powers that colored the give-and-take of daily life at that time but, rather, as we shall see, money's "sterility" as compared with the self-generating capacity of *yɔk*, or cattle (sing., *yaŋ*). "Money," as people put it, "has no blood (*riɛm;* pl., *rim*)," blood being the procreative substance of both cattle and people in their eyes. Similarly, it was the immediate, not ultimate, source of money that defined what many contemporary Nuer considered to be very different sorts of money. People drew a marked distinction, for instance, between *yiou lat,* or "the money of work," and money acquired through the sale of cattle, *yiou yɔɔk,* or "the money of cattle." This dichotomy was balanced by a parallel distinction between two sorts of cattle: purchased cattle, *yɔk yiouni,* or "the cattle of money," and cattle received through bridewealth exchange, *yɔk nyiët,* or "the cattle of girls/daughters."

These four categories of wealth, along with several subsidiary ones, have played an increasingly prominent role in determining relations of autonomy and dependence among contemporary Nuer.

Significantly, the hybrid categorical system of monetary and cattle wealth Nuer developed in recent decades appears to exceed, in both complexity and inner dynamism, anything previously reported in the burgeoning literature on the "commodification" or "commoditization" of human/cattle relations in other parts of Africa (see, for example, Comaroff and Comaroff 1990; Ferguson 1985; Murray 1981; Parkin 1980; Sansom 1976; and Shipton 1989). For unlike the "one-" and "two-way" barrier systems reported among the Basotho (Ferguson 1985) and the Luo (Shipton 1989) respectively, this categorical system did not pivot on a simple opposition between "cattle" and "cash." Nor could it be characterized as an unambiguous "attempt to dam the corrosive flow of cash," as appears to have been the case among the southern Tswana (Comaroff and Comaroff 1990:212). Rather, contemporary Nuer attitudes toward money appeared more ambivalent and contextually differentiated. Although past and present generations of Nuer men and women consciously "resisted" the idea that cattle and money were wholly interchangeable, they simultaneously sought out and used money as a means of tempering perceived instabilities and inequalities within the cattle economy itself. In developing these points here, I attempt to show how the various categories of cattle and monetary wealth they eventually developed facilitated movements of money and cattle between market and nonmarket spheres of exchange at the same time as they affirmed the existence of an axiological boundary between these spheres. This chapter also reflects more generally on how the increasing acceptance of currency by Nuer contributed over the years to a profound reevaluation of the place of cattle in their lives.

My analytic approach is guided in part by theoretical insights offered by both Simmel and Marx. For Simmel (1978[1900]:297–303), money's uniqueness lies in its abilities to extend and diversify human interdependence while simultaneously excluding everything personal and specific. Money distances self from other and self from object, generating within the individual dissident feelings of alienation and self-sufficiency, of powerlessness and personal freedom (307–311):

> In as much as interests are focused on money and to the extent that possessions consist of money, the individual will develop the tendency and feeling of independent importance in relation to the social whole. He will relate to the social whole as one power confronting another, since he is free to take up business relations and co-operation wherever he likes. (343)

The "close relationship . . . between a money economy, individualization, and enlargement of the circle of social relationships" enables the individual to buy himself not only out of bonds with specific others but also, Simmel notes, out of those bonds rooted in his possessions (347, 403ff.). As "the embodiment of the relativity of existence," money drives a wedge between "possessing" and "being": "Through money, man is no longer enslaved in things" (409, 307, 404).

While Simmel welcomes elimination of the personal element of economic exchange as the gateway to "human freedom" (1978 [1900]:297–303), he is acutely aware, nonetheless, of the potential instability, disorientation, and despair generated by money's perpetual wrenching of the personal values from things. The development of a money economy, he remarks, often encourages avarice and other socially detrimental forms of possessive individualism (247). Moreover, as money's empty and indifferent character wears away at the "direction-giving significance of things," individuals often strive to reinvest their possessions with "a new importance, a deeper meaning, a value of their own":

> If modern man is free—free because he can sell everything, and free because he can buy everything—then he now seeks (often in problematical vacillations) in the objects themselves that vigor, stability and inner unity which he has lost because of the changed money-conditioned relationship that he has with them. (404)

For Marx, in contrast, money is a "privileged commodity" to the extent that the congelations of human labor embodied in all other commodities come to express their values in it (1967[1867]:93). The development of "a 'money-form' of commodity exchange" is thus critical, he argues, for the recognition of human labor and productive powers as an abstract totality and thus for the creation of a universal labor market (35–84). Yet in making possible the sale of human labor as a general commodity, "a 'money-form' of commodity exchange" also facilitates relations of exploitation and alienation within the production process by effectively dissociating the value of concrete labor from the value of the products it can produce (167ff., 195–198). The monetization of production relations, in other words, tends to intensify the "fetishism" inherent in simpler forms of commodity exchange by further obscuring the subjective contribution that the producer makes to the product. For it is "just this ultimate money-form of the world of commodities," Marx argues, "that actually conceals, instead of disclosing, the social character of private labor, and the social relations between individual producers" (76). In brief, money plays privileged symbolic as well as material roles in the transformation of "direct social relations between individuals at work" into "material relations between persons and social relations between things," a transformation that, of course, lies at the heart of Marx's analysis of capitalism (73).

Following Marx, this chapter highlights social and economic processes connected with the spread of colonialism and of capitalistic relations of production underlying the gradual empowerment of money in Nuer eyes. Yet it also aspires to a more phenomenological understanding—à la Simmel—of money's "enigmatic" qualities as variously perceived, experienced, and evaluated by Nuer. How have these people been grappling with the allegedly "liberating" and "alienating" potentials of a rapidly expanding regional money economy?

ON THE ONENESS OF CATTLE AND PEOPLE: 1930

According to Evans-Pritchard (1940a, 1951b, 1956), the Nuer of the early 1930s were almost totally absorbed in the care, exchange, and sacrifice of their beloved cattle (see plate 7). Few Nuer at that time understood the concept of currency; fewer still understood the impersonal principles of market exchange; and literally no one parted willingly with a cow for money.[1] Wage-labor opportunities were universally spurned as being tantamount to slavery. Rather, people at that time were bound to their herds in an intimate symbiosis of survival (Evans-Pritchard 1940a:16–50). Mutual "parasites" is how Evans-Pritchard characterized them (1940a:36). Whereas cattle depended on human beings for protection and care, people depended on cattle as insurance against ecological hazards and as vital sources of milk, meat, leather, and dung. Yet cattle were also valued far beyond their material contributions to human survival: Cattle were the principal means by which people created and affirmed enduring bonds amongst themselves as well as between themselves and divinity (*kuɔth*). In sacrificial and exchange con-

---

1. Evans-Pritchard (1956:223–224) characterizes Nuer notions of barter exchange at that time as follows: "Nuer do not regard purchase from an Arab merchant in the way in which we regard purchase from a shop. It is not to them an impersonal transaction, and they have no idea of price and currency in our sense. Their idea of a purchase is that you give something to a merchant who is thereby put under an obligation to help you. At the same time you ask him for something you need from his shop and he ought to give it to you because, by taking your gift, he has entered into a reciprocal relationship with you. Hence *kok* has the sense of either 'to buy' or 'to sell'. The two acts are an expression of a single relationship of reciprocity." By the early 1980s, however, these two acts were linguistically separated—"to buy" (*kokɛ*) and "to sell" (*kɔkɛ*).

Plate 7. Young children celebrating their "oneness" with cattle through dance.

texts, cattle were considered direct extensions of the human persona (Evans-Pritchard 1956:248ff.). Their fertility and vitality were continuously being equated with and opposed to those of human beings. This "cattle/human equation" was perhaps most obvious at times of bloodwealth and bridewealth exchange. However, it permeated myriad other contexts and relations, saturating, as it were, the whole of Nuer social life at that time. Consider, for instance, Evans-Pritchard's sensitive descriptions of the bonds of "identification" uniting a young man with the ox conferred upon him at initiation and his analysis of the "substitution" of "the life of an ox" for that of "man" at the heart of Nuer sacrificial acts (1956:248–271). Or, as I often heard this relationship succinctly expressed: *Yaŋ cäyɛ raan* ("The cow creates the person").

What is perhaps less evident from Evans-Pritchard's descriptions of Nuer social life during the early 1930s, however, is that something was gained by Nuer communities as a whole through the cultural assertion of a fundamental identity between cattle and people. It was because cattle and people were in some sense "one" that individuals were able to transcend some of the profoundest of human frailties and thereby achieve a greater sense of mastery over their world: Death became surmountable, infertility reversible, and illness something that could be actively defined and cured.

This equation gave life (*tëk*), as it were, a second chance. For example, if a man died without heirs, his relatives were able—indeed obliged—to collect cattle and marry a "ghost wife" (*ciek jokä*) in the name of the deceased to bear children for him. Likewise, if a woman proved infertile, she was "free" to become a social man, gather cattle, and marry a wife to produce children for her. And, if not for rites of cattle sacrifice, people would have stood condemned at that time to a passive forbearance of severe illness, environmental crises, and countless other difficulties. But because human and bovine vitality were identified in such contexts, all these experiences of vulnerability and hardship could be lifted to a collective plane where they could be given form and meaning and actively coped with. Last, the ever-present possibility of translating human values into cattle values enhanced people's ability to achieve lasting periods of peace amongst themselves. Although cattle were frequent subjects of dispute among kinsmen as well as non-kinsmen, there is a well-known saying that runs *Thilɛ duer me bääl yaŋ* ("No [human] error exceeds the cow"). In other words, cattle were—and to a large extent continue to be—the conflict resolvers par excellence.

It was thus the ideological assertion of a fundamental "oneness" between cattle and people that enabled Nuer to extend the potency of human action in tempering the perplexing vicissitudes and vulnerabilities of life. And in a social world where procreation, physical well-being, and communal peace were—and continue to be—among the highest cultural values, these "extensions" or "augmentations of life" should not be underestimated. To ignore them or to gloss over them by thinking of cattle exchange and sacrifice solely in terms of "reciprocity," "compensation," and "restitution" would be to reduce, I think, the creative potency of Nuer social life as a whole at that time.

This is not to say that all Nuer benefited equally from this potent equation. Since women and children were excluded in principle, and cattleless men in practice, from full participation in sacrificial invocations and major cattle-transfer negotiations, the added sense of control over the world made possible by the cattle/human equation directly enhanced the social powers of senior, cattle-wealthy men while it intensified feelings of dependence among other household members. In other words, this equation reinforced and extended men's roles as the protectors of women and children and as the defenders of life and the social order—and hence, it bolstered men's claims of physical and moral superiority over women and children as well. Furthermore, it is essential to realize that, without access to cattle, a man could not legally acquire heirs—no matter how many children he sired.

From men's perspective, cattle, not women, "produced" children (Evans-Pritchard 1940a, 1951b). In representing potential rights to the fruits of woman's womb, cattle gathered the procreative powers of both sexes and placed them in the hands of cattle-wealthy elders. Unlike a man, however, a woman did not depend upon their release in order to achieve full parental status: Physical maternity and social maternity were inseparable in the eyes of Nuer. A foster mother who merely cared for, but never suckled, another woman's child established no permanent bond of *maar*, or kinship with that child. Individual fertility, not cattle wealth, was the principal route to self-fulfillment, security, and independence for women. The procreative powers of men, in contrast, were essentially collective: A man's reproductive potential merged with that of his agnatic kinsmen through "the ancestral herd," upon which he and his patrilineal relatives all drew in order to marry, bear sons, and thereby extend the patriline.[2] Male corporate solidarity and continuity were, indeed, founded on this principle of "communal fertility" through shared cattle rights. Hence, cattle were in a very real sense the currency of power among men.[3]

Nevertheless, cattle and people were never equally valued. There was always an element of social asymmetry created by their cross-directional movements. The bride who crossed paths with some twenty or thirty head of cattle was not equated directly with them. Rather, bridewealth negotiations invariably concluded with a declaration by the groom's family that additional cattle would be forthcoming on the marriages of the bride's daughters, granddaughters, and great granddaughters, until such time as the extended debt uniting the two families dissolved (Evans-Pritchard 1951b:78). Or, as this idea was expressed to me, *Kuen thile pɛk* ("Marriage [literally, the counting (of cattle)] never ends"). Similarly, everyone maintained that, despite the successful negotiation and transfer of bloodwealth cattle, blood feuds endured "forever" (Evans-Pritchard 1940a:154). In fact, the bulk of the cattle received was normally reserved for marrying a ghost wife in the name of the deceased, partially in the hope that she would bear a son who would someday avenge his father's blood with that of the enemy (Evans-Pritchard 1940a:155).

2. As Evans-Pritchard explains: "The ancestral herd is a fiction, for the cattle are being constantly dispersed and replaced by others at marriages, but conceptually it is an enduring collectivity" (1956:258).

3. I am less convinced, however, that men's authority over women was rooted on a day-to-day basis primarily in their control over cattle—a point to be elaborated at length in chapter 4.

What I find striking about Nuer culture and social life of the early 1930s, however, is the extent to which these differences between cattle and people were continually underplayed. In dance, song, naming, and speech, people constantly celebrated the fundamental "likeness" of cattle and people. The tremendous cultural energy devoted to the elaboration of this equation is, perhaps, understandable when we realize that the value of "life" itself affirmed it. With each gesture, each metaphor, each burst of artistic creativity in this direction, individuals both proclaimed and enhanced that added sense of control over their lives made possible by the "truth" that "cattle and people are one." With each such act, they also bolstered the dominant position of senior men as well as blurred other social asymmetries founded upon the implicit, if not explicit, recognition that human values could never be fully translated into cattle values.[4] What remains to be seen, then, is whether and to what extent this "truth" survived the subsequent emergence of a radically different equation in Nuer social life—that between cattle and money.

THE CREATION OF CATTLE AND LABOR MARKETS IN NUERLAND: 1930–83

The experience of British colonial conquest (1898–1930), swiftly followed in some regions by that of famine, made the early 1930s deeply disillusioning years for many Nuer. Effectively barred from replenishing their stock through raiding, men stood idle as successive waves of rinderpest decimated their herds (Johnson 1980:496). For the conquering Anglo-Egyptian Condominium regime, in contrast, this was a period of optimism and of rapid political and economic advances. The radical military measures imposed as part of the "Nuer Settlement" of 1929–30, which required, among other things, the temporary separation of the (Lou and Gaawär) Nuer from their Dinka neighbors, appeared to herald a new era of interethnic peace (cf. Johnson 1980). Similarly, the successful elimination or capture of all major Nuer prophets seemed to clear the way for the birth of a new breed of tractable government chiefs (Johnson 1979, 1980:403–467, 1994). Such optimism, though short-lived in most instances, also sparked off scores of government work projects—carried out with conscripted Nuer labor—including the con-

---

4. For excellent accounts of the pervasive intimacy of human/cattle relations at that time, see Evans-Pritchard (1940a, 1948c, 1953e, 1956) and Beidelman (1966) as well as Lienhardt's (1961:10ff) and Deng's (1984[1972]:17ff., 68–86) descriptions of comparable relations among the Dinka.

struction of dirt roads, steamer stations, administrative centers, and the like.[5] Conditions formerly hindering the expansion of northern trade networks into the region also ended abruptly (Evans-Pritchard 1940a:87–88). Improvements in public security and transport greatly facilitated the penetration of seasonal merchants, while cattle epidemics and food shortages ensured the rapid development of a hide-export/grain-import trade.

The extended cattle, grain, and labor markets that eventually developed in the region were in no sense "free." Price controls intended to curb "profiteering" as well as minimize government expenditure on local grain and labor were enforced intermittently throughout the colonial and postcolonial eras. Strict limits on the number of merchants permitted to trade in the area were also maintained through the late 1940s, as were regional quotas on the distribution and sale of cloth, sugar, and other imported consumer items.[6] These restrictions were motivated by a restrained conflict of interests between, on the one hand, profit-minded merchants and, on the other, British administrative officers, who were on the whole deeply conservative and paternalistic in their attitudes toward Nuer. Though frequently at odds, these two groups nonetheless shared a common economic objective: the creation and maintenance of a profitable export trade in Nuer cattle. The greatest difficulty they faced in this regard was to devise adequate ways to tempt, force, cajole, or otherwise pressure Nuer into handing over their largest and fattest oxen for sale to meat markets in the north.[7]

By 1933 seasonal merchants had taken the lead by establishing two modes of cattle extraction, both of them circuitous. The first, a sort of "cow/ox conversion racket," took advantage of interethnic cycles of trade then developing between the western Nuer and their Twic Dinka and Baggara Arab neighbors.

> The Nuer . . . have no desire to sell bulls [oxen] for money but they will exchange them for cow calves. [Baggara] Arabs [bordering the Leek and Bul Nuer in the west] and Twij [Twic] Dinka are willing to sell cow calves. Thus . . . the merchants buy cow calves for money from the former and exchange them to the Nuer and [other] Dinka for big bulls.[8]

5. END 66.A.2., 22 Feb. 1934, "Assistant District Commissioner to Governor."

6. DAK I 49/1/1&2, "Passports and Permits: General Rulings; UNP 1/51/4, 1935, "Nasir District Notes Update."

7. WND 64 B.1, 25 Mar. 1941, "J. Wilson, Assistant District Commissioner, to Governor." Since steamer charges for the northern transport of oxen were calculated on a per capita rather than a per pound basis, export merchants sought to obtain the largest, fattest oxen possible.

8. WND 64 B.1., c. 1933, "Assistant District Commissioner to Governor." The willingness of the Twic Dinka to sell heifers at that time was due to the ease with

In eastern Nuerland, where neighboring ethnic groups were both more distant and more cattle-poor than in the west, merchants relied instead on seasonal fluctuations in local grain supplies to generate a cattle export trade:

> The agents go out to various trading posts in September and October [at harvest time] and buy grain and hides in exchange for trade goods [such as fishing hooks, beads, spears, and cloth] mostly, though occasionally money is used. A second series of posts along the rivers catch the more distant tribes on their way to the dry weather camp. From February to April trade is practically at a standstill but then the reverse flow begins and grain is sold back to the improvident at enhanced prices for animals. Generally speaking, the grain bought from the Nuer is sold for Province requirements, i.e. police, Army, merkaz [town] requirements, and the grain resold to the natives is imported. This naturally depends largely upon prices but few merchants can afford to keep their capital locked up. The turnover is small but the profits are large as the grain and hides, etc., are bought cheap for trade goods acquired at trade prices and imported grain is sold at a profit for animals valued cheaply.[9]

Add to these extractive strategies the confiscation of thousands of cattle in annual tribute-collection campaigns and in court fines and it is not surprising that the oxen-export trade grew rapidly during the 1930s and 1940s.

But individual Nuer were still neither buying nor selling their cattle with money. The mutual convertibility of these two media had simply not been established for them. This situation continued, moreover, despite post-1935 administrative efforts to shift the basis of tribute collection in eastern Nuerland from cattle to cash (officials having discovered early on that this "changeover . . . nearly always ends in more cash for Government")[10] and to provide conscripted Nuer labor with "a small pecuniary reward."[11] Bar-

---

which they could acquire them from the Baggara in exchange for female goats and sheep.

9. SAD 212/13/3, 1930, "Eastern Nuerland, Province Handbook."

10. UNP 1/45/332, 1939, "E. G. Coryton, Handing Over Notes." Unlike itinerant merchants, who stood to gain from a continued barter economy, the colonial administration sought the rapid "monetization" of the regional economy.

11. A note in the Lou Nuer District Annual Report of 1953–54 (WND 57 A. 3.) reveals how long it took for cash to displace cattle in the collection of tribute among the Lou and other eastern Nuer groups: "For the first time [1954] cattle were spared being dragged off for sale by Government, a thing which they never escaped in previous years." Nuer west of the Bahr-el-Jebel, in contrast, were never formally taxed in cattle. Hoping to avoid the bitterness generated by earlier tribute-raiding campaigns among the eastern Nuer, the officer commissioned with opening up western Nuerland to British administration, Capt. V. H. Fergusson, introduced instead compulsory cotton cultivation in 1925. Western Nuer adult males experienced their first annual tax of 5 piasters four years later (SAD 212/14/9,1930, "Western Nuerland, Province Handbook," 1930). The initial

ter continued to dominate the private sector, and government wages remained far too low to permit a ready conversion of coins into cattle.[12]

This situation changed dramatically, however, following the introduction during the late 1940s of government-sponsored cattle auctions for the disposal of livestock acquired through court fines. By that time government chiefs' courts were well established throughout Nuerland and were generating increasingly vital administrative revenues.[13] More important for my purposes, government-fines cattle, unlike tribute oxen, often included a large proportion of heifers.[14] Thus, it became possible for the first time for Nuer to purchase from the government what they desired most: young, fertile heifers to increase their herds. And it was this opportunity that first

---

success of this cotton-for-tribute campaign was short-lived, however, owing to widespread corruption among the (primarily Dinka) cotton cultivation overseers appointed by the local administration. These overseers were in the habit of arbitrarily imposing "cattle fines" on individual Nuer who failed to produce the required cotton. Unable to curb these abuses, the administration revoked the compulsory status of cotton cultivation in western Nuerland in 1934. However, many western Nuer continued to produce significant quantities of cotton until World War II.

12. Throughout the famine era of the early 1930s, thousands of Nuer from the central regions were conscripted to clear, bank, and bridge roads, to raise government "rest houses," and to cut and stack wood fuel for government steamers. In principle, these Nuer were paid for their efforts at the rate of 1 or 2 piasters per day plus grain rations. In practice, however, few coins ever changed hands. As one British officer explained:

> Owing to the people's ignorance which renders them an easy prey for the average Northern accountant, I have been unable to devise any workable system whereby some 10,000 men are given a few pt. [piasters] each, for the purpose of paying it in as tribute after various pieces of different colored paper have been inscribed by a foreigner in an unknown language. So in practice no money changes hands, and each sub-shen [*ciëŋ*] is required to do a definite piece of work every year under the supervision of its chiefs. (SAD 212/14/8, 1930, "Revenue, Zeraf Valley, Province Handbook")

As the years passed and the famine subsided, "normal road maintenance," portage, and other government tasks were increasingly defined as the "normal duty of our tribesmen," and the pretense of a "small pecuniary reward" was dropped (UNP 1/45/331, 1934, "Upper Nile Province Roads"). Yet even when monetary payments were made, at the rate of 1 piaster a day—standard throughout much of the 1930s—a man would have needed the equivalent of 150 days of wages in order to purchase a small heifer in the marketplace. Consequently, the small amounts of money that entered Nuer hands were normally invested in grain and in cloth for mosquito netting.

13. Government cattle fines were routinely imposed as "deterrents" in cases of fighting, homicide, theft, and slander as well as in certain types of adultery and fornication suits (cf. Howell 1954:63, 168).

14. The ratio of cows to oxen collected by the government in homicide cases, for instance, was approximately 7 to 3 (UNPMD, Nov. 1940).

motivated them to enter the cattle market as buyers—and money-paying ones at that. Because these auctions were carried out strictly on a cash basis, individuals wishing to participate were normally forced to sell an ox to a private merchant before the auction in order to have the requisite cash available.[15] Hence, from the government's perspective, these auctions had the added benefit of stimulating the private export trade in Nuer oxen. These auctions were also crucial for the eventual development of a Nuer literate elite. For without such auctions, it would have been extremely difficult for government employees and other salaried individuals to transform their wages into a universally valued and socially essential resource. Eventually, the administration established dry-season public auctions (in which anyone could bring cattle) in various district centers of Nuerland, first on a weekly and later on a daily basis.

It was soon apparent, however, that the long-term success of these auctions depended on two factors over which local administrators exercised little control. The first was a steady supply of female cattle. During some years the number of heifers collected in court fines was so low compared with local demand that prospective buyers grew discouraged and no longer took the precaution of selling oxen before the auction.[16] The second factor, no less troubling than the first, was a constant scarcity of coinage (UNPMD, May 1953). Up until the mid-1960s, Nuer steadfastly re-

15. In a letter to the governor dated 15 Mar. 1947, J. Wilson, the assistant district commissioner of the western Nuer reported: "Two items have a big influence on the cattle trade: 1. the government's sale of fines cattle, which causes people to sell bulls [oxen] to the merchants for money in order to have the ready cash to buy a government cow and 2. famine" (WND 64 B. 1.).

16. British colonial officials were well aware of this stumbling block. In 1946, J. Winder, an assistant district commissioner, proposed to coordinate tribute collection among Nuer with the compulsory sale of female cattle. His plan would have required each taxpayer to provide a heifer that would be auctioned off among the taxpayers of each district for cash. A proportion of the sales "profits" would then be claimed by the government as tribute. Although it was hoped that a small number of female cattle sold would eventually be siphoned off into the general market, the scheme was primarily intended to impress upon Nuer the ready convertibility of money and female cattle and thereby encourage them to value and use money (SAD 541/8, 23 Dec. 1946, "Nilotic Economics"). Not surprisingly, this plan was rejected in-house as much too radical. It was influential, nonetheless, in stimulating a critical review of government policy with respect to the cattle trade. Ultimately, the administration pinned its hopes on the creation of a cattle "surplus" through improved veterinary services. The massive cattle inoculation campaigns against rinderpest and bovine pleuropneumonia that followed during the late 1940s and 1950s were in general highly beneficial to Nuer herds—though some epidemics were spread further and faster as a result of the concentrations of cattle fomented by the inoculation process (UNPMD, Aug. 1948).

fused to accept paper currency for their cattle. In fact, the Nuer term for money, *yiọu* (sg., *yieth*), means any kind of "metal pieces," including spears. *Yiọu waragak* (literally, "paper metal," from the Arabic term for paper, *waraqa*)—was initially rejected for many reasons. As one frustrated British administrator explained:

> If trade is to flourish in Nuerland, large supplies of silver [coins] must be made available. . . . Nuer dislike notes because they cannot keep them safely—they get burnt, blown away by the wind, eaten by white ants, dissolved by heavy rains and torn by rough usage. Quite apart from any conservative distrust of their value, the elements of the ordinary Nuer's existence makes notes unacceptable to him. (UNPMD, May 1953)

Some of these environmental hazards were later overcome by the importation during the 1960s and 1970s of small metal footlockers, equipped with lock and key, that have since become a standard household item. Skyrocketing inflation, which began during the first civil-war era, was another factor contributing to the eventual acceptance of paper currency by Nuer.[17] Until the late 1960s, however, cattle brought to market frequently remained unsold, while others were parted with at reduced rates, owing to a scarcity of coinage alone (UNPMD, May 1953). Despite these nagging difficulties, the regional cattle trade continued to expand in both volume and complexity. As early as 1942 some Nuer had begun to drive their oxen directly to markets in the provincial capital, Malakal. Others sought higher prices for their oxen by butchering them and selling the meat in regional market centers (UNPMD, May/June 1942 & March 1954).

Nevertheless, the two basic cattle extractive strategies established by itinerant merchants during the 1930s had really changed little. Famine continued to fuel the grain-import/cattle-export trade, though coinage had replaced barter to some extent by the mid-1940s. The cow/ox conversion racket, in contrast, had been effectively captured by the government, with many local export merchants benefiting from this "takeover" as well. The net result was that individual Nuer were now replenishing their herds at one another's expense rather than at the expense of outlying neighbors. As far as Nuer were concerned, money remained in such contexts little more

17. Many Nuer also refused to accept paper currency during the 1930s, 1940s, and 1950s because they were unable to read their value denomination accurately—and were thus easy prey to unscrupulous merchants. During this period, some people were allegedly tricked into accepting playing cards in place of paper currency or, more commonly, smaller denomination notes in place of larger ones.

than a means of swapping cattle with the government. In other words, cattle only became money in order to become cattle again: C—>M—>C.

Another major turning point in the gradual forging of the cattle/money equation occurred during the mid-1950s, when thousands of Nuer men were actively recruited by the government to work on private cotton plantations then burgeoning along the upper Nile near the towns of Renk and Geiger. These lucrative investment schemes grew so rapidly during the early 1950s that they soon faced chronic labor shortages at picking time (December through February). By 1959 these schemes required an estimated 15,000 seasonal pickers in addition to more permanent tenant labor (UNPAR, 1959–60). And thus, each year increasingly urgent appeals for additional "Nilotic" labor to migrate to these sites were relayed through local Dinka, Shilluk, Nuer, Atuot, and Anyuak chiefs. Significantly, Nuer men were consistently singled out by scheme owners and government administrators alike as the most desirable "backwater" recruits for reasons made clear in the following quotation:

> Nuers proved the best of the lot. They usually arrived in high spirits and spent the hours proceeding to their station, dancing and singing in the field; they show enthusiasm and interest in their work. Unlike comers from other localities who started grumbling the moment they arrived and when they are transported to the fields it needs a miracle to make them refrain from going on strike [sic]. (WND 57. A., 1959–60, "Eastern Nuer District Annual Report")

Before long, however, these unwitting strikebreakers began venturing further and further north, encouraged by the promise of higher wages. By 1960 scores of young Nuer men reached Khartoum, where they commonly obtained employment as day laborers in the construction industry. Owing to these increasingly lucrative wage-labor opportunities, it actually became possible for a man to earn enough money during a dry season to purchase a cow calf or two upon his return home. And thus, a new relationship between cattle and money was forged: It was no longer necessary for a man to give up a cow in order to get one. Money could yield cattle directly: M—>C.[18]

With the subsequent explosion of the first civil war in Nuer territories

18. Marx (1967[1867]), of course, would not have differentiated this economic phase of the commodification of cattle wealth from the preceding one, since both were part of a money-mediated chain of commodity exchange. However, this second phase was a definite economic "breakthrough" in local terms. For, suddenly, money was empowered in ways previously unperceived or, at least, undervalued by most Nuer.

in 1963–64, all this economic activity ground to a sudden halt. Regional cattle and grain markets collapsed as their northern Arab controllers retreated to heavily garrisoned towns. Scores of villages were razed by rebel-seeking army battalions while local herds were plundered mercilessly by both parties to the conflict. Families living within reach of government roads and towns scattered deeper and deeper into the bush. Hundreds of young men working or studying in the north flocked back to join southern secessionist forces while others fled in the opposite direction. As I explained in chapter 1, Nuer communities east of the White Nile suffered more intensely during these years than their western counterparts. These were the fearful and chaotic years, "when people fled to the bush" (*mee ci nath kai dɔar*) and from which Nuer communities have never recovered.

As part of the negotiated peace settlement known as the Addis Ababa Agreement of 1972, thousands of southern rebels (including an unknown number of Nuer) were integrated into the national army and regional police force. Hundreds of others were offered civilian posts in the newly established southern regional government only to be laid off a few months later due to inadequate funds. These new posts, though temporary in many cases, injected large amounts of paper currency into the region, currency that Nuer were increasingly willing to accept in exchange for their cattle. Bachelors hoping to replenish their war-ravaged herds and thereby achieve a quicker road to marriage also adopted short-term, seasonal labor migration to northern cities on a massive scale. Following employment patterns set by their predecessors, most of these youths became day laborers in the Khartoum construction industry.[19] Indeed, during the early 1980s I often heard Nuer labor migrants assert with pride that they had built Khartoum.

During the post– (or, rather, inter–) civil-war era between 1972 and 1983, the economic vacuum created by the hasty departure of northern merchants during the war began to suck in Nuer adventurers desiring to try their luck at trading. Although some of these would-be merchants initiated their businesses with funds gained through wage labor or the sale of fish, grain, crocodile skins, and other local resources, most relied on a sale of family livestock. Eventually, the more prosperous of these succeeded in penetrating the long-distance grain-import/cattle-export trade previously monopolized by their northern Arab counterparts. Others concentrated on moving dried fish southwards to Juba and Zaire or locally made papyrus mats northwards to Khartoum.

Some of these rising merchants were also assisted by the newly estab-

19. For information on Nuer labor migrants in Khartoum, see Kameir (1980).

lished southern regional government in Juba. In 1975 a capital-loan program was implemented in order to encourage more southerners to take up trading. Scores of would-be merchants (among them many Nuer) were granted fifty sacks of sorghum to begin their businesses. Unfortunately, this development program failed because most recipients simply sold their grain allotments, bought cattle, and married—the southern regional government being thereby forced to absorb the capital loss of these bad debts.[20] The government then devised a program in which some of the more successful southern merchants were granted trucks in the hope of diminishing their dependence on northern truck and barge owners and thereby ensuring more dependable supplies of grain and other goods to outlying areas. Although these mobile merchants were still no competition for those northern traders who, by the mid 1970s, began reestablishing themselves in the area's district centers of Nasir and Bentiu, they certainly wrested much of the latter's control over southern markets, control they had enjoyed since before the first civil war.

As more and more people began to appreciate the enormous profits that could be reaped by driving cattle overland to Kosti or by founding a modest "bush shop," it became considerably easier for a young man to persuade his elders to release a few head of cattle in order to take up part-time trading. This is not to say that local customers benefited from this changeover. On the contrary, many newly established Nuer merchants proved even more rapacious than their Arab predecessors (see plate 8). Markups of over 200 percent on trade goods were standard in many outlying "bush shops" throughout the early 1980s. Furthermore, it was not uncommon at that time to hear ordinary people complain that this newly emerging class of Nuer merchants had begun to adopt strange new attitudes toward money. As David Kek Moinydet (Kɛk Moinydët), an eastern Gaajok Nuer, explained:

> The trouble with these young [Nuer] merchants is that they treat their money like cattle. In the old days you didn't give a cow to just anyone. An [unrelated] man might have to live and work in your homestead for years before receiving a cow. Well, now, these young merchants are taking this same attitude toward their money: If you're not close enough to be "counted" a cow [in marriage], you're not close enough to be lent money!

However, these merchants were not the only ones who had begun to view money in a new light. During this same era between civil wars,

20. Lazarus Lei, personal communication.

Plate 8. During the four months of the year when the dirt roads are dry, many imported commodities are available in small market centers.

scores of rural communities, under the auspices of local chiefs, initiated "self-help" projects, including the construction of primary schools, veterinary stations, and medical dispensaries as well as the repair and extension of local roads. These projects were invariably funded by local cattle contributions—some being more voluntary than others. Tragically, most of these buildings later stood idle, owing to the central government's failure to provide promised staff and supplies. Yet even so, these developments would seem to reflect a definite attitudinal shift. Increasingly, cattle were viewed, in some contexts at least, as potential sources of capital to be invested in specific projects, some private, others collective: C—>M.

And thus, by the time I began investigating these issues firsthand in 1980, the mutual convertibility of cattle and money had become so well accepted that it was not uncommon among the eastern Jikany Nuer for a "generous" father-in-law to accept cash in place of a bridewealth cow or two. In short, money had become a part of everyday social life. As one wry old eastern Gaajak man quipped, "Today everyone wants to die with a piaster in his hand!"

The three basic stages identified in the gradual forging of the cattle/money equation in Nuerland (namely, C—>M—>C, M—>C, and C—>M)[2] are helpful, I think, in understanding the nature and limits of the mutual convertibility of cattle and money as these are revealed through a half century of archival records.[21] They do little justice, however, to the intricacy of cattle/money ties as defined by contemporary Nuer. For the various Ms and Cs of which these analytic phases of commodification consist were by no means interchangeable for them. Rather, contemporary Nuer, as we shall see, defined neither money nor cattle as "things-in-themselves."

THE CIRCULATION OF BLOOD, CATTLE, AND MONEY: 1930–83
First Formulation: "Money Has No Blood"

To what extent did the increased convertibility of cattle and money stimulate Nuer to reassess the inherent logic and general significance of the cattle/human equation so central to their culture during the early 1930s? I begin with the observation that money had penetrated some fields of exchange more thoroughly than others. In exchange for grain, fishing hooks, cloth, guns, and medicines, as well as in the payment of taxes, court fines, school fees, and the like, people gladly substituted money for cattle whenever they could. Indeed, giving up a cow in such contexts was regarded as a truly lamentable loss: Ideally, cattle were reserved for more important occasions such as marriage, initiation, and sacrifice—or, as I would summarize Nuer statements in this regard, reserved for the creation and affirmation of enduring bonds amongst themselves as well as between themselves and divinity. In contrast, the role of cattle as sacrificial victim and as indispensable exchange object at times of initiation, feud settlement, and, to a lesser degree, marriage had scarcely been affected by the massive introduction of currency. This is not to say that people's attitudes toward these rites remained constant between 1930 and 1983. On the contrary, the significance of cattle sacrifice, for instance, was being steadily undermined at that time by mounting waves of Christian conversion, by increased Nuer acceptance of Western medicines and etiologies, and by growing expectations that a host would provide meat for his guests—themes discussed more fully in chapter 7.

Yet even so, money could not replace cattle in these contexts. Nor could it replace the gift of a "personality ox" at initiation, though the overall

---

21. I have, of course, simplified this account of the economic development of this region to a few basic themes. The rise and fall of important export trades such as those in hides, locally grown cotton (1926–45), crocodile skins (1951–56), gum arabic (1953–61), dried fish (1954–65 and 1972–83), and papyrus mats (1965–83), as well as local trades in charcoal, goats, milk, and construction materials have scarcely been mentioned. Yet these, too, generated considerable cash income for Nuer during the colonial and postcolonial eras.

significance of this ox had declined in regions where increasing numbers of Nuer youths rejected scarification entirely—a trend described in chapter 6. Furthermore, most people actively resisted the idea that money was an adequate substitute for cattle in bridewealth and bloodwealth exchange—although small amounts of money, as I noted, had begun to infiltrate eastern Jikany marriage payments by the early 1980s.

I hasten to add that this characterization of the unequal penetration of money into Nuer social life—based as it is upon a distinction between "blood"- and "nonblood"-associated spheres of exchange—is entirely my own construction: Nuer would not use such terms. This idea developed, rather, out of numerous comments made by Nuer men and women (during more general discussions about cattle sacrifice, feuding, marriage, incest, pollution, and other issues) to the effect that "cattle, like people, have blood," but "money has no blood." I interpreted these comments to mean that money was an "inappropriate" medium of exchange in certain contexts because it could not bind people together like "blood"—whether this "blood" be conceptualized as human, bovine, or both in relation to particular types of enduring ties. In order to understand why this was so, we must delve briefly into the symbolism of blood in Nuer culture and social life.

Blood: The Vital Weakness Although not equated with life (*tëk*) itself, blood, or *riɛm*, is the substance out of which each and every human life begins. Conception was understood as a mysterious merger of male and female blood flows, forged by the life-creating powers of Divinity (*kuɔth nhial*). Without the direct participation and continual support of Divinity, no child would ever be born or survive long enough to bring forth another generation. This dependence on the life-creating and life-sustaining powers of Divinity was a reality that could not be ignored in a world where many couples experienced long periods of infertility and where just under half of the children born alive died before reaching adulthood.[22] Procreation,

22. The World Health Organization estimated in 1949 that only 55 percent of children born alive in the Upper Nile Province reached adult life. At that time, mortality rates before weaning were estimated at 284 per 1,000 live births. Tragically, there is little reason to believe that child mortality rates have declined subsequently. The limited community surveys I carried out among the eastern Jikany and (western) Leek Nuer suggest that just over half of Nuer children born alive reached adulthood during the early 1980s. As late as 1983, there were no reliable medical facilities operating in the entire region, and the nearest doctor was in Khartoum. Since then, child mortality rates have soared much higher. It is estimated that more than 250,000 southern Sudanese men, women, and children died of war-generated famine in 1988 alone.

moreover, was the paramount goal of life for every Nuer and the only form of immortality valued by them. Every adult feared "the true death," "the complete death": the death without children to extend one's name and re-vitalize one's influence in the world. For men the immortality sought was motivated in part by strong collective interests: Without heirs, a man ac-quired no permanent position within the patrilineal chain of descendants from which he emerged. For women childbirth was the threshold to adult-hood, future security, and independence. From this perspective, blood may be understood as that which united the greatest of human desires with that profound sense of humility with which Nuer contemplated the transcen-dent powers of Divinity. Indeed, in the eyes of Nuer, a newborn child *is* "blood" and hence was often referred to as such during the first month or two of existence. Milk, semen, sweat—these, too, *are* "blood." It is as though *riɛm* were the mutable source of all human—and hence all social—energy.[23]

As an element of life, blood converged with two other powerful forces of vitality: *yiëëɣ* (breath) and *tiiy/tiei* (awareness). *Yiëëɣ* fluctuates with human energy levels as well, being said to wane (*luär*) with hunger and significant losses of blood. Death was normally identified with a total ces-sation of breath. *Tiiy*, I was told, relates to the idea of "pupil," as in "pupil of the eye" (*tiei waŋ*).[24] Though sometimes translated as "soul" (Evans-Pritchard 1956:155), *tiiy* may also be understood as a generalized concept of perception, understanding, and social awareness.[25] To say that a person is without *tiiy* is to identify him or her as an uncaring, ill-spirited indi-vidual. It is as though such a person were not fully "human" (/*ci ɛ raan*). And since one's *tiiy* necessarily slackens with sleep, lapses with uncon-sciousness, and withers with blindness, Nuer considered all these states to be kinds of "death" (*liaah*).

Blood, however, was unique among these cardinal principles of life in that it was eminently social. Blood passed from person to person and from generation to generation, endowing social relations with a certain sub-

23. Blood, moreover, is inextricably bound up with the seat of human emotions and intellectual capabilities, the heart (cf. Hutchinson 1980:380–386).

24. According to one western Nuer informant, *tiiy* may also be used to mean sperm.

25. Dialectical differences are relevant here. Among the western Leek Nuer, *tiei* and *tiiy*, while related, are two distinct terms, the latter coming closest to our concept of soul. Among the eastern Jikany and Lou Nuer, the second of these terms, *tiiy*, does not appear to exist at all. Although several eastern Nuer recognized that the concept of *tiiy* was common among their western cousins, as far as they were concerned there were just two life principles: blood and breath.

stance and fluidity. It was the gift of blood bestowed from parent to child upon which the authority and respect of the older generation ultimately depended. Similarly, the perpetual expansion, fusion, and dissipation of kin groups were conceptualized in terms of blood's creation, transfer, and loss. The coming of both manhood and womanhood was also marked by emissions of blood. For a girl it was the blood that flowed during her first childbirth (not at puberty) that ushered her into adulthood. For a boy it was that shed during the ordeal of the knife at initiation, when six (and sometimes seven) horizontal cuts were drawn across his forehead from ear to ear. The shedding of blood at initiation also forged a brotherhood (*ric*) among age-mates, ensured the continuity of the patriline, and supported a broader sense of community among Nuer as the "people of the people," the "true human beings," the *nei ti naadh*.

Though imbued with connotations of vital force, blood was not equated with "physical strength" (*buɔm puany*). On the contrary, considerable evidence suggests that *riɛm* was considered the weakest point in the human constitution. Illness, for example, was generally thought to harbor in a person's blood, and hence, Nuer practiced an elaborate art of medicinal bleeding. All emissions of human blood were also swiftly buried for fear that they might be consumed by dogs or other wandering carnivores. Consider also associations between human blood and human vulnerability implicit in Nuer images of *pɛth* ("possessors of the 'red' eye"). These evil beings, who masquerade as true human beings, were said to relish in secretly wrenching out the hearts of others, in draining their blood and milk, in festering their wounds, and in snatching the blood/fetus (*riɛm*) from one woman only to hurl it into the womb of another.[26] It was perhaps due to these connotations of inherent vulnerability that some Nuer argued that "people with relatively little blood are stronger since their blood will soon dry with the sun [as sweat] and their bodies harden." Similarly, many men and women maintained that a person's strength could not be judged on the basis of his or her external appearance. Physical strength was never a matter of blood or "flesh" (nom., *ring*; gen., *rieng*) but derived rather from the inherent hardness (*buɔm*) of a person's bones (sing., *cɔaa*; pl., *cɔu*). More to the point: One's blood linkages with others were the open portals

---

26. Widespread fascination with and fear of "ghouls" (*rɔath*; sing., *rɔdh*)—malicious beings thought to delight in mutilating and consuming corpses—also suggest a close association between human blood and human vulnerability (cf. Howell & Lewis 1947).

through which potentially lethal forms of pollution associated with acts of homicide (*nueer*), incest (*ruaal*), adultery (*kɔɔr*), and other transgressions could enter and spread to endanger the wider community. In the words of one eloquent Lou Nuer man: "*Riɛm* is like a medicine [*wal*] in that it carries all the indirect consequences of other people's actions."

Interestingly, Nuer notions of "weakness," "softness," "fertility," and "vitality" converged in another multifaceted concept: *kɔc* (verbal form, *kɔcɛ*). When used with reference to "the earth" (*mun*; gen., *muɔn*), a state of *kɔc* suggests the "coolness" and "softness" felt underfoot following a long, fertilizing rain. When modifying "the world" (*yɔu*; gen., *yɔaa*), *kɔc* suggests "communal peace," "prosperity," and "well-being" as opposed to "heated" states of war. In association with the body (*puɔny*; gen., *puany*), *kɔc*'s meanings are multiple: A "cool/soft heart" (*kɔai lɔai*) exudes generosity and kindness; a "cool/soft tongue" (*kɔai leep*) favors persuasion and equanimity over coercion and anger. The expression *kɔai puany* ("coolness/softness of the body") is more ambiguous in that it may mean "health, fertility, and well-being" when contextually opposed to "heated/feverish bodily states" (*puɔnydɛ lethɛ*) or "vulnerability/physical weakness" when contrasted with *buɔm puany*.[27] A *puɔnydu kɔc* ("May your body be cool") remained the most common expression people used when blessing and thanking one another. Similarly, when supplicating divinity, people prayed for states of "coolness/softness" in themselves, in their relations, and in the world at large. This pivotal concept thus fused pervasive metaphors of temperature (*leth* vs. *kɔc*) with symbolic oppositions between states of "hardness/power/strength" (*buɔm*) as distinct from those of "softness/vulnerability/weakness" (*kɔc*).

More important for my purposes, the concept *kɔc* was intimately associated with that of *riɛm* in that the ideal or normal state of blood was presumed to be one of both "coolness" and "softness." For example, when I once asked an English-speaking Lou Nuer man to explain to me why newborn children were called *riɛm*, he looked puzzled and said: "Haven't you ever held a newborn child? Ah, a newborn child is so soft and cool like blood." Furthermore, to say of a girl, *Cɛ kɔac* (literally, "She has cooled/softened"), was to indicate that she had become fertile—that is, had experienced her first menstrual flow.[28] Indeed, owing to the strong connec-

---

27. The expression *leth puany*, "body heat," means "sweat." To indicate fever, one uses the expression "his/her body heats"—*puɔnydɛ lethɛ*.

28. This standard euphemism was favored over the more explicit *cɛ thek*,

tion in people's minds between female fertility and states of coolness, it was disturbing when a girl became nubile during the hottest month of the year, *pɛt*. When this happened, the women of the community would strive to counter the intense seasonal heat by pouring cooling water over the newly menstruating girl. Nuer concepts of *kɔc*, like those of *riɛm*, thus fuse experiences of human frailty with people's heartfelt desires for all "the good things of life": health, peace, fertility, prosperity, generosity, procreational continuity, and social harmony. Human vitality and human vulnerability, these concepts declare, are "one."

Because contemporary Nuer equated so many of their aspirations and fears with delicate states and flows of *riɛm*, they often attempted to manipulate blood in ways that they hoped would promote their well-being. They bled not only themselves medicinally but also their cattle. Occasional bloodletting, they argued, helps keep cattle fat, healthy, and fertile by preventing the onset of *nɔɔi*, a mysterious wasting disease that sometimes develops despite abundant supplies of green grass and clean water (cf. Evans-Pritchard 1937:224). Acts of blood-vengeance and rites of initiation could also be seen as motivated in part by a desire to promote specific blood flows.

Direct physical attempts at manipulation such as these were rare, however, compared with the abundance of cattle rites and exchanges thought capable of achieving these objectives indirectly. In my experience the vast majority of cattle sacrificed were offered with the intent of eliciting divine support in the confirmation, facilitation, extension, or negation of specific states and passages of human blood. Among the many types of sacrifices that I would include in this category were those performed at marriages, funerals, difficult births, initiations, adoptions, bloodwealth transfers, and related purification rites in addition to others intended to promote conception and to rid people of the polluting effects of homicide, incest, adultery, and other dangerous "blood states."

Moreover, Nuer frequently stressed the fact that the gestation period of cattle was practically identical to that of human beings. And thus, in repeatedly emphasizing that "cattle, like people, have blood," Nuer were calling my attention to the fact that cattle and people are capable of a

---

literally, "she respects," an allusion to the prohibition on women drinking cow's milk during their menses. This "coolness" metaphor suggests a deeper parallel between feminine fertility and the fertility of the crops—a parallel that is discussed in greater detail in chapter 4.

parallel extension of vitality across the generations.[29] Money, of course, is not augmentative in this sense. If anything, it appears condemned in Sudan to a continual loss of force, to a perpetual withering in the face of mounting inflation. (Except for a few urbanized Nuer, no one during the early 1980s knew of the concept of monetary interest.)[30]

Consequently, insofar as individuals actually succeeded during the 1980s in restricting their use of cash to nonblood- as opposed to blood-related fields of exchange, money was less a challenge than a support for the life-affirmed and life-affirming "truth" that cattle and people are one. As Nyaruol Gaai, an elderly Leek woman, once commented, "Money protects cattle" (*Gaŋkɛ yɔk pịny;* literally, "[Money] delays them on the ground"). People with money, in other words, could keep their cattle longer.

Money could sometimes be used in other ways to protect one's wealth in cattle. For example, there was also a well-known expression that ran *Baa yɔk tolkä kɔam,* which translates literally, "The cows will be broken up into small pieces and stored in the *ambatch* carrying case/shield." This expression was reportedly coined by a man from Fangak District named Kolang Tɔat during the onset of the extended flood era of 1961–72. This man allegedly realized before many others that the forthcoming floods of 1961 were going to be very serious indeed and were likely to devastate the local cattle population. He thus sold his cows and stowed the money in his ambatch carrying case. He was thus one of the few Nuer who were fortunate enough to escape the worst ravages of the floods. The money he stored was later used to purchase a new herd after the floods receded. Since that time other Nuer confronted with cattle plagues or other political or natural disasters have attempted to follow Kolang Tɔat's example. However, the potential benefits of this protective option were increasingly being undermined during the 1980s by a rapidly escalating inflationary cycle that took

---

29. As Evans-Pritchard explained this idea with respect to marriage alliances:

> Marriage is not a single act. It is a succession of interconnected acts leading from courtship to the birth of children, and bridewealth is not a single payment but a succession of payments in response to the changing status of the wife and the increasing maturity of the union. As Nuer see it, these payments continue long after the marriage is fully established in the birth of calves and the progeny of these calves and of their progeny, a constant redocumentation which is balanced by the birth of children to the wife and of children to these children. (1951b:97)

30. Nor would it seem that they are likely to develop this idea in the immediate future: The current Sudanese government in Khartoum regards monetary interest payments as fundamentally "non-Islamic."

hold of Sudan during the mid-1970s, shortly after the end of the first civil war.

Yet why, one might ask, all this emphasis on blood when there are so many other differences between cattle and money that people might have stressed as well? Money is not only "bloodless" (and hence milkless) but also devoid of "breath," "awareness," and individualizing names, colors, temperaments, exchange histories, and so forth.[31] Money is an utterly depersonalized medium in this sense. Moreover, unlike cattle, money can pass in relative secrecy from one little locked metal footlocker to another. In my experience, nevertheless, Nuer men and women did not mention these elements of contrast when debating the nature and limits of convertibility between cattle and money. This is not to say that they did not appreciate them or take advantage of them from time to time; it is to say, rather, that the symbolism of blood that so pervades their culture had been taken up and elaborated once again—this time, it would seem, so as to deny the possibility of a direct equation between people and money. It was as though people were attempting to reassure themselves that, though cattle and people were equated in some contexts and cattle and money in others, money and people were—and always would be—incommensurate. The gulf that divided them ran as deep and broad as Nuer images of "blood" in the generation of life and the continuation of their social world. By stressing the unique blood linkage between cattle and people so as to exclude the intrusive medium of money, many Nuer, it would seem, were also rallying to the defense of all those "augmentations of life" made possible by the ideological "truth" that cattle and people are one. In the process of this denial, however, it would seem that the significance of human/cattle relations was distilled down from the richly varied and diffuse notions of a total symbiosis reported by Evans-Pritchard during the early 1930s to a more explicit "oneness of blood." One wonders whether or not this admittedly hypothetical process robbed human/cattle relations of some of their former intimacy and multiplicity as well.

Everything I have said thus far presumes that cattle and money are discrete units of comparison. But for the Nuer of the early 1980s, as I hinted, these were not "things-in-themselves." Rather, Nuer men and women had successfully crossbred the concepts of money and cattle, bringing forth a generation of hybrid categories that subsequently proved exceptionally adaptable to an increasingly unstable social and economic environment.

31. Comaroff and Comaroff (1990:211) stress many such differences in their analysis of Tswana attitudes toward money and cattle.

And nowhere did these hybrid categories thrive so well as in the vast field of bridewealth exchange. For it was here, in an open environment, where negotiations ranged freely and where there were no rigid rules to mar the horizon, that these categories first came into their own. And it was here, too, that my initial observations regarding the differential penetration of money into blood- and nonblood-associated spheres of exchange could be exposed as excessively static. For in reality, money and cattle were flowing increasingly out, in, and between these opposed spheres of exchange. Before delving into these issues, however, I should first offer a few remarks about fluctuations in bridewealth rates over the last half century.

Changing Bridewealth Rates: 1930–83 The typical number of bridewealth cattle offered in Nuer marriages varied significantly over the years in response to recurring wars, cattle epidemics, floods, and famines as well as structural transformations in the market economy as a whole. Marked regional disparities in bridewealth rates also emerged periodically. During the early 1930s, for instance, Evans-Pritchard reported that some twenty to thirty head of cattle were standard, with final payments sometimes extending over a decade or more after the initial wedding celebrations. At that time it would have been difficult, he noted, for a man to marry with fewer than sixteen head of cattle, owing to the numerous cattle claims held by the bride's extended family (Evans-Pritchard 1951b:83). By the mid-1940s, Howell reported, first marriages were sometimes completed "by payment of as little as 17 to 20 head of cattle and sometimes even less, though the average in 'well-to-do' families [was] usually nearer to 30" (1954:99). Divorcees (sing., *ciek mi kɛay*), in contrast, were often married with fewer cattle (Howell 1954:121). During the trypanosomiasis epidemic of 1946–47, bridewealth rates in some parts of Nuerland reportedly plunged an additional 30 to 40 percent (UNPMD January 1946), only to rebound again by the early 1950s.

During the first civil war, bridewealth rates plummeted to new lows. This was so much the case that, by the late 1960s, some marriages were initiated, I was told, with as few as three or four head of cattle—and, in flood-ravaged sections of western Nuerland, with as little as a sack of grain—together with the expectation that a prenegotiated number of additional cattle would be forthcoming from the groom's family "when the world becomes good again" (*me ci yɔu a gɔaa*). Settlements of between eight and twelve head of cattle, however, were apparently more common during this period.

Considering how far bridewealth rates fell during the first civil war, it is remarkable that rates for previously unmarried girls were in the process of rising again during the early 1980s from between twenty and twenty-five head of cattle to between twenty-five and thirty. Bridewealth rates for divorcees, in contrast, fluctuated between ten and fifteen head of cattle. Or, rather, these were the typical figures cited in situations where the bride was married with the full approval and participation of her kinsmen—and not, that is, by court decree. This latter route to marriage, however, was becoming increasingly popular during the early 1980s, especially in parts of eastern Nuerland, where local government chiefs often considered a payment of ten or fifteen head of cattle sufficient to award a "stolen" or "impregnated" girl to her lover, despite objections raised by the girl's family.[32] As far as many eastern Nuer chiefs were concerned, their first priority was to defuse as swiftly as possible the violent potential of such disputes—and hence their willingness to accept lower bridewealth payments in cases of elopement and impregnation. Western Nuer courts, in contrast, were normally more demanding: A young man was usually expected to muster a full twenty to twenty-five head of cattle before being permitted to marry an eloped or impregnated girlfriend. (I will return to this important regional contrast in court attitudes in chapter 4.)

This remarkable post-1972 recovery in bridewealth rates was attributable in part to a resurgence in the cattle population and in part to the increased velocity with which bridewealth cattle were circulating among Nuer families during the early 1980s. As a result of the massive dislocations and deprivations experienced during the first civil war, many men and women had begun to regard cattle wealth as far too fleeting to be dependable. Hence, it was considered essential for a man to marry or re-marry as soon as the size of his herd made this possible. Were he to delay, I was told, his relatives would be likely to pressure him into doing so with the argument that otherwise his herd might be lost "for nothing": *Bi thul kɛ jiek* ("A stormy wind might engulf them"). Declining confidence in the long-term dependability of cattle wealth was also apparent in the growing expectation, particularly among easterners, that bridewealth settlements would be paid in full on the day of the wedding (*bul nyal*). Hence, the extended bridewealth debts of earlier generations were becoming less

32. It was sometimes possible, however, for the bride's family to gain additional cattle from the groom's family following the birth of a number of children to the union. But as far as eastern Nuer courts were concerned, these frugal bridewealth transfers were sufficient to validate the marriage.

and less common in eastern Nuer regions. As Ret Deng (Rɛt Dɛŋ), an older eastern Gaajok man, explained:

> In the olden days bridewealth cattle came slowly over many years. As long as the woman continued to give birth, cattle would continue to come. Sometimes the last bridewealth cattle were only handed over upon the wedding of the woman's eldest daughter. But now people don't wait so long. A young man who owes cattle will go off to Khartoum, work, save money, and buy cattle to give to his in-laws.

Bridewealth redistribution patterns were similarly affected: Whereas a clash of bridewealth claims among the bride's relatives was typically resolved during the 1930s by waiting for the cow in question to calve, by the early 1980s it was far more common for such a cow to be sold in the marketplace in order to purchase two smaller calves in its place.[33]

The increasing speed with which marriage cattle were circulating among Nuer had not only driven up bridewealth rates but, as we shall see, greatly complicated divorce proceedings. And it is with regard to these complexities that the significance of the system of cattle and monetary wealth categories Nuer devised was most apparent.

SECOND FORMULATION: THE CATTLE
OF MONEY AND THE CATTLE OF GIRLS

I should, perhaps, first check the assumption that money and cattle were wholly interchangeable: Not all money was good, I was told, for buying cattle. There was something called *yiou cieth* (the "money of shit") that allegedly could not be invested fruitfully in cattle. Strikingly similar in some ways to the cattle-harming money of the Kenyan Luo (Shipton 1989), the money of shit was nevertheless defined differently.[34] Whereas the "bitter

33. I discuss the implications of these and other aspects of changing patterns of bridewealth redistribution in chapter 4.

34. Shipton's (1989) stimulating analysis of "bitter money" among the Luo of Kenya draws attention to the fact that people can and often do trace sums of money from source through release in the hope of protecting more treasured possessions, like cattle, from potentially polluting influences. Shipton's development of this important theme might have been even stronger, however, had he explored more fully the interface between cattle and money among the Luo. It would be interesting to know, for instance, whether or not those cattle and sums of money that actually slipped through the hypothetical "two-way barrier system" he constructs blazed a trail, like "bitter money," through Luo social relations—as was the case among contemporary Nuer.

money" of the Luo originated in the sale of specific resources such as land, tobacco, cannabis, and gold, *yiou cieth* was quite literally money people earned in local towns collecting and dumping the waste of household bucket latrines. Following the colonial administration's introduction of bucket latrines during the 1940s, it was difficult, of course, to find people willing to empty them each day—or, rather, under the cover of night. Eventually, the administration came to depend on prisoners for this service. In the interim, however, it would seem that Nuer women and men collectively rejected this type of work by convincing one another that "a cow bought with 'shit money' cannot live" (*yaŋ mi ci kok kɛ yiou cieth, /cɛ bi tek*). What began, I suspect, more as a prideful statement that "we, the people of the people, will not do such work" soon became an accepted fact of social life. Thus, money earned in this way had to be invested in things other than cattle. And since few, if any, Nuer willingly engaged in this work during the 1980s unless forced to do so as unpaid prisoners, the principal way in which this polluted money entered their hands was through the sale of locally brewed beer (*kɔaŋ in boor*) sold in towns where bucket latrines predominated. In Malakal and Bentiu I met several Nuer women selling beer who carefully segregated money collected from non-Nuer clients known to engage in such work from the rest of their incomes. When I asked one of them how she planned to use this money, she smiled and said, "It's going straight to the government."

More interesting still, the notion of *yiou cieth* during the early 1980s extended to include money earned through domestic service in the north. In general Nuer migrants openly scorned such work—"It's work only a Dinka would do"—preferring, as we might say, the more respectable and manly labor of construction. But as if this ethnic slur were not enough of a discouragement in itself, by 1983 many men and women had begun to argue that *Yiou kädamni cetkɛ yiou cieth ɛn ɣöö liu ɣɔɔkien* ("The money of servants is like the money of shit in that its cattle [will] die").[35] In this way individuals sought to prevent the contaminating source of this money from spreading to pollute their cherished cattle, which were, after all, consumed as well as exchanged by them.

In addition to the money of shit there were five basic categories of monetary and cattle wealth prevalent during the 1980s—all of them important for understanding contemporary patterns of bridewealth exchange. The

35. In fact, several people argued that no meaningful distinction between the "the money of domestic service" and "the money of shit" could be maintained since all house servants would eventually be forced to clean their employers' latrines.

first of these, ɣɔk nyiët, the cattle of girls/daughters, referred to bride-wealth cattle received by specific relatives of the bride on the basis of a system of "inheritable rights," cuŋ (sing., cuɔ̠ŋ), and "obligations," laad (sing., lat) (cf. Evans-Pritchard 1951a:74–89; Howell 1954a:97–122).[36] Al-though nominally owned by their official recipient, these cows formed part of the ancestral herd (cf. Evans-Pritchard 1951b:83; 1956:285).

In contrast, purchased cattle (ɣɔk yi̠ouni, or the cattle of money/coins) were less subject to the claims of extended kinsmen. They circulated be-tween extended kinsmen, I was told, more as a "privilege"—that is, as a muc (a "free" gift) or lony (a "free" releasing)—than as a cuɔ̠ŋ or inher-itable right. Their purchaser, in other words, was somewhat freer to dispose of them as he wished—especially if he had acquired them after having established a household of his own.[37] In contrast, it was far more difficult—though by no means impossible during the early 1980s—for unmarried youths residing in their father's household to differentiate effectively be-tween cattle acquired through their own labor and those gained through their sisters' marriages. This was because the father retained formal rights of disposal over all cattle entering his household throughout his lifetime. He could, if he so desired, redistribute cattle purchased by his sons among various wives' households as well as draw freely upon them in meeting cattle obligations toward extended kin. Indeed, it was commonly expected in some parts of Nuerland during the 1980s—most notably in regions west of the White Nile—that bachelors engaged in seasonal labor migration would reaffirm their kinship solidarity upon returning home by freely giving one of the first bull calves purchased with their wages to a favorite maternal uncle, paternal uncle, paternal cousin, or other close relative. This gesture of solidarity was often complemented by a special sacrifice, carried out by a distant patrilineal kinsmen (guạn böthni), that was intended to bless purchased cattle and integrate them into the familial herd. The cattle of money, in other words, could be ritually transformed in these regions into the cattle of girls. Significantly, these expectations and concomitant

36. Regional variations in the transgenerational scope of bridewealth claims will be discussed in chapter 5. What is important to emphasize here is simply that "cattle of girls" were associated with a system of collective "rights" and "obligations"—however those rights happened to be defined in specific instances.

37. Several Nuer have suggested to me that this assertion of more individualized ownership rights associated with "the cattle of money" was not unprecedented. In generations past, people who acquired cattle through the sale of homegrown grain—known as the "cattle of grain" or ɣɔk bɛɛl, were often able to assert more exclusive claims of ownership on the grounds that they had acquired these cattle through their own hoeing efforts.

rites were not, to the best of my knowledge, prevalent among Nuer groups east of the White Nile before the eruption of the second civil war.

Following the father's death, there was far more room for negotiation and dissent among brothers—particularly paternal half brothers—over shared rights in the familial herd. Hence, when I questioned various men and women on this score, I received a wide range of opinions—each expressed with an air of uncompromised certainty. A group of middle-aged, eastern Gaajok men, for instance, assured me that, following the father's death, cattle of money passed only as a "privilege" between paternal half brothers; full brothers, they argued, would normally be more supportive of one another and thus willingly pool all cattle wealth. In contrast, several other Gaajok and many western Leek men and women argued that half brothers retained full rights in one another's cattle, however acquired, until such time as all had married. A third opinion ran that a married man could own purchased cattle individually, regardless of the marital status of his half brothers. Finally, there were some Nuer (notably several western youths in the process of collecting sufficient cattle for their own marriages) who boldly declared that "A cow of your wages is a cow of your sweat and no one has rights in it other than you." In brotherly disputes over rights and obligations held in cattle, the ability to assert one or another of these interpretations of cattle of money would thus seem crucial.[38] Indeed, from this perspective, the concept yɔk yiọuni might be seen as having added yet another twist to what was otherwise a long-standing "zone of contestation" among patrilineal kinsmen by giving hard-working younger brothers and sons a bit of turf from which to begin negotiating for a greater share of status and autonomy within the family fold.[39]

But not all money could be turned into the cattle of money. Besides the exception of the money of shit noted earlier, only money earned as wages

38. Admittedly, relations among these various strains of opinion were, sociologically and historically, far more complex than is suggested here. Failure to work out these relations in any detail remains one of the principal shortcomings of my historical analysis.

39. "Zone of contestation" is a phrase adopted from Ferguson's intriguing analysis of the "category interests" upholding the "mystique" of bovine wealth among the Basotho (1985). He argues that Basotho men value cattle wealth less for its self-reproducing capacities than for its relative immunity, as compared with money, to the claims of other household members—most notably, dependent wives. Significantly, Ferguson's analysis of the key power axes in Basotho society does not mention the possibility of disputes over cattle wealth arising between men of the same household, extended family, or lineage. This, however, was the most important "zone of contestation" shaping contemporary Nuer attitudes toward both cattle and monetary wealth.

or through the sale of grain, gum, fish, crocodile skins, or other goods obtained through self-exertion could become *yɔk yiouni*. Money acquired by these means was closely associated with *leth puᴂny* ("human sweat") and was referred to as *yiou lat* ("the money of work"). This type of money stood opposed to that gained through the sale of collectively owned cattle: *yiou yɔɔk* (the "money of cattle"). Whereas the former type of money was considered individually owned, the latter carried with it all of the collective rights held in the cattle sold. Being an individual possession, the "money of work" could be "requested" (*thieiε*) or "begged" (*liimε*) from its owner by persistent relatives in need of school fees or simply desirous of a refreshing bowl of beer in the marketplace. The "money of cattle" was of a different order. Ideally, it was never squandered on small requests or projects but was reserved instead to purchase younger, more fertile cattle to expand and upgrade the familial herd.

It is noteworthy that this distinction often worked to the disadvantage of those Nuer whose immediate livelihoods depended less on cattle than on wages. As one poorly paid junior administrative official in Bentiu lamented:

> When a man goes to sell a cow [ox] at market, we, the relatives, usually don't bother him because we know that he is going to use that money to buy [female] cattle that will increase the herd. But then that same man can come and pester me here [in Bentiu] to give him money for beer. He may have a thousand pounds in his pocket from the cattle he has just sold. But that money is different; he wouldn't think of using it for beer. Nor could it be begged from him like the money of work. That's why it is so difficult for us who now live in town.

The fifth and final wealth category was also referred to as *yɔk yiouni*, "the cattle of money." However, these were not real cows at all but, rather, sums of money substituted for a usually quite small portion of bridewealth cattle requested. There was no possibility during the 1980s of linguistically eliding the distinction between money parading as cattle and real cattle purchased in the marketplace, despite the fact that both could be referred to as *yɔk yiouni*. This was because real cattle, regardless of their exchange origins, were invariably identified during bridewealth negotiations on the basis of their sex, color, age, horn shapes, and other distinguishing features. Hence, any reference to "cattle of money" in such contexts was unambiguously understood to mean "money cattle" as opposed to "purchased cattle." (For clarity's sake, I will use the term "cattle of money" here to mean purchased cattle and adopt the inverse term, "money cattle," when referring to cash passed in lieu of bridewealth cattle.)

Now, whether a young man could pass money in lieu of a bridewealth cow or two depended entirely, I was told, on the will of his would-be father-in-law. The latter could always refuse, demanding that the young man take his money and buy a real cow instead. Hence, only a "generous" father-in-law, I was told, would accept such a "cow." And for this reason, the number of money cattle transferred in Nuer marriages before the return of civil war in 1983 was remarkably small. With the possible exception of marriages involving the educated elite, I doubt whether more than two or three "money cattle" ever passed in any particular marriage. In fact, the vast majority of Nuer marriages continued to be arranged solely with real cattle. Considering that the bridewealth rates for a previously unmarried girl ranged at that time between twenty and thirty head of cattle, this was not a large percentage. Interestingly, several people remarked that the principal significance of money cattle was that it shifted the burden of finding an appropriate cow to purchase from the wife-takers to the wife-givers—hence the importance of a "generous" attitude among the latter. There was no significant disparity at that time between the "signal" and "market" value of such beasts (Sansom 1976), and, consequently, money cattle were commonly converted into real cattle (classified as the "cattle of girls") by the bride's family. In situations where the bride's father spent some or all of this money instead on guns, grain, clothes, or other goods, he was likely to face greater difficulties mustering the cash as opposed to the cattle portion of the bridewealth payment in the event his daughter was later divorced.[40]

In addition to cattle and money, there were other objects that sometimes passed in bridewealth exchange at this time, including guns, radio cassette recorders, mosquito nets, clothing, mattresses, blankets, and similar items. With the noteworthy exception of guns (and the occasional radio), less expensive items were defined as *pöth* ("honor-bearing gifts") rather than as bridewealth proper. Small—and sometimes not so small—gifts of money were commonly showered on the mother of the bride during the wedding celebration by the groom's entourage in both eastern and western Nuerland. Indeed, it was a well-known fact that eastern Jikany mothers could delay the performance of their daughters' consummation ceremony if their expectations in this regard were left unfulfilled.

40. Significantly, there was no categorical equivalent for "money of girls." Hence fathers and brothers of the bride were often able to shield this "money cattle" from the claims of more distant kinsmen. This was especially true in eastern Nuerland, as will be explained in chapter 5.

In contrast to these smaller, honor-bearing gifts, the offer of a gun—like that of spears in earlier generations—always formed part of the bridewealth settlement proper, being negotiated as so many "cattle of the gun" (*ɣɔk maac*). There were several reasons for this. First, guns were normally purchased with cattle and held collectively by a group of brothers or other kinsmen. Although the cattle value of specific models tended to fluctuate with local supply and demand, there was, nevertheless, considerable consensus among Nuer during the early 1980s as to the value of any particular model at any particular time or place. Second, a gun was sometimes offered in bridewealth exchange as a kind of temporary loan—offered, that is, with the understanding that the groom's family could reclaim "their" gun at some point in the future by replacing it with its cattle equivalent. In such cases it was particularly important that the gun's cattle value be clearly established at the outset of the marriage. Third and finally, guns, unlike money, were seen to share to some extent in cattle's augmentative potential: The cattle-exchange value for most models had escalated so rapidly during the 1960s and 1970s that, by the early 1980s, most people considered the purchase of a gun to be a sound economic as well as security investment. For all of these reasons, the relationship between guns and cattle was an intimate one—especially in parts of contemporary eastern Nuerland. These issues will be explored more fully in chapter 3.

The first thing to note about these various categories of wealth is that they facilitated movements of cattle and money between blood and non-blood spheres of exchange at the same time as they confirmed the presence of an axiological boundary between these spheres. Social principles characteristic of "kinship" exchange were continuously being drawn, together with cattle and money, into the marketplace and vice versa. Consider the following hypothetical—though by no means atypical—series of cattle and money exchanges.

Imagine that an ox, originally obtained as bridewealth, is sold in the market and the money later invested in a young heifer: cattle of girls—> money of cattle—>cattle of girls; Cg—>Mc—>Cg. In this sequence the collective rights and privileges held in the original bridewealth ox are not lost as it is transformed into money and later back again into a cow. As a concept, then, the money of cattle both affirms and protects these collective interests, based as they are on an ideology of shared blood, as cattle pass in and out of the marketplace, a nonblood-associated sphere of social relations and exchange. Conversely, a successful migrant who invests his savings in cattle (money of work—>cattle of money; Mw—>Cm) is able to smuggle principles of personal autonomy and private ownership associated

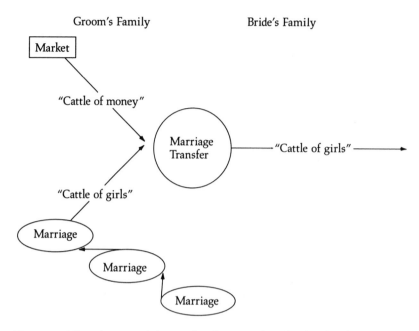

Figure 1.   The relativity of the "cattle of money"/"cattle of girls" distinction.

with market exchange into the realm of kinship relations via the concepts money of work and cattle of money.[41] In this system there are no absolutes: It is always a matter of specific cattle and specific sums of money defined in terms of their immediate sources.

The relativity with which different sorts of cattle and money are classified is readily apparent in bridewealth exchange. For whether a particular cow is collectively defined as a cow of money or a cow of girls depends entirely on the negotiating position of the exchange partners. Whereas the groom and his party are normally quite conscious of which cows are cattle of money and which cattle of girls, from the perspective of the bride's family, all cattle received in the marriage are cattle of girls (see figure 1).

Once having reached the byre of the bride's father, these cattle may be put to a variety of uses. A significant portion of them will probably be

41. The hybrid wealth system of the Nuer raises interesting questions with regard to Bohannan's famous hypothesis (1955, 1959) about money's scrambling effect on traditional exchange spheres among the Tiv. However, I have found Bohannan's thesis difficult to relate directly to my Nuer materials because it is premised on the idea that "things-in-themselves," rather than the social relations through which they flow, differentiate "spheres of exchange."

Bride's Family

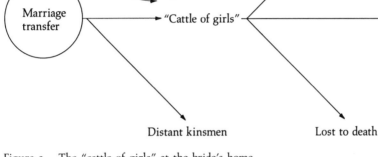

Figure 2. The "cattle of girls" at the bride's home.

redistributed among close agnatic and cognatic kin as *yɔk cuŋni* ("the cattle of rights"). Some of those remaining in the bride's homestead may be sold to purchase "better" cattle, and others may be sold to counter grain shortages, buy medicines, pay taxes, or the like. Still others may be slain in sacrifice or in hospitality, while others may die of natural causes in the bride's homestead (see figure 2).

Bridewealth cattle sold but not butchered in the marketplace will be either siphoned off into the export trade or purchased by other Nuer, in which case they may well pass on again some day in bridewealth exchange. Whether or not they enter their new owners' byres as cattle of money or cattle of girls will depend on the type of money used to purchase them. Of the cattle remaining with the bride's family, several will probably be used in the negotiation of additional marriages.

So, to follow through this ideal-typical series of exchanges, imagine that a brother of the bride desires to arrange a marriage for himself. How will he go about it? What types of wealth might he use? He will probably combine some of the cattle received from his sister's marriage with others collected from paternal and maternal uncles and whomever else he or his father can persuade to assist him. Perhaps he may also add a few cattle purchased with

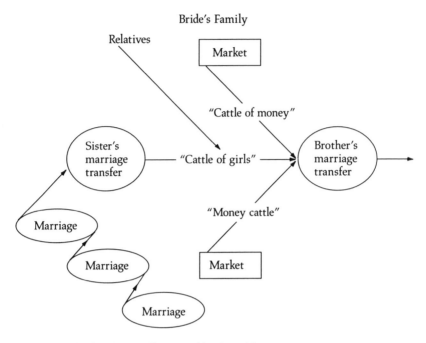

Figure 3.   The brother's collection of bridewealth.

money earned in Khartoum. Assuming that his future father-in-law looks kindly upon him, he may even be able to pass a "money cow" or two. The options before him may be represented as shown in figure 3.

Together, figures 1, 2, and 3 sketch the principal movements of cattle and money within and between kinship and market spheres of exchange. They also reveal how Nuer marriages have tended to build on one another. But what interests, one might ask, has this system of cattle/money distinctions really served? What has been its role, if any, in patterning relations of autonomy and dependence between men and women, young and old, kin and non-kin, wife-takers and wife-givers, the cattle-rich and the cattle-poor, wage earners and nonwage earners, and so on?

With respect to familial and extended kin ties, this system of wealth distinctions certainly enhanced individual possibilities for autonomy by weakening feelings of mutual dependence among agnates and among cognates. With the expansion of the market economy, young Nuer men became far less dependent on the goodwill of their fathers, older brothers, and paternal and maternal uncles in the collection of bridewealth cattle than they were, say, during the late 1930s and 1940s. Consequently, the abilities of senior men to amass power in the form of cattle wealth declined accordingly—though, as I noted earlier, western Nuer elders developed ritual means of muting the cattle of money/cattle of girls distinction. Although these developments could contribute in the long run to the development of sharper wealth inequalities among men, it would be difficult, I think, to convince many contemporary Nuer of this possibility. In fact, several men and women argued that the introduction of money and the creation of local cattle, grain, and labor markets had significantly eased previous social inequalities inherent in the cattle economy itself—most notably, inequalities based on birth order and on relative family size. Whereas a sisterless man was often condemned to a bachelor's life during the 1930s and 1940s, he was "free" during the early 1980s to take up trading and wage labor in order to obtain marriage cattle. The money economy, in other words, was valued by many for having provided industrious individuals with additional opportunities to transcend poverty and misfortune. As one overly optimistic eastern Gaajok youth exclaimed: *Ci caan ŋɔɔk* ("Poverty/misfortune has ended").

Indeed, much to my initial surprise, old men openly expressed admiration for the younger generation's ability to acquire cattle through the marketplace. Once after a long and fascinating conversation with an older Leek man about the dangers he faced as a youth stealing Baggara cattle, he concluded with the words: "Ah, but this is nothing. Today our sons surpass us in their quest for cattle. Haven't you seen? They think nothing of going all the way to Khartoum for a cow!"

The establishment of local markets, together with a system of government chiefs, customary courts, and police posts, also made it considerably easier for unmarried women, widows, and divorcees to maintain independent households. For they could now escape to town, brew beer, earn money, and live under the guardianship of no man. Rebecca Nyaboth, an independent widow who happened to run the biggest beer-selling parlor in Bentiu in 1983, captured the implications of these developments well when she said, *Kɔaŋ ɛ yaandä kä kume ɛ cɔadä kɛnɛ maar* ("Beer is my cow and the government my husband and mother").

Married women, in contrast, did not benefit from emerging market opportunities to the same extent, for Nuer husbands maintained formal rights of ownership over nearly all cattle and monetary wealth acquired by their wives during the marriage.[42] Furthermore, the husband's rights in

---

42. The principal exceptions to this general rule were cattle paid to the wife directly as compensation for some personal injury (e.g., the loss of teeth in a fight)

this regard were staunchly upheld by local government courts—which were run, of course, entirely by Nuer men. Hence, it was impossible during the early 1980s for a wife to sue in court for the return of "beer cows" used by her husband, without her permission, to arrange an additional marriage.[43] Nor could she take such cattle or their offspring with her upon divorce. Although it was thus extremely difficult for married women to assert independent ownership of cattle acquired through their own marketing efforts, they could—and often did—reinforce the cattle of money/cattle of girls distinction with respect to cows purchased by wage-earning sons. Consequently, conflicts between paternal half brothers over rights held in purchased cattle were intimately entwined with the divergent, long-range interests of their mothers.

With regard to affinal ties, these wealth categories had an additional advantage, for they provided farsighted individuals with an opportunity to reduce the risk that their own marriages would someday be negatively affected by the divorce of a close female relative. When one considers the fact that divorce rates among Nuer nearly tripled between 1936 and 1983, this was not an insignificant advantage (for details see the appendix). Indeed, for reasons to be described in chapter 4, Nuer men and women of the 1980s were divorcing not only more frequently than earlier generations but also at later and later points in the marriage process. Whereas Evans-Pritchard claims that during the 1930s divorce was "very unusual" after the birth of a child to the union and "impossible" after the birth of a second (1951b:94), during the 1980s it was not uncommon for government courts to sever unions involving two, three, or even four living children. Recovery of the original bridewealth cattle and their offspring was especially arduous in such cases since the cattle had usually long been dispersed through a multitude of other marriages. If they had not spread too far afield and the woman's husband knew of their whereabouts, he was likely to push in court for the return of those same cows and their calves.[44] If not, the courts maintained that substitutes be provided. Yet sometimes the

---

and bridewealth cattle acquired through the marriages of her natal kinswomen.

43. Hence, when an older, largely independent woman named Nyapuka threatened to sue her husband in court for the return of four beer cows he had seized to marry another wife, he immediately countered with a divorce threat. Nyapuka was thus forced to drop her case.

44. There was a consensus emerging among Nuer chiefs during the 1980s that bridewealth cattle that had passed through more than two additional marriages should be replaced by the divorced wife's family rather than recalled. Nevertheless, all calves born to the original bridewealth cow prior to its passage through the third marriage were subject to recall by the courts.

family of the wife was unable to muster suitable substitutes without re-calling cattle used in other marriages. Although the bride's people were not responsible for replacing cows that died naturally in their own home-stead, they were expected to replace all cattle "that had accomplished some-thing" (*me ci du<u>ɔ</u>r lat*) for the bride's family—including those that had been used to solidify a second marriage, nullify a familial debt, or other-wise further the bride's family's objectives before dying in other people's homesteads. As a result of these rather stringent court-sanctioned inter-pretations of the cattle obligations of the wife's family toward the divorc-ing husband, the rupture of one marriage sometimes weakened others. If the marriage secondarily affected was a relatively recent one, it, too, could end in divorce.[45]

What must be realized, however, is that these potential difficulties could be avoided by farsighted individuals through the skillful manipulation of the cattle/money categories outlined. A young man could attempt to reduce the risk that his own marriage would someday be weakened by the divorce of a female relative by including as many cattle of money in his bride-wealth settlement as possible. For unlike cattle of girls, purchased cattle did not conduct shock waves created by other people's divorces. Since they came directly from the market, they could be reclaimed, in principle, only by the groom himself. During the early 1980s this marriage strategy was especially favored by western Nuer men.[46] There I often heard people ad-vocate the advantages of marrying with cattle of money as opposed to cat-tle of girls with the expression *Yaŋ me ci kok ke yi<u>ɔ</u>u thil<u>ɛ</u> riek* ("a cow bought with money is risk free"). I was also told that a "clever" father would arrange the marriage of a son claimed on the basis of a paternity payment (*ruɔk*) with as many cattle of money as possible so as to decrease the possibility of a future rupture between that son and other sons after his death. For were the adopted son to marry with cattle received through the marriages of his half sisters, it would be very difficult for him to re-ciprocate when it later became time for his younger half brothers to marry since he would have no full sisters to bring in additional bridewealth cattle.

45. I documented three instances of "chain divorce" in the west and two in the east—all of them occurring relatively early in the second marriage.

46. As was stressed in chapter 1, western Nuer migrants were more likely than their eastern counterparts to invest their full wages in bridewealth cattle during the early 1980s. Moreover, for reasons to be explained in chapter 5, western Nuer marriages tended to be more extensively intertwined than eastern marriages since the bridewealth claims of distant kinsmen continued to be fully honored in that region.

Furthermore, several easterners and westerners alike remarked that, though the distinction between cattle of money and cattle of girls was formally lost when marriage cattle passed into the possession of the bride's family, a father might nevertheless prefer to marry his daughter to a man who could offer a relatively large proportion of cattle of money. For the father could then use these cattle in a subsequent marriage for himself or a son, confident in the knowledge that the fate of such cattle, so to speak, depended upon the continuation of only one marriage—that between his daughter and son-in-law. And were that union ever to falter, he would presumably have considerable say in whether or not it actually ended in divorce.

For all these reasons, many men and women had come to regard cattle of money as a more secure form of wealth than cattle of girls. Hence, contrary to what one might have expected, the growth of cattle and labor markets in Nuerland actually contributed in some ways to the stability of marital alliances: The more rapidly cattle of girls were transformed via market exchange into cattle of money, the less likely it was that the rupture of one marriage would adversely affect others. In other ways, of course, the expanding market economy had a profoundly negative impact on Nuer marriages. During the 1980s marriages were often strained to the breaking point by the extended absences of husbands striving to earn a bit of cash in Khartoum.[47] Age- and gender-based asymmetries within the community were also reduced to some extent by the continual transformation in the marketplace of cattle of girls into cattle of money. For in principle, anyone could earn money and purchase cattle—although, as I explained, the rights of bachelors and married women were far more circumscribed in this regard than were those of married men and unmarried women.

At the same time, however, cattle of money were continually being transformed into cattle of girls via bridewealth transfers and special sacrificial offerings. As cattle of girls they could be used to justify and support the same age and gender asymmetries that they would otherwise tend to undermine as cattle of money. In this way Nuer were able to integrate and, in some sense, synthesize practices and principles of monetary exchange with those characteristic of more enduring bonds of kinship and community. The synthesis achieved, however, was based on a perpetual al-

---

47. Furthermore, due to transformations in Nuer customary law wrought by the British colonial regime, it was increasingly easy for long absent husbands to divorce their wives upon their return home on grounds of adultery. This point will be expanded upon in chapter 4.

ternation between the conflicting social principles concerned, not a definitive fusion of them.

From a slightly different perspective, one might argue that men and women had fused the concepts of cattle and money in such a way to permit certain market values to bleed into bridewealth exchange without threatening the uniqueness of the cattle/people equation so fundamental to their social life. One did not actually need to use money in bridewealth transfers in order to take advantage of principles of private property and limited liability associated with it: A few cattle of money would do. Thus, the self-generating aspect of bridewealth cattle, so central to Nuer images of the perpetuation of marriage alliances, was preserved—and all those "augmentations of life" rooted in the cultural assertion of an identity between cattle and people were protected.[48]

Yet money, as I noted, had begun to make some inroads into the field of bridewealth exchange through the concept of money cattle. Though the effects of war, famine, and disease were still limited during the early 1980s, there is every reason to believe that the tremendous hardships Nuer have suffered since the renewal of civil war in 1983 will so decimate their herds that more and more people will be reduced to marrying with money cattle in the future. A major shift from cattle to cash as the dominant medium of bridewealth exchange would require, however, a radical rethinking of the nature and logic of alliance. The notion that alliances are founded on an equation between human and bovine blood and perpetuated through a parallel extension of cattle and people through time would have to be totally reformulated to take account of money's bloodless nature. It remains to be seen whether Nuer communities will transcend their current hardships to create more radical reformulations of their concepts of alliance, descent, and personhood in the future.

CONCLUSIONS

This chapter has shown how Nuer men and women consciously and actively intervened in the broader economic forces shaping their everyday lives. As of 1983, money had not developed into a generalized medium of exchange

48. This continuing commitment to the cattle/human equation in the face of the cattle/money equation was also evident in the fact that there was no categorical equivalent for the money of girls, even though such a category would have been a logical extension of the fact that small numbers of money cattle were sometimes accepted in place of real cattle in bridewealth exchanges in the east during the early 1980s.

among Nuer. Nor had its introduction precipitated the emergence of a "unicentric economy" (Bohannan 1959:501). Rather, Nuer incorporated money into a weighted exchange system in which cattle remained the dominant metaphor of value. This was not simply a process whereby cattle were progressively "commodified" but, rather, one in which commodities were also "cattle-ified." In fact, even cash was cattle-ified.

The elaborate system of hybrid categories of cattle and monetary wealth Nuer devised had provided them with a sense of stability in the midst of change. Cattle and money were able to move freely between "market" and "kinship" spheres of exchange without threatening the cattle/human equation so fundamental to cultural concepts of personhood and transgenerational alliance. Rather, money's powers of effacement were largely checked by an ideological elaboration of the unique blood links uniting people and cattle—an elaboration that was developed, I have argued, so as to preclude the possibility of any direct equation between money and people. At the same time, the hybrid cattle/money wealth categories Nuer developed greatly enhanced the abilities of young Nuer migrants, in particular, to understand and come to terms with the noncattle, "nonblood" forms of sociality increasingly binding them to the world at large.

This is not to say that contemporary Nuer men and women had, by the early 1980s, reached a state of consensus about the "true" differences between cattle and money as everyday media of social exchange. Quite the contrary. Whatever sense of axiological "balance" they maintained by successfully crossbreeding the concepts of cattle and money was based more on a perpetual alternation between—rather than a definitive resolution of—the conflicting social values and practices separating market from nonmarket modes of exchange. But, then, not all problems need to be solved: People can continue to live and work in social and cultural systems that remain fundamentally unfinished. In fact, I suspect that this is more the norm than the exception everywhere.

Although the emergence of the cattle/money equation did not sunder the strong human bonds of identification with cattle, it contributed, nonetheless, to a significant contraction of Nuer concepts of selfhood and sociality. Before the introduction of currency, the sense of self people cultivated through their relations with cattle invariably implied the support and participation of a collectivity of persons, including ancestors and divinities as well as numerous contemporaries. Cattle's role in creating and maintaining this socially enriched sense of self was subsequently diminished, as we have seen, by the emerging opportunities for individuals to acquire and own cattle wealth, opportunities made possible by a " 'money-form' of commodity exchange." Although cattle could now be converted into money and vice versa, the cattle of money and the money of work could not be used to reinforce transgenerational bonds of dependence among kinsmen in the same way as the cattle of girls because, as Nuer put it, money has no blood.

While the wealth system that Nuer developed would appear, from this perspective, to be an ingenious compromise between market and nonmarket forms of consciousness and sociality, it also reflected, as I have shown, major socioeconomic transformations in the relative autonomy and dependence of senior men versus junior men, cattle owners versus noncattle owners, full brothers versus half brothers, wage earners versus nonwage earners, men versus women, husbands versus wives, married women versus unmarried women, wife-takers versus wife-givers, and merchants versus nonmerchants. I pointed out, for instance, how this system of categories contributed to a marked decrease in the abilities of senior men to amass power in the form of cattle wealth. Cattle of money and money of work played key roles in this power shift by giving wage-earning younger brothers and sons a potential basis from which to assert greater autonomy and status within the family fold. From this perspective money was definitely a "liberating" force in Simmel's sense: It enabled more individuals to assert their independence and strength (*buɔm*) through the establishment of their own herds. Moreover, the realization of this cultural ideal became possible at earlier phases in people's lives and in more varied circumstances than before the development of regional cattle and labor markets. With respect to patrilineal connections, these developments significantly aggravated conflicts of interest inherent in the very structure of agnatic descent—namely, conflicts between the collective and individual procreative goals of lineage members. And for this reason, older men and women continued to maintain strong moral pressure on the younger generation to reject formal division of the family's "energy" before marriage and the establishment of an independent household.[49] Moreover, I think it particularly significant that none of my Nuer acquaintances during the 1980s explicitly noted or developed the potential linkages between human blood and sweat, on the one hand, and between human sweat and money, on the other. Although I would not be surprised if these associations were ideologically elaborated

49. Significantly, I learned during a return visit to Sudan in 1990 that the ritual transformation of cattle of money into cattle of girls common among the western Nuer during the early 1980s had subsequently attained popularity among some eastern Nuer groups as a means of affirming familial support in a period of mounting insecurity and hardship.

in the future by individuals wishing to assert more exclusive ownership
rights in cattle purchased with their wages, the fact that these associations
were not explicitly developed by the early 1980s lends support to my earlier observation that the blood bond uniting contemporary Nuer and their
herds continued to be conceptualized primarily in "procreative" terms.
And, of course, human sweat, while eminently "productive," is never in
itself "reproductive."

These controversial issues, however, were far from resolved in 1983.
Moreover, Nuer at that time were profoundly aware of the increasing pre-
cariousness of their social world in general and their cattle wealth in particular with respect to the widening vortex of violence then gaining momentum throughout the Upper Nile. In the years that followed, many Nuer
communities were overwhelmed by government-sponsored Arab militias,
unchecked rinderpest epidemics, intensified air bombardments, and, ultimately, unprecedented famine. As was explained in the prologue, thousands
upon thousands of Nuer were eventually forced to flee their homes in order
to seek sanctuary from the war. Their herds were steadily decimated and
their families and communities increasingly severed and destroyed. This
continuing tragedy will undoubtedly provoke further reexaminations of
their notions of selfhood and sociality in the years to come.

Although it is impossible to predict the ultimate impact this war will
have on Nuer attitudes toward cattle and monetary wealth, I offer a few
tentative remarks about disparities in marriage practices emerging in the
early 1990s between displaced Nuer currently living on the outskirts of
Khartoum and eastern Nuer currently residing deep within the southern
war zone itself. On the basis of brief research trips to these areas in 1990
and 1992, it was immediately apparent that these two sets of Nuer communities were facing very different challenges. Those Nuer who fled northwards were being forced to adapt to a parched, hostile, cattleless world in
which access to money—be it through the generosity of relatives, short-
term wage-labor opportunities, petty trade, begging, prostitution, beer
brewing, or theft—was the central necessity of life. In contrast, the eastern
Nuer communities I visited in the south during 1992 were grappling with
deprivations and hardships that money, even were it readily available, could
scarcely resolve. By that time the extended grain and cattle markets of
eastern Nuerland had been defunct for nearly a decade.[50] Moreover, what-

50. This was apparently less true in parts of western Nuerland, where
long-distance trading networks began to be reestablished in the vicinity of Rup
Nyagai following the successful 1987–88 negotiation of a partial truce between

ever cash these communities may have had at the start of this war had long been absorbed by surviving grain markets operating inside southwestern Ethiopia or in the government-held town of Malakal. Consequently, the distinction between the cattle of money and the cattle of girls was becoming increasingly irrelevant in this area—as was that between the money of work and the money of cattle. And those marriages that continued to take place in that region revolved almost exclusively around cattle and guns. Although continuing insecurity had increased the importance of guns as bridewealth items in the east, the cattle-exchange values for most rifle models were dropping rapidly during the early 1990s, owing to increased local supplies and to the declining cattle population. Moreover, no eastern Nuer marriage was considered valid during the early 1990s without the passage of at least some cows. In other words, the cattle of the gun were insufficient in themselves to cement a marriage: the blood of the cow remained essential.

Displaced Nuer living in Khartoum, in contrast, had responded to the inaccessibility of whatever cattle remained with their extended families in the south by nominally doubling bridewealth rates from twenty-five to fifty head of cattle. Up to half of these cattle could be offered in the form of money cattle (at a mutually negotiated rate that was normally lower than the market value of real cattle).[51] Although the completion of this monetary transfer enabled the union to begin, it did not relieve the

---

SPLA forces in that region and various Baggara Arab communities in neighboring southern Kordofan (Commander Riäk Machar Teny, personal interview, 31 Dec. 1989). A film made by John Ryle and Baping Tim Chuol (1994) and entitled *The Price of Survival* offers images of this bustling market center.

51. I should stress that, although there was little disparity between the nominal and market value of money cattle during the early 1980s, such a disparity subsequently emerged among Nuer war refugees currently camped on the outskirts of Khartoum. These Nuer, of course, had no direct access to cattle. Although I hope to discuss this and other consequences of the second civil war on Nuer marriage practices in later publications, I should, perhaps, note here that this development had major implications for the structure of marital alliances and property relations more generally. To cite a comparable example: Although the Pedi (Sansom 1976) may well have succeeded in "removing the sting of invidious comparison" (Sansom 1976:138) by refusing to distinguish between nominal and real cattle when referring to specific bridewealth settlements, the fact of the matter remains that, with each substitution of a "green-tongued" cow for a real one, the wife-takers' side effectively reduces its exchange obligations toward the wife-givers. It would thus be interesting to know, for instance, whether or not wife-givers among the Pedi and other cattle-raising people in Africa and beyond have attempted to compensate for this disparity by inflating bridewealth demands—as was the case among "displaced" Nuer in Khartoum.

groom's family from the obligation to provide the full balance of twenty-five head of real cattle at some time in the future "when the world becomes good again." Indeed, the general age and sex of all outstanding cattle were fully negotiated by senior members of the families before the wedding celebrations were allowed to take place. Sometimes it was possible for Nuer living in Khartoum to arrange for the long-distance transfer of bride-wealth cattle between southern branches of the extended families concerned. More commonly, however, this cattle debt remained an outstanding obligation on the part of the groom's family. Even so, no marriage could be completed in Khartoum without the ritual slaughter of at least three head of cattle—or, as I suspect was more likely the case, sheep or goats. What was important to these Nuer was that the union should be symbolically sealed and strengthened with a flow of cattle blood.

These war-provoked changes in Nuer marriage practices reveal once again the inherent fluidity of the present and unpredictability of the future. In less than a decade the long-standing historical tendency for wife-takers to complete their bridewealth payments at earlier and earlier phases in the marriage process had been completely reversed in those Nuer communities that had fled to the north. Moreover, it remains to be seen whether Nuer husbands who married while in Khartoum will be able to fulfill their outstanding cattle commitments toward their affines in the future. With little prospect of a viable peace settlement in the foreseeable future, there may well come a time when many of these husbands will be forced to weigh their long-standing cattle obligations toward their wife's people against their economic responsibilities for maintaining and supporting their own growing families.

Doubtless, Nuer evaluations of the binding force of cattle and money will continue to develop in novel ways in the years ahead. However, if there is one conclusion of my analysis that merits special emphasis, it is this: One cannot predict a priori how money will be conceptualized and incorporated by other peoples. Hence, to assume that "global" processes of "monetization" or "commodification" follow some universal logic is not only to distort historical realities but to deny the creative potential of other peoples and cultures.

3 Guns, Warfare, and the State
New Contexts of Power,
Violence, and Leadership

In Nuer historical experience the age of the "government" (*kume*, from the Arabic, *ḥukūma*) and the age of the "gun" (*mac*) were one. From the initial thrusts and parries of British tribute-collecting raids during the 1910s and 1920s, through the early mobilization efforts of southern secessionist forces during the 1950s and 1960s, to the increasingly vicious "jihad" currently being waged against them by the Khartoum government, the gun had dominated the entire fitful history of Nuer accommodation and resistance to the extension of centralized state powers into local forms of authority, cooperation, and coercion (see plate 9).

Contemporary Nuer were entirely realistic about this. Although I sometimes heard older men and women express nostalgia during the early 1980s for the relative peacefulness and security experienced at the height of British colonial rule, the political edge enjoyed by their current overlords, the northern "Arabs" (*jalabni/kareŋni*), was attributed purely to a difference in shooting power. "It's just the Arabs' guns that are bigger," I was told repeatedly. "If we had their guns we would have routed them years ago!" If it were not for the gifts of the gun and of overrule from the British, the northern Sudanese, they maintained, would never have succeeded in gaining dominance over the south.[1]

Significantly, contemporary Nuer perceived a fundamental difference between the force of a rifle and that of a spear: Whereas the power of a spear issues directly from the bones and sinews of the person who hurls it, that of a gun is eerily internal to it. Outside of a minimal effort required to hoist and fire it, a rifle's power was seen to be completely independent of its human bearer—"all a person does is aim it." And thus, the force of a

---

1. Contemporary Nuer frequently emphasized the fact that the current military regime in Khartoum was, like themselves, a mere purchaser—not a producer—of automatic weapons. The production of guns, like that of Western medicines, was attributed, rather, to *nei ti boor*, "white people." Nuer classified northern "Arabs," in contrast, as "brown/reddish people" (*nei ti lual*)—a term that was initially applied to the British as well during the early 1900s.

Plate 9. A government subchief (standing with sash) and his armed policemen.

rifle, they reasoned, demonstrates nothing definitive about the human being behind it. Consequently, the persistent—though at times tantalizingly
narrow—material gap separating their own military strength from that of
successive Khartoum regimes was not interpreted by contemporary Nuer
as indicative of any inherent inferiority on their part. On the contrary,
their images of themselves as courageous warriors remained remarkably
strong throughout the 1980s—even if edged at times with an awareness
that knowledge of warfare may not prove all that effective in a world increasingly dominated by "politics" (*thiyathä*, from the Arabic *siyāsa*). In
the words of Marial Cuol: "We Nuer are ignorant of politics; what we know
is war. War—that is the goodness of our hearts! We do not fear death in
battle—even our women [are brave]." Having been forced to adapt to an
untenable set of externally imposed national borders, the Nuer of the 1980s
took a long-term view of their current political subjugation: "The Arabs
may be our rulers today, but tomorrow we may be theirs!"

Prideful assertions such as these struck me as particularly poignant at
a time when Nuer, along with other southern Sudanese communities, were
plunging uncontrollably into full-scale civil war with the north. Many
people had begun to seek solace in the enigmatic songs of their late
prophet, Ngundeng Bong (Ŋundɛŋ Boŋ, d. 1906), who foretold the coming
of a great war in which Nuer—along with other "black peoples" of the region—would definitively free themselves from external domination. However, there was little more that individuals could do to prepare themselves
for this fully believed eventuality than band together to buy guns. And
this they were doing in ever-increasing numbers throughout the early
1980s—with some men venturing as far as the Ugandan border in search
of more powerful automatic rifles.

The contrast Nuer perceived between the power of guns and that of
spears had not only shielded their warrior ethos from occasional crushing
defeats by government troops but, more important, provoked broader reassessments of the meaning of violent deaths and of the ethics and tactics of
local forms of intercommunity fighting and feuding. *Te kaamdiɛn ke cɔaa*
("A bone exists between them") was the principal Nuer metaphor used for
relations of permanent hostility forged through homicide. The buried
bones of the slain—which remained firm and whole beneath the earth long
after all remnants of flesh had disappeared—were said to create a social
rift so deep, so strong, that relations of commensality, sexuality, and intermarriage between the extended families concerned and their descendants were prohibited, in principle, "forever." Active states of intercommunity warfare (*koor*) and feuding (*tɛr*) could be tempered by a transfer of

bloodwealth cattle and by the completion of special sacrifices of atonement. But relationships of "the bone," like those of agnation (*böth*), endured for as long as they were remembered. However, as firearms burned deeper and deeper into regional patterns of warfare, many people began to wonder whether the spiritual and social consequences of inter-Nuer gun slayings were identical to those realized by spears. Whereas everyone seemed to agree during the early 1980s that to kill someone with a spear was to accept full responsibility for that death, matters were less clear in the case of inter-Nuer gun slayings. Not only were bullets (*dei mac*, literally, "a gun's calves") more prone to unintentional release, but once having been fired their trajectories—and hence fatal consequences—were often difficult if not impossible to trace accurately in the context of major intercommunity confrontations.

To understand the historical significance of this difficulty, it is important to realize that Nuer men and women of the early 1930s conceptualized relationships of the "bone" (*cɔaa*), or feud (*tɛr*), as emanating outwards from a mysterious blood bond forged between slayer and slain at the moment of death. Specifically, they believed that some of the blood (*riɛm*) of the victim passed at death into the body of the slayer, being driven forth, as it were, by a mission of vengeance (*bi riɛmdɛ lɔny ke jɛ*). Were the slayer to eat or drink anything before having this "embittered" blood removed through a small incision (*bier*) made on the upper arm by a *kuäär muɔn* (or "earth priest," also known in the literature as a "leopard-skin chief," *kuäär kuac*), he was sure to die of a highly dangerous and contagious form of pollution known as *nueer*. As Evans-Pritchard explained:

> As soon as a man kills another he hastens to the nearest [earth] priest, who draws the point of a fishing spear down his right arm from where it joins the shoulder and sacrifices a beast, called *yang riem*, the cow of the blood. Were the slayer to eat or drink before this has been done it would be serious *nueer* and cause certain death, for the blood which is drawn is thought to be in some way that of the slain man which has passed into him. . . . It is essential that a blood feud be settled [by the payment of bloodwealth cattle] if the parties to it live in the same neighbourhood, not only for reasons of security, but also on account of the serious danger [of contracting *nueer* in which] both the dead man's kin and the slayer's kin are placed by the homicide, a danger in which the whole community is involved. . . . If either side eats or drinks with the other or from vessels which the other side has used, the penalty is death, and it may be brought on kinsmen on either side by a person who belongs to neither party eating or drinking in the homes of both. This intolerable state of interdiction can only be ended by sacrifice by a priest when compensation has been paid. (1956:293–294)

This association of *nueer* with "dangerous to eat/drink" ran as well through the diverse range of social contexts in which this multifaceted pollution concept surfaced. For though identified first and foremost in people's minds with acts of homicide and of commensality between feuding parties, the threat of *nueer* lingered behind numerous other cultural prohibitions including the ban on cannibalism, the "milking interdiction" (which stipulated that no initiated man could drink milk that he had taken directly from a cow), as well as various taboos surrounding lactation, menstruation, and abnormal births. Indeed, Evans-Pritchard argued in *Nuer Religion* that "*Nueer* is the most important of Nuer sin concepts" (1956:183). My own opinion is that *nueer* would be better defined as a pollution concept governing the social circulation of blood (*riɛm*) and food (*mieth*) as complementary aspects of human vitality. I argue in a separate publication (Hutchinson 1992b) that *nueer* effectively distinguished, via the notion "dangerous to eat/drink," blood flows that were culturally defined as negative, death-ridden, and anomalous from others deemed to be properly mediated, positive, and life promoting.

Although it was my impression that this pollution concept had proven remarkably stable over the years, the one context in which contemporary Nuer were actively debating received notions of *nueer* during the early 1980s was that of homicide. Because of the brutal realities experienced during the first civil-war era, many people had come to doubt that the dangers of *nueer* were equally grave in all cases of inter-Nuer homicide. Some people, particularly easterners, argued that the blood curse of the slain was operative only in situations where assailant and victim were previously known or related to one another. Nor were people in complete consensus about the specific rites required for the removal of such pollution. While it was still widely accepted that inter-Nuer spear killings necessitated the ritual intervention of an earth priest (*kuäär muɔn*), many eastern Jikany Nuer considered the bloodletting rite of *bier* insufficient to eliminate the dangers of pollution when the victim (whether related or not to the killer) had died of bullet wounds. In their efforts to cope with the sheer devastation experienced during the height of the first civil war (1963–72), many easterners adopted new (gun-specific) purification rites that were used first to supplement and, later, to replace the bloodletting rite performed by earth priests. In that region people were turning increasingly to metaphors of temperature—as distinct from those of blood—in attempting to comprehend the mysterious inner force and ambiguous impact of firearms.

Western Nuer, in contrast, continued to rely exclusively on the purifying powers of earth priests in all cases of inter-Nuer homicide during the early 1980s—regardless of the type of weapon used. Following the renewal of full-scale civil war in 1983, however, many westerners began to develop an implicit analogy between bullets and lightning—the deceased victims of both being thought to create a uniquely direct, spiritual linkage with Divinity (*kuɔth nhial*) that could be cultivated through cattle sacrifice and, thereafter, effectively called upon in times of danger by surviving kin. Significantly, western Nuer spiritual practices in this regard were being challenged during the late 1980s and early 1990s by leading Nuer members of the SPLA. The zonal commander of the Western Upper Nile, Dr. Riäk Machar, explained in a 1990 interview with me how he had attempted to persuade local residents that violent deaths resulting from the current civil war should be completely dissociated from the forms of pollution and spiritual consequences of homicides generated by more local occurrences of intercommunity feuding and fighting. In essence the SPLA leadership was arguing that the overarching political context of the current war—which it defined as a "government war" (*kɔ̱ɔ̱r kume*)—should take precedence over the personal identities and interrelations of the combatants in people's assessments of the social and spiritual ramifications of homicide.

The SPLA commander's arguments in this regard were implicitly bound up with Nuer notions of a legitimate governmental authority. Ever since the imposition of British colonial rule, the "government" had claimed the "right" to impose "capital punishment" or otherwise eliminate individuals who seriously challenged its monopolistic claims on the legitimate use of force. And increasingly this "right" was acknowledged by Nuer themselves. Consequently, as greater numbers of Nuer began to participate in the "government" as policemen, prison wardens, government soldiers, and the like, many of them were forced to confront the possibility—if not actuality—of killing fellow Nuer in "the line of duty." Among the earliest people to face this moral dilemma were higher-ranking government chiefs. During the 1930s and 1940s "court presidents" were sometimes pressured into imposing the death sentence on individual Nuer who had been charged under the Sudan Penal Code with "culpable homicide amounting to murder." In such cases, the individual chiefs involved did not see themselves as personally responsible for such killings: They were merely deferring to the will of the government or the *turuɔk* ("foreigners").[2] Following the outbreak of the first civil war in 1955, more and more people were

---

2. The fact that these sentences were normally carried out by prison officers in Malakal undoubtedly helped to mute any lingering feelings of personal guilt these chiefs may have had.

forced to confront these issues in the context of their daily lives. Not surprisingly, both Nuer who fought on the side of southern secessionist forces and those who allied themselves, directly or indirectly, with the national government in Khartoum also denied any personal accountability for homicides carried out under orders from their superiors. However, the efficacy of such denials ultimately depended on whether the families of the slain accepted the southern command structures or the national army as "legitimate" governmental institutions. From this perspective, attempts by the SPLA leadership to dissociate deaths generated by a "government war" from others resulting from local forms of feuding and fighting may be understood as an indirect assertion of authority. In essence Commander Machar was canvassing for public recognition that the SPLA forces under his command constituted a "legitimate" governmental authority.

These controversial issues cut to the core of contemporary Nuer notions of community, ethnicity, and polity—and raised deeper questions about the nature of homicide, the meaning of death, and the role of Divinity in maintaining human morality. They also suggested significant east/west variations in Nuer experiences of gun warfare and of the alternately expanding and contracting powers of the central government. Subtle tensions in people's images of themselves as *nei ti naadh* (Nuer) and as members of a broader community of *nei ti caar* ("black peoples") or *jinubni* ("southerners," from the Arabic, *jānūbīn*) were also thoroughly implicated—as were the moral responsibilities of kinsmen to ensure the "procreative immortality" of relatives slain in battle. In many ways these emerging fields of debate were firmly rooted in Nuer experiences of the recurrent breakdown of the nation-state. Although most contemporary Nuer had come to accept the idea that a government ought to exist, they also retained considerable powers of manipulation and dissent: Witness their continuing military resistance against the Sudanese army. This chapter offers a historical overview of these and related complexities of the gradual intermeshing of state and local power networks in Nuer regions between the early 1930s and early 1990s.

THE IMPACT OF THE GOVERNMENT AND GUNS ON REGIONAL PATTERNS OF WARFARE

No area of Nuer social life had been subjected to greater governmental attempts at intervention and suppression since the early 1930s than that of "the bone" (*cɔaa*), or feud (*tɛr*). Significantly, this form of relationship was not limited to instances of inter-Nuer homicide. During the early 1980s

Nuer men and women often characterized the legacy of violent hostility created during the first civil-war era as "our bone with the Arabs."

Successive governmental regimes had, of course, endeavored to limit the scope and intensity of intercommunity fighting and feuding in this region. Their success, however, had been patchy and their efforts often riddled with contradictions. For example, the Anglo-Egyptian Condominium government imposed an alien system of punishments that stressed the individual responsibility of the slayer while simultaneously preserving a system of bloodwealth compensation based on a principle of collective responsibility (Howell 1954:237). Although the British succeeded in dramatically reducing the intensity of local warfare during much of their rule, they simultaneously created an overarching political situation that foreordained the Nuer and other southern Sudanese to a seemingly endless state of civil war during the postcolonial era. Moreover, once the Nuer had come to depend on centralized governmental institutions for the forcible settlement of violent disputes among themselves, any weakening of state powers was usually accompanied by a rapid surge in the frequency and intensity of intercommunity fighting on a regional level—if not on a national level as well.

Interestingly, many Nuer men and women drew a marked distinction during the early 1980s between what they called "the government of the left" (*kume in caam*) and "the government of the right" (*kume in cuec*). The "government of the left"—being identified with regional administrative networks of government chiefs, courts, police, district officers, and the like—was said to *nhɔk tëy naadh* ("agree/want people to live"). It was defined as a positive, peacekeeping force in that it was capable of containing and defusing outbreaks of intercommunity violence.[3] "The government of the right" or "the army," in contrast, was said to bring only death: *ɛ liaah*. This dualist image of the contradictory impulses of "the government" reveals the extent to which many contemporary Nuer had come to accept the idea of a national state government while simultaneously rejecting current limitations on their abilities to influence its powers in ways that would promote both their immediate well-being and their political objectives in the longer term.[4]

---

3. In fact, many men and women of the early 1980s were actively calling for the reinstitution of capital punishment (which had been effectively suspended in their region after the first civil war) in the explicit hope that this would strengthen "the government of the left" and thereby help to check their otherwise rapidly deteriorating security situation.

4. Nuer impressions of these opposing impulses of "the government" were

In the historical sections that follow, I will be focusing primarily on Nuer participation in and interactions with "the government of the left." However, the activities of "the government of the right" will remain firmly in view.

THE DEVELOPMENT OF THE GUN TRADE AND OF THE "GOVERNMENT OF THE LEFT," 1900–56

The Eastern Jikany Nuer

The eastern Gaajak Nuer were active importers and distributors of firearms since the early 1910s, purchasing successively more powerful models along the Ethiopian frontier and exchanging these for cattle with their brothers further west as well as with Shilluk, Dinka, Nuba, and even Baggara Arab communities. As early as 1912, the British reported a burgeoning Gaajak ivory/Oromo gun trade with well-established meeting points and routes of traffic.[5] At that time a single-shot Abu Gigra rifle with twenty rounds of ammunition could be purchased for a light tusk and later resold to the Lou Nuer for four head of cattle. A second major thrust in this westward flow of arms into the Upper Nile was initiated and controlled by the Anyuak. In fact, setbacks suffered at the hands of the better-armed Anyuak during the early 1910s were what first motivated the eastern Gaajak to seek a reliable source of guns.

Following the gradual buildup of colonial forces in the area after 1898, the British made repeated efforts to curtail the increasingly violent confrontations between the eastern Jikany Nuer and the Anyuak along the Ethiopian (Abyssinian) frontier. Initially frustrated in these attempts, the British unleashed an unprecedented arsenal of machine guns, bombers, and gunboats in 1920 in an effort to impress upon the recalcitrant Gaajak and Gaaguang the futility of resistance. The Gaajak Patrol of 1920 was composed of two army columns totaling some 1,300 troops, supported by Royal Air Force bombers and two gunboats. Between January and May of that

---

heavily reinforced during the first and second civil-war eras (1955–72 and 1983–present). During these wars, major government-held towns were frequently torn apart by all-out gun battles between "the government of the right" and "the government of the left." Resident southern police officers, prison wardens, game rangers, government chiefs, and the like were often forced to take the lead in attempting to shield local citizens (many of whom had been forcibly herded into government declared "peace camps") from the arbitrary army reprisals that so often followed upon government defeats, experienced elsewhere, at the hands of the Anyanya (I) and, later, SPLA forces.

5. "General Note on the Garjak [*sic*] Nuer Country," 1912, DAK 112/13/8.

year, "eight distinct engagements were fought against an enemy armed with [single-shot] rifles and showing considerable power of resistance."[6] The 2,000 Gaaguang and Gaajak fighters estimated to have participated in these engagements were repeatedly routed, however, by a steady stream of machine-gun fire—the first experienced in that region.[7]

Having thus established its hegemony in this region, the Anglo-Egyptian Condominium government adopted as one of its immediate priorities the goal of rupturing the cross-border arms trade and instituting a system of gun licensing. It was hoped that a future disarmament of the general population would become possible once an adequate level of security was assured. However, the government soon discovered that the suppression of Nuer/Anyuak hostilities along the Ethiopian (Abyssinian) frontier provoked an increase rather than decrease in the westward flow of firearms into the province.[8] Although the British administration had earlier awarded Remington rifles to its newly appointed "chiefs," principally as a matter of "prestige," they were soon compelled to extend this "experiment" to the arming of chiefs' police as well. And by 1939, any British optimism about the prospect of a future disarmament of the population in this region was based more on a current scarcity of ammunition than on the establishment of an adequate state of security.[9]

However, it was principally the failure of the British administration to negotiate a coordinated and cooperative grazing agreement with the Abyssinians that bedeviled all their efforts to assert a consistent policy of arms containment. In 1931 there were approximately 2,000 Gaajak who were permanent residents of Abyssinia and an additional 45,000 eastern Jikany who crossed the frontier annually on their way to dry-season grazing grounds. The extension of British administration over these Nuer initially went unchallenged. Chiefs were appointed, tribute collected, and criminals pursued across what was then deemed to be an "unratified international frontier." In 1930, the Abyssinian administration began to consolidate its hold over the region, proclaiming its right to tax its inhabitants

6. "Note on Military Action and Administration in Nuer Country," 1927, DAK 112/18/37.

7. This campaign resulted in some 115 Nuer killed, 17,000 huts looted and burned, 50 cattle camps broken up, and a fleet of canoes destroyed, in addition to unknown losses inflicted by the air force (ibid.).

8. Such was the case, for instance, when a temporary truce established between the Anyuak and Jikany in 1926 resulted in an immediate influx of thousands of rifles into the province (SIR, 26 Apr. 1926).

9. "Handing over Notes," E. G. Coryton, 1939, UNP 1/45/332.

and prohibiting further intrusions by British agents. Reluctantly, the British deferred to these arguments but attempted to salvage the situation by extracting assurances that eastern Gaajak chiefs would continue to attend dry-season court meetings in Sudan. One rather wily Gaajak chief by the name of Koryom Tut soon assessed the political situation and, shifting allegiance to the Abyssinians, simply failed to show up for chiefs' court in 1931. Unable to cross the border to take any action against him, the local British district commissioner was left in an embarrassing situation. In his words:

> This was the beginning of the quote "movement" across the frontier of all Nuer malcontents and cattle thieves who wished to avoid justice. . . . Before that date [1931] the international frontier meant nothing to the Nuer. After that it meant that any Nuer by just crossing the Jekow [Baro River] could defy his chief or the D.C.[10]

When Koryom Tut returned from a trip to Addis Ababa a year later loaded down with gifts of firearms and announcing a special dispensation from the emperor exempting his *ciëŋ* ("extended community") from taxation for five years, the effect was immediate. In 1932 some 2,000 eastern Jikany Nuer simply broke camp, throwing off the unpopular British yoke, and sought asylum across the international border. Numerous Gaajak and Gaaguang sections inside Sudan also refused to pay taxes and to work on government roads. The British then salvaged some of their former prestige with a rapid display of force, but border problems have vexed the administration of the eastern Jikany Nuer ever since. As fluctuations in the relative levels of taxation, security, and arms control became significant to them, eastern Jikany Nuer did not hesitate to shuffle across the border in either direction as this suited their immediate purposes. During an Ethiopian drive to disarm the Gaaguang in 1950, for instance, thousands of people scurried back into the Sudan, while a countermovement occurred during a Sudanese arms crackdown in 1960–61. Add to this the flood of Italian rifles that filtered down to the local population after World War II as well as the English 303 rifles and more sophisticated machinery that flowed into this area during the first civil war, and it is not surprising that the eastern Jikany—and particularly the eastern Gaajak—were exceedingly well armed by the early 1980s. Furthermore, I should stress that the Ethiopian territories of the eastern Gaajak and Gaaguang Nuer harbored the largest and most important rebel training grounds during the first civil war—a trend that continued through the sec-

10. "Notes on History—1930–1935," Nasir District Notes, UNP 1/51/4.

ond civil war up until the fall of Mengistu and his Ethiopian Dergue government in 1991.

The border situation was further complicated by the fact that the banks of the Baro River are lined with some of the richest and most coveted agricultural lands in all of Nuerland because they yield lush crops of maize and tobacco during the height of the dry season with only the moisture that rises from the river (see plate 10). Consequently, a considerable amount of Gaajak ammunition was spent over the years settling competing land claims as various feuding factions shuffled back and forth across the border. During the early 1980s this was the only Nuer region in which major intercommunity fights continued to provoke large-scale migrations.

THE CENTRAL AND WESTERN NUER

In Nuer areas further to the west, guns remained comparatively rare up through the eruption of the first civil war in 1955. Consequently, the British faced fewer administrative challenges in this regard. Among the central Gaawär, Lak, Thiäng, and Lou Nuer, British administrative efforts were directed initially to preventing further Nuer incursions on tribute-paying Dinka communities to their south. During the 1910s and 1920s the Lou and Gaawär Nuer were progressively hedged in by a loose chain of police posts, bolstered by dry-season equestrian patrols. They, like their eastern cousins, were also subjected to periodic tribute-collecting raids, resulting in the loss of many hundreds of cattle. Following the massacre of a small army patrol by Lou raiders in 1916, three large government columns swept through their territories, capturing several thousand cattle, torching villages, and killing over 100 people. This "pacification" campaign did nothing, however, to further the establishment of a viable administration in this area—and, in fact, the Lou Nuer were not revisited by government agents until 1920.[11]

During the first two decades of nominal British rule, government contacts with Nuer communities west of the Bahr-el-Jebel were even more limited and erratic. In 1921 Captain V. H. Fergusson embarked on a program of "peaceful penetration" in which he sought to persuade prominent western Nuer leaders of the potential benefits of government overrule. Hoping to avoid the bitterness created by years of government cattle raids on Nuer groups east of the White Nile, Fergusson introduced a system of

11. "Note on Military Action and Administration in Nuer Country," 1927, DAK 112/13/87.

Plate 10.   Lush maize fields at the height of the dry season, eastern Gaajak.

compulsory cotton cultivation in 1925 in the hope that tribute could eventually be collected in cash. With gifts of cloth and Remington rifles, he conferred governmental recognition on a small coterie of prominent individuals and encouraged them to set up their own courts. This "compliment," however, was rarely reciprocated to his satisfaction. And thus, he, too, was soon calling in the army. Between 1922 and 1926, three separate "punitive" patrols were waged against the western Nuer. The following year, Fergusson was himself speared and slain while on tour among the Nyuong Nuer.

This event—in combination with a Gaawär attack that same year on the Duk Faiywil police post and with mounting government apprehensions that the Lou Nuer were about to revolt—triggered off a massive government offensive, which lasted from 1928 to 1930 and culminated in the Nuer Settlement of 1929–30. This "pacification" campaign—the last to be waged in all of British Sub-Saharan Africa—marked the definitive colonization of the Nuer. The Gaawär and Lou Nuer were ordered to concentrate into specific areas so that a wide swath of "no-man's-land" could be cleared between them and their Dinka neighbors. Yet no sooner had this "peace corridor" been staked out than a series of natural disasters struck the region. Heavy flooding along the Bahr-al-Zeraf coupled with a devastating series of rinderpest epidemics revealed the hardships caused by forcibly segregating communities that had not only rustled one another's cattle but also freely intermarried and intermingled during extended periods of peace. The refusal of several Dinka communities living amidst the Nuer to be "repatriated" across this artificial divide further complicated matters. And eventually the British were forced to abandon their policy of forced "tribal" segregation by officially abolishing the "no-man's-land" in 1936.[12]

Although temporary, the forced concentration of the Lou and Gaawär Nuer did facilitate a number of other administrative objectives, such as the creation of tax lists, the appointment of chiefs, the monitoring of courts, and the conscription of labor for government work projects. Renewed efforts to establish a viable chiefly administration followed.

THE DEVELOPMENT OF GOVERNMENT CHIEFS AND COURTS

> After [the] Nuer Settlement, when new foundations came to be laid, one definite plank of policy, at least east of the Nile, was the negative one of "no big chiefs." . . . They . . . started to build an organisation from the bottom up . . . not top down . . . to work with more and smaller natural leaders rather than through bigger men who largely owed their power to spiritual influences.[13]

The long-term goal of this plan was to develop a hierarchy of "secular" government chiefs patterned after the *tut wec* ("bull of the cattle camp"). The immediate consequence, however, was a vast proliferation of unranked government "chiefs" (*kuäär;* pl., *kuar*).[14] The number of chiefs' *biiyni* ("cloths" or "badges of office") awarded among the eastern Jikany rose from 77 in 1928 to 185 in 1933.[15] Among the central Nuer, the number of

12. For further details of these historical events, see Johnson 1980 and 1994.

13. John Winder, "Note on the Evolution of Policy in Regard to Chiefs, Sub-Chiefs and Headmen," 1942, END 1.F. vol. 1, p. 2.

14. See Corfield, "Handing over Notes," UNP 1/51/4 1935:13–14; Winder, "Note on the Evolution of Policy," 1942:4; Johnson 1980:473.

15. Corfield 1935:13. The first badges of office (*lawa*) conferred on government chiefs were untailored blocks of cloth, about the size of a tablecloth, which were worn draped and tied over one shoulder. These were soon replaced by colored "sashes" that hung from the shoulder and extended across both back and front. Over the years these sashes were redesigned to reflect the evolving hierarchy of government chief ranks. During the early 1980s, lower-ranking headmen wore sashes of a dark blue cloth edged in white. Subchiefs sported red sashes, which were also edged with white strips. Executive chiefs and court presidents wore red

"jealous independent heads" recognized by the government had swollen to 200 by 1936, with some representing as many as 1,300 tax-paying men and others as few as 80.[16] An arbitrary halt was declared in 1933, but the scramble for government chiefs' cloths continued. As the centripetal forces of Nuer political groupings gained momentum, leaders of smaller and smaller Nuer communities sought to bolster their authority and autonomy by seeking representation on the chiefs' councils responsible for the settlement of intercommunity disputes. Between 1933 and 1934, five major fights erupted over "rivalries over the question of Chiefs' 'cloths' " among the eastern Jikany alone (Corfield 1935:17). Increased labor demands for the completion of government "public work" projects also necessitated the involvement of smaller community leaders. Working as de facto government agents, many of these local leaders eventually lobbied for and received government recognition on the grounds that this would greatly facilitate their administrative activities. The practical question then became, as one British colonial officer put it: "How far up the hierarchy of *ciengs* must we go to find a unit which is not too small to be used as an administrative unit but which is not yet too large to have lost its inherent authority due to lack of cohesion?"[17]

When British administrators initially sought to rank these chiefs hierarchically so as to create a clear chain of authority and command, they often encountered staunch resistance. In 1929 the British district commissioner of the eastern Nuer conferred newly designed "sashes" on some of his more prominent chiefs with the intention of eventually awarding one such sash to each of the twenty "secondary sections" under his administration. He also announced at the time that future recipients of government cloths would not be incorporated on the same basis as earlier chiefs but would serve, rather, as the latter's assistants (sing., *wakil*, an Arabic term, or subchiefs) and would receive "slightly different 'cloths.' " Although this scheme appealed to those eastern Nuer already holding government offices, it proved a public relations fiasco.

> A large number of them [the *wakils*] maintained that they were in no way inferior to a number of chiefs who had the "superior" clothes, they had merely appeared on the scene a little late. This in many cases was true . . . [and] feeling over the matter was so strong that in 1932 they refused to accept the "inferior" clothes, and from that year no distinction was made. The recognition

---

sashes that were differentiated from those of subchiefs by an additional central stripe or two of white running the length of the sash.

16. Winder, "Note on the Evolution of Policy," 1942:2.

17. Ibid.

of further chiefs was inevitable but it opened the flood gates, as almost every family leader considers himself a potential chief.[18]

This unwieldy situation continued, with minor modifications, well into the 1940s, when a large number of chiefs were finally eliminated on the basis of a minimum taxpayer rule.[19]

Among Nuer west of the White Nile, where a tendency toward appointing fewer chiefs and endowing them with greater governmental authority was established during the 1920s, the creation of viable chiefly hierarchies proceeded more slowly.[20] In 1933–34 the British discovered, much to their alarm, that several western "head chiefs" had developed into "tyrants of the first order."[21] There were as yet no formal court councils in this region nor any system of registering verdicts reached by individual chiefs. Largely free of government supervision, many western chiefs sought to enrich themselves by the imposition of arbitrary cattle fines, while others routinely demanded "a certain proportion of cattle or money from every successful litigant." Consequently, "very few cases were heard."[22] In an effort to curb these abuses, the administration raised the salaries of local chiefs "considerably" and appointed court clerks to keep track of all cattle and money awarded. The tradition of appointing "head chiefs" for entire Nuer "tribes," however, never died in that region.

By the early 1940s, the government was beginning to discover many of the difficulties it faced in attempting to mould Evans-Pritchard's elegant model of the segmentary lineage structure of Nuer territorial groupings into a viable system of indirect rule. As early as 1934, one British district commissioner warned: "[There] may be a tendency to integrate up the scale and assume that every unit however large has its recognized head and that every Tertiary Section has say the same characteristics. But this is not so. . . . [Still] we should 'go gently on.' "[23]

A drive toward standardizing administrative approaches to the appointment of Nuer chiefs began at the Nuer district commissioners' meeting of 1943. There it was formally agreed that a three-tiered hierarchy—consist-

18. Corfield, "Handing over Notes," 1935:21.
19. During the early 1980s a subchief needed a minimum of 500 taxpayers and a headman, at least 60.
20. For summaries of regional contrasts in this regard, see M. Parr, "Handing over Notes," 1936, UNP 1/45/331, pp. 1–15, and P. Coriat, "Report Western Nuer," 1934, DAK I 112/15/99, pp. 1–4.
21. Coriat, "Report Western Nuer," p. 2.
22. Ibid.
23. Ibid.

ing of a court president (*kuäär bok/kuäär in diit*), subchiefs (*kuäär lamä/ kuäär kaarä*), and headmen (sing., *gattuot*; pl., *gaattut/gaatuuni*)—would be instituted in all Nuer regions on the basis of "the *gaat diila* system of aristocratic lineages. Chiefs that were not *diel* (members of locally "dominant/aristocratic" lines; sing., *dil*) were to be replaced by ones who were. By 1947, however, the government became increasingly frustrated by the fact that the rise and fall of *dil* personalities rarely coincided with administrative needs. And gradually, a system of local elections was established in which any taxpaying male, regardless of his genealogical heritage, could run for chiefly offices.

Over this same period, the British also began to realize that their long-term administrative objects were marred by several basic contradictions. Their efforts to create a chiefly hierarchy "from the bottom up" were directly undercut by the process of community fragmentation set in motion by their suppression of local warfare and by their development of regional grain and cattle markets (Howell 1954:232–234). Moreover, the idea that government chiefs could serve as impartial judges who were nevertheless expected to prosecute their own people was unrealistic from the start. As one district commissioner observed:

> . . . a young chief who enforces obedience and the carrying out of chiefs' court decrees automatically becomes unpopular amongst his own people, though much respected and liked by neighbouring clans. His own clan, though, feels that he is being thoroughly untribal in enforcing decisions against them, and unless he can square them in some way he is going to be very unpopular and have a rather miserable life. Consequently, I think we want to compensate him by giving him a really good pay. Generosity and open handedness go a long way amongst the Nuer, and the chief who is free with his Government money and gives beer parties etc. on a large scale, regains to a great extent the popularity lost through enforcing court decisions.[24]

Despite recurrent pay hikes, the problem of executing court judgments lingered on. In some areas British agents began fining government chiefs who failed to carry out court judgments within three months. Additional allotments of chiefs' police were awarded in the hope of strengthening the "executive" powers of local chiefs.

Finally, in 1942, a more radical administrative solution was proposed: the creation of a new government office—that of "executive chief" (*kuäär lat/bok in tot*). As originally conceived and developed by the British assis-

---

24. H. Romilly, assistant district commissioner of the eastern Nuer, to Marwood, 14 June 1938, Civsec 1/43/114.

tant district commissioner of the Zeraf Region, John Winder, this appointee was to be "purely a government man," responsible for the collection of tribute, the conscription of labor, the suppression of fighting, and, most important, the execution of local court rulings.[25] Although nominally equal in stature and pay to the "court president," the "executive chief" was not to involve himself directly in judicial proceedings. This new office was subsequently adopted by other British district commissioners, principally because it allowed them to channel their administrative directives through a few carefully chosen personalities. Nevertheless, the conceptual division between the "executive" and "judicial" authority of government chiefs proved difficult to maintain in practice. Intense rivalries often developed between the court president and executive chief of specific areas. As one retired district commissioner explained:

> The Executive chief became the main link between the District Commissioner and the Sub-Chiefs and Headmen in all administrative matters. It was also, however, regrettably plain that the Nuer themselves did not regard the Executive Chieftainship as equal in status to that of the Court President. . . . This factor led to repeated and often delicate situations where a strong Executive Chief would attempt to oust the Court President by making trouble in the Court in order that he might occupy what was generally considered to be a more worthy and influential position. . . . This meant that it was seldom possible to have the strongest personality in the area at the disposal of the Government except at the cost of internal dissension within the Court. (Roussel n.d.:8–9)

These rivalries were exacerbated following the departure of the British and the establishment of the Southern People's Regional Assembly at the end of the first civil war in 1972. For once Nuer members of the literate elite began vying for public offices in the southern regional assembly at Juba, and, in the national parliament at Khartoum, they often sought to unseat government chiefs who had failed to support them in regional elections—a point that will be developed more fully in chapter 6.

By 1943, early administrative policies directed toward the forced segregation of the Nuer and the Dinka and the imposition of fixed "tribal" boundaries were declared "retrogressive." A new vision of the future was proposed: the gradual buildup of a "Nilotic Federation" in which the Nuer and neighboring Dinka communities would be administratively merged.[26] British district commissioners hoped that this would help to check the "in-

25. Winder, "Note on the Evolution of Policy," 1942:6.
26. "Minutes of the Nuer District Commissioners' Meetings, February 1–5, 1943," Civsec 55/13/137. See also Johnson 1980:471.

cessant splitting" of local communities generated by the imposition of *pax britannica*. This policy objective was soon undercut, however, by higher-level political decisions culminating in the abrupt reversal of the so-called Southern Policy, or the policy of a "separate development" for the south. Between 1930 and 1946, all administrative decisions in the south were guided by this policy, which severely restricted communications and contacts between northern and southern Sudanese civilians. Its abandonment was followed by a last-minute scramble to educate, organize, and otherwise prepare the Nuer and other southern Sudanese for a future union with the north.

"It was like guilt," one contemporary Nuer commented: "The British suddenly realized that they would soon be leaving and that they would need people to replace them, so they started rushing around grabbing children to put them in school." Before this policy reversal, the colonial administration had taken no independent initiative whatsoever in the field of education in the Upper Nile. The few Nuer primary schools in existence at that time were entirely mission run (cf. Passmore-Sanderson and Sanderson 1981:256–290). In 1946 however, approximately 100 Nuer boys were rounded up on a quota system from among the central and western Nuer and sent to open a new government primary/intermediate school at Atar. These were later joined by eastern Nuer youths proceeding from the American Presbyterian mission school at Nasir.[27] In 1950, the first crop of Atar graduates entered Rumbek Secondary School, founded only two years earlier. Rumbek was the only secondary school to be established in the southern Sudan prior to independence in 1956. Hence, it was from among the small pool of boys fortunate enough to graduate from Rumbek before

---

27. The American Presbyterian Mission, founded at Nasir, eastern Nuerland, in 1916, and the Verona Fathers Catholic Mission, founded at Yoinyang, western Nuerland, in 1924, both established a four-year vernacular primary school during the 1920s. The combined graduating class of these schools rarely exceeded twenty-five students during the 1930s—and most of them were immediately employed as mission teachers, court clerks, translators, and government trainees of one sort or another. Two or three graduates were usually sent on to distant intermediate schools—Catholic candidates proceeding to Sir Lee Stack Memorial Intermediate School at Bussere in the Bahr-el-Ghazal Province and Protestants proceeding to Nugent Intermediate School at Loka in Equatoria Province. A third elementary school was opened by the Church Missionary Society at Ler, western Nuerland, in 1931. However, few of its graduates ever qualified for admission to intermediate schools. Enrollment in all these schools was voluntary, with a majority of students coming initially from fatherless, cattle-poor, or otherwise unfortunate families. Sons of government chiefs, though sometimes cajoled into attendance, rarely completed the four-year course at that time.

its forced closure and subsequent transferal to the northern Sudan during the first civil war that the Nuer literate elite emerged.

In line with the Marshall report of 1949, which advocated an emergency acceleration of the establishment of local government institutions throughout Sudan, the first "provisional" Nuer District Council was created in 1951. Nurtured with great paternalistic care by its British overseers, the Zeraf Island Rural District Council (Central Nuer) was founded with the objective of giving its members "as much experience as possible in handling their own affairs" before Sudan's independence. Four "purely advisory" rural councils were also established among the eastern and western Nuer by 1954. Despite the avowed purpose of these new administrative appendages, the British were reluctant to bestow any real powers on their councilors-in-training, entrusting them "only with those tasks they either *want*[ed] to perform or [could] be completely trusted to perform adequately" (Roussel n.d.:29). It is thus doubtful whether their members gained any real skills or knowledge from the few administrative tasks permitted them. And shortly after the "Sudanization"—or, rather, "northern Sudanization"—of the regional administration just prior to independence, these experimental councils were abruptly dissolved.

As a growing nationalist movement swept through northern Sudan, many southerners welcomed the idea of independence on the condition that their calls for federation within a united Sudan would be given due consideration in the future. Although the British talked extensively about the creation of political safeguards for the south, none were instituted. And in August 1955, five months before Sudan unilaterally declared its independence, a battalion of southern soldiers mutinied in Torit, Equatoria Province, thereby sparking off the first civil war.

NEW PROCEDURES FOR THE RESOLUTION OF HOMICIDE CASES INSTITUTED DURING THE COLONIAL ERA

Before the standardization of "Nuer customary law" and the introduction of various British legal precepts regarding homicide, bloodwealth was not fixed but rather subject to a complex series of negotiations by an earth priest (or "leopard-skin chief" in Evans-Pritchard's writings). Circumstantial details of the slaying, such as the nature of previous relations between the families of assailant and victim, their territorial proximity and ancestral affiliations, the type of weapon used in the slaying (whether club [*kɛɛt*], fishing spear [*bidh*], fighting spear [*mut*], or gun [*mac*]), as well as current rates of bridewealth all influenced the likelihood, speed, and amount of bloodwealth exchanged. It was generally agreed among the central and western Nuer, for instance, that deaths resulting from fishing spear wounds were to be compensated with fewer cattle than those involving fighting spears, though this distinction was by no means rigidly applied (Howell 1954:48). The guiding compensatory principle, however, appears to have been "a wife for a life"—with bloodwealth rates being closely linked to those of bridewealth (Howell 1954:60). Bloodwealth cattle were offered primarily as a gesture of goodwill intended to assuage the "embittered hearts" of the dead man and his kinsmen by enabling them to marry a "ghost wife" in the deceased's name. Ideally, every bloodwealth settlement culminated in marriage and the birth of sons—sons who it was nevertheless hoped would someday avenge their father's death with the blood of his enemies.

The actual transfer of cattle, when it occurred at all, often extended over many years, during which time the return of violence remained a strong possibility. Moreover, according to Evans-Pritchard (1940a:121), the possibility of bloodwealth compensation did not extend beyond the boundaries of specific Nuer "tribes" (*rool/door*). All acts of social interaction between the feuding parties were severely restricted throughout this period, especially those of commensality and sexuality. Interestingly, contemporary Nuer maintained that were a woman to conceive a son with a man with whom she was separated by a "bone"—however ancient or distant—that child would tear open her womb before birth (*baa jiidε rεεt*), thereby allying himself with his father's people. In contrast, the conception of a daughter, I was told, would not endanger the mother's life—blood-vengeance being the responsibility of males, not females. Although blood feuds could be permanently defused by a special sacrificial ceremony called "the breaking of the bone," it was extremely unlikely for this to occur during the 1930s—or, for that matter, during the 1980s—unless the parties to the feud were close relatives (*nei ti maar*).

Nuer fears of *nueer* supported these precolonial settlement procedures in important ways. Widespread belief in the "avenging" blood of the slain greatly reduced the likelihood that a slayer would attempt to cover up his deed. As one contemporary Nuer put it: "*Nueer* keeps people vomiting out the truth—you can't hide the fact that you have killed a man!" By thus ensuring revelation of the deed even in the most shameful of circumstances, this concept helped set in motion the complex series of rites and negotiations overseen by an "earth priest" that ideally culminated in a peaceful transfer of bloodwealth cattle (Evans-Pritchard 1940a:152–158; Howell 1954:44–67). As a concept of shared risk, *nueer* also shifted the significance of the slaying immediately to a collective plane. All persons within the extended communities concerned were forced to ally themselves with one side or the other—if only in matters of food and drink. Only persons with neither direct nor indirect contacts with the families concerned could afford to contemplate the homicide from a position of indifference. Consequently, smaller, more tightly knit communities, as Evans-Pritchard explained (1940a:157–162; 1956:294), were under greater pressure to resolve their feuds peacefully and rapidly than were larger, more far-flung ones. Dread of *nueer* also reinforced the moral obligations of close kinsmen and neighbors to support each other in times of armed conflict as well as in the collection of bloodwealth cattle. Fear of *nueer* must thus be understood as one of the primary forces motivating reconciliation or, alternately, migration prior to the coming of the British. As one contemporary eastern Nuer put it: "*Nueer* was one of our 'chiefs' of the past."

The dangers of *nueer* were also associated at that time with a definite code of fighting ethics that precluded recourse to tactics such as killing or capturing women and children, burning huts, raiding stock, and robbing grain in all inter-Nuer confrontations. Ideally, these brutal methods were reserved for confrontations with Murle (*jäbɛni*), Anyuak (*bär*), Burun (*cai*), and, to a lesser extent, Dinka (*jaaŋ*) communities. For it was generally assumed that these people could be slain without incurring the blood curse of the deceased and without provoking lethal states of *nueer*. It is noteworthy, however, that some Nuer communities during the early 1930s regarded the blood of Dinka victims scarified in the Nuer fashion as sufficiently similar—or potent, as it were—to provoke deadly states of *nueer* (cf. Evans-Pritchard 1934:48). The rite of *bier* was thus sometimes performed after major raids on neighboring Dinka groups—some of which had, of course, intermarried with their Nuer neighbors.

This general code of fighting ethics further prohibited the use of spears in conflicts among close kinsmen and neighbors—clubs were the only honorable weapons in such circumstances. Although "this convention," Evans-Pritchard remarked:

> . . . is most easily explained as making homicide a less likely outcome than if spears were permitted and, should it happen that a man be killed, of making a settlement easier to bring about on the grounds of absence of intent; but there may be a different, or at any rate an additional, reason for it. It may be that behind it is the notion that not the same responsibility is felt if the life-blood does not flow as it would from a fatal spear wound—that in a sense the man has not taken the life, that the death happened of itself, as Nuer would put it. That Nuer have some such idea is shown by the fact that a ghoul may be killed with impunity, but only if he is beaten to death with clubs and his blood is not shed. (Evans-Pritchard 1956:213)

Without an actual blood flow at death, the physical bond created between slayer(s) and slain remained highly ambiguous and diffuse—an observation that would seem to support the centrality of blood flows in the creation and control of *nueer* (for details, see Hutchinson 1992b).

With the imposition of British colonial rule, many of the social and circumstantial factors previously critical in determining the likelihood, speed, and amount of bloodwealth cattle offered among Nuer were eclipsed. Once the British regime set about fixing cattle compensation rates for homicide and other wrongs and enforcing these through the agency of government courts, the scope and meaning of Nuer kinship relations changed. The parallelism in Nuer thought between the scope of bloodwealth obligations and that of bridewealth claims at the heart of their concepts of kinship was gradually eroded. Not surprising, many Nuer resisted initial governmental attempts to dissociate these two aspects of their social system. When the district commissioner of the eastern Nuer first sought to promote the rapid resolution of local feuds by lowering and setting bloodwealth compensation at twenty head of cattle during the early 1920s, many people objected on the grounds that bloodwealth and bridewealth rates should be either standardized at the same rate or not standardized at all (Evans-Pritchard 1951b:98).[28] And when the British later raised bloodwealth compensation rates in that area to fifty head of cattle in 1945 so as to bring them into line with those of other Nuer districts, the effect on local bridewealth rates was immediate and palpable. Local bridewealth rates surged, and government chiefs became reluctant to sever relationships of *maar* that had grown weak with the passage of numerous generations (Howell 1952:20; 1954:63–64). Adopting the cattle logic of the Nuer, Howell (1952:20) explained that: "since more distant kinsmen must necessarily be brought into the orbit of bloodwealth claims, they are entitled

---

28. In a revealing exchange between the district commissioner of the eastern Nuer and the governor of the Upper Nile Province in 1936, the governor rejected the former's suggestion that bloodwealth rates should fall together with bridewealth rates. "Brideprice is reduced to make earlier marriage possible," the governor argued, whereas "compensation for killing should only be reduced if the herds have been so reduced in numbers that the payment of x cattle is an improper penalty" (M. W. Parr, Governor of the UNP to DC Nasir, 9 Apr. 1936 [END 66. A.2]). Significantly, this exchange was touched off by the district commissioner's suggestion that the administration support two recent suggestions made by a prominent Gaajak "man of cattle" (*wut yɔɔk*) named Joklou Gaac. The latter had appealed for a reduction in local bridewealth rates and argued that young men who seduce girls should be encouraged to marry them and not threatened with death by angry relatives (Extract, Eastern Nuer District Diary, Feb./Mar. 1936, END 66. A2).

to press more vigorously their corresponding and equally remote claims in the bridewealth system," thereby driving up bridewealth rates. Likewise, the declining frequency of *dak maarä* ("kinship division") was part of a conscious attempt by government chiefs to preserve the widest communities of kin in the belief that "the more so-called relatives there are available to collect blood-money [cattle], the better" (for details, see Howell 1954:64).

By the time I began investigating these issues firsthand in 1980, the eastern Nuer no longer questioned the great disparity between bridewealth and bloodwealth rates introduced in 1945—the latter typically running some twenty to thirty head of cattle higher than the former. In fact, this gap had become so well accepted that one older Gaajok man, whose bridewealth negotiations I attended in 1981, countered what he regarded as the exorbitant cattle demands of his would-be affines with the quip: "But I didn't kill her, all I want to do is marry her!" Although there are good reasons to believe that the community of kindred called upon to contribute bloodwealth cattle was broader than that united by bridewealth claims, even prior to government intervention (cf. Howell 1952:19), the disparity between these two sets of kinship obligations—these two aspects of *maar*—broadened considerably during the colonial era. By the early 1980s, bonds of *maar*, Nuer argued, were divisible solely with respect to bridewealth claims. Bloodwealth rates, in contrast, continued to operate as a quasi-defense pact uniting more extended communities of kin (cf. Howell 1954:64).

Once the British declared acts of inter-Nuer homicide crimes against the state, punishable by imprisonment and fines, court evaluations of the relative "morality" of the deed became the single most important criterion in determining the possibility and extent of bloodwealth exchanges. And in 1945, bloodwealth compensation was standardized in all Nuer districts at fifty head of cattle, forty of which were considered bloodwealth proper, and ten of which were imposed as a fine payable to the government. Unless there were exceptional mitigating circumstances, a term of imprisonment varying from one to six years was normally imposed on the killer as well. In contrast, persons charged with "culpable homicide amounting to murder"—that is, of premeditated acts perpetrated by stealth rather than in a fair fight—were subject to the death penalty (in which case bloodwealth cattle were not transferred), though this was usually remitted to life imprisonment (in which case bloodwealth cattle were transferred [Howell 1954:66–67, 235–237]). Such cases were removed from the jurisdiction of the chiefs' courts and tried, instead, under the Sudan Penal Code by a major court consisting of three magistrates, two of which were usually Nuer chiefs specially appointed for this purpose (Howell, personal communication).

In a comprehensive study of the impact of colonial policies on Nuer patterns of feud settlement, Howell documents these and other procedural innovations introduced during the 1930s and 1940s. Among the most important changes he noted were: the elimination of the dimension of negotiation and compromise in bloodwealth exchange; the introduction of capital punishment, terms of imprisonment, and collective fines as "deterrents"; the abolition of several putative forms of homicide previously liable to claims of compensation; and, most important, the realization of a major reduction in the frequency of vengeance attacks (Howell 1954:61–67, 230–237; see plate 11). Gradually the "modern procedure" for the forced resolution of feuds took shape, involving: (1) the swift suppression of hostilities by government chiefs, backed up when necessary by state police; (2) the massive seizure of local cattle, pending the arrest, trial, and sentencing of all "killers" as well as all "those who participated in or instigated the affair"; (3) the imposition of collective cattle fines once the "relative guilt" of the parties was determined; and (4) the transferal of bloodwealth cattle and the performance of "indigenous ceremonies of composition" by a court-appointed "earth priest" (or "leopard-skin chief"; Howell 1954:66–67).

Despite the severity of some of these sanctions, Howell stated, it was rare during the mid-1940s for a killer to attempt to conceal his guilt: "even if in the heat of battle there are no witnesses, [the killer] will usually give himself up to the nearest authority after performing the necessary purificatory ritual with a Leopard-Skin Chief" (1954:66). He also explained that when penal sanctions were first introduced, the British faced considerable difficulty in convincing Nuer chiefs why they were needed at all (Howell 1954:62, 235).

Sometimes it was possible for Nuer to manipulate the contradictory impulses of government agents by playing off the collective and individual responsibilities of warring factions to their own advantage. Consider the following amusing incident reported to me by Gabriel Gai Riam.

> There was a fight that broke out among the people of cieng Yol [of the eastern Gaajok Nuer] and one man was killed. The [British] District Commissioner (*mabetaic*) ordered the police to discover who the killer was and to jail him. Only one man was to be jailed. The police rounded up some twenty men who had gone to the fight [on the winning side] and brought them before the *ma-*

Plate 11.   A war rally: preparing to reopen an old feud, eastern Gaajok country.

betaic. As each man came in [to the DC's office], he was asked whether or not he was the killer. The first man answered, "I killed him," the second man also said, "It was I," as did the third man—and so on down the line until all twenty men had [proudly] claimed responsibility for the homicide. Angry and perplexed, the *mabetaic* ordered that all twenty men be jailed. The attending Nuer police officer warned him that if all of these men were jailed there would be a fight. But the *mabetaic* insisted that they all be jailed. Once inside the prison, the men [intentionally] started an argument over who was the real killer. One said "I did it." Another said, "Why are you disregarding me?" [*dhọali ni yä?*]. And so it went, until they started fighting amongst themselves. In the end the *mabetaic* was forced to release them all.

Interestingly, the district jailhouse was soon regarded by many Nuer as the contemporary equivalent of the earth priest's sacred homestead. By the early 1980s, many Nuer argued that killers were imprisoned for a few years primarily in order to protect them from the avenging spears of the dead man's kin. And just as a slayer who wandered beyond the limits of the priest's homestead was formerly subject to ambush, so, too, prisoners were sometimes killed in the 1980s while engaged in government work projects outside the perimeter of the jail. There was absolutely no stigma attached to ex-prisoners—especially if they had been jailed on account of their fighting skills. And it was becoming common at that time for some local chiefs to accept a cow in lieu of each year of imprisonment awarded.

The idea that a feud originates in a physical blood relationship between slayer and victim that extends outwards through bonds of shared food and blood was also weakened during the colonial era by the imposition of fixed bloodwealth rates. And once the British began to extend the enforcement of bloodwealth compensation beyond the territorial limits of named Nuer groupings—or "tribes" in Evans-Pritchard's definition—to all Nuer communities and, later, to neighboring Dinka, Murle, Anyuak, and Shilluk groups as well, they effectively ruptured the former relationship obtaining between the scope of *nueer* and restrained fighting tactics, on the one hand, and the possibility of bloodwealth exchange, on the other. In 1945 the colonial administration also rejected the idea that the type of weapon used in the slaying (i.e., whether club, fishing spear, fighting spear, or gun) should influence court sentencing—a decision that further undermined the ethical code of warfare binding Nuer communities as well as the cultural premise that *nueer* originated in a direct spilling of human blood. Certainly, British notions of culpability clashed sharply with indigenous attitudes toward the collective clubbing of "ghouls" and *pɛth*. In 1945 the colonial administration also eliminated the possibility of bloodwealth compensation in several situations formerly subject to such claims. A lover, it was decided, could no longer be held responsible for the payment of cattle compensation in situations where his unmarried, impregnated girlfriend died during childbirth (*thɔŋ yiikä*). The payment of cattle compensation for delayed deaths caused by old wounds (*nyindiit*) was similarly abolished.[29]

The "collective liability" aspect of *nueer* was further weakened by the fact that governmentally enforced feud settlements between communities socially and physically distant from one another soon proved easier to impose than settlements between communities with closer ties. Howell, in an insightful passage, drew attention to this inversion of precolonial trends:

> Generally speaking, the nearer the social relationship of the opposed groups, the greater the likelihood of a permanent settlement [in the past]. This observation applies theoretically, but only in the sense that in the initial stages feuds between less closely related groups were more likely to continue and no action be taken to bring about an agreement. In fact, they do not often continue nowadays because the Government intervenes and acts as a purely

29. Howell (1954:55–56, 65).

artificial and new medium through which hostile groups are brought together. Paradoxically enough, it is nowadays often the case that feuds between closely related groups are more difficult to deal with. The reason is, I think, that feelings of hostility receive the permanent reminder of almost daily communication, while the primary sanction for composition, the threat of aggressive action by other groups, is much modified by the action of the Government in maintaining peace. (Howell 1954:61)

What Howell defines here as the primary sanction for composition—the threat of external aggression—was as inseparable from Nuer notions of *nueer* as the need for alliance was from the alliance itself. Interestingly, Howell himself suggests that fear of contamination by *nueer* might be interpreted as a psychological expression of the fear of retaliation (1954:222 n.2). Whereas the external and internal pressures for reconciliation worked in relative harmony among Nuer prior to colonial conquest, the significance of extended political alliances, as we have seen, was subsequently undermined, with the result that many Nuer communities began to fracture into smaller and smaller autonomous units with more widely spaced homesteads (Howell 1954:233).

Although it is difficult to trace specific stages in the evolution of the purification rites required for the removal of *nueer* in situations of homicide, it is clear that the colonial administration initiated a process of ritual streamlining that continued well into the 1990s. Of the complex series of sacrifices and cattle exchanges described by Howell (1954:44–48) as essential for the complete restoration of harmonious relations between feuding parties, only one rite was intentionally "preserved" by the colonial administration—the sacrifice of *yaŋ kɛthä/ruath kɛthä* ("the cow [bull-calf] of the gallbladder") marking the formal transfer of the bloodwealth cattle (Howell 1954:45–47). As far as colonial administrators were concerned, this rite marked the definitive conclusion of a feud. Anyone who dared break the peace after its performance was treated "as the worst kind of murderer" and severely punished by the courts.

In precolonial times, the bull-calf of the gallbladder was speared by the presiding earth priest in the bush surrounding the homestead of the deceased man's kin upon the delivery of the bloodwealth cattle. As soon as the beast collapsed, the kinsmen of the deceased rushed upon it and butchered it in a mad scramble (*kuak*), with each man carrying off as much meat as he possibly could (see Evans-Pritchard 1956:295–296). "It was like war," one contemporary Nuer observed. The blood of the victim was thus vindicated in part by a counterflow of cattle and in part by a ritualized act of blood vengeance performed on a bovine surrogate for and from the enemy. Yet whether or not this sacrifice removed all risk of *nueer* remains a moot point. According to Evans-Pritchard, the ban on commensality between the parties to the feud was formally lifted with this sacrifice—though he stated that, for "reasons of sentiment," the feuding factions often refrained from eating together for many years afterwards (1956:295–296). Howell, in contrast, reported that, among the central and western Nuer, the sacrifice of *yaŋ kɛthä* was merely a sign that the kindred of the deceased had accepted cattle compensation (1954:46–48). The ban on commensality, he argued, could be removed only many years later following a second cattle exchange initiated by the kinsmen of the deceased, the handing over of the "cattle of appeasement" (*yɔk palɛ lɔai* [1954:46–48]). However, this cattle exchange was abolished by the colonial administration in 1947 (Howell 1954:65). Though these differing accounts probably represent regional variations—the concept of "appeasement cattle" apparently being alien to the eastern Nuer at that time (Howell 1954:46 n.1)—one is still left wondering whether British attempts to simplify compensation rituals did not help to create some of the ambiguities apparent in contemporary Nuer controversies over the meaning and limits of *nueer* in situations of inter-Nuer homicide.

Be that as it may, the British certainly undermined the former stature and authority of earth priests. As early as 1930, an alarm was sent out by the assistant district commissioner of the eastern Nuer following an incident in which two governmentally appointed Gaajok chiefs allocated to themselves the ritual responsibilities of earth priests in the settlement of feuds.[30] The ADC stepped in, seized the cattle involved, reprimanded the chiefs, and reassured the local earth priest that his powers would be respected and protected. Two years later, however, after extensive conversations with Evans-Pritchard on the subject, the governor of the Upper Nile Province observed in a letter to the civil secretary:

> The administrative authorities in this Province realise that there are leopard skin chiefs and other functional experts among the Nuer and other tribes and are already aware of their value and encourage the exercise of their functional powers in so far as these powers do not run counter to the authority of recognised chiefs and courts, e.g. homicide cases. I agree there is some danger of the Government tribal court replacing the functional experts to too great an extent and further attention must be paid to this matter.... A leopard skin chief unrecognised by Government may remain a tribal functional expert, but if Government authority supports his powers the position is altered at once. ... Though I agree to the fullest use being made of all tribal institutions yet

30. "Note from the UNPMD, 1930," Civsec 1/43/113.

> I see no reason to doubt that Government has the right to introduce chiefs'
> courts and not try to run the tribe through a number of functional experts
> whose customary and hereditary powers would have been completely changed
> by the sanction of Government authority and support.[31]

If the earth priest was ever anything more than a "functional" or "ritual"
expert," he was certainly nothing more than this following the consolidation of British rule. And in subsequent years, even his control over the sacrifice of *yaŋ kɛthä* was reduced by the secularizing thrust of government
intervention. On the two occasions I witnessed this sacrifice among the eastern Gaajok in 1981, a court-appointed "earth priest" (who, much to my
amusement, was decked in a full set of government khakis complete with
beret in addition to a prominently displayed leopard skin) speared the bull-
calf on a small stretch of bush just outside the local police station. Gathering
some of the blood (*riɛm*) and undigested contents of the beast's stomach
(*wau;* the victim's blood and food, as it were), the earth priest ceremoniously
flung these over the rest of the bloodwealth cattle—an act, I was told, that
ensured that the relatives of the deceased would not *nueer* from direct contacts with these animals. No oration was made. The police immediately
moved in to carve up the carcass and to distribute its meat among "the
people of the government," *jikume* or *jituruɔk*. Amidst a flurry of arguments
and counterarguments, the court president as well as attending subchiefs,
policemen, headmen, court scribes (*bulkamin*), medical dispensers (*kimni*),
and even local school teachers (*ŋieec*) stepped forward to claim a cut of the
meat as their *böth* right as members of the administration. On the one occasion I witnessed this rite among the western Leek—where, I might note,
extensive orations were made—even the *maböthni* (or occupants of the local
jail, "the guests of the government," so to speak) were awarded the neck, the
portion formerly bestowed on Dinka captives. As for the kinsmen of the deceased, in the west, they received a full leg. In the east, however, I was told
that they would have to "go begging" (*bikɛ wä lim*) if they hoped to receive any meat at all—probably an exaggeration of the truth. Clearly, the
meaning of this sacrifice had changed considerably between the 1930s and
1980s, although I was unable to pinpoint the exact period in which local
administrative agents succeeded in capturing and twisting the symbolism of this rite into one of solidarity among "the people of the government."

---

31. "Governor of the UNP to the Civil Secretary," 12 Feb. 1932, Civsec
1/43/133. Governor Pawson's letter makes explicit references to conversations
with Evans-Pritchard on this subject.

The bloodletting rite of *bier* was also modified during this period. The two deft cuts drawn along the upper arm of the killer, which Evans-Pritchard likened to the "mark of Cain" (1940a:152), were gradually abandoned in favor of more discreet operations. By the early 1980s, earth priests, when consulted at all, usually sought a bit of the slayer's blood from between the thumb and forefinger of his dominant hand or from beneath a fingernail—or even, claimed one eastern Gaajok, from behind a back molar. The fact that these ritual innovations spanned the geographical extremes of Nuerland at that time suggests that they emerged before the worst years of the first civil war. For, as we shall see, many regional variations in contemporary Nuer attitudes toward the dangers of *nueer* may be traced back in large part to their differing experiences of gun warfare and violent deaths during the turbulent first civil war.

THE IMPACT OF THE FIRST CIVIL WAR ON REGIONAL PATTERNS OF FEUDING AND FIGHTING

All Nuer regions experienced a serious escalation in the viciousness of intercommunity combat following the abrupt departure of the British in 1955–56. Many individuals took this as an opportunity to settle old scores by force of arms. Consequently, the number of intercommunity conflicts escalated rapidly—especially along the ungovernable Ethiopian frontier. At first, few Nuer were directly involved in confrontations with the newly established Sudanese state. Indeed, it took years for some Nuer communities to become convinced that the government army was their principal enemy. Nevertheless, once it became clear that the Sudanese government intended to impose a policy of forced "Arabization" and "Islamization" on the south, growing numbers of Nuer joined the incipient secessionist movement. Democracy came and went and the Nuer, along with other southerners, were soon confronted with an increasingly intolerant and brutal military establishment. Although there were as yet very few Christian converts among Nuer (outside the small, missionary-trained literate elite), many people viewed the burning of a southern Christian church in Khartoum and the eviction of all foreign missionaries in 1964 as crucial turning points in their attitudes toward the central government and hence in their willingness to take up arms against it. Interestingly, when I asked Nuer villagers during the early 1980s to explain why that war developed, they often attributed it to an insult: "The Arabs called us dogs and slaves and said that we were no better than the dirt under their feet." Other individuals stressed their desires for political autonomy: "The British have their government and the

'Arabs' theirs, so we, southerners, decided that it was time to have our government, too!"

When the first members of what later developed into the southern Anyanya army began to infiltrate Nuer regions in search of arms and men during the early 1960s, they faced considerable skepticism on the part of the older generation about the prospects of successfully "overturning the government": *dee turu̱ɔk lɔɔc?* According to accounts gathered during the early 1980s, a Nuer by the name of Daniel Yiec Diu was responsible for the early mobilization of the eastern Jikany—which he allegedly accomplished by first enlisting the support of local women. I was told that he would gather the women of the local community and then tell them that their husbands and boyfriends were not men at all. Rather, the real men were the "Arabs," because they were out there raping and killing, while Nuer men stood by and did nothing. This "shaming" strategy proved eminently effective, and larger numbers of eastern Nuer, together with their rifles, began to join up. Yiec then tired out his new recruits by leading them day after day in search of the enemy. When some of his new recruits later asked to be released, Yiec agreed to their request but stipulated that they would have to leave their guns behind for other recruits who were willing to engage with the northern Arabs. And this condition was accepted. For guns, as I shall explain more fully below, were considered collective possessions to some extent in that they were used for the protection of extended communities in situations of external attack. As the war escalated and as greater numbers of rifles flowed in from across the Ethiopian border as well as from successful raids on government posts, many eastern Nuer youths joined the secessionist movement for the express purpose of acquiring access to guns. The ideological and material linkages between guns and masculinity thus developed swiftly in this region—a point to which I will return shortly.[32]

32. Interestingly, when I recounted Daniel Yiec Diu's enlistment strategy to the current SPLA leader of the Upper Nile in 1990, Commander Machar commented that, though he had not previously heard the story, it was very believable since he, too, had experienced the profound impact of women's views on recruitment patterns while working among the western Nuer during the late 1980s.

> After 1986, if a citizen went to a dance and it was found that he was not a soldier, the girls would reject him, saying: "I don't want to talk with a woman!" They challenged them, and that boosted the number of recruitments a lot! But when the girls later found out that soldiers were dying, some of them revised their question, asking instead: "How can I talk to a ghost?" This is now causing problems in recruitment.

By the mid-1960s, a predictable pattern of violence emerged: swift attack-and-retreat rebel raids on government-held positions during the rains countered by massive dry-season retaliatory campaigns in which the army, bolstered by the Egyptian Air Force, plundered and razed the surrounding countryside. Of the estimated one half to one million southerners slain during this seventeen-year civil war, the vast majority were civilians caught in the cross fire between Anyanya and government forces. Local patterns of intercommunity fighting and feuding were also exacerbated and frequently manipulated by both government and Anyanya troops. English 303 rifles and more-powerful weaponry were also distributed widely among the eastern and central Nuer by both sides in the conflict in an attempt to consolidate local support. Many Nuer, particularly easterners, were also trained, formally and informally, in the laying of traps and the mining of roads. This was a war of hidden enemies—of paid spies and coerced informants—in which the major lines of conflict were often unstable and unclear. Several powerful Nuer prophets emerged among the central and eastern Nuer, some aligning themselves with the Anyanya rebels and others with government arms suppliers. As the level of violence continued to mount between 1969 and 1972, Israel played an increasingly important role in supplying and training Anyanya troops. More than a million southerners were driven from their homes, scattering as far as possible from government-controlled roads. Of these, approximately 40,000 were eastern Nuer who sought sanctuary across the Ethiopian frontier. Large sections of the western Nuer, in contrast, were shielded from the worst effects of this war, as I explained, by a decade of extremely high floods (1961–72) as well as by the inscrutable military priorities of the time.

The Addis Ababa Agreement of 1972 granted the south "regional autonomy" and ushered in a brief, eleven-year period of relative calm. A new southern capital was established at Juba, and the work of reestablishing regional administrative structures began. A general amnesty was proclaimed—something that necessitated the reinstatement of many Nuer chiefs who had been rejected by their constituents or had aligned themselves with government troops during the war. Public elections were also held for many new chiefs, under the guidance of Peter Gatkuoth Gual and other leading Nuer members of the newly established High Executive Council and Southern Regional Assembly. Thousands of ex-Anyanya fighters were also absorbed into the national army, most continuing to serve in the south. Thousands more were incorporated into the regional police force and other branches of the newly established southern administration. Bitter disappointments, however, followed swiftly. The millions of Sudanese pounds earmarked for the infrastructural development of the south allegedly came and went, leaving little in the way of lasting benefits for the rural masses. And many of the schools, medical dispensaries, and other infrastructural improvements built independently by local communities during the 1970s were still inoperative in 1983, owing to the central government's failure to supply them. In June 1978 work began on the highly controversial Jonglei Canal Project, despite the fact that many southerners remained unconvinced that the massive social, economic, and environmental disruptions it would cause would be compensated by any direct benefits (Howell 1988). And the regional High Executive Council and Southern People's Assembly were soon bogged down by bitter leadership struggles and sharpening ethnic divisions. Following the discovery of massive oil deposits in the Western Upper Nile and Sobat valley regions by Chevron and CPF-Total Corporations, respectively, the question of whether or not the southern regional government had direct revenue claims in the mineral wealth of its territories became an increasingly contested and divisive national issue. These and other political factors discussed in the prologue eventually exploded into a renewal of full-scale civil war in 1983.

The extent to which the first civil-war era permanently altered the ethics and tactics of local patterns of inter-Nuer community feuding was readily apparent during the early 1980s. By that time, the fighting club had been abandoned in all Nuer regions. Spears were now the dominant weapon in violent disputes among close kinsmen and neighbors. Indeed, spear wounds were sometimes acquired at that time in domestic conflicts between husbands and wives. Furthermore, it was increasingly common for men who had fallen wounded in intercommunity confrontations to be subsequently slain and mutilated by the repeated spear thrusts of their attackers—an operation called *cɔk*, which was considered extremely unethical among Nuer a generation earlier.

The degree of this escalation was most apparent in those Nuer regions that had been heavily devastated by the first civil war. The fighting spear, for example, remained the dominant weapon of local feuding and fighting among the western Leek Nuer through the early 1980s. Nevertheless, the heavy, smooth-curved blade of earlier generations had given way to lighter models adorned with numerous back-bending prongs that created exceptionally grievous wounds when extracted. Due to the exceptional lightness of these locally crafted spears, skilled warriors could hurl as many as three or four with a single thrust, thereby making it impossible for opponents to parry them all. This fighting technique was said to have been an innovation by the youngest age-set at that time. The buffalo and crocodile hide "shields" (or *kotni;* sing., *kot*), standard during the colonial era, had likewise been replaced by sturdier metallic models called *zinki,* which were hammered out by local craftsmen. And yet, the logistics and general ethics of inter-Nuer warfare among the western Leek appeared to have changed little from the British colonial era. Major intercommunity battles continued to take place only during daylight hours and only after all warriors had queued up next to their closest of kin to form two parallel fighting lines. Leek women, moreover, continued to accompany their menfolk to battle where they encouraged them with shrill war cries, retrieved spears, and, most important, protected and carried away the wounded. Although Leek Nuer communities possessed a small but growing arsenal of guns, this was reserved for the most part for confrontations with their northern Baggara Arab neighbors and, to a lesser extent, with their better-armed Bul Nuer neighbors to the west. Significantly, many contemporary westerners argued that the power of a fighting spear (*mut*) was actually "greater" (*diitni jɛn*) than that of a gun (*mac*). As one young Leek man explained: "People respect the spear, its importance exceeds that of the gun because it's the spear that splits the cucumber, the spear that kills the cow of divinity, and the spear that is stowed above the entrance of the cattle byre." In other words, the sacrificial role of spears was seen to enhance their military significance in contradistinction to the purely defensive powers of the gun. In this region in the early 1980s, guns were neither fired off on sacrificial occasions nor offered in bridewealth exchange.

Although all westerners I met continued to maintain during the early 1980s that the bloodletting rite of *bier* was essential, regardless of the type of weapon used, gun slayings were increasingly being differentiated from spear slayings in that victims of the former were said to create a uniquely direct, spiritual linkage with Divinity (*kuɔth nhial*) that could be cultivated through sacrifice and thereafter called upon in times of danger by surviving kin. Persons killed by bullets were categorized by western Nuer together with those killed by lightning as *col wic.* These deaths, in other words, were equated with the direct intervention of *kuɔth nhial,* or the all-powerful, overarching "Divinity of the sky." The Nuer, as Evans-Pritchard explained, were a profoundly monotheistic people in the sense that all manifestations of lesser divinities of the air and earth were interpreted as refractions of a single, distant transcendent "God." Nevertheless, communications with this ultra-human power were predominantly indirect, being channeled through sacrificial appeals for assistance to specific "air divinities" and their prophets as well as to lesser powers of the earth.

The only direct linkage between human beings and *kuɔth nhial* was, in fact, the *col wic* guardians of specific lineages that could be called upon for assistance in life-threatening situations. As Evans-Pritchard explained:

> When a person is killed by lightning Nuer are resigned. They say that God has struck him with his fire and that as God has taken him there is nothing to be said. God would be angry were they to grieve too much for someone whom he has taken away. . . . Sacrifices must be made at once. . . . It is believed that unless sacrifices are made at once the *col wic* may return, bringing death to man and beast. Also, the close kinsmen of the dead are so unclean that relatives and neighbours may not eat or drink in their homes before they have sacrificed; animals must follow the dead before the people can rest in peace. Nuer say *"Caa je kir ka det kene ruath."* "He (the dead man) was expiated with goats (and sheep) and oxen." The sacrifices cleanse the kith and kin of evil and ward off from them further misfortune.
>
> Some weeks or months later a ceremony is held in honour of the *col wic*. (Evans-Pritchard 1949b:7)

Col, as Evans-Pritchard pointed out, was a term for the "divinity of lightning," who was said to have a "black head" (*col wic*; see plate 12).

> I think that the Nuer do not separate in their minds the man killed by lightning and the god of lightning who killed him. They say the *yie*, the life [breath], has been taken by God and has become part of God. It is only the *ring*, the flesh, which they cover up. The *col wic* is in the sky: "He has been taken by God into the sky." (1949b:8–9)

When properly honored with periodic sacrifices and a small shrine, consisting of a mud hearth screen (*buɔr*) and a small wooden stake taken from a *nyɔat* tree, the spirit of a *col wic* could be transformed into a force for good. The wood of a *nyɔat* tree was an especially appropriate symbol for the enduring spiritual presence of the *col wic* because it often sprouted of its own accord with the onset of the rains.[33] Although other deaths caused by drowning and fires, as well as those that occurred deep within the bush without apparent cause, were also assimilated into the category of *col wic*, the paradigmatic case was that of lightning victims. And in this respect, it is noteworthy that the Nuer term for gun means "fire"—this being a shortened version of a linguistic distinction drawn in earlier decades between *mut taŋ* ("a spear with a wooden shaft") and *mut mac* ("a spear of fire"). Moreover, the fire of a gun, like that of lightning, is always followed by a thunderous roar. This western Nuer analogy between bullets and lightning also

---

33. Evans-Pritchard reported that "*Col* is associated with rain, the *yir nhial*, the river which Nuer says [sic] runs through the sky, and the *nyɔat* tree, of which it is said that 'God loves it'" (1949:8).

Plate 12. Sacrificial commemoration of a *col wic* spirit, western Leek Nuer.

played on mythological associations between "fire" and divine agency. Human knowledge of and access to "fire" were portrayed in Nuer origin myths as direct gifts of Divinity, conveyed by a burning stick tied to the tail of a dog. As early as 1918, moreover, the superior fire power of the "pink" foreigner (*nei ti lual*) had been incorporated into Nuer creation myths as a direct and discriminatory gift from God (Westermann 1912:116).

Although I witnessed the special *col wic* mortuary ceremonies performed upon the death of a pregnant woman slain by lightning among the eastern Jikany Nuer in 1982, as well as attended memorial services for several *col wic* spirits among the western Leek in 1983, I never attended a mortuary ceremony for a person slain by bullets. Gun slayings were still exceedingly rare at that time among the western Leek Nuer. Consequently, I am uncertain whether or not the burial and mortuary ceremonies of such victims followed the same form as those of the lightning victim in the east. Nevertheless, contemporary western Leek were unanimous in the opinion that all *col wic* were capable of protecting their supplicants from life-threatening situations—even those involving bullets. I should also note that *col wic* spirits would sometimes possess people who had neglected them or otherwise manifest themselves through serious illnesses. During the early 1980s attacks of appendicitis were widely interpreted by the west-

ern Leek as manifestations of angry and sacrificially neglected *col wic*.
More important, the obligations kinsmen shared in helping one another
achieve personal immortality through the birth of heirs was considered
especially strong with respect to *col wic*. Every *col wic* expected that surviving kinsmen would marry him/her a ghost wife and that this kinship
obligation would take precedence over all other marriages. Failure to fulfill
this divinely sanctioned obligation invited the justified wrath of the spirit
concerned.

With the return of civil war in 1983, the western Leek Nuer experienced an unprecedented escalation in the frequency of gun deaths. Government-sponsored Baggara Arab militias raided deep into their territories,
burning villages, stealing grain, capturing thousands of cattle, and carrying off hundreds of women and children in the process. By 1987, the SPLA
had succeeded in tempering these raids south of the Bahr-el-Ghazal, where
the vast majority of Leek Nuer had taken refuge in late 1983. The SPLA
commander of the region soon became aware of the fact that rural villagers
categorized the many hundreds of victims who had been shot and killed
during these devastating raids as *col wic* and, consequently, as persons for
whom the marriage of "ghost wives" was deemed essential. Fearing that
this conceptual equation would "cheapen" the idea of *col wic* spirits, which,
he argued, were supposed to be extremely rare phenomena, the commander embarked on an ideological campaign to rupture this linkage between bullet and lightning victims. He argued that contemporary victims
of government guns should not be equated with *col wic* but, rather, dissociated entirely from the social and spiritual consequences of homicides
generated by local forms of fighting and feuding. The bloodletting rite of
bier, he maintained, was likewise unnecessary in the context of a "government war" (*koor kume*). The dangers of *nueer* simply did not exist in such
contexts. This revolutionary redefinition of the meaning of violent deaths
implied a weakening of Divinity's overarching role as the guardian of human morality, and of the obligation of kinsmen to provide ghost wives for
their relatives who died heirless. The commander's arguments could also
be interpreted, as I suggested earlier, as an implicit bid for public recognition of the SPLA as a "legitimate government" in its own right.

Just how persuasive these arguments proved among the western Nuer
is difficult to judge since I was prevented, for security reasons, from reaching that area during my return to the Upper Nile in 1992. Although the
commander appeared convinced in 1990 that his radical reinterpretations
of the meaning of violent death in the context of a "government war" were

gaining acceptance among rural western Nuer, I suspect that his ideas were not as readily appropriated as he believed. For their acceptance would imply a temporary—if not permanent—abandonment of some of the strongest moral obligations binding communities of kin. Moreover, I think that it would take more than a "government" order to convince ordinary Nuer villagers that they could ignore divinely sanctioned prohibitions with impunity in any context. Be that as it may, these ideological developments certainly marked a potential turning point in western Nuer attitudes toward both the government and guns. It remains to be seen whether or not these ideas will generate broader reassessments of the dangers of *nueer* in that region in the future.

Contemporary controversies over the scope and potency of *nueer* were developing in very different directions during this same period among eastern Nuer communities. During the early 1980s guns were rapidly replacing spears as the dominant weapon of intercommunity combat throughout the east—a trend that developed quite early, as we have seen, among those Gaajak Nuer sections straddling the turbulent Ethiopian frontier. This was so much the case that the fighting spear was increasingly regarded by the eastern Jikany Nuer as a weapon of ambush, valued primarily for its silence. Unlike the western Leek Nuer, the eastern Gaajak and Gaaguang Nuer no longer queued up during the early 1980s in opposed fighting lines. Rather, they tended to adopt instead scattered and prone firing positions—a fighting tactic apparently introduced by Anyanya forces during the first civil war.[34] Consequently, it was no longer safe for eastern Jikany women to accompany their sons and husbands into battle: "It is awful," one eastern Gaajak exclaimed, "today the dead and wounded are left to the birds." Night battles, moreover, were not uncommon in this region during the early 1980s, and ambush attacks were frequent.

Eastern Nuer interpretations of the nature of the relationship created between slayer and slain at the moment of death changed as a direct result of their experiences during the first civil war. The brutal realities of everyday life during that war led many easterners to suspect that the blood curse of the slain was operative only in cases of homicide between "relatives" (*nei ti maar*). Hence, the rite of bier, many argued, could be safely

---

34. During the early years of the first civil war, many eastern Nuer reportedly resisted the scattered and prone firing positions being urged upon them by Anyanya leaders as both humiliating and cowardly. They preferred a one-kneed firing stance in full view of their opponents. As the death toll rose, attitudes changed.

dispensed with when slayer and victim were previously unknown to each other. Consensus on this matter, however, was by no means reached by the early 1980s. Some easterners continued to argue that the rite of *bier* was essential in all cases of inter-Nuer slayings. While discussing this controversial issue with a governmentally recognized Gaajok earth priest in 1982, I discovered, much to my surprise, that he had performed the bloodletting rite of *bier* only once during his entire career. Significantly, that case involved a Nuer policeman who allegedly shot and killed a fellow Nuer in the line of duty. Judging from the number of individuals killed each year in local feuding and fighting, this admission was, to my mind, quite striking. It certainly dramatized the declining powers of eastern Nuer earth priests in the resolution of blood feuds as well as the contracting social scope of *nueer* in that region. Because this particular earth priest was often summoned by the local chiefs' court to perform incest sacrifices and other services, he was probably viewed as a less desirable ear for homicide confessions than were other earth priests less closely associated with local administrative structures. Unfortunately, the most prominent *kuäär muɔn* of the immediate region was brutally murdered just days after we had arranged to hold extensive discussions about his religious responsibilities. Hence, I am uncertain as to whether or not his experience of homicide confessions was more extensive than that of the "government" earth priest mentioned.[35]

Furthermore, as a direct result of the massive dissemination of guns during the first civil war, most eastern Jikany Nuer had come to the conclusion that recourse to the bloodletting rite of *bier* was insufficient to eliminate the risk of *nueer* when the victim (whether related or unrelated to the slayer) had died of bullet wounds—though some people suggested that this rite could be carried out as a secondary precaution. The principal purificatory rite, however, was called *piu thorä* (or "the water of the cartridge shell"). The slayer, I was told, must pour some water (preferably mixed with a few grains of salt, if available) into an empty cartridge shell and drink it—and that is all. This simple rite would seem to suggest that gun slayings involved a cross flow of "heat" between victim and slayer (either in addition to or in place of blood) that needed to be negated or "cooled" by the water of the cartridge shell if the slayer were to survive. This association between "cooling" and "curing" was also evident in the bloodletting ceremony of *bier:* the drawing of blood and the ingestion of

---

35. The context of this murder will be discussed in chapter 5 in conjunction with violent disputes over contemporary definitions of incest.

the priest's spittle (cf. Hutchinson 1992b) were explicitly directed toward restoring the bodily "coolness" (k_ɔai pu_any) or "health" of the slayer. Indeed, all curative operations involving the extraction or transfer of bodily fluids were spoken of by Nuer in terms of the removal of "heat" (sickness or pollution) from the body of the afflicted. From this perspective, a shift from a metaphor of blood to one of temperature was not as revolutionary as might be supposed. The central prohibition on drinking water at the heart of this state of pollution was incorporated into the curative rite of piu thorä along lines similar to preventive inoculations in Western medical practices. From a historical perspective, it is not surprising that a purificatory rite that could be performed by anyone, anywhere, at any time, without disclosing the identity of the slayer, would have been "discovered" during the first civil-war era and thereafter avidly adopted in the east. Significantly, the rite of piu thorä was unknown among the western Nuer in 1983—though it may well have spread to that region with the violence of the second civil war.

Nevertheless, the rite of piu thorä did not eliminate the dangers of *nueer* associated with acts of direct or indirect commensality between the families of slayer and slain. It was thus fully expected during the early 1980s that an eastern Nuer killer who failed to confess his deed publicly (*mi caa raan luç*) would secretly warn his family of the dangers of *nueer* in which they shared. *Te kɛ mi caa y_ar,* he might say: "Something has gone awry." If the slayer had small children and lived in the immediate vicinity of his victim's family, he was likely, I was told, to devise a discreet excuse to move quietly away.

All of the above assumes, of course, that the slayer actually realized that he had killed someone. But in major community gun battles, it was often difficult, if not impossible, to know from whose gun the fatal bullet was fired. Unlike individually crafted spears, a bullet lodged deep in someone's body could not be easily recognized or traced. A further degree of ambiguity and distance was thus introduced into eastern Nuer definitions of relationships of the "bone": At times, it was difficult to establish the exact boundaries of a feud and, consequently, the focal intensity and scope of the dangers of *nueer*. The rite of piu thorä was eminently suited to these changing circumstances. Warriors in doubt as to whether or not they had killed someone could easily take the precaution of sipping some water of the cartridge shell and thereby avoid the immediate danger of *nueer*.

The increasing ambiguities surrounding the identity of slayers resulting from the expanding use of guns among the eastern Jikany had similar ramifications on the collection and transfer of bloodwealth cattle. In situations where the fatal bullet could not be traced accurately, the responsibility for contributing bloodwealth cattle was generalized to fighting communities as a whole. There were times, moreover, when the death toll was so high on both sides that local chiefs extracted cattle compensation only when the number of deaths on one side exceeded those on the other. The expression *cikɛ yɔat* was introduced to signify a balancing of the deaths on each side—a metaphor that played upon the idea that the object of pounding grain (*yɔal*) was to homogenize its texture—that is, to create particles of equal size. According to one informant, this strategy of compensation was first used in the aftermath of a major gun fight between cieng Cany and cieng Wau of the eastern Gaajak during the mid-1950s in which twenty-nine men were killed in a single day.[36]

The extraordinarily rapid spread of Christianity after the first civil war in the east further complicated these developments in that "the people of the church" (*jiluay kuɔth*, literally, "the people of God's cattle byre") emerged as a formidable peacekeeping force in some areas. Armed with the commandment /Co raan na̱k ("Thou shalt not kill"), Christian converts began to challenge the entire ethos of Nuer warriorhood on moral grounds. In 1981 for example, a major confrontation between two communities of eastern Gaajak was prevented at the last moment by a small band of hymn-singing, banner-waving converts who took it upon themselves to march up and down between the opposed warring sections. A few years earlier, a long-standing feud between two closely related and contiguous Gaajok communities of cieng Gaac, a constituent of cieng Laang, was allegedly defused by recourse to mass Christian conversion. In 1968–69 a fight broke out between two "brothers" (read: paternal cousins) of cieng Mändholi and cieng Mänlony following the death of their "father." Shortly thereafter, one of cieng Mändholi's supporters was found murdered by an unknown killer. Suspecting the worst, the "bull" of cieng Mändholi immediately mustered a war party and attacked cieng Mänlony. Since cieng Mänlony lost two men in this attack to cieng Mändholi's one, expectations of future violence remained strong even though full bloodwealth payments were transferred under pressure from the local chiefly administration. Tensions simmered for several more years until one of the leaders of cieng

36. Among the contemporary western Nuer, this generalization of compensation responsibilities extended to the payment of government fines imposed for fighting. In that region, families that had no members who attended the fight were nevertheless expected to contribute to cattle fines in turn—something that created considerable resentment in some quarters. Among the eastern Nuer, in contrast, persons who had attended the fight were often arrested and fined individually.

Mänlony—a man who had lost a full brother and a father's sister's son in the attack by cieng Mändholi—was elected "executive chief" (*bok in tot*) of the extended region. As a newly appointed government officer, this man was, of course, expected to keep the peace; but he was also under a strong moral obligation to vindicate his brother's death with the blood of his foes. The conferral of chiefly offices on persons who might otherwise be expected to break the peace was a well-recognized election strategy among contemporary Nuer both east and west of the White Nile: "If he wants to fight, make him a headman!" ran their political motto. During the early colonial period government chiefs were often appointed or promoted on the basis of having demonstrated unusual restraint by not avenging close kinsmen who had been slain. Consequently, our man of cieng Mänlony was not the first Nuer "chief" to have been caught between his administrative responsibilities on the one hand and his moral obligations to avenge the death of a close kinsmen on the other. The way in which he eventually resolved this dilemma, however, was unusually creative. It just so happened that shortly after his election, a man of cieng Mändholi was "accidentally" speared while visiting his affines, who were themselves deeply embroiled in a separate feud. Being merely an affine as opposed to a paternal relative of that family, this man was not an ethical target of ambush in this second feud. He was, nevertheless, wounded with others while sleeping in his mosquito net at night outside his father-in-law's cattle byre. Though he survived a serious head wound, he subsequently suffered from bouts of insanity. It was at this point that our "executive chief" took the initiative. Guided by a dream, he summoned his wounded and insane foe to his homestead along with his immediate kinsmen and declared before them that *kuɔth* had spoken to him, saying that all of them should convert to Christianity and thereby terminate the feud that had divided their extended family once and for all. This announcement was followed by numerous prayers and a mass rally at the local church. Not everyone of cieng Mänlony and cieng Mändholi ended up adopting the Christian faith. Nevertheless, everyone who was morally obliged to wreak blood vengeance did so. Following this extraordinary event, the ban on commensalism between the two families was lifted.

These dramatic incidents reveal the extent to which Christian conversion was being seized upon by the eastern Nuer as an opportunity to rethink the meaning of violent deaths and the nature of relationships of "bone" more generally. Nevertheless, the Christian leadership in the east had yet to articulate any explicit policy regarding the dangers of *nueer*. On the one hand, its vehement rejection of all forms of cattle sacrifice made it difficult for converts to submit to the purification rituals performed by earth priests. On the other hand, an explicit denial of the existence of *nueer* would have been counterproductive to Christian efforts to suppress inter-Nuer slayings on moral grounds. Although the novel use of Christianity in the settlement of the feud between cieng Mändholi and cieng Mänlony would seem to suggest that the rite of conversion itself had some potential for defusing the dangers of *nueer*, this issue remained shrouded in uncertainty in 1983. On the few occasions I asked leading Nuer evangelists about the church's position in this regard, I was told that this was, indeed, a good question. One pastor tried to assure me that a Christian killer would never attempt to cover up his deed. Otherwise, I elicited no definitive statements. While discussing the dangers of incest (*ruaal*) and menstrual taboos with lay members, I sometimes heard people claim that baptized Christians were immune to the spiritual consequences of transgressions of these prohibitions. However, I never heard anyone express this opinion with regard to the pollution generated by inter-Nuer acts of homicide. Were a more open and generalized debate about the nature of *nueer* to develop in the near future, I am quite certain that local church leaders would play a crucial role in its evolution. However, as things stood in 1983, the church had yet to resolve this issue.

The message of nonviolence eastern Christians were preaching during the early 1980s, I should stress, was directed primarily toward the suppression of local feuding and fighting. Though many eastern converts took pride in the fact that the Sudan Council of Churches and the World Council of Churches had been instrumental in setting up the peace negotiations that culminated in the signing of the 1972 Addis Ababa Agreement ending the first civil war, they were, not surprisingly, among the most active and vociferous opponents of more recent governmental attempts to impose Islamic shari'a law as the law of the nation. This rapid, post-1983 politicization of religious identities in Sudan will be taken up in chapter 7.

SPLA INITIATIVES: THE ADMINISTRATION
OF THE WESTERN UPPER NILE, 1985–90

By the time SPLA forces began to assert a measure of control over the Western Upper Nile during the mid-1980s by preventing further incursions by Arab militia south of the Bahr-el-Ghazal, they were confronted with many of the same administrative problems formerly faced by the British colonial regime during the 1920s. Although I am unable at present to offer any independent assessment of the efficacy of the administrative policies that the

SPLA introduced in this region, I include a brief summary of them here (based on official documents and interviews provided by the SPLA leadership of that region) in order to highlight some of the ways in which they converged with and diverged from administrative precedents set by the British.

The immediate administrative priorities of the SPLA were to limit the frequency and intensity of intercommunity confrontations, to establish an effective system of indirect rule, to introduce a system of arms controls and gun licensing, and to conduct a population survey of the extended region. Between 1983 and 1986, much of the Western Upper Nile was terrorized by individual "gun toters," who, having acquired firearms early on, proceeded to use them to expand their herds and to settle personal vendettas with other citizens. Interestingly, the better-armed eastern Jikany Nuer demonstrated far greater restraint in this regard during this same period. Having endured much of the brunt of the first civil war, the eastern Jikany Nuer were more reluctant than their less experienced western cousins to deplete their limited ammunition supplies in interpersonal struggles as distinct from collective confrontations with government troops, SPLA forces, or neighboring Anyuak, Murle, and other peoples.

In an effort to curb individual recourse to firearms in the west, the SPLA leadership doubled the bloodwealth compensation rate for bullet victims to 100 cows, 20 of which were claimed by the administration as a fine.[37] A seven-year term of imprisonment was also standardly imposed. It was further announced that persons convicted of particularly grievous gun assaults were liable to be sentenced to death by a firing squad—the SPLA equivalent of the hangings earlier introduced by the British.[38] The cattle compensation rate for spear slaying perpetrated in declared sectional fights, in contrast, remained at 50 head of cattle, 10 of which were payable to the administration as a fine. A prison term of five years was also stipulated in such circumstances. The SPLA further declared that anyone caught firing off a gun as a celebratory act was liable for a one-cow fine.[39]

These administrative decrees had the effect of further accentuating the disparity developing since the colonial era between the community of rela-

37. Compensation for blatantly provoked gun slayings was normally reduced to eighty head of cattle.

38. The use of a firing squad in such contexts undoubtedly further weakened people's belief in the dangers of *nueer*.

39. And should such celebratory acts result in the accidental death(s) of persons in attendance, bloodwealth compensation was set at fifty-five head of cattle for adult victims, fifteen of which were awarded to the administration as a fine.

tives bound together by common bloodwealth obligations and that connected by shared bridewealth claims. However, in differentiating gun slayings from spear slayings, the SPLA effectively reversed earlier British practices of ignoring the type of weapon used in the sentencing of killers as well as in the assessment of bloodwealth compensation rates. The SPLA reinstituted the possibility of compensation for deaths attributed to old wounds (*nyindiit*), although a two-year limit on such claims was specified. And in some cases, the SPLA acknowledged that suspected *pɛth* ("possessors of the evil eye") and *rɔath* ("ghouls") killed by clubs were not subject to bloodwealth claims—thereby contradicting British decrees in this regard.

The SPLA also carried out an extensive population survey of the area in conjunction with an assessment of critical food shortages. According to the regional commander, this "indirect" census yielded a population figure of well over a million Nuer in the Western Upper Nile alone. The SPLA administration's survey technique was innovative in that it defined households in terms of their female heads, with husbands being counted as members of their youngest wives' households. All previous population estimates in the Upper Nile were made either on the basis of male taxpayer lists multiplied by an estimated figure of between 3.5 and 4.5 dependents per household or on the basis of questionnaires in which adult males were asked to specify how many wives and children they had—methods that, the SPLA leadership argued, had resulted in serious and pervasive undercountings.

Surprised by the population densities uncovered by this survey, the commander proceeded to divide the chiefly administrations of the Nyuong and Dok into eight separate courts with the aim of facilitating individual access to local chiefs. By 1989, five regional appeals courts had been established, one for each of the principal subdistricts, composed of a permanent judge and the relevant head chiefs of the cases concerned. The SPLA also encouraged women to participate as voters in the election of (invariably male) government chiefs—a pattern that was subsequently extended to the eastern Nuer in 1992. The annual tax was shifted from a cash to a grain basis and set at three tins (roughly 12 kilos) per adult male. In addition, SPLA soldiers were ordered to establish individual as well as collective farms so as to ensure adequate grain supplies for themselves and for other SPLA forces moving through the region.

Following the negotiation of a local truce with various northern Arab militia in 1987, Arab merchants began to bring sugar, clothes, medicines, and other consumer items from south Kordofan, with the support of newly established SPLA economic officers. These merchants obtained most of their trading goods through black markets operating in the north. These goods were then sold to hundreds of local Nuer traders who had begun to open small "bush shops" throughout the district. In 1988 the annual licensing fee for "normal [retail] trade" was set at 180 Sudanese pounds and at 360 Sudanese pounds for merchants operating cattle auctions or slaughterhouses.[40] Cattle were generally sold for currency at the principal auction markets established at Ler and Rup Nyagai (set up as a substitute market for the government-held district capital of Bentiu), with most cows being passed on to export merchants in southern Kordofan.[41] Three months after the old Nimeiri-faced currency became obsolete in the north, the SPLA organized a districtwide currency exchange for the new bills—a daunting administrative task that was reportedly accomplished in only fifteen days.

This administrative model, being the first established by the SPLA in the Upper Nile, was later adopted and extended by the SPLA leadership of Bor and Central Nuer Districts in 1987 and 1988, respectively. Nevertheless, I have little information at present about how well these administrative structures held up in the Western Upper Nile following the transfer of their principal architect, Commander Machar, to the eastern Nuer region in 1990 and the subsequent renewal of government-sponsored Arab militia attacks along the Bahr-el-Ghazal.

THE NONMILITARY SIGNIFICANCE OF GUNS AMONG THE EASTERN JIKANY NUER, 1980–90

Above and beyond their increasing importance as weapons of intra- and interregional warfare, the eastern Jikany Nuer had adopted guns as key value referents in the definition of many contemporary social relationships and distinctions. Commonly used as an element of bridewealth payments during the 1980s, an offer of a rifle sometimes conferred a competitive advantage over offers of full cattle transfers from prospective grooms. Moreover, the ever-resilient trade in illegal firearms remained one of the few long-distance exchange networks in this region that continued to operate independently of established market and transport centers. With the cattle exchange values of most models having doubled between 1969 and 1981, guns were increasingly regarded as sound economic as well as sound security investments.

40. "Western Upper Nile Zonal Command: Conduct of Trade Regulations," 2 Aug. 1988, SPLA/SPLM Archives, Nairobi, Kenya.
41. Images of this bustling market are available in *The Price of Survival*, a documentary film by John Ryle and Baping Tim Chol (1994).

Interestingly, the eastern Jikany Nuer had also developed guns as a fresh focus for a culturally creative aesthetic deeply entwined with local concepts of male potency, beauty, and strength. Their phallic forms were scarified onto women's bellies, their golden bullets were girded to the right arms of men—indeed, gun displays had even replaced the imitation of cattle in male dance forms throughout the east by the early 1980s. Similarly, it was not unusual at that time to find young boys armed with artfully molded mud rifles staging elaborate war games at the perimeter of a village. The ability of a boy to hold and aim a rifle was, in fact, one of the principal prerequisites for initiation in that region at that time. The temperature symbolism of guns had also been tapped by the eastern Nuer for medicinal purposes as diverse as soothing teething pains to eliminating eye infections. In brief, the avid absorption of guns by these self-characterized warriors had not only revolutionized the battlefield but also contributed to a reevaluation of cattle, spears, and other important foci of Nuer culture as recorded by Evans-Pritchard during the early 1930s.

Significantly, guns were not considered individual possessions but rather were owned collectively by families—*mac ɛ duŋ ciëŋ*—or, most commonly, by groups of brothers. With the exception of rifles conferred as symbols of office on government chiefs and police, the communal ownership of guns was characteristic of Nuer communities both east and west of the White Nile throughout the 1980s. In fact, many western Nuer communities secretly collected cattle in order to purchase powerful machine guns, which, while stored in the homes of respected community leaders, belonged to the contributing community as a whole. Everyone agreed, in other words, that such guns would be taken out only in the event of generalized attacks by the army or neighboring peoples. The protective force of guns was also generalized by eastern Nuer communities—something that should be clear from the successful mobilization strategy adopted by Daniel Yiec Diu during the first civil war. Although spears, too, were used in sacrificial contexts to symbolize community bonds of support and identification, particularly among communities of agnates (cf. Evans-Pritchard 1956:231ff.), they were essentially individual possessions. Guns, in contrast, were collective objects through and through. And thus, unlike the "money of work" and the "cattle of money," guns directly reinforced a socially expanded sense of self and of community in that rights of ownership were identified with the shared cattle rights invested in their purchase. Moreover, the fact that the exchange value of most rifles varied between five and twelve head of cattle at that time greatly reduced the possibility of individual purchases. Their increasing usage in bridewealth exchange throughout the east—but not the west—further accentuated their collective status. Although it was impossible at that time to legitimate a marriage solely with the transfer of guns, the bridewealth value of a gun was always negotiated as so many "cattle of the gun" (*yɔk maac*). Sometimes the groom's family retained latent ownership claims in the rifle offered. That is, the groom's party could negotiate the right to reclaim the gun through the subsequent bestowal of its cattle equivalent. Thus, it was very important that the cattle value of the gun be fully agreed upon at the time of the marriage.

Among Nuer communities west of the White Nile, neither guns nor money were common elements of bridewealth exchange during the early 1980s—a trend that continued into the early 1990s partly as a consequence of concerted SPLA efforts to restrict this use of guns among the western Nuer. The local SPLA leadership feared that the introduction of firearms into the local bridewealth system could provoke increased attacks on individuals for the sole purpose of obtaining their guns. However, the centrality of guns as bridewealth items was, by that time, so firmly established in the east that there was little hope that SPLA directives could reverse this trend. Indeed, Commander Machar cited an incident in which he was eventually forced to release a 404 rifle in order to enable one of his eastern Nuer lieutenants to marry after the bride's father adamantly refused to accept its cattle equivalent.

Whereas the use of guns in bridewealth exchange carried with it the collective interests of the groom's extended family in the procreative powers of the woman married, when it came to the redistribution of "cattle of the gun" among the bride's relatives, conflicts often developed. This was especially the case when the cattle value of the gun exceeded the number of cattle the bride's father and brothers could legitimately claim. For though the bride's father was obliged to sell the gun for its cattle equivalent in situations where the additional bridewealth cattle offered were insufficient to satisfy the outstanding claims of more distant relatives, in practice, "cattle of the gun" were invariably "eaten" by the bride's immediate family. As will be explained in chapter 5, this trend was contributing to a contraction both in the scope of bridewealth claims honored in that region and, concomitantly, in people's estimations of the transgenerational boundaries of incest and exogamic prohibitions.

The relationship between guns and bridegrooms in the east went far beyond bridewealth negotiations themselves. Rifles were also an increasingly important aspect of courtship display, often being fired off at cattle camp dances as celebratory acts of self-affirmation. The elaborate personal songs (*tuari/wieea*) eastern Nuer men composed to attract the attention

and admiration of local girls were often filled with laudatory self-refer-
ences to the power of their guns as evidence of their marriage worthiness.
Among the earliest published evidence of this trend appeared in a delight-
ful and revealing set of eastern Jikany Nuer songs collected during the
mid-1970s by Terese Svoboda (1985). One of these songs (sung by Daniel
Cuol Lul Wur) was aptly entitled by Svoboda "Strutting with My Rifle."

> I met Galuak at the dance
> where my gunshots are always heard
> with the shots of Gac, Bol Dean
> and Cuol Tungcuor.
>
> We carry our rifles like those of Waldeth,
> like the cavalry, like the Congolese army,
> like the Anyanya guerillas. Girls run away,
> smoking like cigarettes when we fire.
>
> Smoke from poor guns smells like exhaust.
> Girls hate these guns like they hate
> the monitor lizard. The dance is ruined
> even if everyone keeps the beat.
> Girls hate these guns like they hate
> the monitor lizard.
>
> The belly of an ox, Bil Rial,
> is the color of the skullcap of an Arab.
>
> The belly of an ox, Bil Rial,
> is the color of the skullcap of an Arab.
>
> His hide is like the sun itself:
> he is the ox of the moonlight.
> Whenever I find that ox, a bull comes along.
> It's true, Tuitui,[42] the ox is like moonlight.
> Whenever I find that one, a bull comes along.
>
> Tunyang, this gun, a rifle with two shots,
> made a man back down. Nyang Nyakong
> and Nyang Nyankaat, I make men anxious

42. This age-set was initiated during the early 1960s when the water hyacinth
(*tuitui,* Eichhornia crassipes) was multiplying at such a rate that it was seriously
clogging boat travel along the upper reaches of the Nile.

like those of the town "To be anxious,"
strutting with my rifle like an Egyptian.
The gun is a tawny thing like my ox
whose horns meet overhead.

(Svoboda 1985:19)

The images of guns and oxen were thus increasingly fused as complementary symbols of wealth, physical strength, and, hence, marriage worthiness. Moreover, as I discovered during the early 1980s, Nuer women were increasingly incorporating derogatory references to a man's gun in their personal songs as blatant attacks on his virility. I collected a number of cross-sex teasing songs (*ruathni*) among the western Leek Nuer in which wives humorously complained about the fact that husbands' guns were "plugged" or useless owing to a shameful scarcity of "ammunition." Hence, even in a region where guns were still comparatively rare, their significance as symbols of male potency and impotency was being avidly developed by both men and women through song.

Nevertheless, it was only among the eastern Nuer that guns were considered indispensable elements of marriage ceremonies themselves. In that region the prospective groom and his accompanying age-mates and relatives publicly announced their intentions to marry a particular girl by shooting off a gun at night over her home while delivering the first engagement cattle. Consequently, the eastern Jikany referred to the engagement ceremony as "having fired a gun off [over the head of a girl]." Similarly, an engaged girl was someone "whose head had been fired over" (*Caa widɛ duac mac*). Guns were also routinely sounded at the conclusion of bridewealth negotiations and as collective gestures of affirmation and support at major sacrificial invocations in the east during the 1980s. The piercing sound of a bullet's ring was said to help give the speaker's words "bitterness" or "bite" (*ruaidɛ bɛ kɛc*)—this being the predominant Nuer metaphor for "accurate," "potent," and "incisive" speech. Although individuals offering sacrificial invocations continued to clasp a spear, bullets were becoming an increasingly important element of collective sacrificial offerings that complemented rather than displaced the primacy of spears.

Nevertheless, I could not help but think that the elaborate ideological development of guns as symbols of masculine potency and collective strength among the eastern Jikany was in large part defensive. Men, it would seem, had latched onto guns as a fresh rallying point for their otherwise flagging sense of self-esteem vis-à-vis both their dependents and the wider world. For the fact remained that the firearms and ammunition to which they had access were profoundly inadequate to the protective challenges they faced. The increasingly destructive intentions and capacities of the "government of the right" meant that, regardless of their self-laudatory displays, Nuer men experienced "the age of the gun" as contributing to a decline in, rather than augmentation of, their abilities to fulfill their primary social role as the protectors of women and children and defenders of homestead and herd. No amount of ideological bravado could cover up the fact that the material gap separating their own military capabilities and those of successive state regimes had widened considerably between 1930 and 1990.

CONCLUSIONS

We have seen how "the age of the government" and "the age of the gun" were intimately entwined in Nuer experiences of some twenty-five years of colonial rule and two major civil wars. Despite concerted governmental attempts to suppress them, relationships of the bone (*cɔaa*) or feud (*tɛr*) remained fundamental determinants of evolving Nuer concepts of selfhood and sociality. Indeed, many of the administrative policies adopted by the British and extended later by the SPLA accentuated the centrality of homicide relative to more peaceful modes of interaction in Nuer understandings of their expanding social world. With respect to inter-Nuer community relations, for instance, the British radically altered the meaning of *maar* by rejecting the indigenous compensatory principle of a "wife for a life" in favor of artificially inflated and fixed bloodwealth rates. With bloodwealth compensation standardized at, roughly, twice the average rate of bridewealth offers, homicide became a stronger point of political cohesion than did marriage. Moreover, as recourse to guns became increasingly common in inter-Nuer community confrontations, collective bloodwealth liabilities were sometimes generalized to broader administrative and community units. This was especially the case in situations where gun warfare made the individual identification of the slayer impossible. Nuer men and women, as I explained, eventually responded to these pressures by redefining the concept of *dak maarä* (or the formal severing of kinship relations) as solely applicable to shared bridewealth claims. Nevertheless, there is little concrete evidence to suggest that the governmental enforcement of more "punitive" bloodwealth rates was effective in reducing the frequency of homicide among Nuer (cf. Howell's [1954:63] critical observations in this regard). With respect to expanding regional confrontations with the Sudanese state,

Nuer images of "the bone" proved eminently capable of encompassing wider political oppositions between north and south. In brief, the transgenerational strength of relationships of permanent hostility forged through homicide gradually overshadowed the scope of patrilineal, affinal, cognatic, and, indeed, national identities.

These trends were accompanied by a radical secularization of the procedures for feud settlement as well as by a significant contraction in Nuer assessments of the dangers of *nueer*. Prior to the imposition of British colonial rule, this pollution concept was, as one contemporary eastern Jikany man put it, "one of our 'chiefs' of the past." Backed by the transcendent powers of Divinity (*kuɔth nhial*), these concepts reinforced Nuer images of an overarching suprahuman moral force that revealed itself through specific instances of illness, misfortune, and death. In the context of inter-Nuer homicide, *nueer* was also bound up, as we have seen, with an ethical code of fighting, which precluded recourse to the most destructive weapons and tactics in interpersonal confrontations among kinsmen and neighbors.

Following the introduction of guns and the government, however, many of these ethical restrictions began to chafe. This was especially the case in those Nuer regions heavily devastated during the first civil-war era. As one contemporary eastern Gaajok man explained: "No one stood up during the war and said 'I killed someone'—death was everywhere!" Consequently, many Nuer, particularly easterners, seized upon changing circumstances arising from the widespread dissemination of guns, the declining prestige of earth priests, and the introduction of Christian doctrines as opportunities to reexamine the relevance and reality of pollution risks with respect to their experiences of death and destruction during the first and second civil wars. The relationship between the blood curse of the deceased and the ban on commensalism between the families of slayer and slain became increasingly frayed and loose, particularly in the east. The mediating powers of the earth priest were also increasingly eclipsed by secular government chiefs, who eventually succeeded in twisting the principal sacrificial rite of feud composition into a celebration of the unity and efficacy of "the people of the government" (*jikume*).

Some of these developments derived from the materiality of guns themselves. The former centrality of human blood flows in triggering off states of *nueer* was increasingly marginalized by the sheer "fire" force of guns. Both the elaborate analogy drawn between bullet victims and lightning victims in the west and the adoption of "the water of the cartridge shell" rite in the east represented major shifts away from metaphors of blood to those of temperature in people's attempts to comprehend the mysterious inner force and ambiguous impact of guns. In both cases Nuer experiences of increasing vulnerability to gun warfare were symbolically transformed into assertions of greater individual control over the social and spiritual consequences of homicide. Nevertheless, the fact that these conceptual developments occurred at a time when the frequency of violent deaths was rising and local cattle stocks were being depleted meant that people's abilities to ensure the "procreative immortality" of individuals slain in battle were being severely strained. Subsequent attempts by the SPLA leadership to dissociate the social, spiritual, and moral ramifications of homicides generated by inter-Nuer community feuding and fighting from the alleged "finality" and "individuality" of deaths occurring in the context of a "government war" would seem to add impetus to this trend toward a weakening of the procreative obligations binding communities of kin.

Because guns were collectively owned by families and because their exchange value was rapidly increasing, they shared to some extent in cattle's socially binding and self-augmentative capacities. In this sense, guns were perceived and incorporated by contemporary Nuer in strikingly different ways than was money. Even so, the penetration of guns into eastern Nuer networks of marriage exchange may be seen to have contributed indirectly to a contraction in the transgenerational scope of bridewealth claims—a point developed further in chapter 5. Whereas the "cattle of money"/"cattle of girls" distinction tended to divide the bridewealth contributions of the groom's extended family at the same time as it reinforced the collective cattle rights of the bride's side, the "cattle of the gun" did just the opposite—that is, they effectively conveyed the collective interests of the groom's extended family in the bride's procreative powers while simultaneously reducing the likelihood that the bride's immediate family would be able to satisfy fully the cattle claims of more distant relatives. Were the exchange value of guns ever to drop low enough to make widespread individual purchases possible, the "cattle of the gun" in bridewealth transfers would probably share the individualizing impact of "the cattle of money" on Nuer concepts of personhood and of sociality. However, as things stood in 1992, guns continued to reinforce the socially expanded sense of self identified with "the cattle of girls" and "the money of cattle."

Interestingly, there was some evidence to suggest that money might be developed in the future by some Nuer, at least, as a means of tempering the transgenerational risks of *nueer* in the context of homicide. This hypothesis is based on the arguments proposed by two eastern Gaajok Nuer in 1983, both of whom claimed that the *nueer*-backed prohibition on the return of bloodwealth cattle (or their offspring) to the byres of the slayer's extended family through marriage or other forms of exchange could be effectively avoided if the returning cattle were immediately sold in the market and other cattle purchased in their place. By passing through a brief monetary phase, the pollution state carried by these cattle, these Nuer claimed, could be ruptured because "money has no blood." I found this ideological assertion particularly intriguing because it suggested an implicit parallel between money (*yiou*) and the earth (*mun*) as terminal points at which cycles of blood and food begin afresh. Nevertheless, when I reported this claim to several other eastern Nuer, they vehemently rejected its veracity, arguing instead that the money obtained from such cattle would be equivalent to the "money of shit." Such money, in other words, would conduct the pollution characteristics of the original blood-wealth cattle into their replacements. Clearly, no consensus on this provocative issue had been reached.

The evolution of Nuer assessments of the risks of *nueer* was ultimately attributable to a conscious, creative, and collective effort on people's part to comprehend the meaning of violent deaths and the spiritual and social ramifications of homicide in a world where the powers of the government and of guns had increasingly displaced those of Divinity as the creators and destroyers of their social world. And all indications in 1992 were that Nuer confidence in the efficacy of divine supplication and in the powers of political compromise and persuasion would continue to decline in the context of a seemingly endless state of civil war.

4 Cattle over Blood
The Changing Symbolism of Gender, Marriage, and Filiation

Nuer sometimes characterized relations between the sexes as an ongoing tug-of-war. As one eastern Gaajok man jokingly remarked:

> Between men and women is an old braided grass rope. Women pull together on their end of the rope while shouting, "We have the right!"; men pull back on their end while shouting, "No, we have the right!" Though this rope is very old and frayed, it has not yet snapped.

Presumably this rope will never snap, no matter how vigorous the tug-of-war becomes. Nevertheless, indications are that the strain of this rope had increased considerably between the 1930s and 1990s. Nuer men, in particular, appeared to have suffered a rapid loss of ground vis-à-vis women ever since their most vital of social roles—that of the protectors of homestead and herd—was first challenged by government guns. Their actions and decisions regarding their dependents' welfare had likewise become increasingly subject to the scrutiny of government courts and the approval of distant administrative officials. Yet women, too, had experienced serious setbacks over the years. Whereas recurring wars and famines—together with expanding peace-time patterns of male labor migration—had frequently impelled them toward greater self-sufficiency in the production and acquisition of essential supplies (grain, milk, meat, medicine, and money) for their families, few women succeeded in establishing definitive control over these resources within marriage. Nor could they take such resources with them upon divorce: *Ciek me kɛaɣ jalɛ kɛ tetdɛ* ("A divorced woman [invariably] leaves [her husband's home] bare handed").

In the context of these rapidly changing circumstances, it is perhaps not surprising that my impressions of the "outward harmony" of Nuer family life differed sharply from those of Evans-Pritchard during the 1930s (cf. Evans-Pritchard 1950:32). Although Evans-Pritchard noted the existence of a "latent hostility" between the sexes, he apparently witnessed no concrete eruption of it.

Nuer have told me, though they do not like to speak of it, for it touches on death, that there is what we would call a latent hostility between husband and wife, and indeed between man and woman. They say that when a man has begotten several children by his wife he wants her to die, and may even pray for this to happen, for he does not want to die before her and another man to cohabit with her, rule in his home, use his cattle, and perhaps ill treat his children and rob them of their birthright. Men say also that women in their heart of hearts wish for their husbands' deaths. Whatever may be the significance that should be attached to these statements and to stories in which similar sentiments are expressed, family life among the Nuer is remarkably harmonious on the surface. I attribute this, in part at any rate, to the unchallenged authority of the husband in the home. (1951b:133)

Yet wherever I traveled in Nuerland during the early 1980s, it seemed I heard men grumbling about the difficulties they faced in attempting to influence the behavior of their daughters, sisters, and wives: *män ci wäŋkiɛn baɽ* (literally, "women's eyes have grown long"; that is, women have become farsighted in their search for lovers); *ɛn täämɛ nyier lökɛ ruac ciëŋ mani* ("girls today refuse to obey their parents and natal kin"); *kɔn wuuni, kuiyne ciaŋ mään* ("we men are ignorant of women's ways . . . we don't understand them"). Women, in contrast, often complained bitterly of unprovoked beatings, of abandonment, and of household resources seized without their consent (e.g., goats "borrowed" but not returned). Disputes involving the beating of wives, the elopement of daughters, the disappearance of both husbands and wives, as well as domestic conflicts over the allocation of resources were extremely common in Nuer courts at that time. Moreover, two marital surveys, documented in detail in the appendix, suggest that jural divorce rates among Nuer may have trebled between 1936 and 1983.

Interestingly, many Nuer of the early 1980s—particularly easterners—identified conflicts over women as the principal cause of violence among themselves. Whereas the cow was allegedly viewed as the critical focus of armed confrontations during the 1930s, many contemporary men and women argued, rather, that "it is girls [or women] who bring war" (*kɛ nyier kiɛ män kɛn tin nööŋkɛ koori*). After hearing scores of eastern Jikany men and women cite elopement, impregnation, adultery, and the "stealing" of wives as the most common causes of local fighting and feuding, I once ventured the question "But don't people fight over cattle?" "Cattle?" responded my middle-aged, eastern Gaajok informant. "Why should we fight over cattle? We Nuer are not cattle thieves!" The implication was, of course, that Nuer were "women thieves," and this, indeed, many young men proudly admitted to. Nevertheless, since cattle and women were so closely associated in daily life, and since all disputes over women were, in principle, resolvable through cattle, this "change" would seem to reside more in people's minds than in their actions toward one another. It represents, I think, a major shift of perspective, attributable in part to the declining significance of cattle in Nuer social life and in part to a perceived increase in the self-assertion and independence of many Nuer women.

This chapter traces these shifting relations of autonomy and dependence between Nuer men and women with particular reference to the transformative impact of government chiefs' courts on local patterns of courtship, marriage, and divorce. Divided into three parts, the chapter begins with a symbolic analysis of the relationship between blood and food as complementary sources of human vitality and human vulnerability. I argue that "acts of commensalism" (*nyuak*)—symbolized primarily by the sharing of food (*mieth/kuan*)—were a third powerful means by which Nuer men and women perpetually defined, created, and affirmed enduring bonds of *maar* ("kinship"). Building on themes developed in chapter 2, I then go on to explore how blood, cattle, and food were experienced and valued in different ways by Nuer men and women throughout the life cycle and across the generations. More specifically, I show how enduring social asymmetries based on distinctions of age, gender, and parentage were rooted in the "cattle over blood" value principle—that is, the principle whereby the social circulation of cattle was seen to take precedence over that of human blood in determining the significance, hierarchy, and scope of interpersonal relations among Nuer. And yet this principle was much less relevant to women's experiences of daily social life than it was to men's. Whereas men's experiences of personhood and sociality were closely bound up with the social circulation of "cattle" and "blood," those of women, I argue, were more closely associated with symbolic linkages between blood and food.

Following this paradigmatic sketch of the symbolic and material bases of gender relations across the generations, the chapter shifts to a discussion of historical discontinuities in Nuer concepts of gender, marriage, and filiation. In particular, I show how historical transformations in "Nuer customary law" brought about by the establishment of government chiefs' courts and the subsequent infiltration of various British legal concepts had significantly undermined the centrality of the "cattle over blood" value principle in the resolution of contemporary courtship, marriage, and divorce disputes.

THE SOCIAL CIRCULATION OF BLOOD
AND FOOD: GENERAL PRINCIPLES

In many ways, *riεm* and *mieth* were conceptualized by Nuer as alternate states of a single force: the force of human vitality in the world. Like blood, food was essential for human life. Its social circulation was thus intimately bound up with Nuer experiences of sexuality and procreation, illness and health, strength and weakness, aging and death—as well as with the life-generating and life-sustaining powers of Divinity. Fundamental distinctions of age, gender, descent, and community were likewise inseparable during the 1980s (as well the 1930s) from the daily gathering, giving, and sharing of *mieth. Mieth yiene naadh:* "Food binds people together." Ideally, I was told, "people who live together as one community hoe together, eat together, and go to war together"(*Jiciëŋ kεl, pfurkε kεl, miethkε kεl, ke wä kε koor kεl*). Though I sometimes heard individual Nuer complain that "the thinnest people are often the ones who hoe the hardest, while those who hardly hoe at all grow fat," there was, in fact, no socially acceptable way of excluding less productive community members from "the common bowl." Generosity in the giving and sharing of food among friends and relatives was a divinely sanctioned obligation from which no Nuer felt he or she could escape. Hunger was associated with the world of "the bush," not that of "human beings."[1] Consequently, members of any particular community tended to experience the same cycles of scarcity and abundance. To experience severe hunger implied, therefore, both personal failure and a state of social isolation. And for these reasons, famine victims were never buried but, rather, dragged off and abandoned in the bush (*baa kε yɔac dɔɔar*)—an ignominious death that, tragically, has befallen many thousands of Nuer men, women, and children since the renewal of civil war in 1983.

When times were better and food more plentiful, however, divinely sanctioned obligations to share cooked food extended as well to unaffiliated strangers in need of hospitality—to *jaal kuɔdh* (or "the guests of divinity"). During the early 1980s, Nuer men, women, and children alike took great pride in their regional reputation as being a magnanimous people, among whom strangers could wander freely without fear of either hunger or unprovoked attack.[2] People's attitudes toward sharing food was

1. The sharing of food was what distinguished most clearly the social world of human beings, the world of *ciëŋ*, from that of animals and the bush, *pan/dɔɔr*, in numerous Nuer folk stories and myths.
2. Hence, Nuer did not carry supplies of food or drink with them during their

thus quite different from their attitudes toward sharing cattle. "Sorghum," people stressed, "is never counted." Nor did people differentiate linguistically during the 1980s between locally produced grain and grain acquired through the marketplace. In other words, there was no grain equivalent for the "cattle of money"/"cattle of girls" distinction so central to contemporary definitions of cattle rights. Although basketsful of grain were commonly offered to needy community members with the expectation of a future repayment in kind, it was notoriously difficult to extract repayment from recalcitrant kinsmen and neighbors—even in situations where the original grain was purchased with cash. Government chiefs, moreover, adamantly refused to hear disputes over food. Whereas it was becoming increasingly common during the 1980s for people to sell surplus beer, milk, grain, and fish in local town centers (*rɛi rɛɛk,* literally, "within the fence"), the selling of cooked meats or porridge (*kuan*) was universally condemned in all contexts. This was so much the case that, in 1983, there was only one market stall in all of eastern Nuerland that sometimes doubled as a crude restaurant—and that was owned and run by a resident northern merchant. Otherwise, the only ready-to-eat food available in local market centers, besides the occasional package of bug-infested crackers, was *kɔaŋ in boor* ("white beer")—a thick, nourishing form of undistilled sorghum or maize beer that was normally brought to established "beer parlors" by women from the surrounding countryside.

I did, however, hear tales of one Nuer man named Puol, who brazenly transgressed this taboo as well as restrictions on the cooking of food by men by opening a small restaurant in the distant provincial capital of Malakal during the early 1980s. This event sent shock waves throughout the entire Nuer community. Although Puol's restaurant apparently proved popular with local Dinka, Shilluk, and northern Arab residents, no Nuer— or so people claimed—had ever deigned to eat there. Indeed, it was a common joke during the early 1980s for rural Nuer women in the west to respond to complaints of a stomach ache by a friend with the question, *Ci mith dhor Puol?* ("Have you eaten at Puol's place?").

Like blood, moreover, Nuer experiences of food sharing blended human aspirations for increased vitality with fears of inherent vulnerability. Although many Nuer men and women adamantly maintained that fear of death in battle was "pointless" (*thile luɔt*), because "a person with many

---

travels to visit distant kinsmen—except in situations where entire communities were forced to relocate on account of war or some other emergency. And I followed Nuer practices in this regard.

wounds may live while another with only a small wound may die," they openly admitted to fears of "poisoning" (*luëëŋ*) and of deaths caused by the legitimate wrath of Divinity as the ultimate guardian of human morality. Fear of death in battle was irrational, I was told, because the time of a person's death was determined by Divinity at the time of conception. "Life and death are both things of God."

This generally espoused conviction, however, was tempered by the idea that one's time of death could, nevertheless, be accelerated by intentional or unintentional "poisoning" and by the breach of divinely sanctioned interdictions. For example, a malicious "ghoul" (*rɔdh*) could threaten an entire community by purposely poisoning its water supply with bits of human flesh taken from an unearthed corpse. So, too, an embittered wife could attempt to poison a disregarding husband by secretly adding a bit of lizard's meat (*kirkir*) to his porridge. A casual meal in the home of distant relatives could likewise prove fatal if a person from whom one was separated by a relationship of "the bone" had previously eaten there. Indeed, a mother could unintentionally poison her suckling child if, unbeknownst to her, another suckling woman of the community had sexual intercourse prior to weaning her own child. Hence, bonds of food sharing, like those of blood, also conveyed the negative consequences of other people's actions. And for this reason, most Nuer men and women were, in my experience, extremely cautious about what, where, and with whom they ate.

More interesting still, Nuer regarded blood as generated from food and food from blood. The nutritional qualities of different types of food were, in fact, assessed in terms of their relative blood content. Some foods, such as *kɔaŋ in bǫǫr* (white beer) and *bɛɛl* (sorghum), were considered far richer in blood than were *kɔaŋ in caar* (black beer) and *maintap* (maize).[3] Milk (*caak*), of course, was the perfect food—the food that could support human life unassisted. Indeed, one need only trace the swollen veins running along the underbelly of a cow toward its udder to conclude, together with Nuer, that "milk is blood." Even agricultural products were considered blood-based in this sense. A man who had sweated day after day while tilling the soil could refer to his crops, once harvested, as "my blood" (*kɛ riɛmdä*). Or as I sometimes heard Nuer men and women express this idea, *Riŋ dial kɛ juaac* ("All flesh is grass").

3. Complex dietary evaluations were also extensively used in the curing of illness. Individuals suffering from malaria, for example, were strongly encouraged to increase their intake of "bitter" (*me kɛc*) and "sour" (*me wac*) foods while simultaneously restricting their consumption of red meat and fresh milk and other "sweet" (*me lim*) foods.

From this perspective, the perpetuation of human social life depended on the continual transformation of blood into food and food into blood. Nuer concepts of *maar* (kinship) were, in fact, founded on this idea: ideally, "relatives" (*nei ti maar*) celebrated their "oneness of blood" through the constant sharing of food. It was only after a child had both matured and begun to develop the unique blood bonds acquired at birth with counter-gifts of food that he or she achieved the status of a true relative among relatives.[4] "We eat our children," parents said quite bluntly. For example, I was told that a father would never announce, "I have a son," until such time as the boy had begun to fish and hunt, returning home with generous gifts of meat for his family. There was also a well-known proverb that ran *Rɔmaai lɛnyɛ gat me thil lɔac kɛ kuur kɛl* ("A string of fishing hooks is a hundred times better than a heartless son [that is, an 'irresponsible son' who is ignorant of his alimentary responsibilities toward his parents and kinsfolk]"). Daughters, in contrast, were said to be "eaten" at marriage, whereupon their families rejoiced in the abundant milk and meat their bridewealth cattle provided. Or as Nuer more commonly expressed this idea: *Nyal ɛ tɔc* ("A girl is a lush riverain grazing ground")—the idea being that "you [or, more directly, your herd] will find something to eat there."

Newly created affines, in contrast, normally avoided one another completely in matters of food and drink until some time after the birth of a child solidified the union. A man would not so much as request drinking water from his wife during the first months of marriage if he could possibly avoid it: "You don't want to get too close too soon or to expose your weaknesses too quickly." Whereas the social bond created through bridewealth cattle was potentially reversible, the birth of a living, healthy child was taken as indisputable evidence of a successful fusion of different types of blood. Consequently, restrictions on commensalism between the families concerned were thereafter gradually relaxed. Until then, there was no socially recognized blood bond between the families and hence nothing to be solidified and affirmed, as it were, through the sharing of food. But as long as a child of the union survived, a relationship of *maar* existed between the families of the husband and wife—even in situations where the marriage itself later faltered and ended in divorce and the return of bride-

---

4. The unique blood bonds acquired at birth thus remained, in a sense, latent throughout early childhood. "A small child is the child of everyone." All adults shared in the responsibility of ensuring that he or she was well nourished and well brought up. When destined for the bellies of young children, food could even be begged freely from strangers without fear or shame.

wealth cattle.[5] There was a well-known riddle that captured this gradual assimilation of bonds of affinity to those of *maar*. "What is forced to be kin but is not kin but later becomes kin?"—the answer being *wut kɛnɛ ciek* ("a man and a woman/wife").

The "blood brotherhood" forged between age-mates at initiation, *maar ricä*, also carried with it expectations of uninhibited commensalism. In fact, the blood men gained from the common bowl was explicitly identified with that later spent in acts of mutual defense and communal work projects. Indeed, one eastern Gaajok youth went so far as to suggest that food sharing in itself created a quasi-blood bond between people: "If I have a little food and I share it with you, that means we are brothers. Once we have eaten together, we should not marry each other's daughters nor kill one another." *Maar* thus combined an ideology of shared substance, shared vitality—shared food and blood—with expectations of exogamy and communal peace.

This ideology was complicated, however, by veiled associations between commensalism (*nyuak*) and aggression. The metaphor "eating is warring" was a highly pervasive one in Nuer social life. For instance, I was told that men ate more voraciously than women because "they need more blood" in order to carry out their primary social role as the protectors of homestead and herd. Boys were also taught from an early age never to let their hands drop to their sides while eating—the fear being that a boy who withdrew from his peers while eating would do the same someday on the battlefield. A young boy who thoughtlessly backed away from the communal bowl before finishing his meal was therefore likely to be hit by a concerned adult—normally, the boy's mother. The polite way for an adult to indicate satiety and thus to withdraw inoffensively from his eating companions was to say /*Ci tetdä luaŋ* ("My hand/arm is no longer capable [of raising the food to my mouth]"). "It is as if you were battling with the food," explained Gatluak, an eastern Gaajak youth: "you can [legitimately] grow tired." For a man—or a woman, for that matter—simply to announce *Cä riäŋ* ("I'm full") would arouse suspicions that he or she had already eaten secretly elsewhere. This expression was thus studiously avoided. Similarly, were a man to arrive at a cattle byre only to discover that his male friends had just finished eating, he could be greeted by his host with the words *Ɛ jin guạn baaŋä* ("You are lucky")—the implication being, as one westerner

5. For example, a man was prohibited from marrying a sister (or any close relative) of a deceased wife if the latter was survived by a child born to the union.

explained, "You are lucky because otherwise you would have been killed in the battle of eating. But you came after the battle: so we are the ones killed and you are spared."

Although these particular expressions and practices pit the community of eaters against the food, people recognized that the eaters were also, in a sense, pitted against one another. In fact, several Nuer mothers I knew admitted openly to provoking fights over food among their children in order to test their relative tenacity and courage in "battle." The task of raising fearless fighters, after all, fell first and foremost on Nuer mothers. Consider the following incident.

I arrived at dusk one evening with several eastern Gaajok friends at a distant homestead just as the women were preparing the evening's porridge (see plate 13).[6] Upon first seeing me, a small boy about the age of four was completely overwhelmed by fear. He, like so many other young children before him, ran off screaming to his mother's knees. She, however, responded curtly, publicly chiding him for his cowardice and pushing him away. Moments later, his half sister, who appeared to be just a bit younger than he, received a hefty spoonful of porridge from the boy's mother. Approaching his sister silently, the boy eyed the spoonful of porridge hungrily. The woman encouraged the girl to share her porridge. "Go ahead, give your brother some," she prodded, "I'll give you more." Reluctantly, the little girl held out her shell spoon. However, just as the boy drew close enough to get a taste, she grabbed it back and bit him hard on the hand, whereupon he immediately burst into tears. For a moment all that could be heard were the boy's piercing shrieks. His mother then flew into a rage, picking up a stick and threatening the boy with a beating if he did not cease his cowardly crying immediately. The boy, once again overwhelmed by fear, ran, of all places, straight into my lap. At that point, he clearly feared his mother's threats more than the pale-faced, wild-haired monster who had settled in quietly by the fire. "Look at that coward," the exasperated woman railed on: "I've had it with him! He's nothing but a cry baby—he can't even stand up to his younger sister!" She then threatened the boy with abandonment—a common motherly ploy. "If you like Nyarial so much, perhaps you would like to go with her to the place of the white people," she taunted. Not a word of reprimand was uttered about

6. This is an example of what was called "arriving with the good leg/foot" (*cop ke ciok me gɔaa*) as opposed to "the bad one," since food would soon be made available.

Plate 13.   A mother, surrounded by her young children, prepares the evening porridge.

his sister's unwillingness to share her food. On the contrary, the little girl's behavior was explicitly praised by the mother: "Unlike her brother, that girl really knows how to fight!"[7]

7. Incidents such as this always took me aback. For though I understood the value judgments underlying them, they nevertheless continued to grate against my cultural image of mothers as "peacekeepers." Whereas little boys who consistently showed themselves to be cowards in food spats with their peers were a source of profound embarrassment to their mothers, those who demonstrated a certain "strength of heart," willfulness, and independence swiftly won their mothers' respect and admiration—although this admiration was often expressed in veiled forms. For example, I once watched a young eastern Gaajok mother, armed with a large stick, attempt to shoo away a group of curious young children from the doorway of her house in which I and another woman visitor had entered. While retreating, the woman's five-year-old son turned suddenly, picked up a broken brick, and heaved it toward her. She did not react outwardly to her son's defiant gesture. There were no strong words uttered and no rush with the stick.

The fact that many mothers consciously sought to inculcate the virtues of courage, self-assertion, and independence in their children by provoking sibling rivalries through giving and withholding food must have carried over to some extent into adult experiences of commensalism as well. After all, there was a certain finality about food, especially that shared from a common bowl: It ends up either in your stomach or in mine.

Nuer metaphors of power and authority were likewise expressed in terms of people's willingness or unwillingness to share food. A community leader was, first and foremost, someone who "helps others to eat" by freely extending hospitality to all and sundry while simultaneously restricting his reliance on the hospitality of others. "A greedy man" (*raam me daar/cueer mithä*), in contrast, "soon finds himself sitting alone." Moreover, several men and women remarked that "the best way" to criticize the character or behavior of a close relative was to accuse him or her of avarice in matters of food. Whereas charges of, say, cowardice, debauchery, or thievery would inevitably reflect back upon the family's reputation as a whole, every adult man and woman was seen to be personally responsible for his or her eating habits.

Feelings of power and aggression, however, shaded rapidly into those of physical weakness and spiritual vulnerability in situations where acts of commensalism extended beyond the boundaries of *maar* or kinship. Al-

---

However, no sooner had she accomplished her mission and returned to her guests than she smiled proudly and said: "Did you see that? My little son threw a brick at me! His heart is truly strong." Although the boy was out of earshot when these words of praise were uttered, he undoubtedly noted the tacit approval of his aggressive act in his mother's reaction—or, rather, nonreaction—to it. On another occasion I was chatting with a group of western Leek mothers when one of them casually reported that her six-year-old son had, for no apparent reason, the day before given his older sister a sound beating that had resulted in some significant bruises. Without a trace of condemnation in her voice, she commented, "Ah, that boy really knows how to fight!" This is not to say that Nuer mothers invariably supported violent outbursts from their children: I often saw them run to break up fights between children when it appeared that someone might be seriously hurt or when an older child was bullying a much younger one. Yet there appeared to be considerable consensus among Nuer mothers and fathers alike that a boy who was permitted to explore freely the negative and positive thrusts of his violent impulses would soon "find his head" and thus develop into a more stable, cool-tongued, and even-tempered adult. As boys grew older, it was also expected that they would demonstrate greater independence and stubbornness in relation to their fathers by refusing to carry out certain orders or perform certain tasks. Such passive resistance was regarded as an important sign of a boy's readiness for initiation. Acts of physical defiance—of the brick-heaving variety—were totally unacceptable, however, in a boy's interactions with his father and father's age-mates.

though there was nothing shameful about eating or drinking in the company of relatives, to be caught in the act of satisfying one's hunger or thirst before a stranger was everyone's nightmare. For to do so was to admit lack of self-control and physical dependence in a situation requiring firm displays of outward dignity and inner strength.[8] Beidelman captured the central logic of these concepts and prohibitions quite well when he wrote:

> The principle of kinship (commensality and prohibitions on sexuality) gains force because of its medial component, affinity (problematic commensality and licit sexuality), that principle allowing kin to generate more kin by going beyond themselves to incorporate strangers. Here is the counterpoint between natal kin, affines, and strangers played out negatively through feud, positively through marriage and expressed commensally. (Beidelman 1981:146)

What remains to be seen, then, is how these ongoing cycles of blood and food in Nuer social life cross-cut the symbolic linkages between blood and cattle (explored in chapter 2) in Nuer interpretations and experiences of gender relations.

BLOOD, CATTLE, AND FOOD: A PARADIGM OF GENDER RELATIONS

Cattle over Blood: A Reconsideration of the Cattle/Human Equation

We have seen how contemporary Nuer men and women continued to use cattle exchange and sacrifice in order to empower human blood bonds, despite the ever-increasing importance of money in their daily lives. Cattle, I argued in chapter 2, remained the dominant medium through which people rendered the mysterious powers of human blood both socially significant and stable. The perpetual superimposition of "cattle flows" over "human blood flows" continued to reinforce the dominant social position of senior, cattle-wealthy men at the same time as it reduced possibilities of autonomy for women and other household members. The power and authority of men over women and of senior men over junior men thus depended in large part on the perceived efficacy of cattle exchange and sacrifice in indirectly controlling specific states and passages of human blood, as this was assessed and acknowledged by Nuer communities as a whole. As Peter Gatkuoth Gual, a

---

8. Girls and women had to compensate for their role as the food providers by showing special sensitivity, as it were, to the relative weakness of men in this regard. For example, they, too, would feel shame if they accidentally discovered an older man eating.

highly respected Lou Nuer, summed up this continuing dependence of men on the mediating role of cattle in 1983:

> Without the blood of the cow, there would be nothing moving in Nuer society. It is the blood of the cow [shed in sacrifice] that brings in the good and takes away the evil. If I were alone without the cow, I could not build new relationships. What this means is that, without the cow, I would not be worth much.

Indeed, it would seem to be in the long-term interests of men in general—and cattle-wealthy elders in particular—to play down the existence of social asymmetries generated by the fact that "human values" could never be fully translated into "cattle values." It would also seem advantageous for them to try to tip the ideological balance of this equation, so to speak, in the opposite direction—that is, in favor of cattle, rather than human blood, as the dominant force in the creation, specification, and affirmation of enduring bonds of *maar*. For hanging in the relative balance of this equation were a multitude of crucial social issues such as: (1) whether or not a father (read: pater) would be able to secure the long-term support and loyalty of his children over and against their mother's (or genitor's) kinsmen; (2) whether or not the older generation would succeed in curbing and manipulating the sexual desires of the younger so as to further its own moral, political, and economic objectives through the latter's marriages; and (3) whether or not senior men would be able to resolve specific feuds peacefully and permanently through bloodwealth payments, despite passionate calls for blood vengeance from the youth. Furthermore, to the extent that various sacrifices were acknowledged, albeit in retrospect, as having successfully elicited divine support in the manipulation of particular states and passages of human blood, the dominance of cattle over blood would seem to stand confirmed.

As for relations among men, the preeminence of cattle exchange and sacrifice over the social circulation of human blood appeared scarcely challengeable. Certainly every man realized at an early age that, in matters of procreation at least, cattle transfers definitely took precedence over human blood flows in the tracing of agnatic descent. Physical paternity was not a necessary condition of fatherhood as socially defined: Cattle transfers alone assured a man heirs who would carry on his name and line. Without cattle, moreover, a man was effectively barred from participating in the two most exclusive and honorable of masculine activities: the negotiation of political alliances through cattle exchange and the supplication of divinity through cattle sacrifice. In this light, the status of "manhood" itself might be seen as an ancestral "gift" passed down from generation to generation together with communal rights in the familial herd.

The notion that human blood states are effectively and collectively manipulable through cattle exchange and sacrifice was experientially much weaker, however, for generations of Nuer women. This was not only because women were normally barred from initiating collective attempts at such manipulation but also because their very biology forced them into a relationship with blood designated by Nuer as polluting. A menstruating woman was prohibited from drinking a cow's milk lest the cow become barren (*bɛ bot*)—though she could continue to milk cows for others as well as consume goats' milk herself. The mere act of stepping over (*baal*) a cow's tethering cord during menstruation was thought to endanger the cow's health (*dee nuer*).[9] Similarly, a woman was expected to refrain from sexual intercourse during the height of her menstrual flow for fear that some of her blood might penetrate her mate's penis and thereby increase his susceptibility to illness, misfortune, and death—particularly death in battle.

Nevertheless, women did not need access to cattle in order to realize their procreative potential. Bonds of maternity, unlike those of paternity, were forged solely through a direct, substantive contribution of blood to the child—whether in the form of congealed uterine blood, breastmilk, or both. Hence, a foster mother who merely cared for another's child (without at some point actually breastfeeding it) established no permanent bond of *maar* with the child. There simply was no feminine equivalent in Nuer culture for the blood/cattle split so crucial in the determination of descent lines among men.

Indeed, this "blood"/"cattle" contrast in the ways women and men procreate was in fact the crux of gender distinctions in Nuer culture. Just as a man without cattle was not fully a man in Nuer eyes, so, too, a woman without children was not fully a woman. The comprehensive term for "woman/wife" in the Nuer language—*ciek* (pl., *män*)—was conferred only on those women, whether married or not, who had experienced childbirth. *Ciek* could also be used as a verb to describe the full-fledged maturation of sorghum heads and other agricultural crops just prior to harvest. It conveyed an image of the bursting forth of inner seeds—that is, of a fully realized state of fruition. This metaphorical linkage between feminine fertility and agricultural maturation was also apparent in the term used for

9. For similar reasons, women, whether menstruating or not, were extremely careful to avoid stepping over a reclining man.

an unmarried mother and a divorcee: *ciek mi kɛaɣ*. *Kɛaɣ* takes its imagery, I was told, from a small enclosed gourd (*kɛak*) which, when rattled, revealed the presence of inner seeds—the idea being, as one young woman explained, that "the woman's seeds are there, all she lacks is a husband (*cou*)." Barrenness, though common, was attributed to some moral breach or spiritual disturbance that could be rectified through proper divination and sacrifice. Should such curative operations fail to restore the woman's fertility, people would begin to suspect that the woman's blood was somehow incompatible with that of her husband or lover—a situation often resolved during the 1980s, as it was during the 1930s, by a change of mates. The basic assumption remained, however, that all "women with blood" were by their very nature capable of conceiving and bearing children. The strength of this conviction was also apparent in Nuer beliefs regarding childbirth. Adultery (*dhöm*) or some other unconfessed misdeed was thought to prolong labor and cause other birthing difficulties. Women in the throes of childbirth were thus urged by female attendants to reveal any hidden transgressions in the hope of minimizing the pain of delivery.[10] But it was always an external disturbance that was seen to impede what was otherwise considered to be the innate capacity of every menstruating woman.

Because fertility, not cattle wealth, was the principal route to self-fulfillment, security, and independence for Nuer women, the cattle-over-blood ideology appeared more ambiguous and problematic when viewed in light of their everyday experiences and life-orientations. The social powers of women, as we shall see, were bound up more with cultural interpretations of the relationship between blood and food than with that between blood and cattle. Before pursuing this line of thought, however, I should first clarify the sociological ramifications of what I am suggesting here to be an essentially "viricentric" representation of the relationship between cattle and blood.

Cattle Links: The Father-Child Relation

Nowhere was the preeminence of cattle flows over human blood flows more obvious or crucial to men's lives than with respect to the "genitor"/"pater" distinction. The significance of a man's substantive contribution to his child was effectively muted by this dichotomy: As far as men were concerned,

---

10. This was also, I was told, one of the reasons women usually preferred to give birth to their first and, if possible, second child at their natal homes (where such confessions were secrets that could be swiftly buried).

cattle—not blood (whether conceived of in terms of semen or its uterine counterpart)—were the true source of heirs. Although the contribution of semen from a child's genitor (when distinct from that child's pater) was always publicly acknowledged through the extension of incest prohibitions and bridewealth claims,[11] the thrust of the genitor/pater distinction was to undercut the significance of semen (or male blood flows) in the creation of enduring bonds of *maar*. A boy born of an adulterous union, though vulnerable to occasional insult, could nevertheless hold his own at his pater's homestead and could even come to rule over his father's biological children when he matured.

The potential "benefits" of this method of tracing agnatic descent for men in general, and cattle-wealthy men in particular, were many. By obscuring the importance of semen in tracing patrilineal descent, men were able not only to extend their procreative ambitions beyond the grave but also to diminish their sense of personal dependence on the procreative powers of women. Since the payment of bridewealth was considered to "guarantee" the husband a minimum of two children, he could potentially divorce any wife who failed to produce them. Moreover, in some parts of contemporary western Nuerland, it was allegedly possible for a man to divorce a wife who had failed to produce a son—even in situations where she had already given birth to two, three, or even four daughters. Consequently, the personal vulnerability married men felt with respect to problems of conception and birth was greatly reduced. Occurrences of infant mortality simply did not weigh as heavily upon Nuer husbands as upon their wives because the former had the option of transcending them more easily through divorce and remarriage. In contrast, women who menstruated but failed to conceive and those whose children died before reaching adult life were doubly unfortunate: Not only was their status as full-fledged adults, as "women/wives," seriously undermined by such events, but so, too, were their chances of achieving positions of security and stability in their husbands' homes. During the early 1980s, they often became wanderers of land and of spirit—being the first women to drift into town, the first women to convert to Christianity.

There was, for instance, a young woman in eastern Nuerland whose third and only surviving child I watched die slowly after he had apparently

11. The genitor of a child—when distinct from that child's pater—had the right to claim one cow, the "cow of loins" (*yaŋ letä*), upon the child's marriage, if a girl, or, alternately, upon the child's maturity or initiation, if a boy. Failure to give over this cow endangered the child's health and fertility.

swallowed a clump of tobacco that had fallen from someone's pipe. Within moments, the boy of seven months was in convulsions. His mother immediately rushed him to a female *tiet* or diviner; a special sacrifice was recommended and performed. Yet the child continued to sicken. His mother later confessed to me in an extreme state of despair, "If this child dies as well, there will be nothing left for me to do but go wandering in the bush" (Mi wee wä liu, thilɛ me bä lel, bä wä jal ni dɔar). Two days later the child was buried, and shortly thereafter the young woman left her husband's home for her natal homestead in order to do, she said, she knew not what. Though her husband undoubtedly suffered from this tragedy as well, I had little reason to believe that it prompted in him the soul-searching questions and aching self-doubts that it did in his wife. Certainly his life and dreams were less shattered by it: He had other wives and other children, as well as the hope of acquiring more of both through cattle exchange.

In thus diminishing men's sense of personal dependence upon the procreative powers of women, cattle also served to reinforce alliances among men, especially fellow agnates. Just as cattle stood firmly between a man and his desires to achieve personal immortality through the birth of progeny (preferably sons), so, too, did all those men whose cooperation and consent were necessary for the collection and release of sufficient cattle for him to marry. In Nuerland, these male bonds of mutual dependence were strongly biased in favor of agnates—it being generally agreed that paternal half brothers, as distinct from maternal half brothers, alone shared rights in cattle. Hence, unlike the procreative powers of women, those of men were neither innate nor exclusive but, rather, collective. As far as men were concerned, "marriage," as one senior Gaajok man explained, was "really a matter of names"—that is, a matter of "keeping alive" through progeny the names of all males born into a particular family.

The procreative prospects of men were thus skewed not only in favor of the cattle-rich but also in favor of senior men as well as in favor of the deceased. Younger men's willingness to give priority to the procreative ambitions of their genealogical seniors was, of course, bound up with their sense of indebtedness for cattle received from them as well as with their faith in their own juniors' willingness to perform the same procreative service for them should it become necessary.[12] In brief, the overwhelming importance of age and generation in determining relations of power and

---

12. Failure to carry out this divinely sanctioned obligation invited the wrath of the dead man's spirit.

authority among men was rooted firmly in the cattle-over-blood principle of patrilineal descent.

A man's fundamental need for a woman as mother of his children was thus transformed via cattle exchange into a broadened and deepened dependence on other men. Just how far these male bonds of dependence extended varied, of course, with such factors as the age, wealth, and birth order of the man concerned, the number of kinsmen to whom he could legitimately appeal for cattle contributions, the number of bridewealth cattle demanded, and the period over which such payments were expected to extend. Furthermore, these factors were progressively linked, as we have seen, to emerging opportunities for the individual acquisition of cattle and to the complex system of categories of cattle and monetary wealth described earlier.

Moreover, it is important to realize that in this system young men as well as girls could sometimes be coerced into marrying against their wills. For instance, I knew a man in western Nuerland whose father eventually succeeded in curtailing his son's lengthening stays in far-off Khartoum by selecting and marrying a wife in his son's name without consulting him. Although the young man had rejected earlier requests by his father to marry and settle down in his home community, he returned one dry season only to discover that a wife was awaiting him. "What else could I do?" the young man later explained: "I couldn't just reject the girl; I now had a wife to take care of—and a man with a young wife cannot be running back and forth to Khartoum."

Since cattle and blood were alternate means of acquiring children, gender inversions were sometimes possible. Not only was it sometimes possible for barren women to become social men and to marry wives in their own right, but, in principle, any mature woman who died without having given birth to a child could be turned into a man and married to a "ghost wife" posthumously. If such a woman were married at the time of her death, she was sometimes categorized by western Nuer as a *col wic*—in which case the obligation to contribute bridewealth cattle for her "ghost marriage" fell upon her husband's family as well as upon her natal kinsmen.[13]

---

13. For a more general discussion of this spiritual category, see Evans-Pritchard (1949b, 1956). Although I have reported this western Nuer practice as it was explained to me, I am in doubt as to how the cattle rights of the relatives of the "ghost wife" married to the female *col wic* would be reconciled with those of the deceased woman herself with respect to any daughters born to the union. To the best of my knowledge, this practice was not observed by the eastern Jikany Nuer.

And just as a barren woman sometimes acquired heirs through cattle exchange, so too an impoverished genitor sometimes succeeded in reproducing posthumously by having a natural son marry a "ghost wife" in his name.

I also uncovered a fascinating note in the archives that suggested that sperm itself could sometimes be transformed directly into bridewealth cattle:

> Information was received of a new way by which the young cattleless men of Lou [Nuer] can make a living, namely by going into stud in Murle country. Murle men have difficulty in begetting children [due in part to widespread venereal diseases among them] and the Lou are notably proficient in this respect. Therefore elderly Murle widows who have not borne children and have become disillusioned as to the progress of their own menfolk, entice the Lou across to oblige. A "ghost" marriage is performed and the Lou man is given a young Murle girl by whom to raise children in the name of the childless widow (similar to Nuer "ghost" marriage). As though this was not enough, the Lou man receives five cattle at the time the agreement is made and another ten after the birth of the third child, after which he is free to return to Nuerland plus his cattle. (Annual Report, Lou Nuer District, 1954/55, WND 57.A.3)

By the 1980s relations between the Murle and the Lou Nuer were marred by an increasingly violent series of drought-induced raids and counterraids, and hence there was little opportunity for peaceful exchanges of this sort to occur. Nevertheless, this archival note underscores the fact that blood and cattle were potentially interchangeable means of acquiring heirs for both men and women.[14]

Blood-Links: The Mother-Child Relation

More important for our purposes, the entire nexus of concepts and practices associated with the predominance of cattle over blood in tracing patrilineal

---

14. Among the contemporary western Nuer, a married woman had the right to receive a special "cow of divinity" from her natal family after she had successfully given birth to three or four children at her husband's home. This cow and its calves became her personal property—or, rather, her personal divinity's property—and as such were outside her husband's control. According to Nuer, everyone receives a personal divinity at birth that subsequently demonstrates its relative strength or weakness by protecting or impeding, sustaining or undermining, that person's life and objectives. The personal divinity of a mother of many children has clearly demonstrated its support and thus deserves to share in the woman's success as well. I do not know whether this tradition existed among the contemporary eastern Jikany. However, its existence in the west reveals yet again how thoroughly entwined people's experience of "blood" and "cattle" were.

descent accentuated the unique strength of the blood connections binding mother and child at the same time it undercut the social significance of a man's substantive contribution to his child. Nuer were not of the opinion that a steady supply of sperm was necessary for the healthy growth of the fetus. Consequently, a man considered it his right to suspend sexual relations with his wife at any point he wished following conception. Although some men continued to have sexual relations with their wives during early pregnancy, most men abstained after about month five or six. Men also distanced themselves from the delivery process, which they considered to be repugnant and polluting and attended only in emergencies requiring immediate sacrificial or medical intervention. Indeed, a father would not so much as hold his newborn child for a period of a month or two after birth. This fatherly avoidance, men insisted, was not grounded in pollution fears per se—though it is interesting to note that it was normally relaxed about the time the child ceased to be called blood. Rather, several men confessed that they would feel awkward holding such a small child because they realized that they had nothing of significance to offer "since all the child wants is the breast." The weaning taboo, which prohibited sexual contact with lactating women, further distanced the father from both mother and newborn child. During the early 1980s, this period normally extended for some fourteen to twenty-four months, with sickly children sometimes being nursed considerably longer.[15] A violation of this taboo, called *thiaŋ*, was thought to endanger the health not only of the infant concerned but of all other suckling children of the community (cf. Evans-Pritchard 1956:188; Howell 1954:177).

These prohibitions and patterns of avoidance did more than justify men's polygynous urges: They also promoted the creation of strong bonds of mutual affection and identification between mother and child. A lactating mother was not considered polluting by men but, rather, inviolate. It was as though the intimacy of the nursing period depended on an exclusivity of relations that could not be disturbed. And for this reason it was often a delicate matter when the husband began to suggest, directly or indirectly, that his wife consider weaning their child. In the case of several younger wives I knew, this transitional period had the air of a second courtship—and one that was not necessarily any less anxiety provoking

15. Whereas in generations past children were rarely weaned before they could speak, it became increasingly common during the 1980s for parents to resume sexual relations after the child was walking well—a reduction of approximately one year.

than the first. For example, Nyatut, the youngest wife of my western Nuer host, Kelual Nyinyar Rik, shared with me a horrifying nightmare she had shortly after her husband first proposed weaning their first child, who at that point had just started to walk. Disturbed by what she felt to be the prematurity of this suggestion, Nyatut dreamed that her daughter, Nyakiir, had fallen into a deep pit in the earth. Screaming and sobbing, Nyatut ran to her rescue—but though she strained and strained, she could not reach her. Then, suddenly, her husband appeared before her in her dream. "What's all this commotion about?" he chided. Reaching down into the pit, he pulled out the child and presented her to Nyatut, saying: "Here's your daughter, she hasn't died—take her." Several months later, the child was weaned.

In many ways, the strong bonds of identification uniting mother and child were comparable to those uniting men and cattle[16]—or, more specifically, men and oxen (cf. Beidelman 1966). For a woman, her child was the living symbol of an inner state of self-realization. Her experience of full femininity was inseparable from her experience of the child itself. So, too, a man's self-image was intimately linked with the ox he received from his father upon initiation. It, too, was a tangible symbol of his masculinity, a direct extension of his social personality (Evans-Pritchard 1956:50–55).[17]

This is not to say that the physical blood tie uniting genitors and their offspring carried no social importance whatsoever: Everyone expected children to resemble (*cät*) their genitors in both features and character. This was so much the case that, in questionable cases of adultery involving pregnancy, members of the local community often waited until the child in question was born and its features noted before taking sides with either husband or wife. Yet when one considers the sheer volume, requisite nature, and duration of the blood flow binding mother and child—a flow that gained momentum during pregnancy as well as throughout lactation—in light of the fact that no blood whatsoever need pass between pater and child, it would certainly seem that the blood of motherhood was in some sense primary.[18] I found that whenever people compared the presumed

16. This idea was originally stimulated by Paul Riesman's study of the Fulani (1977).

17. Furthermore, whereas women were responsible for the procreation of children, men were responsible for the procreation of cattle. Men assisted cows in labor and would even reach into the cow's womb to turn the calf if necessary—an act they considered too defiling to perform on human beings.

18. Significantly, Evans-Pritchard states, "A man is said to respect his as yet

closeness of maternal kin with the thinly veiled rivalry characteristic of relations between paternal half kinsmen, this metaphor of the "unity of blood" surfaced. Full siblings were said to be of "one mother," "one breast," or "one blood," whereas no blood connection could be assumed between paternal half siblings.[19] Indeed, as Evans-Pritchard remarked: "In a sense all kinship is through the mother, even kinship with the father and hence with the paternal kin" (1951b:156).

In many ways these dual blood/milk bonds of motherhood were the strongest in all of Nuer social life (see plate 14). Whereas a rupture of patrilineal relations was possible through a formal severing of cattle obligations and rights (a process known as *dak maarä*), descent connections through women were considered unbreakable. For no matter how strained they might become on an interpersonal level, a blood-based bond of *maar* continued to exist.

The stability and cohesion of Nuer families, in fact, depended far more upon these maternal connections than, say, upon relations between husband and wife. Recurring frictions between paternal half brothers, the cross-pull of loyalties between maternal and paternal kin, and the proverbial divisiveness of co-wives (*nyak*, literally, "rivals") all stemmed directly from the inherent strength of these mother/child bonds of *maar*. Indeed, the very word for "relationship" or "kinship" in Nuer (*maar*) appears to be identical to that for "my mother" (*maar*).[20]

Unfettered by the rigid age hierarchy governing interpersonal relations among men, Nuer mothers were often able to forge more personal, egalitarian, and openly communicative ties with their children. Whereas a father's love was said to be contingent upon the child's obedience and conformity to certain moral standards, that of the mother was presumed more constant and less judgmental. In the words of Lam, a middle-aged Gaajok man:

---

unconceived children by abstaining from congress with his wife while she is menstruating" (1956:179).

19. I was told, for instance, that it would be unwise for a man to go lion hunting with his paternal half brothers lest he be abruptly abandoned to an attacking beast. Full brothers, in contrast, were said to make excellent lion-hunting companions since their mutual loyalties would be total and beyond question.

20. This linguistic linkage, first noted by Evans-Pritchard (1951b:156), remains hypothetical. The late Peter Gatkuoth Gual argued that that there was no conscious connection between these two ideas in people's minds. In his opinion, the words were mere homonyms.

Plate 14.   Despite a dominant patrilineal ideology, the dual blood/milk ties a mother creates with her children are the strongest social bonds of all. Notice the vicarious sucking of the child's older sister.

> A mother has the right to defend her child no matter what. Even if the child is a thief, she has the right to defend him in court. A father would never do such a thing. [And for this reason,] a father will quarrel with his wife.

Unlike fathers, moreover, mothers were not directly responsible for the extraction of material benefits from their children. This fact was first impressed upon me by a middle-aged, western Leek Nuer man, who described how profoundly disappointed a father would feel were he to learn that one of his sons, having caught a single fish, proceeded to grill and eat it with his friends in the bush instead of presenting it, as he should, to his father or one of his father's age-mates. When I then asked whether the mother would not be disturbed by her son's action as well, Gatmarial looked perplexed and said, "What has she got to do with it?" Similarly, mothers were not held directly responsible for securing bridewealth cattle for their daughters. Although a mother stood to gain cattle upon her daughter's marriage, she could also freely side with her daughter against her husband in situations where the man her daughter loved had fewer bridewealth cattle than were normally demanded. For whatever the cattle outcomes of her children's marriages, a mother knew that the strong mutual bonds of affection she cultivated with her daughters and sons were the best assurance that she would be loved and cared for in her old age.

Due to the presumed intimacy of these maternal bonds, a father often sought to influence his children through their mother. Marriage proposals were usually relayed through her, as were her daughters' replies. Moreover, most men firmly believed that their wives were privy to their children's most intimate secrets. For example, it was often assumed that a mother knew of an unmarried daughter's pregnancy or a son's elopement plans long before these became known to their father and the rest of the community. Yet, due to the intense love a mother bore for her child, she rarely—or so men claimed—alerted her husband to these impending crises voluntarily. A mother would sometimes beat her daughter upon first discovering her pregnant and might even attempt to deny her milk if she strongly disapproved of her daughter's choice of a mate. After this initial outburst of anger, however, mother and daughter were usually reconciled in a pact of silence. Hence, when the father eventually discovered the truth for himself, he was likely to vent his rage by beating both mother and daughter. Should the daughter succeed in eloping before this happened, the father's fury usually descended full force upon the mother.

The profound vulnerability men felt vis-à-vis these often powerful maternal alliances was especially obvious in parts of contemporary eastern Nuerland, where the older generation was becoming increasingly frustrated in its attempts to oversee the younger generation's selections of mates. In fact, local chiefs, overwhelmed by irate fathers anxiously seeking to discover the whereabouts of "stolen" daughters or the names of their impregnators, had adopted a new tactic in the hope of swiftly resolving such mysteries: Arrest the mother.[21] This procedure, which was rapidly becoming standard during the 1980s in cases of elopement in that region, was usually justified by presiding court officials and other attending men on one of two grounds: Either it was assumed that the mother was willfully withholding information from the court—"Even if she doesn't know where her daughter is, she should know with whom"—and thus deserved some form of public admonishment; or it was hoped that news of the mother's plight would rapidly reach the wayward couple, forcing them to return or, at least, announce their whereabouts so as to permit the mother's release. Sometimes the mother of the young man who staged the elopement, when known, was arrested as well in an effort to coax the couple's return.[22] Yet

21. This "strategy" was not practiced in the west.
22. When the identity of the man was known, the courts—in both eastern and

in my experience this strategy—however rationalized—normally proved ineffective. In the four incidents of arrest I followed among the eastern Gaajok, the mothers were all released after spending a few days in "jail," despite the fact that the eloped couples in question had yet to be located. Often the mother's arrest was little more than symbolic, since most of these women were permitted to continue their normal activities at home during the daytime so long as they reported back to the chief's compound or to the local police station—to "jail"—each night. Yet even so, the very fact that eastern Nuer court officials so often resorted to this tactic, despite its apparent inefficacy, is indicative, I think, of the tremendous frustrations men felt when attempting to manipulate these maternal bonds of affection or when attempting to control women more generally. As one Gaajok chief observed, "The real problem begins when mother and child unite in court, for then the father's powers plummet earthward."

A certain amount of conflict between husband and wife over their children's actions was perhaps inevitable in older marriages, if for no other reason than the long-term interests of husband and wife were so clearly opposed. Whereas men strove to achieve autonomy through the creation and maintenance of a personal following of dependents, women normally gained independence by helping others (primarily their own children) become independent themselves. There was thus a point in the evolution of many marriages in which the balance of power between the spouses began to shift rapidly in favor of the wife. If the man had no younger wives, he felt this power shift all the more intensely—hence the "latent hostility" between husbands and wives in later marriage noted by Evans-Pritchard. For an elderly man who had lost control over his sons through the dispersal of the familial herd, old age was often a time of bitterness and loneliness. An elderly mother, in contrast, often experienced old age as bringing with it a marked rise in status. Freed from the defiling rhythms of her reproductive processes, she could begin to take on "masculine" tasks. She could wield a digging stick when planting. She could also participate in sacrificial invocations, in which case the fighting spear normally clutched at such times by men was replaced by a grass reed. And once a son was initiated or a daughter married, she could approach her husband and other men with far greater equanimity—and, by the time she became a grandmother, she

---

western Nuerland—would also seize a significant number of cattle from the young man's family in order to forestall the possibility of violence erupting between the families concerned. The family of the eloped girl normally regarded her lover's actions as a direct insult to them.

could say just about anything she liked to anyone she wished without fear of chastisement.

Because maternal bonds were neither created nor ruptured with cattle, the cattle-over-blood ideology was especially weak and problematic when it came to male attempts at influencing these feminine linkages. Although the passage of bridewealth at marriage established a man's rights to his wife's procreative powers to the exclusion of other men, it by no means guaranteed him control over the strong mother/child bonds of blood forged at birth. Presumably, the husband could exercise a certain degree of control over these mother/child bonds during early marriage by wielding threats of divorce. For in essence he could threaten to disrupt his wife's relations with her own children and hence undermine her long-term ambitions of achieving greater independence and security through them. Whereas men considered a wife who had not yet borne her husband a child as potentially "stealable," a young mother was usually far more reluctant to run off with a lover and leave her child in the care of others. Consequently, divorce threats were more likely to have an impact on a woman's behavior after the birth of a child. There was a common expression women used to convey their commitment to their husbands through the child: /*Caa dee bany jɔk burä*—"I couldn't go away leaving him/her abandoned behind the mud cooking screen." For it was generally assumed that the abandoned child would be subtly, if not blatantly, spurned and ignored by any *ciek guan*, or stepmother. The potential sting of this verbal whip, however, was not long enduring: Each new child the woman brought forth solidified her position within her husband's home. By the time a son was initiated or a daughter married, she could freely talk back to, swear at, or even beat her husband without fear of divorce.[23] One witty man explained the situation thus: "By that time, the wife will have her own house, her own fields, and her own cattle—there is nothing more she needs from her husband. She becomes like a sister to him . . . or more like a brother."

It was thus children, not bridewealth cattle, that bound a woman to her husband's home. One eastern Gaajok woman, upon hearing that in the United States children often remained with the mother upon divorce, immediately interjected, "Oh, we Nuer thought of that [possibility] long ago but rejected the idea because, if the children were to remain with the

---

23. Among contemporary western Nuer, older wives were often jokingly categorized by their husbands as *gatgualen* ("son of my paternal uncle"). For like paternal cousins, an elderly couple could hurl elaborate insults at each other without threatening their relationship itself: *dekɛ rɔ lɛɛŋ*.

mother, all wives would leave their husbands—and so, with us, it's always father who keeps them." If the woman's children were still quite young at the time of the divorce, she could keep them with her for a period. But her ex-husband retained the right to reclaim his children at any time, provided that he had retained paternity rights in them through the payment of a cattle fee (ruɔk) of between four and six head of cattle to his ex-wife's family.

Yet even when mother and child were forcefully separated through divorce, the strength and existence of their kinship connection were never called into question. Her brothers retained rights to a portion of the bride-wealth cattle of any daughter born during her marriage. Her sons would also seek their maternal uncles' assistance when collecting cattle for their own marriages. Furthermore, the divorced mother herself had the right to return to her ex-husband's homestead and live together with her children once they matured. At most, then, divorce drove a temporary wedge between mother and child—and painful as this might be, a blood-based relationship of *maar* continued to exist between them as well as between the extended families of ex-husband and wife. For an older woman who had experienced numerous procreative difficulties or infant deaths, this wedge could indeed usher in an extended period of deprivation and hardship. A young woman confident of her fertility, however, might view the possibility of divorce after the birth of children with far greater equanimity—or, indeed, as a potential step forward onto something better. One young woman conveyed this attitude well when she said, "A young mother need not fear divorce, since she can always have more children with her next husband; a woman might have three husbands during her lifetime, bearing children with each of them."[24]

There is a well-known Nuer myth, first recorded by Evans-Pritchard, that conveys many of the complexities and ambiguities inherent in men's attempts to influence these mother/child bonds of *maar*:

> It was then that man began to kill, and his first killing seems to have been that of the mother of cow and buffalo, or rather that of the mother of cattle,

---

24. This attitude could negatively affect the marriage prospects of daughters born to a multiply married and divorced woman. Prospective husbands could be more suspicious of a prospective bride whose mother had proven flighty. Such a girl was referred to as a *nyaciek*, "the daughter of a woman"—the implication being that she had received little or no paternal supervision. Although this situation could be overlooked if the girl's mother was living happily at the time with her third or fourth husband, the young bride-to-be risked being dubbed as improperly brought up.

for at one time cows and buffaloes were the same. This led to a feud between men and cattle, buffaloes avenging their mother by attacking men in the bush and cows by causing men to quarrel and slay one another. (Evans-Pritchard 1956:269)

Man's troubles originated with his first act of killing, for the loyalties between the mother of cattle and her children were transformed upon her death into a legacy of unforeseen vengeance. Although man was able to dominate the mother of cattle herself—ultimately through superior force—he was incapable of subordinating the loyalties of her children to his own purposes. This myth makes clear that the bonds uniting a mother and her children were perpetual, that they continued long after death, and that men were incapable of controlling them completely—no matter how effective their controls over women.

Ultimately, then, a woman's ability to realize her innate, individuated potential for bearing children—whether accomplished within or outside of marriage, with one mate or with many—determined her future status within society. Men, it would seem, implicitly recognized the general weakness—or, from the point of view of women, quasi-irrelevance—of the cattle-over-blood ideology with respect to maternal bonds: Disputes over adultery, the impregnation of unmarried girls, and the paternal affiliation of children were considered by men and women alike to be primarily cattle affairs among men.

Blood-Links: Initiation and Mastery of the Self

The rite of scarification at initiation played an especially crucial role in this regard. For through this rite men collectively usurped the force of these feminine blood bonds, redefining and redirecting it in order to buttress cattle connections and age-based distinctions among themselves. Permanent blood bonds were forged during scarification between the initiate and his agnatic kinsmen as well as between him and fellow age-mates. As a medium of social bonding, blood suddenly took on an entirely new set of "masculine" (exclusively intermale) connotations and orientations for the initiate—all of which were, of course, fused with the additional rights, privileges, and responsibilities he took on at this time as a man among men. Only after the forging of these masculine blood bonds were a man's agnatic kinsmen morally obliged to "kindle a fire" in his name should he die without legal heirs. And only then did a young man gain rights, extending beyond his own death, in his pater's herd. He also became a member of a formal *ric* (age-set), being integrated thereby into the slowly evolving age hierarchy so fundamental to relations of authority among men (see plates 15 and 16).

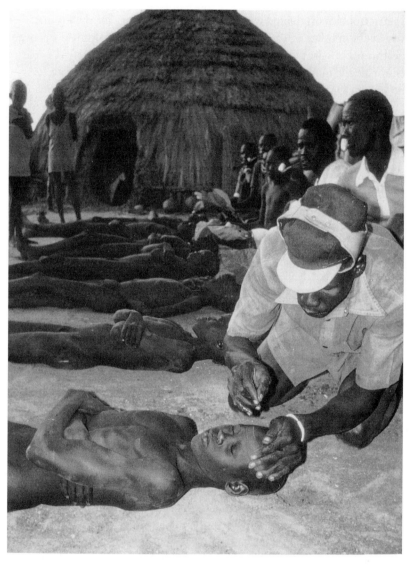

Plate 15. Cutting the marks of *gaar,* western Leek Nuer.

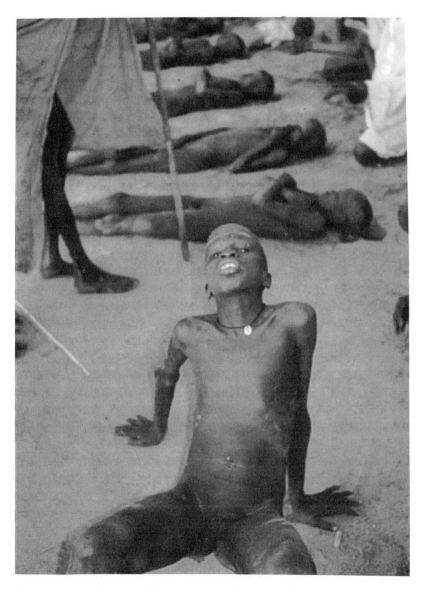

Plate 16. A newly initiated man moves to the recovery house.

In this light, the rite of scarification might be understood as a powerful symbolic maneuver on the part of men to overcome (or at least disguise) the inherent weakness of the cattle-over-blood ideology with respect to the well-recognized ability of women to aggravate frictions within the male hierarchy through the manipulation of their children's loyalties. Implicit in this rite was the assertion that men's powers as "blood controllers" were superior to women's powers as "blood producers." And it was on the basis of this ideological claim as well as of cattle transfers at marriage that men justified their rights to their wives' sons over and against their sons' maternal kinsmen. With regard to daughters, a father's claims remained centered, as we have seen, on bridewealth cattle.

For the initiate, this expanded and enriched appreciation of blood was experienced on at least two levels. On the one hand, the rite of scarification drew him into a network of exclusively male blood connections, and, on the other, it formalized his new status as a warrior/defender of the community and as an exchanger/sacrificer of cattle—a transformation symbolized by his "fathers' " conferral of fighting spears and oxen, respectively. He thus became someone potentially capable of—in fact, responsible for—controlling and protecting the lifeblood of others. The metal fighting spear (*mut*)—which also symbolized the initiate's right to invoke its verbal equivalent, the patrilineal spear name or call (*mut*)—remained, even in an age of automatic rifles, the prime symbol of agnatic continuity and solidarity throughout the 1980s (cf. Evans-Pritchard 1956:238–240).[25] To become a man was thus to embrace the entire complex of cultural practices and principles upholding the cultural "truth" that human blood is effectively manipulable through cattle exchange and sacrifice.

For the young man, this change of status was articulated through a radical transformation in his relations with cattle. During the long period of convalescence following the ordeal of the knife, initiates were forbidden all contact with cattle—though they could continue to drink cow's milk. They temporarily acquired the status of "hornless [and hence harmless] cattle" (*cöötni*) who could ignore ordinary rules of social propriety. They would often fashion elaborate mock spears out of mud and sorghum stalks and charge about the community in groups experimenting with their soon-to-be-formalized rights to upbraid their juniors and seduce girls. Immediately following the closing rite, in which the initiates were driven (*duac raar*)

---

25. The quick thrusts of the spear with which men punctuated invocations were, as Evans-Pritchard (1956:231) observed, "an integral part of the expression of intention" so crucial to sacrificial acts.

at dawn to a nearby stream from which they reemerged as men (*wuuni;* sing., *wut*), they were joyfully reunited with cattle. No longer responsible for milking cows, cooking meat, or gathering and drying cattle dung, the initiate adopted a totally new stance toward cattle, one that emphasized their dependence upon him as herdsman and sacrificer rather than his dependence upon them as sources of milk and meat—that is, one that played upon the material and symbolic associations between cattle and blood rather than upon those between cattle and food. Blood, the only substance men took directly from the herd, was drawn solely in contexts of sacrifice or hospitality—or less commonly for the health of the cow itself.[26] The distance a man maintained between his role as the protector/slayer of cattle and his dependence upon them for the satisfaction of physical needs was a major source of masculine dignity and strength. For it represented not only a mastery over cattle but a self-mastery as well: a source of inner pride as well as outward dignity.

The onset of the milking interdiction marked not only a major transformation in men's relations with cattle but also the formal inception of courtship and sexual relations with women.[27] From that point on men were encouraged to view women as consisting of two basic sorts: those from whom they might seek sex but not food and those from whom they might seek food but not sex. A man would endure extreme hunger rather than be caught eating or drinking by an unrelated girl. In fact, rules of exogamy, as we have seen, were stamped by this principle: Unrelated men and women avoided each other completely in matters of food and drink. For to be seen satisfying one's hunger or thirst in such contexts was to demonstrate lack of self-control and physical weakness in situations requiring displays of self-mastery and inner strength. Furthermore, this avoidance extended, as I explained, into early marriage. Affines (including husband and wife) "respected" (*thɛk*) one another completely in matters of food and drink until sometime after the birth of a child cemented the union.

Similarly, the milking interdiction as applied to girls and women had the effect of driving an experiential wedge between their nurturing responsibilities and their blossoming procreative powers. The two most exclusive of feminine gifts—cow's milk and procreative blood—were thus experientially segregated and symbolically opposed. That this was not

26. Occasional bleeding, men maintained, helped cattle stay fat, energetic, and fertile.

27. This association between the cessation of milking and the onset of sexual relations with women was eminently direct.

purely a taboo revolving around women and cattle is clear from the fact that household heads sometimes designated the milk of a specific cow, called *yaŋ me ŋuɔt*, exclusively for menstruating (and nonmenstruating) women. A cow thus dedicated was not in danger of becoming barren. However, no man would drink its milk, even if, as one man put it, "it were the only lactating beast in the herd!"[28] The weaning taboo prohibiting sexual relations to lactating mothers carried this duality of feminine roles into marriage and, as it were, into the body of the woman herself.

Whereas the nurturing powers of cattle and women were thus continuously fused in the daily organization of cattle-related tasks, men, through their controls over blood, were able to maintain dominance over the reproductive gifts of women and cattle through the rites of initiation and sacrifice, respectively. Moreover, women, as we have seen, rarely achieved this heightened sense of autonomy in their relations with cattle. Nor were they normally permitted to interact with cattle as symbolic counters for human blood. Unable to control even the flow of her own blood, a woman was, in the eyes of men, profoundly incapable of bearing that symbol of intention, self-mastery, and control over blood—*mut*, the metal fighting spear.

From the perspective of men, women's exclusion from these masculine domains was justified primarily on the grounds that they remained uninitiated. However, lurking behind this argument was a well-developed ideology of male superiority in which women were depicted as inherently weak and lacking in self-mastery. The natural biological rhythms of menstruation and childbirth not only remained permanently beyond a woman's control but were also highly vulnerable to external disturbances. In addition, they were considered potentially polluting for both men and cattle.

Unlike the maturation process of men, that of women went ritually unmarked. The initiation of a young girl into adulthood was, as it were, left to nature. For only after a girl had experienced childbirth did she become a woman (*ciek*). Although the coming of both manhood and womanhood could be seen to involve acts of submission, a girl deferred to inner biological forces whereas a boy deferred, instead, to a social hierarchy. A boy acknowledged the superior authority of his elders by submitting to the ordeal of the knife. This gesture of submission was counterbalanced, however,

---

28. I was told that a cow whose milk had been declared "for women only" could later be purified and returned to a normal status by having its owner lead it back and forth across a river.

by a simultaneous act of daring and strength: Initiates were expected to show neither fear nor pain during their trial with the blade. The six parallel scars running across a man's forehead from ear to ear remained as a permanent symbol of this moment of self-mastery.[29]

Ultimately, then, it was the ability of a man to master himself that enabled him to complete the weakness of a woman and so dominate her to the degree that she could not dominate herself.[30] The intimacy of this association between self-mastery and initiation was impressed upon me by an incident that occurred shortly after I witnessed my first scarification rite. On seeing me return home after the ceremony, Gatnyinyar, who was sitting and chatting with a large group of men beneath a tree, called over to me: "So, tell us, Nyarial, what did you think of scarification?" I responded honestly:

> Though I am sure that the operation is very painful and that the boys are very brave to endure it, I was surprised how quickly it was completed. Each boy was cut within a matter of moments. And if I compare scarification with the difficult birth I attended the other day—well, there's no comparison: the birth was much harder.

The men immediately burst into laughter. "Aie, Rial, that girl!" they chuckled appreciatively, having taken my comment as yet another indication of my willingness to engage in a bout of cross-sex teasing. Encouraged by this response, I added, "Besides, a man is only scarified once whereas a woman gives birth again and again"—a comment punctuated with another surge of laughter. In answering Gatnyinyar's question as I did, I was consciously testing these men's reactions to what I believed to be a implicit parallel between the maturation experiences of men and women. And much to my surprise, these men partially agreed with me. "You're right, Nyarial," Gatnyinyar remarked while fingering his own marks of manhood:

> We men know that these scars are not a big thing in themselves. But you must realize that initiation is still harder/stronger (*bumni jɛn*) than birth because, once a man is scarified, he must do many things. If a war breaks out, he must run and join the battle; or if there is a wild buffalo or a lion, he must go and face it.

29. Moreover, unlike the rhythms of childbirth that remained forever beyond a woman's control, the boy himself arranged the time of his initiation with the man who was to scarify him. Moreover, the blood that flowed from his forehead was not considered to be polluting in any way.

30. This insight was initially stimulated by Paul Riesman's discussion of gender relations among the Fulani (1977).

Whereas I had been implicitly comparing initiation and childbirth in terms of the relative degree of pain endured, Gatnyinyar and his associates were thinking of them rather in terms of the mastery of fear—especially, the fear of death. When I later discussed this issue with several women, they unanimously agreed that no woman ever overcomes the fear of childbirth completely, no matter how many times experienced. This is not surprising, considering how many Nuer women die in childbirth each year.

Childbirth: Weakness and Femininity

Yet even when a woman successfully realized her procreative potential, she was seen to be permanently weakened in the process. The experience of childbirth—no matter how personally exhilarating or rewarding for the mother—was followed, men and women agreed, by an unenviable and unavoidable state of extreme exhaustion (see plates 17 and 18). Ideally, "a woman who had recently given birth" (*ciek mi pay dap*) was excused from as many household tasks as her circumstances allowed for a period of months after delivery. Others were supposed to cook for her, help care for her older children, gather wood for her, and so forth, until she felt capable of taking on these tasks fully once again. Although this cultural ideal was not always realized, owing to an absence of younger sisters, co-wives, or other women assistants, there was a definite public status accorded to a woman who had recently given birth. A man could honorably inform a would-be house guest that, regrettably, there was no one capable of preparing a meal for him since "the only woman/wife here has recently given birth." I have also heard young mothers jokingly attempt to evade certain chores by claiming the status of *ciek mi pay dap* while pointing to their "newborns" who were by that time old enough to scamper merrily around their mother's knees. Although a mother recovered much of her former strength as her children grew and were weaned, there was still no comparison, people argued, between the vigor of a mature "girl" and that of a "woman" who had experienced childbirth. The strength of the former was equated with that of young men: Both sexes were considered ŋuɛatni (sing., ŋuɛat) during the prime of their youth—a term that conveys images of endurance, strength, beauty, grace, and self-restraint (especially in matters of food). Since the experience of childbirth, not puberty, separated "women" from "girls," the full flowering of a girl's femininity was equated directly and unambiguously with a reduction in physical strength—a reduction sometimes spoken about by women in terms of the loss of blood itself.

Not surprisingly, men made much of this association between femininity and physical weakness. For example, when several eastern Gaajok men were asked why women were excluded from formal positions of leadership, they immediately pointed to the postdelivery exhaustion of women (rather than to the experience of pregnancy or the stain of menstruation) as most crucial. One middle-aged Gaajok man, upon hearing that the *liŋlith*, "the English," were currently headed by a pair of women (i.e., Thatcher and the Queen), exclaimed:

> Ah, but that could never happen here. A woman's speech would not be heard [by men]; her words would not have weight. A woman might get pregnant; and then, can you imagine a woman who has recently given birth commanding/ruling (*ruacɛ*) men?

Now, to the extent that a woman experienced her own blood—her own fertility and procreative processes—as something beyond her control and, as such, something highly vulnerable to outside disturbance, she was doubly dependent upon men as "the protectors of life." When a girl failed to menstruate or a woman to conceive, or whenever grave difficulties were experienced during pregnancy or delivery, women turned to men and men turned to cattle as objects of divine supplication and sacrifice. The protective responsibilities of men extended, moreover, through the woman to her children.

This last point was driven home to me by an unknown middle-aged man, who suddenly shouted at me from across a crowded byre: "Who does more for the child, its mother or its father?" By that time I had learned to expect and even enjoy such impromptu invitations to a bout of cross-sex teasing as one of the more entertaining aspects of the art of conversation between mature men and women. Although I usually responded to such queries with an appropriate defense of my sex, on this occasion, being curious to discover on what grounds this man would base his defense of fatherhood without prodding from me, I said simply, "I don't know; what do you think?" "Why, it's the father, of course," he answered:

> When the child falls ill, isn't it the father who sacrifices a cow? Or, if the child needs medicines, doesn't the father sell a cow to buy them? What can the mother do at such times? All she can do is forebear (*ruut*). Besides, when she herself becomes ill, doesn't her husband kill a cow for her as well? The meaning of this is that man is the divinity of woman (*wut ɛ kuɔth ciek*).

This was, I had to admit, a clever and strong defense. "But do you think mothers would agree with you in this?" I countered. "Of course not," he responded, "they would say: 'We give birth to them and we suckle them—

Plate 17.   The pain of childbirth.

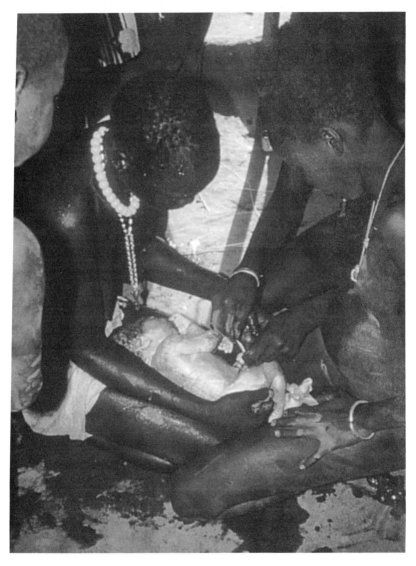

Plate 18. Tying the umbilical cord.

we do much more for our children than their fathers.' " And on that note our conversation ended as abruptly as it began.

Ultimately, then, it was the effectiveness with which men were able to shield women and children from danger and misfortune that bolstered male claims of physical and moral superiority over women. Women brought forth children but could not then defend them; they were the producers but not the protectors of human life. Most people assumed that, without the constant attention of men as warriors and as sacrificers, women and children would not long survive.

Images of women as physically weak and incapable of self-mastery were thus all of a piece with male-oriented assertions of the dominance of cattle flows over human blood flows in the creation of enduring social bonds. Otherwise expressed, both women's sense of dependence upon men and men's corresponding sense of authority over women would have been reduced were not cattle exchange and sacrifice regarded as effective means for coping with problematic states and passages of human blood.

The conversation quoted above also reveals the extent to which men's protective powers were rooted firmly in their monopolization of the symbolic means by which the life and blood of human beings were "indirectly" manipulated and controlled. Men's abilities to use their exclusive powers as the exchangers and sacrificers of cattle so as to dominate women were limited by several important factors, however. Though I have argued that cattle, as objects of bridewealth exchange, effectively shielded men from the negative consequences of a wide variety of procreative ills and, as objects of sacrifice, gave men the edge in defining and interpreting human realities, this is not to say that by manipulating cattle men somehow got women to do what they wished. Current crises in the marriage system belie any such simplistic notion: Cattle traced the movements of women, not women the movements of cattle.

Food-Links: Women as Mediators

Women, moreover, had their own exclusive field of dominion with respect to the life-creating and life-sustaining powers of cattle. For women, the cow was a powerful ally in disputes with men in that nearly all the vital nutrients she provided passed through women's hands before reaching men's stomachs. Women, assisted by their uninitiated children, were responsible for the milking of cows, the churning of butter, and the cooking of meat. This sexual division of cattle-related tasks was especially rigid, as we have seen, with respect to milking: An initiated man was prohibited from drinking milk that he had directly taken from a cow on pain of death by *nueer*.

Hence, were a long trek to necessitate that a man milk, he never did so for his own consumption but rather exchanged his milking gourd for that of another man—preferably, a man belonging to a different age-set.

Just as cattle mediated between men and the procreative powers of women, so, too, women mediated between men and the nurturing powers of the herd. The nurturing responsibilities of women extended, moreover, beyond cattle to the preparation of grain, the cooking of porridge, the brewing of beer (*dhiem kɔaŋ*), the conveying of water—in short, to the preparation and distribution of nourishment in all forms. Normally, women were expected to prepare two meals a day for their households—meals consisting for the most part of sorghum porridge topped with fresh or soured milk. Each meal required many hours of "feminine" labor, including the milking of cows, the carrying of water and the collection of firewood. Before reaching the cooking pot, the sorghum or maize also had to be cleaned, pounded, soaked, ground, and reshaped into thousands of minute, evenly sized balls (see plate 19).

These last steps required the use of a special, hollowed-out gourd bowl (*baal*) that was replete with feminine symbolism. On the one hand, the mediating role of this bowl was explicitly compared to that of cattle: "The *baal* is the cow of the cooking world because everything must pass through it before reaching the cooking pot." On the other hand, the *baal* was intimately linked to women's procreative processes. Not only was it the place where agricultural grains budded and swelled, but, more uniquely, the *baal* shared to some extent in women's menstrual restrictions. "The *baal* is like a woman with her period," I was told: "Were it to come in contact with milk, butter, or any other dairy product, the cow concerned would become barren."

Following these preparations, meals were normally shared by a woman with her younger children, older daughters, and female visitors inside the house (*duël*), with additional bowls of food being served to the woman's husband, older sons, and male guests inside the cattle byre (*luak*). When delivering cooked food to their menfolk, women partially compensated for their de facto control over the family's food supply by adopting a highly deferential attitude. They courteously bowed their heads and kneeled before placing bowls of cooked food before men, after which they gracefully retreated backwards on their knees for a few paces before silently rising, turning, and departing. In polygynous households younger co-wives were especially conscious of their husband's attention at such times. They often donned their favorite dresses or otherwise paid special attention to their appearance when presenting cooked food to their husbands. Older co-wives, in contrast, often sent a daughter or younger co-wife in their place. But

Plate 19. After pounding, a young wife grinds sorghum flour in preparation for the morning meal.

regardless of who presented the food, co-wives competed consciously for their husband's affections through the preparation of especially delicious meals. Consequently, it was considered a great honor if one of them was assigned exclusive responsibility for housing and feeding a guest: "for a guest must have the best." Conversely, it was a grave insult for a man to disdain his wife's food. For this act was tantamount to refusing her bed—and, when sustained, could seriously jeopardize the woman's procreative goals. For instance, Gatnyinyar had steadfastly refused to accept the food of one of his younger wives following allegations that she had conceived their second child in adultery. The poor woman could do nothing. Although she had weaned the child more than a year earlier, she was faced with the discouraging choice of either remaining together with her two daughters in her husband's home with little prospect of conceiving a third child or, alternatively, of abandoning her husband for another man, in which case she would only confirm his suspicions and, ultimately, be forced through divorce to separate from her young daughters. Of all the Nuer women I met, this young wife was the most visibly depressed. When I left the region more than a year later, her situation was still unresolved.

It is important to realize, moreover, that husbands were the formal "owners" of all grain supplies produced by their households—even those planted, weeded, and harvested entirely by their wives and unmarried sons and daughters. In polygynous households it was also common for a man to maintain a separate field, independent of his wives, so that he might build up a special grain reserve for purposes of hospitality, beer brewing, sale, or the like. Because this reserve was rarely tapped before his wives had exhausted their own supplies, the head of the household usually retained full control over whatever grain surplus his extended family produced from year to year.

Nevertheless, a husband's control over his family's food supply was in many ways more formal than real. For ultimately it was women who decided when and how much their menfolk ate. As the principal mediators between men and the life-sustaining powers of cattle and the fields, women could, and often did, express their anger and disillusionment with their husbands, brothers, and sons by simply neglecting to prepare them meals. *Ci jiǫk tɔɔc thoɣ maac*, "the dog lay down by the fireplace," was the expression commonly used to indicate that, for whatever reason—sheer laziness being the implied motive—no supper would be forthcoming. (Literally, this expression played on the idea that the cooking hearth, not having been lit since morning, would make a warm and agreeable place for a dog to settle in for a rest.) As one eastern Gaajok man pointedly remarked, "Food is a very dangerous weapon in the hands of women."

Significantly, a woman's failure to prepare meals for her husband was not considered sufficient grounds for divorce by Nuer courts—even in situations where feminine protests of this nature endured for months or even years. I recall one occasion, for instance, when a middle-aged Gaajak man, who was deeply frustrated by his wife's repeated refusal to cook for him, attempted to sound out the local head chief about the possibility of a divorce. The chief, however, merely laughed and dismissed the idea as hopeless. "Do you think all my wives cook for me?" he countered.

Although feminine protests of this nature were often undermined by competition among co-wives as well as by patterns of meal sharing among men, they could sometimes be used to great effect.[31] For example, I was told of a major feud between two eastern Gaajak sections during the 1940s that ended abruptly after the women of that region collectively refused to

---

31. Sometimes co-wives coordinated their "food strikes." For example, Kelual Nyinyar Rik, my principal host among the Leek, was forced to go without supper on the third day after his return from—what all his wives agreed—was an irresponsibly long stay in the district capital of Bentiu.

cook for their menfolk until the fighting ceased. Similarly, when I asked one young man in Leek Nuer country why he had rushed off to join a spear fight before having any idea of what it was about, he confided that his greatest fear was for his supper. "Well, if I hadn't joined in," he confessed, "the porridge might have run short." When I later questioned his wife about whether or not this was so, she smiled and said, "The porridge of a coward might well run short." One witty older Gaajok man, with whom I discussed these issues, summed up the situation thus: "Look around you, Nyarial, and you will see that the bravest Nuer men are always henpecked husbands."

Polygyny, collective-eating patterns among men, and ideals of hospitality went a long way, however, in tempering the abilities of individual women to give weight to their opinions through the denial of food. "The wife of one is the wife of all [except in bed]" and "Women and children may eat alone, but we men always eat together" run two well-known Nuer sayings. In much the same way as the bridewealth system shielded men from the full impact of procreative misfortunes experienced by their wives, masculine patterns of food sharing greatly reduced their sense of personal dependence on the nurturing responsibilities of specific women.

Commensalism was a pattern encouraged in men from early youth: Boys were taught to develop a sense of solidarity with their peers through the daily sharing of food. Women, in contrast, tended to express favoritism and exclusivity in the giving of food, since it was primarily as nurturers that they won the long-term support and affection of their husbands, brothers, and sons. Moreover, women rarely ate together in large groups. A daughter usually remained together with her mother and sisters inside the house long after her younger brothers had joined their paternal half brothers, cousins, and peers for collective meals inside the byre.

Although men ate together more frequently than did women, male bonds of food sharing rarely bridged senior and junior age-sets. In general, fathers ate only with fathers and sons only with sons. Solely among agemates was a man able to cultivate bonds of equality, competition, and comradeship through acts of food sharing. Just as the union of interests fostered among kinsmen by shared cattle rights was circumscribed by a strict hierarchical structure of deference based on age, generation, and descent, so, too, were patterns of commensalism among men. Patterns of food sharing among women, in contrast, were not normally age-graded. Celebratory bowls of beer, porridge, and meat passed quite freely at weddings, for instance, among women of all ages.

Once scarified, moreover, a man was expected to demonstrate greater self-control in matters of hunger and thirst by conforming to an elaborate set of "table manners" designed to suppress all signs of *daar* (greed). The spoon that touched his mouth could never be chock-full; nor could the bowl he left be scraped and empty. Similarly, he would be subject to public ridicule were he ever to fill both sides of his mouth at once or break a spoon while eating. Though women, too, strived to demonstrate self-control over their hunger and thirst before unrelated men, and to suppress all signs of greed when eating with relatives, they were not expected to conform to the strict rules of etiquette followed by men. The porridge left clinging to the unscraped bowls and unlicked spoons abandoned by men was, after all, destined for their bellies and those of their children. Women frequently did not set aside separate bowls of food for themselves but rather awaited the unconsumed portion of meals first offered to their menfolk.

Furthermore, there were times when a man was not supposed to participate in the feast following sacrifice—as, for example, at the mortuary ceremony of an age-mate. The weakness the death represented for the entire age-set had to be countered by an added show of strength by surviving members. Similarly, the groom who fasted during his wedding celebrations demonstrated a degree of self-control that bore witness to his future dignity as a husband and father. Any failure to maintain this image before his affines would have been a deep source of shame. For the groom would be admitting a double weakness since the wedding ceremony itself was a confession of his dependence: He was situationally demonstrating, perhaps, his greatest weakness of all—his need for a woman.

The close cultural association between manhood and acts of self-restraint in matters of food—especially cow's milk—was evident in the names of two of the scars acquired during initiation: "never again to suckle the udder" and "never again to lick milk froth from one's fingers." The milking prohibition could thus be seen as part of a more generalized attempt by men to reduce their sense of personal dependence on the nurturing powers of cattle and the fields. By systematically avoiding relating to cattle and nature as physical dependents, men enhanced their feelings of dominance, personal autonomy, and self-control. But the fact that, in so doing, men necessarily increased their dependence upon women as milkmaids, water bearers, and cooks was a potential source of uneasiness and shame. One young man conveyed the deep sense of embarrassment a man would feel if caught satisfying his hunger or thirst before unrelated girls with the hyperbole *Mieth ɛ buaar nhiäm nyiët*, "Eating in front of girls is a scandal."

The shame men associated with eating was in many ways comparable to that women felt with respect to menstruation. In both cases, there was an underlying experience of not being totally in control of the situation or of oneself. Moreover, it is striking that the experience of hunger—and the ability to withstand it—were associated directly with the experience of menstruation as well. The polite way to ask a woman whether she was menstruating was *Ti kɛ buɔth?*, "Are you with hunger?" (or, alternately, /*Ci te caak?*, "Are you not taking milk?")—alluding thereby to the ban on menstruating women drinking cow's milk. Were the question about the woman's hunger pure and simple it would be phrased as some variant of: *Nak buɔthi?*, "Is hunger killing you?"

The rite of sacrifice was another important means by which men attempted to dissociate the act of slaying the victim, one implying superiority and independence, from the consumption of its flesh for the satisfaction of their bodily needs, one implying weakness and dependence. The tremendous shame attached to the nonsacrificial slaughtering of cattle for purposes of meat consumption—though having grown considerably weaker with the expansion of cattle markets and the introduction of Christian doctrines—continued, nevertheless, to soften the identification of cattle with food for most Nuer, thereby enriching the associations between cattle and blood.[32] By helping men maintain a respectful distance between themselves and the reality of their dependence upon cattle as sources of food—by freeing them so they could relate to cattle primarily as symbolic counters for human blood—women provided a crucial source of masculine dignity and strength. They underwrote that whole complex of concepts and practices supporting the cattle-over-blood value principle, whereby the social circulation of cattle took precedence over that of human blood in determining the hierarchy and scope of enduring bonds of *maar*. And it was precisely this ideological premise that reinforced and extended the potency of men's actions in the world.

Nevertheless, to move from the idea that "cattle are greater than blood" to "men are greater than women" was not difficult in a world where the mediating premise, "men are greater than cattle and cattle greater than women," was structured into the daily organization and execution of all cattle-related tasks. The extent to which Nuer used cattle to transform re-

---

32. The reluctance of Nuer to bleed cattle solely for the purposes of food—except during times of extreme famine—is further evidence of a more general cultural tendency to segregate the blood and food dimensions of human/cattle relations.

lations of gender complementarity into ideologies of male dominance is made clear in the following incident. One day while walking alone along a footpath in eastern Gaajok country, I came across a young herdsman driving three docile-looking cows toward me along the same path. As we were about to meet, the young man suddenly cried out to me, "You're going to be gored." When he realized that I didn't understand his intent, he was more explicit: "You should clear the path for a cow." By that time, however, the approaching cows had already stepped aside and passed me. "Oh," I said, "why is that?" "Because cattle say 'it is we who bring women,' " he explained, "and for that reason women should give way." "And what about men?" I asked. "No, for men it's different; the cow will respect/fear (*dual*) a man and move aside."

CATTLE OVER BLOOD: A PARADIGM IN PERIL

Yet just how resilient had this cattle-over-blood ideology really proven over the years? How were relations of mutual dependence and independence between men and women and between young and old working themselves out in terms of ongoing cycles of blood, cattle, and food? To what extent were these cycles and idioms themselves in flux? In grappling with these questions here, I shall concentrate on changing patterns of courtship, marriage, and divorce—paying particular attention to east/west variations in contemporary gender relations as well as to more general transformations in marriage practices wrought by the infiltration of Western legal precepts into Nuer customary law.

The general image I wish to convey is of a world in which senior men were gradually losing control over the definition and negotiation of blood relations. The significance of blood—conceived as a highly versatile and dynamic medium of social bonding—was rapidly outstripping that of cattle in a number of crucial social contexts. And thus, while the cattle-over-blood ideology continued to dominate relations of power and authority between the sexes and among various age groups during the early 1980s, there were numerous indications that the general force of this ideology was fast dissipating and, along with it, that added sense of control over the world previously shared—albeit unequally—by Nuer.

Chapter 2 described some of the mounting obstacles senior men had begun to face in this respect by the early 1980s. The introduction of currency, together with the rapid expansion of labor and cattle markets, made it far more difficult for senior men to amass power through controls over cattle wealth. And as ever-increasing numbers of cattle spun off into exchange networks devoid of human blood associations, the general significance and scope of the cattle-over-blood value principle was necessarily reduced. Although many Nuer sought to reinforce the centrality of the "cattle/human equation" in the creation of enduring bonds of *maar* by calling attention to money's "bloodless" nature, the inevitable negotiations and compromises characterizing shared cattle rights were increasingly bound up with more generalized controversies over the meaning and application of key new wealth categories such as the cattle of money and the money of work. As issues of power became fused with those of definition—fused, that is, with disputes over who had the right to define the "type" of cattle or money in question—individual rights in cattle became less clear-cut, less collective, and less age stratified.

The growing number of cattleless "marriages" initiated by youth and of those requiring fewer cattle than before according to Nuer courts—was another clear indicator of the declining significance of the cattle-over-blood value principle in important areas of Nuer social life. Eastern Nuer elders, in particular, often complained bitterly during the early 1980s about what they saw as the general intransigence and irresponsibility of contemporary youths—as well as about the short-sighted laxity of the courts in such matters. One eastern Gaajok elder, who had worked for nearly twenty years as court scribe, characterized the changing situation in his region as follows:

> In the old days, a girl would get pregnant. If her lover had no cows, she would be married by someone else. But now, a girl who is impregnated clings to her lover, even when there are no cattle. There will be a court trial. There's no longer any fear of death [from the girl's kinsmen]. What's more, the courts will often give the girl to her lover, telling her family that the bridewealth cattle will come later.

One consequence of this trend was a decline in the age at which many contemporary Nuer youths were marrying—or so, at least, many people alleged. Whereas a generation earlier, young men rarely married before their late twenties or early thirties, during the 1980s many men succeeded in acquiring wives before the age of twenty-five. Interestingly, many members of the older generation cited this decline in the typical marrying age as contributing directly to rising rates of divorce. These young husbands, many elders alleged, often took their conjugal responsibilities less seriously than they should.

More important, many young women of the early 1980s were actively resisting the idea that cattle exchange should take precedence over all else in determining their marriage partners. Whereas earlier generations of Nuer women often took great pride in the fact that they were married with many cattle, it was precisely this sense of pride that, by all accounts, was declining, especially in parts of eastern Nuerland. For instance, I knew a young Gaajok woman in her early twenties who repeatedly evaded her parents' attempts to marry her to a man with cattle by running off with a series of lovers. Shortly after she was first engaged, Nyadak was impregnated by another man. This second relationship, however, soon collapsed as well. While still pregnant, Nyadak then eloped with a third man—a certain Majak, whom I knew well. When she later returned to her parents' home to give birth, it was discovered that Majak had insufficient cattle to marry her. A year later her parents arranged her marriage to a fourth man, who completed his initial bridewealth payments. Three days after the consummation ceremony (*muɔd nyal*), however, Nyadak eloped again. The immediate suspect was her former lover, Majak, who was promptly arrested in spite of his vehement denial of having had anything to do with Nyadak's disappearance. Nyadak's sister was also summoned by the court and publicly whipped in the hope that she would reveal the whereabouts of her wayward sister—but to no avail. After languishing a week in jail, Majak was eventually released on the presumption that Nyadak had run off with a fifth—and as yet unknown—"husband." When I left the region several months later Nyadak's family had yet to locate her. And with no way of identifying her new lover, the courts could do nothing for them. Her discouraged parents were thus forced to return her bridewealth cattle to her official "husband" and await Nyadak's reappearance. Though Nyadak's case was more complicated than most I encountered, it amply reveals the obstacles many contemporary parents faced in attempting to influence their children's choice of mates as well as to secure bridewealth cattle for their daughters.

Sometimes parents were saddled with multiple elopement or impregnation cases at once. One frustrated eastern Gaajok father whom I knew well attempted (unsuccessfully) to enlist me in a campaign to persuade his eldest daughter, who had already borne a child to a cattle-poor "Anyuak," to accept a marriage proposal from a Nuer man with cattle so that her brother, who had recently impregnated a girl, could also marry. But the man's daughter steadfastly refused to cooperate in the hope that the father of her child would someday obtain sufficient cattle to marry her. "Love/agreement (*nhok*)," she stressed, "is not a matter of cattle." Similarly, it was not unusual to hear young men pleading in court for more time to gather marriage cattle for their eloped or impregnated girlfriends in order to pursue similar cattle suits against their sisters' lovers. As one exasperated Gaajok mother complained: *ɛn tääm ɛ, lum lenyɛ kuen kɛ gɔi* ("Today, sexual love exceeds marriage in goodness [in the eyes of youth]").

Significantly, marriages carried out with the full approval and participation of the extended families concerned were marked during the early 1980s by a special term: *kuen luääɣ* ("cattle-byre marriage"), the bride's family's byre being the traditional place where bridewealth settlements were negotiated. The related term "house marriage" (*kuen duëël*) was sometimes used to indicate a parentally supported and negotiated marriage in which fewer cattle were demanded owing to the bride's status as a *ciek mi kɛaɣ*. By implication, any union that was neither a "byre" nor a "house" marriage was not a "real" marriage at all (that is, it was a union in which the "wife" had few or no "cattle on her back"), or, alternatively, one in which the couple "feuded for each other" (*cikɛ rɔ tɛr*) and eventually succeeded in pushing their case through the courts despite parental opposition.

With cattle-byre marriages rapidly becoming the exception rather than the norm in eastern Nuerland, court officials often felt pressured into lowering their bridewealth standards so as to defuse as swiftly as possible the violent potential of elopement and impregnation disputes. If the young man concerned could immediately produce ten or fifteen head of cattle, the court almost always ruled in his favor—provided, of course, the union was not judged "incestuous" (*ruaal*). For a young man with limited cattle resources, elopement or impregnation seemed an economically rational way of voicing marriage proposals at that time in the east. As one eastern Gaajok youth optimistically remarked: "The world is fast approaching the point where girls will be taken for nothing!" But as another youth explained: "It's not so hard to get a girl these days, but cattle remain a problem—for if you don't have cattle, her children will not be yours."

These trends were far less apparent during the early 1980s among the western Nuer, where cattle-byre marriages remained the norm and where local chiefs normally required a full transfer of between twenty and twenty-five head of cattle for the marriage of a "stolen" or impregnated girl. This east/west contrast was also evident with respect to "house marriages": whereas bridewealth settlements for a girl previously eloped or impregnated were usually negotiated in the east at rates lower than those standard for the marriage of a *nya mi nyaal* (literally, a "girl girl"), westerners tended to reduce bridewealth rates only in situations of repeated impregnation or prior divorce. Indeed, several westerner men stressed that a woman who had already proven her fertility through childbirth and had maintained formal custody of the child might be seen as a particularly desirable marriage partner by an older man with few or no children of his own. Such a match would be less desirable, however, in situations where the genitor had already asserted paternity claims in the child through the payment of some four to six head of cattle (*ruɔk*).[33] For in that case, the woman's relationship (*maar*) with her former lover could not be ruptured definitively through separation and remarriage.

Western Nuer court practices in this regard were subsequently modified during the late 1980s and early 1990s by officers of the SPLA. As part of his more general efforts to reconstruct local administrative networks following the extended devastations wrought by government-sponsored Arab militias during the mid-1980s, the zonal commander of the Western Upper Nile proposed to limit the amount of bridewealth cattle that could be claimed in court for the marriage of a previously eloped girl whose original suitor had failed to marry her.[34] Although informal bridewealth agreements between the families concerned could be larger than the maximum limits set by the courts, bridewealth rates for previously eloped girls were officially reduced in 1988 from twenty-five to fifteen head of cattle. This decision, the commander stated, was "enthusiastically" endorsed by young western men, who saw it as an "economic opportunity" at a time when local herds were seriously depleted by years of civil war.[35] In effect this decree extended the category of *ciek mi kɛay* to "stolen" girls (*nya mi caa ɛ kual*) who had not borne children and had not been divorced. In explaining the reasoning behind this decision the zonal commander argued that either "the parents of the girl were forcing her to marry someone against her will and thus deserved to be punished" or "the girl had herself made a mistake, in which case her market value should go down because suitors would begin to doubt her [character/motives]." It was further stipulated that bridewealth for a *kɛay* ("unmarried mother/divorcee") with one child should be limited in court to ten head of cattle and that of unmarried women with two children reduced to six. As for a woman who had borne

33. Paternity payments in the east were standardized at five head of cattle for a boy and four for a girl. In the west, they were normally six head of cattle for a boy and four for a girl. Lower fees for girls were locally justified on the grounds that the mother's kinsmen would be receiving additional cattle upon the girl's marriage.

34. "Customary Laws of WUN [Western Upper Nile]," 8 Feb. 1988. This is a thirty-page unpublished manuscript that documents current efforts by the Sudanese People's Liberation Movement to standardize customary law in that region.

35. Personal communication with Commander Machar.

three or more children, the courts proclaimed that a man need place only
"one cow on her back" in order to establish exclusive rights in her sexuality. Such a woman, the commander explained, was "really a concubine."
But even so, that one cow was extremely important because, as he put it,
"Suppose you get lucky and have an industrious wife. Without that cow,
nothing that she produces belongs to you—but with it, everything she produces [be it grain, children, beer, or money] is yours!" When I asked him
whether, under these conditions, a woman might not prefer to reject such
a minimal payment and thereby retain full rights over the products of her
labor, the commander said, "Well, that may be so, but her husband is her
protector and she needs him." "Besides," he added, "if no cow were paid
for her and she later died, there would be confusion over who should bury
her and over who should receive her property."[36] Nevertheless, SPLA administrative decisions in this regard clearly continued to reinforce men's
legal rights in the products of their wives' labor, even in situations where
the bridewealth-cattle basis of such claims had been greatly reduced.

Regional courts also differed markedly during the early 1980s in the
sanctions applied in cases of elopement in which the "stolen" girl (*nya mi
caa ɛ kual*) died of illness or accident before being returned to her family's
homestead. Whereas eastern Nuer chiefs took the attitude that the girl's
lover was personally responsible for her death—"it's as if he killed her
with his own hand"—and thus held him liable for twenty-five head of
cattle in bloodwealth compensation, western Nuer chiefs tended to argue
that such a man was not accountable since, as one of them put it, "the girl
did what she did out of love." Whether or not the harder line adopted by
eastern chiefs was a recent innovation intended to curb spiraling rates of
elopement in that area is difficult to know. However, it appeared during
the early 1980s that western Nuer courts could soon be forced to adopt a
similar policy, if for no other reason than to close what amounted to a
major loophole in their moral code. My impressions in this regard stem
from public reaction to an unusual elopement case I followed among the

---

36. If she were divorced from her first husband and not yet married to her
current mate, the latter, being an "unrelated" man, would have to pay a cow—*yang
muɔn*, "the cow of the earth"—to have her buried. The commander further
explained that the courts would, in such a case, normally permit the former
husband to revive the former marriage by paying two head of cattle to the
deceased woman's parents—an exchange known as "the placing of an ax" (*lath
jɔp*)—thereby establishing definitive rights in any property she may have had at
death as well as rights in whatever cattle she would have received from the
marriages of her daughters. This was, however, possible only if she had borne at
least one son to her former husband.

Leek Nuer in 1982 in which a wily young man attempted to circumvent his poverty in cattle by first running away with a girl and later reporting fallaciously to her parents that she had died of illness. It was a full year before rumors that the girl was alive and well and had recently given birth reached her parents. By that time, however, the burden of proof lay with them—the chief's hands were tied until the girl could be located. Since this was apparently the first time anyone had used this elopement strategy in that area, many people could not help but admire the young man's ingenuity. "Now there's a plotter among plotters," commented the presiding subchief.

COURTSHIP: BECOMING LOVERS

One reason that elopement and impregnation cases were escalating more rapidly in the east than in the west during the 1970s and 1980s was due to regional variations in contemporary courtship practices. Unlike their western Nuer cousins, easterners had by the early 1980s developed an elaborate ideology of "declared love" in which a man and a girl could formally commit to a relationship of "love" before an assembly of at least six other youths. Public declarations of this sort were often preceded by months, and sometimes years, of courtship in which the young man, supported by his close friends and relatives, attempted to convince the girl of his unswerving love for her. Upon first approaching the girl, the man, I was told, would utter phrases such as *Ɛän göörä ji, nhɔkä ji ɛloŋ, ɛ jin nya mi gɔaa, göörä ɣöö biaa lumdä* ("I want/need you, I love you very much, you are a beautiful girl, I want you to be my love"). It was fully expected, however, that the girl would reject such statements, initially refusing to listen to the young man. At that point it was common practice in the east for the young man to withdraw temporarily in order to allow time for his brothers and close allies to wear down the girl's resistance. Whenever one of them encountered her he would impress upon the girl the sincerity and depth of his friend's affections, praising the man highly: *Ɛ wut pany mi nhɔakɛ ji ɛ loŋ kä ɛ ŋuɛat,* "He's a real man who loves you very much; he's a clean/well-dressed/self-respecting person." The man would have no cause to suspect his friends' intentions, for there was an extremely strong ethic of mutual support and loyalty in such matters among close male friends throughout the east. Ideally, men who participated in the same dancing chain (*dep*) never competed simultaneously for the affections of a girl: *Jidep kɛl, /cikɛ dee rɛk* (see plates 20 and 21). Similarly, every girl had her own close circle of female companions in whom she confided. Should the girl eventually become convinced of the depth of the man's love—or, as local youths put it, should he succeed in "getting into her blood"—she and her closest friends would agree to meet with the man and his friends at some isolated place, where her brothers were unlikely to intrude. There, before an assembly of youths, the girl would formally announce, "*Cä ji nhɔak*" ("I agree to you/I love you"), and exchange gifts with her newly declared love. Whereas twenty years earlier she might have offered a long, decorated tassel (*dhuor*) for him to hang on the horn of his prize ox as a sign of her affection in exchange, say, for some colorful beads (*tiik*), during the early 1980s gifts of purchased mirrors, soap, perfume, and other grooming items were more common. Although the girl could continue to resist the man's sexual advances, neither she nor her friends would consider it shameful if she later became pregnant by him. In the subculture of contemporary eastern Nuer youths, pregnancy brought shame upon a girl only when realized outside a relationship of "declared love".[37]

Although a man could not assume that a formal declaration of the girl's love implied her consent to engage in sexual "play" (*ŋar*), men's expectations in this regard appeared to be hardening during the early 1980s. If the girl continued to resist her "lover's" sexual invitations with statements such as "sex isn't everything" or "I love you but that doesn't necessarily mean that we can play together," he could threaten to break off their relationship by returning her special gift. Force, I should stress, was not considered an option in such circumstances. Courtship revolved, rather, around the art of conversation (*muɔŋ*) in which men would attempt to overcome feminine resistance through the skillful construction of compliments, arguments, and counterarguments. As one young man explained, "It is the girl who determines how far things go, for if she says no, what can the man do?" Rape, though not unknown, was regarded as an extremely serious offense that could easily result in the immediate mustering of a war party. This attitude has continued into the 1990s. During the latter 1980s Commander Machar, for instance, adopted a severe policy of court martialing and executing by firing squad any enlisted men convicted of this offense. What many courting men did seem to worry about during the early 1980s was that they might initiate a type of sexual play with which the girl was unfamiliar and thus offend her. At that time many Nuer youths, inspired by foreign films seen in northern cities, were experimenting with the phenomenon of kissing (*ciim*). Although kissing had long been used

37. Were this to happen, the girl's friends could justifiably insult her, saying that she was no better than "beads" to be "begged" by a man.

Plate 20. A chain of male dancers: The flamboyantly colored dance leggings, sneakers, and tight, pocketed shorts have become essential display items for young eastern Gaajok men.

Plate 21. A chain of girl dancers: Books, flashlights, and other imported display items can be held in place of dancing rods by eastern Gaajak girls. The girls' skirts are made of twisted grass topped with a chain of cattle tails.

by parents to express affection for small children, most adults continued to disdain the idea of kissing their spouses on the mouth—an act they considered tantamount to a ludicrous infantilization of them.[38] The younger generation, however, was becoming more open to the experience.

Despite superficial appearances of egalitarianism and reciprocity between the sexes, contemporary eastern courtship practices were marked by a strong double standard in that a girl was expected to have only one declared love at a time whereas a man could have many. Indeed, a man who succeeded in winning over several girls at the same time was openly admired by his contemporaries, both men and girls alike. Such a man was a *balaŋ* (pl., *balaaŋ/balaaŋni*)—a term that was never applied to girls in the east and that originally meant, amusingly, "expert fisherman"/"hippopotamus hunter" (Kiggen 1948:28). Although a man would be in deep trouble with the courts were he to impregnate more than one of his girlfriends at once, his reputation as a *balaŋ* would only soar. There was one young Gaajok man I met, for instance, who proudly claimed to have impregnated five girls in succession without marrying any of them. When I asked him how he managed to evade their brothers' spears, he smiled and said, "with cleverness (*pɛl*)." He explained that when each of the girls' relatives approached him about marriage cattle, he readily agreed to marry the girl but stressed that he must first complete his secondary school education: "For I knew that the girl would eventually grow tired of waiting and would accept another lover. When that happened, I would confront the girl, saying angrily, 'Why didn't you wait for me?' After that, I could [legitimately] break off the engagement." Although I suspect that the number of girls this young man claimed to have treated in this manner was sheer hyperbole, he clearly grasped the exploitative potential of the sexual double standard embedded in eastern Nuer concepts and practices of "declared love" (*luɔm*).

Once the proud girl publicly revealed the identity of her "lover" through her songs or actions, it became extremely difficult for her to meet openly with him—or with his best friend/ally (*kiiɣdɛ*). Often the couple would refrain from greeting each other in public and from dancing together at night. For if they were to be seen together by the girl's father, brothers, or cousins, a major fight was likely to ensue. For the girl's relatives knew that, were she to elope or be impregnated by her lover, her bridewealth value, so to speak, would be seriously threatened, if not re-

---

38. Among contemporary western Nuer, close girl friends would often greet one another with a kiss if they had not seen each other for a long time.

duced. It was thus the girl's responsibility to notify her lover of potential opportunities to meet safely with her.

More important for my purposes, the girl considered herself morally obliged to consult with her "declared love" in the event that another man approached her or her father with a marriage proposal. Her lover was expected to respond in either of two ways. He could formally release the girl, explaining that he was unable to marry her at that time because, for instance, one of his older brothers had not yet married or because of a shortage of bridewealth cattle. In that case it was considered essential that he and the girl's husband-to-be dance together before her at some point during her wedding celebrations. Alternatively, the man could refuse to release the girl, arranging instead—via his best friend (*kiiɣde*)—to elope with her, if his cattle resources were inadequate to arrange an immediate cattle-byre marriage. Moreover, the ethics of eastern Nuer courtship practices were such that the girl felt morally compelled to run away with him, if he so proposed. In the event she subsequently became pregnant, the young man's negotiating position vis-à-vis her family and the courts would only be strengthened—though he still risked ambush by her relatives if caught with her.

In the tightly spun rural communities of eastern Nuerland it was not difficult for residents to surmise the motives of young, unknown couples traveling through their territories. Although unrelated individuals usually turned a blind eye to what was going on, they could also mock a wayward couple on occasion, playing upon their ignorance and vulnerability, as a way of expressing moral condemnation of rising elopement trends. For instance, I was told, amidst peals of laughter, of a practical joke played on an eloping couple by a small eastern Gaajok community of cieng Yol that bordered the banks of a large stream. An unknown eloping couple, having forded the stream in the direction of the community, was immediately met by an agitated group of villagers who stated that the couple had deeply offended the spirit of a man who had drowned at that place several years earlier. "It's a place of divinity," the villagers exclaimed, "which must not be crossed without first offering an appropriate sacrifice." "Normally, we require the sacrifice of an ox, but since we see you have no cattle," the villagers added pointedly, "there is a rite you must perform to negate your offense." The frightened couple readily agreed to conform to their request, whereupon the villagers explained that the rite required the man to bend over and expose his anus to the girl, who must then penetrate it with a wooden spear shaft (*taŋ*) several times while solemnly repeating *liel cɔadä, ɛ jɛn liel cɔadä* ("my husband's anus, this is my husband's anus"). The girl, however, became extremely embarrassed at this suggestion and pleaded for some other way of appeasing the divinity's anger.[39] The villagers, however, were adamant that no alternative rite existed. And after much persistent persuasion the girl finally agreed to comply. But no sooner had she poked her husband's anus and pronounced the words *liel cɔadä* than the villagers burst into laughter, whereupon the humiliated girl burst into tears. "She just couldn't take it," commented Gai.

The concept of "declared love" did not extend into western Nuerland during the early 1980s. In that region the concept *luɔm* revolved, rather, around the idea of a "mutual acquaintance" established between a man and a girl through a formal exchange of names. When a western Nuer man met an attractive girl he would ask to know her name. If she agreed to reveal it and asked for his name in return, he would later embroider it with compliments and weave it, together with the names of other girls he had met, into the *wieea*, or personal song he would sing at the climax of evening dances. And since a relationship of "love" was associated first and foremost with the praising of individual names, western girls as well as men could acquire reputations as *balaaŋ/balaaŋni* ("expert hippopotamus hunters").

Nor did contemporary western youths share eastern Nuer expectations of mutual cooperation and allegiance among friends in their love affairs. Courtship in that region was a more individualized affair in which older and younger brothers sometimes competed directly for the affections of the same girl. Unlike eastern Nuer dances, where it was common to see entire chains of men (*dep*) dancing and singing in unison before a single girl, male dance lines in the west swiftly broke up in order to allow each man space to sing his personal songs—and, hopefully, attract around himself as many admiring, female dancing partners as possible. At the conclusion of western dances, therefore, some men found themselves dancing with many girls and others with none.

Whereas it was the girls who selected their dancing partners in the west, the reverse was true in the east. Indeed, among the eastern Gaajok, a man would often attempt to force his attentions on a particular girl by "accidentally" knocking into her while leaping backwards in mock duel with a male partner—a custom that I found not only annoying and disruptive but downright painful at times. In fact, at some of the eastern Nuer wed-

---

39. The anus is the most private part of a person's body. Consequently, to invoke it was one of the most potent insults imaginable. Some people said that were a wife to curse her husband's anus, her children would go blind.

dings I attended the bride and her girl friends were forced to retreat some 30 or 40 yards away from the center of the dance and to form a tight defensive pack in order to be left at peace long enough to sing the personal songs they had collectively composed for the occasion. Even so, determined young men, with heads craned backwards over their shoulders, would follow with a clumsy rearward hop—all for the privilege of potentially bruising a girl in the front row. Much to my relief, nothing comparable existed at western Nuer dances during the early 1980s.

The more individualistic tendencies of western Nuer courtship practices were also evident in the absence of collective action among marriageable girls—girls who were, as a result, far less demanding of their male suitors than were their more organized eastern Jikany sisters. A western girl could shame a young man into demonstrating his courage and commitment with the question *Tekɛ yaan jaani mi ci nööŋ?* ("Have you brought back a Dinka cow?"). Were he subsequently to fail in capturing a Dinka cow, she could justifiably reject him, no matter how many other cows he might have. "And that's why," as one young western man commented, *buut nath liaaɣ* ("people [men] spend the heat of the day [wrestling] with death"). But outside of this standardized request, western Nuer girls did not require their suitors to acquire purchased display items such as the elaborately colored dance leggings, tight pocketed shorts, sun glasses, white plastic dancing sneakers, beads, hair lotion, mirrors, foot lockers, blankets, foam mattresses, and opaque cotton mosquito nets increasingly demanded by their eastern counterparts. In the east, men who fell short of these everchanging fashion expectations were frequently subjected to insults and ostracism by well-organized bands of local girls. One man in his thirties described how humiliated he felt as a youth when a group of local girls refused to speak with him and called him an animal simply because he had no shoes. "I couldn't stand it," he remarked. "I went and sold an ox the very next day so that I could buy some shoes." Another eastern Nuer man recounted how he had been ridiculed for having acquired a stuffed cotton mattress instead of the more expensive foam ones preferred by local girls. One girl disdainfully compared the stuffing of his mattress with the "undigested contents of a cow's stomach": *ɛ jiec wau.* Yet another man recounted being rejected because he had failed to obtain the sunglasses deemed essential display items by local girls that year.

The vulnerability of young eastern Nuer men in this regard should not be underestimated—nor should its impact on local patterns of labor migration be ignored. When questioned as to why they first ventured off to Khartoum, many young eastern Jikany migrants cited their desire to obtain specific courting paraphernalia, rather than the need to purchase bridewealth cattle, as primary. And when I once asked a group of young eastern Gaajok girls whether they would prefer a poorly dressed man with a beautiful display ox to a well-dressed man with none, they laughed and unanimously agreed that a well-dressed man would be far more attractive. Nevertheless, I don't wish to give the impression that the courtship demands of eastern Nuer girls were invariably material. One of the questions eastern Nuer girls were beginning to ask their suitors in 1982 was *Caa wiidu lak?* ("Are you baptized?")—a trend that undoubtedly added impetus to the wave of Christian conversion gaining momentum in the east at that time.

Last, I should stress that contemporary eastern and western Nuer men alike took the attitude that "a girl belongs to everyone" (*nyal ɛ duŋ naadh dial*). Consequently, there was absolutely no excuse in their eyes for a girl to refuse to converse with a man who politely solicited her attentions. The strength of this conviction was impressed upon me by an eighteen-year-old eastern Gaajok youth named Paul, who was a good friend of mine. One day, while walking along the market street of Ulang, Paul suddenly turned to me and whispered, "Do you see that girl over there—well, next time I meet her, I'm going to punch her!" Taken aback by the sudden intensity of his anger, I asked: "What did she do? Did she steal from you?" "No," he responded sullenly, "last night after the dance I grabbed her wrist because I wanted to converse (*muɔŋ*) with her [this being the standard male invitation] but she just shook off my hand and refused!" "Perhaps she wished to converse with someone else," I ventured. "But that's still no excuse for rejecting me!" Paul exclaimed. "Look at me, what's wrong with me? I have a good body, my clothes are good—and I have cattle. If she were to become pregnant, I could marry her. Is there anyone who exceeds me in goodness (*gɔi*)!" "Well, it seems to me," I joked, "that everyone around here thinks that there's no one better than himself!" Then Paul relaxed a bit and said, "I suppose that's true—but, still, I feel like punching her!" In brief, no complicating tie could possibly justify a girl's rejection of another man's request to converse with her. Other men might drop away in situations where a girl had already declared her love for a particular man, for they knew she could easily defeat them in conversation with the assertion *Nhɔk ɛ kɛl* ("Love is one"). A flat refusal, however, not only seriously jeopardized the man's sense of self-worth but also invited acts of verbal, if not physical, retribution. One of Gatnyinyar's nephews composed a thirty-minute song after being similarly shunned by a girl after a dance in which he gave full vent to his wish that the girl in question would die!

Although members of the older generation were highly critical of the growing tendency of young men to insult girls viciously through song, their verbal condemnations appeared to have little impact.

Paternity, Legitimacy, and Adultery

For young Nuer men it was becoming easier not only to railroad marriage propositions through courts but also to reject girls they had impregnated while simultaneously asserting claims of paternity over the children conceived. With respect to the "legitimation" of children born of unmarried girls, the evolution of Nuer customary law since the 1930s had been dramatic. Whereas prior to the creation of government chiefs and courts it was apparently impossible for a man to claim formal paternity of a child conceived by an unmarried girl whom he failed to marry (Evans-Pritchard 1951b:121), his "right" to claim that child through the payment of a cattle fee (*ruɔk*) was increasingly upheld by the courts—even in situations where the young man himself originally denied in court that the child was his so as to avoid marrying the mother (Howell 1954:175–176), though in the latter cases higher *ruɔk* fees could be demanded. "Second thoughts" of this nature were impossible only in situations where another man had already laid claim to the child by marrying the mother (Howell 1954:175–176). A belated paternity claim of this sort was not likely to be supported by the courts, however, if the man had not paid compensation of two or three head of cattle (*ruɔk nyal*) to the girl's family after having impregnated her. Otherwise, the child would be incorporated into the girl's patriline, with her father deciding whether the child would later "be married" together with the mother to another man or, alternately, remain a member of the girl's own natal family.

This subtle yet, to my mind, highly significant shift in the legal code must be understood, I think, as part of a more general decline in the social prominence of the pater/genitor distinction in Nuer social life, both within and outside of marriage. This trend was evident not only in changing legal norms concerning the "legitimation" of the children of unmarried girls but also, as we shall see, in hardening court attitudes toward adultery.[40]

According to Evans-Pritchard, Nuer husbands did not take the infidelity

40. Nuer concepts of adultery (*dhöm*) applied, in principle, whenever a man had sexual relations with another man's wife (including ghost wives and leviratic wives). With respect to widows, however, a pro-husband could claim only one cow in adultery compensation, called *yaŋ kolä*, "the cow of the sleeping hide." It was normally sacrificed to remove any pollution resulting from the act.

of their wives all that seriously during the early 1930s because there was little importance attached to the physiological paternity of children at that time. "Men prefer to beget their own sons, but it is not ignominious to nurture children begotten by others. Nuer pay little regard to the manner of begetting so long as the legal fatherhood of the child is well established" (1951b:120).

Indeed, Evans-Pritchard reported being "struck . . . both by the frequency of adultery and the infrequency of quarrels or even talk about it" (1951b:120). At that time adultery compensation varied—when it was obtained at all—between three and six head of cattle, depending on the relationship between the men concerned. One of these cows—*yaŋ kolä* ("the cow of the sleeping hide")—was normally sacrificed in order to sever the adulterous relationship and to protect the husband from the onset of *kɔɔr*, a form of pollution that usually manifested itself as aching pains in the husband's lower back. The other cattle compensated the husband for the infringement of his sexual rights in his wife. When the adulterous affair culminated in the birth of a healthy child, however, these latter cattle were always returned to the adulterer lest the adultery-compensation payment (*ruɔk ciek*) be confused with a paternalization fee (*ruɔk gatä*; Evans-Pritchard 1951b:120; Howell 1954:156). In no circumstances was the adulterer permitted to claim paternity rights in such a child (Evans-Pritchard 1951b:121). Compensation cattle were also returned to the adulterer in situations where the husband subsequently divorced his wife, thereby relinquishing all claims in her. Moreover, according to both Evans-Pritchard (1951b:134) and Howell (1954:141), it was extremely rare for a woman to be divorced on adultery charges during the 1930s and 1940s unless she persisted in relations with one man or many. And even then her husband could not divorce her if she had already fulfilled her procreative obligations to him by having borne two children to his name (Evans-Pritchard 1951b:92–93; Howell 1954:148–149).

Following the establishment of government chiefs and courts, however, adultery was increasingly defined by local British officials and newly appointed Nuer chiefs alike as "a threat to the stability of marriage as well as to public security" (Howell 1954:167). Hence, as part of their more general efforts to standardize Nuer customary law, British officials encouraged Nuer chiefs to apply more stringent legal sanctions on adulterers in the hope of curbing what many Nuer perceived to be a disturbing decline in the fidelity of wives, evident in the rising number of adultery suits reaching the courts.

In an excellent discussion of evolving legal practices in this regard, Howell explained how adultery, originally a "private delict," was gradually transformed under British rule into a "public delict" and into a "criminal offence" in cases where the husband subsequently decided to divorce the offending wife (1954:236).[41] Through what he termed a "curious admixture of traditional Nuer law . . . and European legal concepts" designed to strengthen Nuer marriages by reinforcing the husband's exclusive sexual rights in his wife, Nuer chiefs were eventually prevailed upon to institute the following jural innovations:

1. A man who committed adultery repeatedly with the same woman, while subject to the payment of cattle compensation fees only twice, remained liable to government imposed fines and prison terms of six to twelve months.

2. A man who had sexual relations with an unmarried woman who cohabited on a stable basis with another man was punishable by imprisonment and fines even though cattle compensation could not be awarded to the man who had unsuccessfully claimed to be the woman's husband.

3. Compensation cattle were not to be returned to the adulterer when a healthy child was born of his act.

4. In the event of divorce, cattle received by the husband as adultery compensation became government property. (Howell 1954:167–169)

The first two innovations were directed primarily toward expanding the punitive powers of the courts beyond the scope of civil liabilities. But in the process it would seem that the definition of "adulterous acts"—and hence the rights men formally held in the sexual and procreative capacities of their "wives"—was expanded as well (Howell 1954:155). The third and fourth innovations were adopted after a British administrator vehemently objected to the return of adultery-compensation cattle on moral grounds: The adulterer, he argued, must not be allowed to benefit from his act under any circumstances—and particularly when it resulted in divorce (Howell 1954:167).

By the time I began investigating these issues firsthand during the early 1980s, government officials had begun to categorize adultery with homi-

41. Significantly, Howell attributed increased litigation over sexual rights in wives at that time not only to dwindling fears of forceful retaliation by these women's husbands but, more interestingly, to expanding legal definitions of "adultery" as such (1954:155).

cide and theft in that a conviction of any of these "crimes" was considered sufficient to disqualify a man from running for high-ranking chiefly offices. And in the east, where Christianity was spreading rapidly at that time, evangelists frequently harangued their congregations about the evils of adultery along with those of homicide and cattle sacrifice.

More important, many contemporary eastern Nuer chiefs were actively defending—or rather extending—men's claims of sexual exclusivity in highly questionable circumstances in an apparent effort to curb feminine infidelity. For instance, I followed an "adultery" suit among the eastern Gaajok in which a pregnant, unmarried woman (*ciek mi kɛaɣ*) was publicly "divorced," whipped, and jailed after she had attempted to leave her first lover, with whom she had borne a child and had lived in concubinage for many years, in favor of another. Although I suspect that political collusion and bribery were important factors in the brutal resolution of this case, I was surprised how swiftly certain segments of the population swung behind the chief's decision. Though many men and women were appalled by the chief's decision to lash a woman in her seventh month of pregnancy, several middle-aged and younger men with whom I discussed the case argued—some of them quite vehemently—that the woman nevertheless deserved some form of punishment. The most respected elder of the community, however, a man who had served as head chief of the region for nearly thirty years before being forced to retire in 1976, viewed the decision as scandalous since it was well known that the woman, as he put it, "had no (bridewealth) cattle on her back." This view was also voiced by many, but not all, of the women with whom I spoke.

Among contemporary western Nuer, where adultery suits continued to be regarded solely as cattle affairs among men, women were neither lashed nor imprisoned when convicted of this offense. Rather, the extension to women of punitive sanctions for adultery originally intended solely for men appeared to be a recent innovation by eastern court officials, motivated no doubt by their desire to restrain what seemed to be a long-standing historical trend in that region toward increased litigation over sexual rights in women. Howell, who first noted this trend during the 1940s, attributed it largely to the government's prohibition on armed retaliation by the offended husband—an important factor often defined by more contemporary Nuer as "a loss of fear" or, otherwise, as "the spoiling (of people) by the government" (*ɛ nyiɛth kume*). In view of the more general social disruptions caused by labor migration and recurrent war over the last thirty-five years, it is perhaps readily understandable that adultery accusations appeared to be on the rise. Significantly, Kun Thoän, a prominent eastern Nuer prophet, built much of his fame during the 1970s and 1980s around a powerful stick, which he claimed enabled him to divine whether a woman had committed adultery.

This is not to say that western Nuer courts remained unaffected by these trends or by accompanying shifts in public opinion. In that region as well men appeared to be pursuing adultery suits with greater tenacity and bitterness during the early 1980s than was common a generation earlier. Whereas Howell reported that it was rare during the 1940s for a man to divorce a wife on grounds of adultery unless she persisted in relations with one man or several, during the early 1980s a single offense was often regarded by government chiefs as sufficient grounds to justify divorcing a wife against her will, even in situations where there were several living children involved. Among the Leek Nuer, for instance, I followed a controversial divorce case in which a middle-aged widow was divorced against her will on charges of adultery by her late husband's brother after having borne her husband four children—two of whom were living at the time of the trial. Of the four children she bore, the first two were fathered by her late husband, the third by his brother, and the fourth (which had died during delivery) by a lover. The widow defended her decision to take a lover on the grounds that her husband's brother was unable to fulfill his procreative obligations toward her since he traveled frequently to Khartoum, often remaining there for a period of years before returning to visit her. All she desired from the court was permission to remain together with her two daughters in her late husband's home and to bear additional children in his name by her lover. Her late husband's brother, however, was adamant about divorce: "My heart refuses her, I no longer want her [around]." Although during the 1930s and 1940s this case would almost certainly have been resolved in favor of the widow, especially since she had two surviving children at the time of the trial, the court eventually ruled—albeit reluctantly and only after numerous attempts to dissuade her late husband's brother from his suit—in favor of divorce. Paradoxically, the court reached this decision despite the fact that the deceased husband's brother had no right to claim adultery compensation from the widow's lover. Having already borne her dead husband several children, she was "free" in principle to seek a lover of her own choosing: *Ciek jokä /caa ɛ ruɔk* ("A widow [with children] is not subject to adultery compensation"). In explaining the reasoning behind their decision, several chiefs expressed fear that a continuation of the marriage could lead to bloodshed between the families concerned. "The woman's brother and her husband's brother are on the verge of killing each other," one remarked. Indeed, the widow had already suffered a superficial spear wound in a fight with her husband's brother. Yet the fact that the six presiding court chiefs ultimately decided to dissolve the union rather than to protect the widow's rights to remain at peace in her home reveals, I think, the legal difficulties many women were facing when attempting to assert a greater measure of autonomy—sexual or otherwise—within later marriage. For in essence the court undercut, while simultaneously recognizing, the widow's legal right to separate rights held in her procreative powers from claims held in her sexuality. Moreover, this trend was magnified, as we shall see, through expanding court definitions of the procreative obligations of wives toward their husbands and their husbands' kin.

Divorce

According to Evans-Pritchard, it was practically impossible during the 1930s for a man to divorce his wife after she had fulfilled her procreative obligations toward him—obligations which, at that time, apparently did not extend beyond the birth of the second child (Evans-Pritchard 1951b:91–92). Were the wife subsequently to commit adultery or otherwise neglect or abandon her husband, it would have been extremely difficult for him to reclaim his bridewealth cattle from his in-laws since "cattle that have children on their backs cannot be returned."

> Whatever the circumstances [of the spouses' separation] are, the husband has a right either to his cattle or to the children his wife may bear to other men, but it sometimes happens that whereas he wants his cattle back to marry again, since he cannot have a home without a wife, the wife's people tell him he is responsible for the separation and must be satisfied with the children. They would not refuse him his children. If they tell him this—and they would not do so unless she had already borne him a child and had lived in his home—he has to accept their decision. There are no courts he can appeal to and his kinsmen would be unwilling to support him in resort to force. There is nothing he can do. (Evans-Pritchard 1951b:92–93)

The husband was thus forced to resign himself to an indefinite state of separation, suffering loss of a mate, cook, housekeeper, beer brewer, and so forth while at the same time retaining rights of paternity in whatever children his wife conceived thereafter "in the bush." In other words, the rights he gained in his wife's sexuality and domestic services through marriage payments could be effectively withdrawn by the woman herself (Gough 1971).

If the abandoned husband had no other wife or any hope of obtaining one in the near future, he felt this loss intensely indeed. Consequently, states of jural divorce—as distinct from states of conjugal separation—were apparently quite rare during the 1930s. Indeed, Evans-Pritchard claimed that he had "never known, or heard of, a case of divorce, or even of separation, after the birth of a second child" to the union (1951b:94). One of the principal reasons for this, he argued, was the dominant negotiating position maintained by the bride's relatives as the keepers of the bridewealth cattle.

On the basis of a marital survey Evans-Pritchard conducted among thirty-two western Leek women in 1936, it would appear that only 6.25 percent of the women sampled had ever experienced divorce. And of the divorces he uncovered, only one (or 3 percent) involved a living child (see the appendix). Following the establishment of government chiefs' courts and police, however, jural divorce no longer depended entirely upon the willingness of the wife's kinsmen to cooperate in the return of the bridewealth cattle. New power elements were introduced, as were new discursive possibilities. One of the immediate consequences was a rapid rise in the number of divorce suits appearing before Nuer courts, a trend first documented by Howell (1954:145) during the mid-1940s and subsequently corroborated by a major marital survey conducted by myself among 122 western Leek women in 1983. The latter survey, documented in full in the appendix, suggests that the proportion of ever-married women who had been divorced in that region rose from 6.25 percent in 1936 to 12.29 percent in 1983. And when the mean number of marriages ending in divorce is expressed as a proportion of all marriages that had taken place minus those that had ended in death (a calculation known as divorce ratio C and widely regarded as the most revealing figure for comparative purposes), this rise in the frequency of jural divorce among Leek Nuer women appeared even more striking: 13.0 in Evans-Pritchard's 1936 survey as compared with 38.2 in my own 1983 sample. Furthermore, 35 percent of the divorces reported by Leek Nuer women in 1983 involved living children as compared with only 3 percent of those registered in Evans-Pritchard's earlier Leek Nuer survey.

In an insightful passage, Howell hypothesized that the surge in divorce suits that developed shortly after the introduction of government courts was due

> not so much [to] the possibility of legal enforcement as the general recognition that divorce is possible at all, particularly after the *muot* [or marriage consummation ceremony] and after children have been born of the union.

> ... Added to this is the fact that union of peoples required for political security is less necessary than in the past, and therefore intermarriage does not serve the same purpose as it did then. (1954:145)

Once government courts admitted this possibility, it became necessary, as Howell explained, for the administration to establish certain standards regarding the exact point at which a woman's procreative obligations toward her husband were to be considered fulfilled. Although British officials actively encouraged local chiefs to establish a consensus of opinion on this matter, this was not easily accomplished. Nuer chiefs often disagreed over the number of children necessary to preclude the possibility of jural divorce—although British administrators apparently sought unsuccessfully to establish the limit at two (Howell 1953a:139; 1954:143). The issue of infant mortality proved especially thorny:

> Nuer consider that the dissolution of marriage, instituted by either party, is impossible if the wife has fulfilled her procreative obligations. Generally speaking, though this point is sometimes controversial, two living children constitute fulfillment in this respect. Three are always sufficient. . . . In particular, the question whether children who have died in infancy should count is a controversial one. Among most Nuer tribes it is generally accepted that those who die in early infancy should not be so counted. From the legal point of view a small child is not considered a being at all, and if it dies before cutting its second teeth no mortuary ceremonies will be performed. Nor will a "ghost-wife" be married to its name, though there are many exceptions to this rule, especially when there are few adult males to represent the lineage. The test ultimately lies in whether mortuary ceremonies have been performed or not, and the situation is not uncommon owing to the high rate of infant mortality among the Nuer. Opinion, however, is often divided. (Howell 1954:148–149)

Since Evans-Pritchard did not address the issue of infant mortality directly, stating only that a woman could not be divorced after having borne two children in her husband's name (1951b:92), it is impossible to know whether the issue of infant mortality was weighed as heavily before as after government intervention.

This is not, however, an insignificant issue. Knowledge of the earliest point in the marriage process when it became feasible for a wife to leave her husband without at the same time jeopardizing the cattle resources (and, potentially, the marriages) of her natal kinsmen is crucial in assessing longer-term shifts in relations of power and authority within marriage. As Gough perceptively pointed out years ago, it was the very possibility of separating rights held in a woman's sexual and domestic services from others held in her procreative powers that afforded Nuer women greater personal autonomy in later marriage without threatening the legal principle of agnatic descent (1971:111).

Viewed from the perspective of the wife, marriage could be seen to involve a lengthy period of probation during which she was under pressure, if committed to the union, to defer to her husband's will, publicly and privately, until such time as her procreative obligations toward him were unambiguously fulfilled.[42] However, once a woman's position within her husband's home was fully secured through the birth of several children, she could assert her desires and opinions more forcefully, talking back to or quarreling openly with her husband if he failed to live up to her expectations. That she should do so was readily understandable to contemporary Nuer, who often explained growing tensions between husband and wife in later marriage in terms of a progressive loss of *pöc* ("shyness") or, alternatively, *dual* ("fear") on the part of the wife toward her husband.

What is important to realize here, however, is that this "probationary period" was gradually extended through the agency of government courts.[43] This was so much the case that, by the early 1980s, the existence of three or even four children was no longer considered sufficient grounds by court officials to reject the possibilities of divorce and of the forced return of bridewealth cattle. On the contrary, the adoption of increasingly

42. Indeed, it was uncommon at that time for a bride to take up residence at her husband's home before giving birth to their first child. She remained instead at her natal home, where her husband was free to visit her at night. During these visits, she was not expected to cook for her husband or perform any other wifely duties other than that of potential procreator. Consequently, a woman normally entered her husband's household with the status of both a wife and a mother.

43. This "probationary period" was not only extended but also intensified between the 1930s and 1980s by a growing tendency for Nuer brides to take up residence in their husbands' homes at earlier and earlier stages in the marriage process. During the early 1980s, it was not uncommon for the bride to be taken to her husband's home shortly after completion of the wedding ceremony. This trend reportedly began during the first civil-war era when it was more risky for husbands to travel at night to their wives' natal homes. Many fathers also believed that their daughters would be more secure under the full-time protection of their husbands during this period. It was also during this period that some Nuer husbands began to view marriage as a kind of "purchase." Consequently, they began to argue that the domestic and procreative rights acquired in their wives through the payment of bridewealth cattle should be fully awarded to them immediately upon completion of the wedding celebrations. And in many cases these arguments were deferred to. Consequently, many Nuer brides began to enter their husband's home in a comparatively weak position. This in itself increased the likelihood of domestic conflicts. Not only were the bride's procreative powers as yet unproven, but her domestic skills and general personality were subjected to the critical scrutiny of her husband's family at an earlier phase of the marriage process.

rigid and punitive adultery sanctions had made it far more difficult for
Nuer chiefs to condone—let alone defend—states of conjugal separation as
distinct from jural divorce under any circumstances. Moreover, it was my
experience that court officials tended to ignore the issue of infant mortality
entirely in favor of a simple count of how many children were living at
the time of the divorce trial. Add to this the fact that divorces were being
granted more easily at that time on grounds of wifely infidelity (even after
the birth of numerous children to the union), and it is not surprising that
many women were finding it increasingly difficult to achieve stable states
of conjugal separation as opposed to jural divorce. I recall, for instance, a
divorce suit in which a middle-aged western Leek woman wished to take
a lover but feared that he would be fined and jailed on adultery charges.
She thus felt she had no choice but to push for a formal divorce through
the courts, even though she had already had four children with her husband, all of them living at the time of the trial. Throughout the court
hearing she adamantly rejected her husband's attempts to salvage the
union. "Even if I never give birth again," she exclaimed, "I want a divorce."
Whereas this dispute would certainly have terminated in a state of conjugal separation prior to the introduction of government courts, the presiding
chiefs eventually decided in favor of divorce and immediately embarked
upon the complex task of retracing the fates of the original bridewealth
cattle and their offspring. Belated divorce suits of this nature, of course,
made the return of bridewealth cattle especially arduous. Moreover, we
have already seen how the conceptual distinction between cattle of money
and cattle of girls was becoming increasingly significant in this respect.

As far as most Nuer chiefs of the early 1980s were concerned, the option
of jural divorce lapsed only after the marriage or initiation of a child from
the union. Nevertheless, the de facto limits of divorce could be earlier. Once
the number of cattle required to retain paternity rights in the children
born to the union equaled or exceeded those the husband could hope to reclaim from his affines, he would be highly unlikely, many people stressed,
to agree to a formal divorce. When I asked how many living children this
would mean at prevailing bridewealth rates during the early 1980s, most
men and women I spoke with came up with the number five, basing their
calculations on current paternalization fees of five head of cattle for a
daughter and six for a son in the east or, alternately, four head of cattle for
a daughter and six for a son in the west.

Now, to the extent that Nuer husbands and contemporary court officials
actually rationalized the economics of marriage and divorce in this way,
the efforts wives devoted to the daily maintenance of their husbands and

households, as distinct from their labors as procreators, were implicitly devalued. Upon divorce it was primarily a woman's accomplishments as the provider of children that were formally recognized in the redistribution of bridewealth cattle. In other words, increasing numbers of Nuer were beginning to equate bridewealth payments directly with childwealth payments. And as issues of adultery were given greater emphasis by the courts, the fate of specific marriage alliances began to revolve more and more around the circulation of human blood rather than of cattle. Moreover, in two divorce cases I witnessed the husbands tried—albeit unsuccessfully—to avoid paying *ruɔk* (the cattle paternalization fee) for some of the children born to their wives during the marriage on the grounds that they had been conceived in adultery. Although the court rejected this request in both instances, the very fact that any man would seek to disown a child born to a legally married wife on the suspicion that he or she had been conceived in adultery reveals, I think, the extent to which the pater/genitor distinction was being questioned and reassessed—a reassessment that was inseparable from a more general decline in the significance of cattle flows relative to human blood flows in the creation and maintenance of *maar*.

All of these developments shifted the fulcrum of power and authority within marriage in favor of the husband. Since unions involving as many as four living children could now be dissolved through the courts, the point at which the procreative fortunes and misfortunes of husband and wife were permanently welded together was also effectively delayed. Consequently, the burden—and hence vulnerability—of bringing forth the next generation began to weigh even more heavily upon wives than it did in the past. Put bluntly, in a world where almost half of the children born alive died before reaching adulthood, it was one thing to expect a woman to raise two children through early childhood and quite another to expect her to raise four or five. As was made clear in the case of the divorced widow discussed earlier, older wives with few surviving children were especially vulnerable to being divorced against their will in late marriage. Many women with whom I discussed this issue cited rising mortality rates among children as an important contributing factor to rising divorce rates. Although a total void of reliable census data precludes any definitive judgments in this regard, I have little reason to believe that child mortality rates dropped since the World Health Organization first estimated in 1949 that only 55 percent of children born in the Upper Nile Province reached adult life. Yet even if child mortality rates remained fairly constant through the outbreak of the second Sudanese civil war in 1983, it would be quite understandable, given changing court attitudes toward the procreative obligations of wives, if women felt such losses more intensely as a result of their increasing vulnerability to jural divorce.

Moreover, I should note that contemporary eastern Nuer women did not feel that they could sue directly in court for divorce. Rather, they felt forced to provoke their husbands into such suits by abandoning them or by eloping with other men. Eastern Nuer chiefs were on the whole extremely reluctant to proclaim in court that any wife had "the right" in a marital dispute with her husband. Most voiced the attitude that *Ciek thil jɛ cuɔŋ* (literally, "A wife never has the right [against her husband in court]")—the explicit fear being that a wife publicly awarded "the right" against her husband might consider herself equal to a man (*dee rɔadɛ paar kɛ wut*). Hence, a married woman, I was told, could win a case against her husband only indirectly—for although eastern Nuer chiefs would not chastise a man in court for mistreating his wife, if her case were especially strong they would not hesitate to do so in private after the trial. Needless to say, this well-recognized chiefly strategy did not encourage eastern Nuer women to view the courts—which were, of course, controlled entirely by men—as a potential source of support in domestic disputes. Indeed, of the many hundreds of cases of abandonment, divorce, wife-beating, and adultery I followed in that region, I never once saw a married woman publicly given "the right" against her husband. Unmarried girls and divorcees, in contrast, were frequently awarded "the right" in disputes with their fathers and other men. But when it came to married women, whether young childless wives or leviratic widows, eastern Nuer courts invariably supported the husband's authority over his wife.

These attitudes were far less apparent during the early 1980s among western Nuer chiefs. I readily recall my amazement upon attending my first western Nuer court case in the vicinity of Adok when the chiefs openly awarded a widow "the right" in a suit against her late husband's brother (and current pro-husband) over three goats he had allegedly confiscated without her permission. Although the accused man countered this charge with a divorce threat and with complaints that the widow had recently taken a lover, the three presiding chiefs concluded the case by publicly threatening to evict the man from his late brother's home if he persisted in abusing the widow's properties. Never before had I seen a case resolved in this manner. Moreover, when I later settled into the home of the head chief of Leek Nuer, I could not help but be struck by the steady procession of battered and abused wives who sought sanctuary there until their husbands could be summoned and their domestic difficulties aired in court. In that region many women seemed to regard the courts as a sort of marriage counseling service in which they could expect to receive a just hearing. In my experience western Nuer chiefs did not hesitate to upbraid husbands in court, and women were permitted to sue directly for divorce. Although I cannot offer a fully historicized "explanation" of these regional differences in court attitudes here, I suspect that they may be linked to a more general decline over the past half century in the status and negotiating powers of wife-givers in the east. This theme will be developed more fully in chapter 5.

From Wife-Takers to Wife-Givers

By extending the period during which jural divorce remained a viable option, eastern and western Nuer courts effectively delayed the point in the marriage process when the interests of the extended families concerned began to take precedence over the state of conjugal relations in determining the fate of the union. Whereas during the 1930s the second childbirth principle ensured that these priorities shifted relatively quickly to a collective plane, the British initiated a process whereby—as one Nuer put it—"the fate of marriages was placed increasingly in the hands of the two people who never agree about anything." What was formerly a procreative bond uniting two families was redefined under British rule as a matter of "personal commitment" in which the husband's exclusive rights in his wife's sexuality became the key issue.

By implicitly devaluing the alliance interests of the extended families concerned, the courts thus tipped the balance of power not only in favor of the husband but, more dramatically, in favor of the wife-takers over the wife-givers. The powerful negotiating advantage formerly enjoyed by the latter group as the keepers of the bridewealth cattle was suddenly lost and replaced by increased vulnerability to government-enforced cattle recalls during later and later phases of the marriage. The wife-givers experienced this power reversal all the more intensely because paternalization fees were not automatically deducted from the bridewealth cattle prior to their return upon divorce. As a result of legal precedents established during the colonial era (Howell 1954:154 n. 1), government courts sought to separate divorce suits, normally pursued by the wife-takers, from paternalization suits, normally raised by the wife-givers. The standard procedure during the early 1980s was for the wife-givers to return or replace the original bridewealth cattle (minus those that had died naturally while in their possession plus any offspring the husband knew about) before being allowed to sue the husband for paternity fees for children born during the union. Although some Nuer chiefs remarked that this procedure—which clearly favored the wife-takers—could be relaxed in situations where the husband's bad behavior provoked the divorce, it normally operated during the 1980s as a kind of credit system for the divorcing husband. In essence, the ex-wife's people were expected to provide the husband with a short-term cattle loan to facilitate his prompt remarriage. It was only fitting, several chiefs commented, for the ex-wife's family to assist him in this way so that he might all the sooner find someone to care for the children left behind by the wife. Normally the husband gained de facto custody of all weaned children upon divorce, regardless of whether the formalities of the paternalization fees had been completed. Moreover, the husband's right to legitimate his children never lapsed, even were he to delay for years before handing over the required *ruɔk* fees. Should he put off payment until the marriage of a daughter, these fees, I was told, would be deducted from his portion of her bridewealth cattle.

The wife-givers were further disadvantaged by the fact that their responsibilities as well as liabilities vis-à-vis the wife-takers grew together with the wife's procreative obligations toward her husband. Not only were the husband's people now guaranteed, as it were, more legal heirs for their cattle than was true in the past, but their claims in the wife's sexuality and domestic services expanded together with the "probationary period" of the union. This was not simply a matter of a change in the timing of the same rights but rather one of more extensive rights in women being acquired earlier and being retained longer by the husband's family than was true before the establishment of government courts and the standardization of "customary law." Together these juro-political changes effectively reduced the autonomy of women within marriage at the same time as they leveled—if not reversed—the former asymmetry of affinal alliances. Furthermore, as I will explain in the next chapter, the declining power of the wife-givers was further magnified in the east by an increasing reluctance among the wife-takers to honor transgenerational obligations toward the wife-givers in the redistribution of bridewealth cattle received upon the marriage of the brides' daughters, granddaughters, and great granddaughters.

Although the courts had made it increasingly difficult for women to establish a greater measure of economic and sexual independence within marriage, there is little doubt in my mind that they greatly enhanced women's possibilities for autonomy outside marriage. Girls, as we have seen, were able to use the courts effectively in choosing the men they would marry, thus overcoming parental objections. Moreover, the establishment of a stable administrative network of government chiefs, courts, and police—together with a rapidly expanding regional market economy—made it much easier for unmarried women, divorcees, and widows to found and maintain independent households in which they could live under the guardianship of no man. Women now had the option of brewing beer for sale as well as of appealing to the local courts and police for the protection of themselves, their property, and their dependents. Furthermore, due to the rapid spread of Christianity in the east after the first civil war, and following the outbreak of the second civil war in the west as well, women's dependence on men's religious role as the sacrificers of cattle was seriously undermined by an ideology of individual prayer—a revolutionary change to be explored fully in chapter 7. As far as contemporary Nuer courts—and, indeed, many individuals—were concerned, *Ciek mi thil wut ɛ wut* ("A woman without a man is a man"). For some women, the status of independent divorcee undoubtedly appeared more attractive than that of formally married wife. For as far as the economics of household management were concerned, women's legal property rights within marriage had not kept pace with their material contributions to their families' welfare. The courts never awarded a divorced woman even partial rights in property obtained during the union from the sale of grain she had grown, goats she had raised, or beer she had brewed. On the contrary, it seemed that local courts had swung completely behind male ideological claims that "there is no such thing as a wealthy wife; a woman only becomes wealthy/full [*riäŋ*] by dint of her husband's efforts." And for this reason, it is perhaps not surprising that some women appeared during the early 1980s to prefer the status of independent divorcee rather than that of legally married wife.[44]

I should also mention a more recent development associated with the

44. This trend was readily apparent in a comprehensive marital survey conducted in 1983 among 122 Leek Nuer women and set forth in the appendix. However, I should perhaps note here that comparisons between this survey and an earlier marital survey of 32 Leek Nuer women conducted by Evans-Pritchard in 1936 suggest that the percentage of widow concubines surveyed dropped from 19 percent in 1936 to only 3 percent in 1983. Furthermore, the 1983 survey uncovered two "new" categories of women: independent divorcees and divorcees living in their natal homes, composing 3 and 1 percent of the 1983 female sample respectively.

postwar spread of Christianity in the east that may well prove highly corrosive to the cattle-over-blood value principle in the future. Unlike the court-
promoted trends discussed earlier, this challenge centered on the issue of
"ghost marriage": Church leaders, both east and west of the White Nile,
had begun to argue by the early 1980s that to marry a wife in the name
of a deceased relative was a fundamentally un-Christian act. One pastor
justified the closure of this option to Christians on the grounds that "A
dead body is not a soul; a dead body should no longer become your god."
Another evangelist justified it in terms of—as yet unheeded—Christian
calls for monogamy. But in condemning the practice of "ghost marriage,"
the Christian church was also threatening to destroy the procreative obligations binding kinsmen to one another—especially fellow agnates. At risk
were not only individual aspirations of transcending the "complete death"
but, more significantly, the transgenerational strength and organization of
contemporary relations of *maar*. For were the growing Christian community ever to succeed in suppressing the possibility of "ghost marriage," it
would no longer be possible for families to expand and reconstruct kinship
networks ravaged by war or cursed by recurrent procreative misfortunes.
Nor would heirless men and women be able to extend their procreative
ambitions beyond the grave. However, it remains to be seen whether this
increasingly rigid evangelical stance will be accepted, modified, or ignored
by the expanding Christian congregations in the future.

Blood over Cattle

The current situation is far clearer, however, with respect to the genitor/pa-
ter split: Recent SPLA court policies have continued earlier court practices
of muting this distinction in favor of a blood-based definition of paternity.
My impressions in this regard stem primarily from extended interviews I
had with Commander Machar in 1990 and 1992. At one point in our discussions I asked him to describe some of the most difficult civil disputes he
had faced in recent years in his capacity as the final authority of all appeal
decisions in the Western Upper Nile. Of the many fascinating cases he recounted, two related directly to the importance of blood relative to cattle in
determining patrilineal descent. The first, which the commander urged me
to include in my book, revolved around a lesbian incident between two unmarried women.

Before recounting this case, I should emphasize that, unlike sexual relations between men, female homosexuality was not considered pollut-

ing or degrading by Nuer. Whereas sexual intercourse between men was widely seen as a recent introduction brought about by increased contact with northern Arabs (often in situations where unscrupulous soldiers and employers forced young Nuer boys into submission), female homosexuality was recognized as an indigenous practice. And though not particularly encouraged, it appeared to be taken lightly by men and women alike. Some people gave me the impression that they did not consider female homosexuality a form of sexual intercourse at all, while others expressed open tolerance of the idea that two women might, on occasion, "help each other with their hands" in the absence of men.[45]

To return to our case, it so happened that an older western Nuer girl had sexual relations with a younger girl shortly after having had sexual intercourse with a man. Her female sexual partner promptly became pregnant. When the parents later discovered her condition, they pressed her to reveal the name of her impregnator. She insisted, however, that she had never in her entire life had sexual relations with a man but confessed to her sexual interlude with her girl friend. Upon hearing this news, her female friend immediately announced her intention to claim paternity rights in the child through the payment of a cattle fee (*ruɔk*) to the girl's parents. Confused and perturbed by this turn of events, the parents of the impregnated girl brought the case before the courts. During the initial trial, presiding court officials inquired as to whether the woman asserting paternity rights had had sexual relations with a man shortly before engaging with the girl. She answered in the affirmative and named a man, who happened to be in attendance. The man immediately stood up and announced his intention to assert paternity rights in the child. The court was immediately thrown into a quandary since "nothing like this had ever happened before." Could a woman credibly claim the role of genitor? If not, how could the court award a child to a male genitor who had never had sexual contact with the child's mother? Unable to reach a consensus, the regional chiefs referred the case to Commander Machar. Although the commander stressed that he had great difficulty reaching a verdict, he ultimately decided to deny the woman's paternity claim in favor of the man's. "What woman," he asked, "has ever produced sperm?"

Yet the fact that women do not produce sperm had not in itself disqualified them from assuming the role of pater in other circumstances.

45. See also Francis Mading Deng's discussion of female homosexuality in his biography of his late father (1986).

There was a long tradition, as I explained, of Nuer women becoming paters through cattle exchange.[46] It would thus have been possible, at least in principle, to have resolved this dispute by proclaiming the woman both pater and genitor—or, alternately, as pater alone, with the original source of the sperm being recognized as genitor. Considering the unusual circumstances of the case, this second option would seem a viable compromise.[47] Be that as it may, the commander's decision reveals quite clearly a continuing tendency for court officials to mute the cattle-based distinction between paters and genitors in favor of a blood-based interpretation of fathers' rights.

The premise was even more apparent in the resolution of the second paternity case the commander cited as particularly difficult. It so happened that a man married a girl who, unbeknownst to him, was already pregnant at the time of the wedding. A daughter was born and raised to maturity. All the while the husband assumed that he was both genitor and pater of the girl. However, just as the man was about to formalize his daughter's marriage by invoking his ancestral spear-call, his wife, fearing divine punishment, revealed the name of the true genitor of the girl. This confession immediately threw the marriage negotiations into turmoil, and eventually the case was brought before the commander. After carefully considering the evidence, Commander Machar ruled that the girl's genitor should assume full paternity rights over the girl by paying a cattle fee (*ruɔk*) of four cattle to her mother's natal family. Following this transaction, the girl's genitor was to receive all the bridewealth cattle that would otherwise have gone to the man who raised her. This decision also stipulated that the girl's former father could reclaim four cows from the bridewealth originally offered for her mother. Upon hearing this verdict, I suggested that the case might have been resolved without rupturing the long-standing relations between the girl and the family of the man whom she had considered since birth to be her father. This could have been done by acknowledging the genitor's right to claim "the cow of the loins/begetting" (*yaŋ letä*) upon the girl's marriage while leaving her pater's rights intact—a

46. Although the vast majority of such women sought progeny through cattle because they were unable to conceive themselves, as far as I am aware personal barrenness was not a prerequisite in this regard. For instance, I met one woman who became a "man" somewhat later in life and eventually married three wives of her own. Prior to making this decision, however, she had allegedly been married and had borne a child to her former husband.

47. Interestingly, the marriage of the impregnated girl was not an issue in either of these paternity suits.

pattern that, I argued, was more the norm in situations where the bride's genitor was other than her pater. The commander, however, disagreed. Whereas my proposal was rooted in the idea that paternity relations based on cattle exchange should take precedence over those established through common blood, the commander's resolution of the case appeared to be guided by the premise that, whenever possible, a child's genitor and pater should be the same person.

CONCLUSIONS

In this chapter I have argued that (1) the increasing ease with which men were able to assert rights of paternity over children born to unmarried girls, (2) hardening court attitudes toward the infidelity of wives, (3) the decreasing frequency with which formal bonds of alliance based on cattle exchange endured in spite of conjugal separation, (4) emerging Christian condemnations of the practice of "ghost marriage," and (5) SPLA attempts to modify Nuer customary law—all were indicative of a long-standing tendency for Nuer courts to mute the distinction between paters and genitors in favor of a blood-based interpretation of fathers' rights. Consequently, the general significance of the cattle-over-blood ideology was being eroded in matters of courtship, marriage, and divorce. Increasingly, men's rights in their children were being defined in the same blood idiom as those of mothers.

The impact of these—primarily court-instituted—changes on relations of autonomy and dependence between the sexes within marriage was profound. Prior to the introduction of government courts, there was a good deal of flexibility that allowed a wife certain liberties after she had borne children to her legal husband. These liberties, however, were gradually eroded by increasingly burdensome court interpretations of women's procreative and sexual obligations within marriage. These court-instituted changes in the balance of power between the sexes within marriage also effectively shifted the balance of power in favor of the wife-takers over the wife-givers. The ability of the latter, the wife's kinsfolk, to determine divorce decisions through control over the bridewealth cattle was considerable prior to the introduction of government courts. Since that time, however, bridewealth narrowed in its character to the point that it was frequently equated during the early 1980s with childwealth payments pure and simple. Consequently, the husband and his kinsmen were now in a position to pursue divorce claims against the wife through government courts more easily, and at a later stage in the marriage, than was previously possible. Although many Nuer women may have personally welcomed these increased opportunities for divorce, the overall thrust of evolving court policies and practices in this regard would seem to run counter to women's more general interests.[48] Moreover, that added sense of control over the world formerly made possible by the unchallenged strength of the cattle-over-blood value principle was being increasingly lost to all.

48. Nevertheless, there is no doubt in my mind that women had experienced a relative rise in status and independence vis-à-vis men over the last half century. Men's exclusive control of the courts and of formal positions of local authority, however, had significantly tempered women's gains within marriage. Yet it would be a mistake to assume that whatever power and authority men lost was necessarily gained by women. Local government administrative institutions laid claim to much of the directive and protective powers formerly concentrated in the hands of senior household heads.

5 "Incest Is Blood and the Cow"

Struggles over the
Control of Reproduction

In 1981 an unprecedented event occurred among the Nuer: A pair of full siblings began living together openly as husband and wife, something that sent shock waves throughout the extended rural community in which they lived. At first their neighbors said nothing. However, when it became apparent that this was not a temporary affair and that the couple intended to raise a family together, the regional chiefs intervened. Summoning the incestuous couple before an assembly of scandalized elders, headmen, and subchiefs, the court president demanded that the brother explain his relations with his sister. However, the young man responded with a firm counterquery of his own: "Who is raising this case against me?" "The government," replied the court. "Who?" the brother retorted: "Is my sister the daughter of the government?" The chiefs responded with an uneasy "yes." "Well, if she's the daughter of the government, then who am I?" challenged the young man. When the elders of the court heard this, they realized that these were profound questions indeed and thus softened their stance: "Tell us, son, how did this situation come about?" The young man explained that he and his sister were cattleless orphans who had little hope of marrying in their own right. Although they had a living maternal uncle, he had no daughters and three unmarried sons—and hence there was little prospect of acquiring bridewealth cattle through him. His sister's marriage prospects, he explained, were no better than his. She was considered an undesirable bride because she had no extended family upon which her in-laws could call upon in times of need; and his only hope of acquiring marriage cattle rested with her. Consequently, he and his sister eventually decided that, since they were "dead" anyway, they had nothing to lose if they were later killed by *ruaal* ("incest"). Moreover, by taking that risk, there was a chance that they might actually succeed in bringing forth children—in transforming a situation of death into one of life. Overwhelmed by the reasoning behind the couple's decision, the court assembly unanimously decided not only to drop its case but to confer its formal blessing on the union. Although the court did not declare the couple's relationship "nonincestuous," it was deeply moved by the couple's plight and thus offered special prayers in the hope that Divinity would likewise bless the union.

This remarkable event cut to the very core of Nuer marriage practices and concepts of incest: "Nothing like this had ever happened before!" In responding to the young man's arguments as it did, the council of elders was acknowledging the fact that the force of "incest prohibitions" ultimately rested with Divinity as the guardian of human morality. Although received notions of the transgenerational scope and relative intensity of various incest taboos provided an indispensable guide for human action, they were not beyond challenge: Exceptions could be made. This incident also reveals the extent to which the court considered it the natural or divine "right" of every human being to seek "procreative immortality" through the birth of progeny. Although this "right" was subject to moral constraints, there were times when it took precedence over all else. This incident further shows how the marriage prospects of a man were intimately bound up with those of his sister or sisters. Ideally, this, too, was a blood tie that would be reinforced and extended by the passage of bridewealth cattle as the siblings matured. Indeed, the transgenerational scope of *maar* (in the sense of "cognatic kinship") was conceptualized, as we shall see, in terms of the extension of an apical brother-sister tie through relations of shared blood and shared cattle rights.

Although this incident was utterly unique, there is considerable evidence to suggest that it formed part of a broader process of self-questioning taking place among Nuer at that time. By the early 1980s many men and women had begun to wonder whether their assessments of the limits of incest and exogamic prohibitions were accurate reflections of Divinity's will. Increased exposure to Christian doctrines had led some people to suspect that some of their "incest" fears were unwarranted. Furthermore, growing awareness of the fact that, among "Arabs" (*jalabni/karɛŋni*), "close relatives" (*nei ti maar*) often marry and bring forth living healthy children was especially thought provoking in this regard. For Nuer, this was a phenomenon that required an "explanation" since it was generally assumed that similar unions among themselves would prove infertile—if not fatal. In essence, people were asking themselves why Divinity should tolerate "incest" among the "Arabs" but not among themselves. Was it because the "blood" (*riɛm; pl., rim*) of the Arabs was somehow different? Or was it because the Arabs married with money instead of cattle?

In fact, it seemed that, wherever I traveled in rural Nuerland during the early 1980s, one of the first questions I was asked upon meeting new faces was always the same: "Where you come from do people marry with cattle or with money?" This question was never easy to answer since it inevitably spun off into an extended discussion either about divorce ("Who gets the children?") or about incest and exogamy ("Can relatives marry each other? Is there *ruaal* [incest] where you come from?"). After a while the course of this conversation became so predictable that I actually began to gauge my progress at language learning by how well my "answers" succeeded in drawing out and satisfying what appeared to be a remarkably deep-rooted cultural curiosity of Nuer in this regard. Gradually, however, I began to realize that these all-too-recurrent questions formed part of a much broader cultural debate concerning the nature and limits of incest prohibitions (*ruaal*).

This chapter explores the relationship between this emerging debate and apparent changes in Nuer definitions of the scope and relative intensity of various categories of incest and exogamy from the early 1930s through the 1980s. I am especially interested in exploring the extent to which such questioning may be seen as partial or incomplete—that is, as highly selective in its focus on particular categories of kin. To what extent did this controversy ignore as well as reveal dynamic aspects of Nuer social organization over this period?

A HISTORICAL PUZZLE: SEX AND THE CROSS-COUSIN

My research interests in these issues were piqued by a startling contrast I uncovered between contemporary eastern and western Nuer attitudes toward incestuous relations between siblings on the one hand and cross-cousins on the other. I simply could not understand why contemporary eastern Jikany Nuer considered sexual relations between a man and his father's sister's daughter (FZD, *nyawac*) to be worse than incest with his own daughter or full sister. This was not the case among Nuer men and women living west of the White Nile, where current opinion regarding the relative gravity of incest accorded with Evans-Pritchard's summation of Nuer attitudes some fifty years earlier. In his words:

> Incest with kinswomen on the paternal side is not thought so bad as incest with kinswomen on the maternal side. It is worse with the uterine sister than with the paternal half-sister, and it is worse with a mother's brother's daughter than with a father's brother's daughter, and with a mother's sister's daughter than with a father's sister's daughter. In all categories of incest it is considered much worse with a near kinswoman than a distant one. (Evans-Pritchard 1951b:40, 1949f:95)

The underlying logic of this ordering made perfect sense to me: In general, maternal bonds of blood were considered by contemporary western Nuer to be "closer"—or more "intense"—than paternal bonds of cattle. Indeed, the very term for "incest" (*ruaal*), I discovered, derives from the transitive verb *rualɛ*, meaning to "dry up." It was as though people equated incestuous relations with a dangerous "withering up" or "contraction" of one's blood.

And yet, contemporary eastern Jikany and Lou Nuer firmly maintained that sexual relations with the last of these categories of kin—the father's sister's daughter (*nyawac*)—had the most serious consequences. Whereas a timely confession by the parties concerned, followed by the ritual splitting of an ox by a Nuer earth priest (*kuäär muɔn*), was believed effective in tempering, if not neutralizing, the misfortunes caused by other types of incest (including relations between a man and a full sister or daughter), it was impossible, contemporary easterners argued, to counteract the negative consequences of incest with the father's sister (*wac*) or with her daughter (*nyawac*; see plate 22). *Bi liu*, I was told: "You will die." Or, as this conviction was more commonly expressed, *Ruaal nyawaidu, /caa yaandɛ juoc* ("The cow of incest with your father's sister's daughter is never seen"—literally, "it can't be rushed [to the place of sacrifice] fast enough [to save lives]"). And since a sacrifice of purification and atonement was believed futile in such circumstances, normally none was made.[1]

Now if one assumes that Evans-Pritchard's account of the relative severity of various categories of incest was once accurate for the eastern Jikany and Lou Nuer as well—and considering that he carried out the majority of field research in that area and that contemporary easterners readily acknowledged that their notions of incest were changing, I think this especially probable—then surely one must wonder why this apparent "hardening" of incest norms with respect to women related through the father's sister has occurred. And why only in the east? And why sometime over the previous half century? Before delving into these historical complexities, however, I should first sketch some key differences between the eastern and western Nuer and discuss principles of incest and exogamy more generally.

---

1. Presumably, were a case of "father's sister's daughter" (FZD) incest to come to the attention of the courts, a sacrifice of atonement would be performed. Although eastern Jikany Nuer usually spoke of this type of incest in terms of the FZD, incest with one's FZ was believed equally fatal. Incestuous relations between mother and son, in contrast, appeared to fall below the horizon of the imaginable and thus were not the subject of an explicit taboo (cf. Evans-Pritchard 1951b:40).

Plate 22. The ritual severing of an incestuous relationship: A live ox is split down the middle by an earth priest as the parties to the incest hold opposite legs.

THE CONTRACTING SCOPE OF KINSHIP TIES:
EAST/WEST REGIONAL VARIATIONS

As I explained in chapter 1, the forefathers of the contemporary eastern Jikany Nuer assimilated large numbers of Dinka and Anyuak captives and immigrants during their nineteenth-century migrations eastwards across the White Nile. Collectively known today as *jaaŋ* (sing., *jaŋ,* literally, "Dinka" and by extension all other assimilated "foreigners," including Nuer "latecomers" from other regions [*röl*]),[2] these absorbed peoples and their patrilineal descendants were initially at a disadvantage vis-à-vis the original Nuer settlers (*diel;* sing., *dil,* or the "dominant clansmen/tribal aristocrats" in Evans-Pritchard's accounts) in terms of both cattle wealth and opportunities for community leadership. Although western Nuer also dis-

---

2. Significantly, contemporary eastern Jikany no longer drew a marked distinction during the 1980s between *jaaŋ*, the descendants of Dinka, Anyuak (*bär*), and other "foreign" elements, and *röl* (sometimes spelled *rul*), or later Nuer immigrants from other "tribal" regions (*rool*). All such people were referred to as *jaaŋ*. Among contemporary Lou Nuer, in contrast, the distinction continued to be used.

tinguished between "assimilators" (*diel*) and "assimilated" (*jaaŋ*) at that time (a distinction more commonly defined during the 1980s as that between "bulls" [*tut*] and "tied" [*yien*]), Evans-Pritchard tells us that this dichotomy was far less pronounced in that region than it was among the more recently settled eastern Nuer communities. The long establishment and natural increase of "latecomers" in the west had reduced any overt privilege that resident "first comers" might have claimed to a vague prestige. The clearest indication of this contrast in the relative status of the descendants of "assimilators" and "assimilated" related to bloodwealth claims: Whereas prior to British colonial rule bloodwealth compensation was allegedly negotiated in the east at a higher rate for the descendants of "original Nuer settlers" than for the descendants of assimilated "Dinka," no such distinction was evident during the 1930s among western Nuer (Evans-Pritchard 1940a:215–218).[3] I mention this precolonial regional contrast here because it will be significant for aspects of the analysis to follow.

The historical tendency toward greater cultural continuity in the west, also discussed at length in chapter 1, was particularly evident during the 1980s in matters of incest and exogamy. Whereas contemporary western Nuer continued to respect the wide range of incest and exogamic prohibitions first recorded by Evans-Pritchard in the 1930s, contemporary easterners appeared to be taking a much more "flexible" approach to these issues. And as a result, the transgenerational scope of incest and exogamic prohibitions in that region appeared to be contracting more rapidly than among contemporary western Nuer groups.

Consider the following synopsis of Evans-Pritchard's account (1951b:29–43) of Nuer incest and exogamic prohibitions during the early 1930s. A man could not marry (1) into his agnatic "clan" (*tut*)—a prohibition that extended back some ten to twelve generations in the patrilineal line; (2) into his mother's "maximal lineage" (with a six- to eight-generation limit); (3) any "cognate" related to him up through six or seven generations (*nyier nyiët*); (4) into his genitor's "maximal lineage," if his genitor was other than his pater; (5) any natural kinswoman up through three or four generations; (6) a sister or close paternal kinswoman of a woman married to his brother or close paternal cousin; (7) the daughter of an age-mate.

I should note that sexual relations between a man and the daughter of an age-mate were not considered "incestuous" (*ruaal*) but, rather, transgressions of *maar ricä* ("age-set relations"). Otherwise, incest prohibitions

---

3. See Gough's (1971) important reanalysis of these issues.

extended in principle to all women whom a man was forbidden to marry—
though the force and extension of this prohibition varied across categories
of kin.

In addition to the above limits, incest prohibitions, extended during the
1930s for a man to the following two groups.

a. The wives of his living fathers, full brothers, mother's brothers, and
mother's brother's sons. Incestuous relations with these women were, in fact,
considered especially grave during their husbands' lifetimes since these connections were seen to involve maternal linkages.[4] (Nevertheless, these were
some of the men on whose behalf a man could marry a woman in "ghost-
marriage" after their deaths or with whose widows he could cohabit in the
levirate.)

b. The wives of his father's paternal half brothers, his own paternal half
brothers, and first paternal cousins during their husbands' lifetimes. This
category of incest was considered much less grave than category (a) since it
derived from paternal connections. (These were also men on whose behalf
a man could marry a woman in "ghost-marriage" and whose widows he
could take in the levirate.) Sexual relations with the wives of more distant
agnatic kinsmen (*tut*; sing., *tuut*, literally, "bulls") were considered either
"incestuous peccadilloes" or not incestuous at all.[5]

---

4. This interpretation stresses the fact that, in the first case, a man was connected
to his father's wives not only through his father but also through his mother.

5. For a detailed discussion of these categories, see Evans-Pritchard (1951b:29–48
and 1949f:85–103). Also see Gough's (1971) brilliant reanalysis of Evans-Pritchard's
data. With reference to prohibition (2), Evans-Pritchard tells us "that a man cannot
marry the daughter of a woman of his own maximal lineage even though the lines
of himself and the mother converge at a point more than six generations back"
(1951b:31; see 1934:7–13 for ethnographic examples). I can neither confirm nor
deny the general validity of this statement. This is because among contemporary
Lou Nuer (where Evans-Pritchard appears to have gathered the ethnographic
evidence for this prohibition) cognatic kinship (*nyier nyiët*) was traced in an
anomalous fashion. In that region the existence of a common ancestor or ancestress
up through generations five or six constituted, in principle, a bar to intermarriage.
If the genealogical link was established in generations seven through nine (some
Lou say six through eight), marriage was permissible, but if it was established
after that point (i.e., in generations ten through twelve), marriage was once again
prohibited. Contemporary Lou Nuer stated that at this point "They [the couple's
families] have become related again," *Cikε rɔ nyɔk ke maar*. I have yet to meet
a Lou Nuer who could explain the logic behind this method of tracing *maar*. My
own hunch is that it relates to the specific pattern of genealogical ties among the
diel of that region. My knowledge of Lou alliance patterns, however, is insufficient
to explore this hypothesis. Whether this same system existed at the time that
Evans-Pritchard carried out his research remains a moot point.

In addition to restricting sexual intercourse between "relatives," incest prohibitions forbade two close "relatives" from having overlapping sexual relations with a third party. Furthermore, in certain cases this prohibition extended to the witnessing of what might otherwise be considered licit sexual relations. For instance, it was incestuous for a woman to be present in a house where one of her sons or daughters was making love with his or her spouse. In witnessing the event the mother was considered to have participated in it to some degree. The heavy cotton mosquito nets many Nuer had acquired through migrant labor had helped to temper the obvious inconvenience of this prohibition to some extent. For, by the early 1980s, the younger generation had begun to treat the thick opaque walls of the mosquito net as if they formed a separate house within a house. As one older Gaajok man summed up this growing trend: "The mosquito net is becoming a very dangerous concept."

Now, by and large, contemporary western Nuer adhered to the basic principles of exogamy and incest outlined by Evans-Pritchard. For them, the outer limit of exogamy as traced through the male line continued to hover during the early 1980s between ten and twelve generations. Among the eastern Jikany, in contrast, some marriages had begun to take place between distant agnates after a genealogical lapse of seven or eight generations. However, this trend toward a contraction of agnation was not accepted by everyone. Rather, most easterners maintained that descendants of "first comers" (*diel*) should not intermarry under any circumstances, even when they were genealogically separated by more than ten generations—and, according to some, even when no exact genealogical relationship could be traced at all. There was even a special term for this exogamic principle: *maar diilä* ("relationship of the *diel*")—a term that was not recognized by contemporary western Nuer. Indeed, an explicit exogamic concept of this sort would have been superfluous in the west since restrictions upon intermarriage between *diel* and non-*diel* alike continued to encompass the full scope of most patrilineal genealogies. Yet in eastern Nuerland, where the limits of agnatic kinship were shrinking, *maar diilä* could be seen as a means by which the descendants of "first comers" had sought to reaffirm their uniqueness and social solidarity vis-à-vis the descendants of " 'Dinka' latecomers"—a point to which I will return shortly.

This is not to say that marriages among distantly related *diel* never occurred among contemporary easterners. Couples occasionally succeeded in getting around this prohibition by asserting that one of them was not really *dil*. A man could claim, for example, that one of his paternal ancestors was really a "Dinka" by asserting, Ɛ *yän jaŋ, matkɛ ni yä ke mut*

("I'm an [adopted] Dinka, who was assimilated through [the conferral] of a [patrilineal] spear [call]"). Otherwise, he might claim that either he or a close paternal ancestor was sired by someone other than his official pater—*Ci caar rɔ goŋ* (literally, "the umbilical cord has curved in on itself")—indicating, thereby, that his agnatic heritage was not as straightforward as it appeared.

Moreover, since many contemporary eastern men and women readily admitted that they really didn't understand why exogamic prohibitions should extend longer for the descendants of "first comers" (*diel*) than for assimilated "Dinka" (*jaaŋ*), some easterners had begun to suggest that *maar diilä* could be safely reduced to a seven- or eight-generation limit as well. However, as far as the vast majority of contemporary easterners were concerned, *maar diilä* remained an accepted if puzzling exogamic principle.

I do not wish to imply that the concept of *maar diilä* was necessarily "new." On the contrary, I suspect that it developed during the nineteenth century as a means of buttressing the social cohesion of the advancing Nuer groups and of facilitating their rapid assimilation of "Dinka" captives and immigrants. One of my more sociologically minded Nuer friends, David Kek Moinydet, ventured the following hypothesis:

> Not everyone who came across with Latjɔɔr [the legendary leader of the Jikany migrations] was related to him. He took a few brothers from this camp and a few more from that. But once they crossed the Nile they had to present a united front before the Dinka. Had they started to marry amongst themselves, the Dinka would have quickly realized that relations between them were not strong; they would have appeared weak. So Latjɔɔr and his people decided to prohibit intermarriage amongst themselves, thereby creating the [exogamic] principle of *maar diilä*. People later forgot how *maar diilä* began, and thus most people today do not understand it. But those of us who know why it was created can see that it is something that is really not necessary any more.

A parallel process of contraction was also occurring among easterners in the scope of cognatic kinship—the limits of which were usually conceived of as generating out of an apical brother/sister tie and as extending across the generations through "the daughters of daughters/girls" (*nyier nyiët*). Consider figure 4, adapted from Evans-Pritchard (1934:13).

The limits of cognatic kinship (*nyier nyiët*) may be understood either in terms of a progressive thinning out of blood connections through generations of women or in terms of diminishing bridewealth claims. However, because the state of a person's blood was not immediately apparent, the exogamic limits of cognatic kinship were more easily traced, as Evans-Pritchard noted, through shared bridewealth claims—the principle being

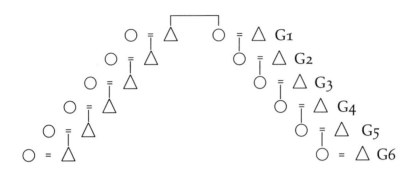

Figure 4. The limits of *nyier nyiët* (cognation).

that no man could marry a woman upon whose marriage he had the right to claim some portion of her bridewealth. Otherwise expressed, Nuer definitions of cognatic kinship were inextricably bound up with the "cattle over blood" value principle outlined in chapter 4.

Consider the following hypothetical example. Upon the marriage of the original sister (G1) represented in figure 4, some twenty-five to thirty cows travel, as it were, through this apical sister/brother tie to be distributed among the bride's extended family. However, this settlement does not fully compensate the family of the brother for having given over the procreative powers of the sister to the family of her husband. And thus, upon the marriage of this woman's daughter (G2), approximately ten more cows flow through the apical brother/sister connection to be distributed among the maternal relatives of the bride. In the third generation, one cow passes in the same direction, and in the fourth, some goats, and in the fifth, some spears, and so on until after some six, seven, or, in some areas, eight generations no bridewealth claims are honored. At that point the transgenerational bridewealth "debt" stemming from the marriage of the original sister (G1) ends, and with it the prohibition on intermarriage. I should note that one and only one bridewealth cow passes in the opposite direction. That cow, "the heifer of the father's sister," is claimed by the apical sister herself upon the marriage of her brother's daughter. Contemporary eastern Jikany Nuer, in fact, considered that cow to be the first and most important bridewealth obligation to be met by the groom's family. Contemporary western Nuer, in contrast, stressed the rights of the bride's *näär* (or "mother's brother") as taking precedence over all others in bridewealth negotiations with the prospective groom's family: Without the full approval of the bride's *näär*, a marriage simply could not take place in that region. Now, whereas contemporary westerners continued to respect the exogamic limits of cognatic kinship for at least six generations, there were several eastern Nuer I met who argued that a lapse of only three generations was sufficient to avoid risk of *ruaal*. Hence, they reasoned that intermarriage after that point could be permitted. A generational limit of four or five steps, however, was far more widely accepted in that region during the early 1980s.

This trend toward a contraction of cognatic ties in the east was inseparable from a more general collapse of bridewealth claims in that region. For a variety of historical reasons to be discussed in greater detail below, bridewealth claims were rarely honored among the eastern Jikany during the early 1980s beyond three or four generations, with the bride's immediate family gaining additional cattle and related items at the expense of more distant kinsmen.

The scope of affinal and of "natural" kinship ties was likewise being challenged and gradually reduced by contemporary easterners, especially those who had been heavily influenced by Christian doctrines. Among the eastern Gaajok, for example, I documented a case in which two full brothers married two full sisters and a second case in which a man married the natural daughter of his paternal uncle. The first of these marriages was less "shocking" than the second. For it was sometimes possible for a younger sister to step into the marriage of an older sister after the latter's death. Moreover, incestuous liaisons between a man and his sister-in-law were relatively common—though still condemned—as compared with many other types of incestuous relations. Nevertheless, I suspect that both of these marriages would have been simply inconceivable fifty years earlier. And as it was, they remained highly controversial: Many eastern men and women voiced apprehensions that these marriages were still "too close" to avoid risk of incest (*ruaal*). Yet though rare and controversial, marriages such as these reveal the extent to which previously accepted principles of incest and exogamy were being actively challenged in the east.

The Challenge of the Younger Generation: Fertility Testing

This gradual easing of exogamic prohibitions, a trend well recognized by contemporary eastern Nuer themselves, was not accepted by everyone. Many eastern Jikany continued to abide during the 1980s by the more comprehensive exogamic principles outlined by Evans-Pritchard a half century earlier. The courts, moreover, were an important conservative force in this regard since most chiefs, in my experience, tended to side with the weight of tradition in defining exogamic limits. The conservative influence of the courts would have been greater, however, were it not for the rising frequency of elopement and impregnation in the east. It was not at all uncommon during the early 1980s for a couple frustrated in its desire for marriage by official decrees of incest to run off shortly after the trial. If the union proved fruitful and the child thrived, the couple could later return to their families confident that some sort of marriage arrangement would be made. If not, the lovers usually separated voluntarily. None of the marriages cited above—namely, those between the two brothers and two sisters and that between "natural" paternal cousins—took place without strong, initial resistance from their families. In each case the lovers "feuded for each other" (*cikɛ rɔ tɛr*)—that is, they defied public opinion and eventually overcame their families' reluctance by eloping and bringing forth a healthy child. In the case of the two sisters it is doubtful whether bridewealth would have been accepted even so were it not for the fact that they were fatherless orphans and professed Christians.

One reason this mode of "feuding" was so effective was that most contemporary Nuer, easterners and westerners alike, regarded any union that proved fruitful as divinely blessed and thus, in some sense, free of *ruaal*. Viewed from a slightly different perspective, one could say that the limits of incest and exogamy had an experiential correlate in Nuer eyes: "Incest children" (*gaat ruali*) were expected to reveal their dangerous origins through illness, abnormality, and early death. For this reason, the fecundity of couples who willingly risked possible illness, infertility, infant mortality, or other misfortunes in order to challenge received notions of *ruaal* usually proved more powerful in shaping public opinion than did official court decrees.[6] It was the fortune or misfortune of such couples, closely watched and commented upon by all, that was later cited as evidence either for or against the validity of particular incest and exogamic prohibitions.

Of course, this method of testing the limits of "divine tolerance" in matters of incest and exogamy was nothing new. The existence and relative

6. In cases of serious incest it was not only the offenders and their offspring that were endangered but sometimes also their nearest of kin, particularly small children. For a full discussion of the types of misfortunes associated with *ruaal*, see Evans-Pritchard (1956:183–185 and 1951b:30).

severity of different categories of incest had long been revealed to Nuer through the experience and interpretation of affliction. *Ruaal,* as Evans-Pritchard noted, refers not only to the act of incestuous congress itself but also to subsequent hardships attributed to it (1956:183–184). Moreover, Nuer had long recognized an element of arbitrariness in the outer limits of different categories of kinship. Evans-Pritchard described several ritual means by which people could manipulate the generational scope of various prohibitions during the early 1930s (1951b:31–36; 1934:11–15). Sometimes a gourd was split, sometimes a sacrifice was made, or the spear-calling rite marking the successful conclusion of the bridewealth negotiations was modified or suspended to remove any taint of *ruaal.* These rites continued to be used during the 1980s as well.

What appeared to have changed over the intervening decades was, rather, the frequency and pragmatic consciousness with which many members of the younger generation were now questioning incest limits. Moreover, it was no longer simply a matter of debating the exact generational scope of specific prohibitions but rather of grappling with the underlying logic, nature, and meaning of incest itself. People were wondering: "What is it 'made' of? Why is there such a thing?"

ARE INCEST PROHIBITIONS ROOTED
IN HUMAN BLOOD OR IN THE COW?

The first thing that I should stress is that the distinction between incest and exogamic prohibitions, although crucial in the anthropological discourse, was normally glossed over by contemporary Nuer. This was because they almost always explained marriage prohibitions in terms of incest rules: "Why can't they marry? They can't marry because it is *ruaal"* ran the standard refrain.[7] And thus, in the generalized debate about *ruaal* that emerged, people were especially interested in understanding the logic of incest as it related to exogamic prohibitions. They began with the premise that *ruaal* mirrored

7. See Evans-Pritchard 1951b:43. The marriage prohibition concerning the daughter of an age-mate was rarely brought up in the generalized discourse about *ruaal* outlined here. Yet that "nonincestuous," exogamic prohibition was being challenged during the 1980s on a different basis. Since "men" who had rejected scarification had no official *ric* or age-set (though the age-sets they would have belonged to had they submitted to scarification were easily determined), it was becoming debatable whether this prohibition should apply to them. However, most unscarified men continued to honor this prohibition at that time. The factors that motivated some Nuer men to abandon initiation by the early 1980s will be explored in detail in chapter 6.

maar—*maar* being an equally ambiguous and fluid notion of "relationship" or "kinship." Both "kinship" and "incest" were in turn said to be based primarily upon shared blood and shared cattle: *Ruaal ɛ riɛm kɛnɛ yaŋ* ("Incest is blood and the cow"), I was often told. With regard to certain types of relationships, it was the binding power of cattle that was stressed: "What is the relationship between a man and his adopted son? Is it not the blood of the cow sacrificed [upon his adoption]?" In other relationships, the notion of shared human blood was emphasized, as, for example, with respect to the bonds of *maar* created through breastmilk or through ties of genitorship.

What is striking about Nuer concepts of sociality, however, is the extent to which shared human blood and shared cattle were complementary modes of defining the same relationships, the same categories of *maar*. Although the primacy of human blood linkages was often stressed, the fact remained that these linkages were invariably reinforced and specified by shared cattle rights or bridewealth claims—in line with the cattle-over-blood value principle discussed in chapter 4. For example, just as the limits of cognation discussed earlier could be conceived either in terms of blood passing and thinning out through chains of women or in terms of bridewealth claims honored across the generations, so, too, the *maar* binding close affines could be seen in terms of the social circulation of both blood and cattle. In this context, the union of blood binding close affines was realized through the birth of children into the families of both parents (cf. Evans-Pritchard 1951b:32–34). Similarly, the bonds of kinship uniting a genitor and his offspring were both blood and cattle based: A genitor had the right to claim the "cow of begetting" upon the marriage of his natural daughter or, in some cases, upon the maturity of his natural son as well. So, too, a woman who had suckled and raised another's daughter could claim the "cow of nurturing" (*yaŋ romä*) upon the girl's marriage.[8] Even the prohibition on intermarriage between a man and a daughter of his age-mate, which, as I explained, was not strictly speaking an "incest" bar, had its blood and cattle correlates. Nuer maintained that a kind of "blood brotherhood" (*ric*) was established among young men who were initiated together. And under certain circumstances an age-mate had the right to claim a special cow—"the cow of the age-mate"—upon the marriage of his *ric*-mate's daughter (see Evans-Pritchard 1951b:33–34). It was thus only with respect to bonds of distant agnation (*böth*) that the overlapping

8. However, this claim was likely to be resisted by the groom's family if the "natural mother" was a close maternal or paternal relative of the bride who could be expected to be awarded a bridewealth cow on that basis.

blood/cattle bonds of *maar* withered with time into those of "shared [sac-rificial] meat" (*böth*)—that is, into those of the "blood of the cow" con-sumed, as it were.[9] This exogamic relationship was also reinforced and maintained by a shared agnatic spear-call (*mut*) that was invoked by pat-rilineal kinsmen during times of war, sacrifice, marriage, and other im-portant events.[10]

However, the key question that contemporary eastern and western Nuer were debating during the 1980s was "Is *ruaal* based primarily on human blood or on the cow? Or is it, perhaps, the blood of the cow that is crucial?" This public rethinking of incest prohibitions was motivated in part, as I suggested, by increased awareness of northern Sudanese marriage practices and of Christian concepts. Without attempting to capture the full range and subtlety of the diverse strains of contemporary opinion held on this matter, I shall nevertheless sketch here the reasoning behind the three most influential interpretations of *ruaal* being expressed at that time.

The first and second of these attempted to account for the fact that, among "Arabs," "close relatives" intermarry and yet bring forth living, healthy children. For Nuer this was an especially perplexing phenomenon since it was assumed that similar unions among themselves would prove infertile. "If 'Divinity is [everywhere] one' (*kuɔth ɛ kɛl*), then why should Divinity punish us for committing incest but not the 'Arabs'?" Not sur-prisingly, there were two main hypotheses advanced, one focusing on blood and the other on cattle.

"Their bloods are different" (*rimkiɛn kɛ göl*) ran the first interpretation. "Haven't you seen that the Arabs eat raw meat?[11] They also circumcise their men and their women, but we don't do these things. Clearly their blood is different and that is why they don't have incest." The nature of blood is here viewed not simply in terms of parentage but also in terms of a person's experience with blood in all of its myriad manifestations. This

9. For those readers unfamiliar with Evans-Pritchard's discussions of agnatic ties, it is important to realize that such ties were always recognized in the distribution of sacrificial meat. Specific parts of the sacrificial cow were reserved for specific categories of kin.

10. For a detailed discussion of the significance of agnatic spear-calls, see Evans-Pritchard (1956:231ff).

11. There is a special dish (*mararä*) prepared with raw liver and spices that northern Sudanese enjoy. Otherwise, they prefer their meat well cooked. Nuer, however, were keenly aware of this uncooked specialty since they were sometimes put in the situation of slaughtering a cow in hospitality for northerners. At such times the raw liver was usually reserved for the preparation of this delicacy by the guests themselves.

quasi-racist notion reveals much about the current state of relations between northern and southern Sudanese: I often heard Nuer men and
women argue that the blood of "we the black people" (kɔn nei ti caar),
or "we the southerners" (kɔn jinubni), was distinct from that of northern
"Arabs."

The second hypothesis advanced to account for the "absence of incest"
among "Arabs" focused on the cow or, more specifically, on the blood of
the cow. Northern "Arabs," it was argued, marry with money rather than
with cattle, and money, unlike cattle, is "bloodless." Hence, Nuer reasoned
that "It is the blood [of the cow] that kills people [who commit incest]."
Indeed, many men and women freely hypothesized during the early 1980s
that, were they to marry exclusively with money instead of cattle, "incest
might become nothing" for them as well: Dee ruaal thil. This fascinating
hypothesis was widely shared at the time by easterners and westerners and
by school-educated and nonliterate Nuer alike. Personally I doubt whether
these people were thinking at the time they made these remarks about the
ties between a mother and her children, which are, after all, neither created
nor ruptured through cattle exchange. Nevertheless, many of them clearly
believed that money, being bloodless, could not bind people together like
cattle. Money's ascendancy was thus associated with a world of transitory
ties, a world that had neither a center nor boundaries. Were such a revolutionary change in Nuer marriage practices ever to occur, I do not doubt
that these people would change their minds about the basis of incest taboos
somewhere along the way. Nevertheless, the strong identification in people's
minds between cattle exchange and enduring social bonds could hardly
have been more starkly expressed.

The third hypothetical interpretation of ruaal being explored during the
early 1980s was intimately associated with the burgeoning Christian community, which at that time was still confined largely to the eastern Nuer.[12]
Like the second interpretation, it, too, rejected the equation of incest with
human blood in favor of the cow: "Did not the children of Adam and Eve
intermarry?" Moreover, some eastern Nuer Christians had begun to add
the rider, "Perhaps we could use different cows." Indeed, a few eastern
Christians with whom I spoke were beginning to wonder whether purchased cattle (yɔk yiɔuni, or "the cattle of money") were equally effective
in forging and extending relations of maar as cattle acquired through

12. See chapter 7 for a discussion of regional variations in the relative impact
of Christianity on Nuer communities during the colonial and postcolonial eras.

bridewealth or inheritance (*yɔk nyiët*, or "the cattle of girls"). Perhaps the risk of incest, they reasoned, could be reduced if people married exclusively with "the cattle of money."

This intriguing idea, which I heard expressed only on a few occasions by eastern Nuer men who were members of the literate and Christianized elite, flowed directly out of broader ideological controversies over the mutual convertibility of cattle and money as media of exchange, an issue that was explored in chapter 2. To paraphrase Gabriel Giet Jal, a highly educated eastern Jikany Nuer, were a man able to marry a woman using cattle of money exclusively, when it later became time for his daughter to marry, he could justifiably argue that no one other than himself had rights in her bridewealth cattle. For he could claim that those relatives who would normally have shared rights in his daughter's bridewealth cattle had failed to honor their earlier obligations to contribute cattle toward the marriage of the girl's mother.

However, this idea was not beyond challenge. For instance, James Mabor Gatkuoth, an educated Christian Nuer from the west, vehemently rejected the cattle reasoning behind this argument on the grounds that, even though a man's kinsmen were not formally obliged to contribute bridewealth cattle to his second marriage, they nevertheless retained full rights in the marriage cattle of all daughters born to that union. Although these arguments and counterarguments remained entirely hypothetical, they clearly reflected very different attitudes toward the collective and individual rights conveyed in "the cattle of money."

Upon hearing individuals suggest that the adoption of cash bridewealth payments might lead to an "absence of incest" amongst themselves, I would sometimes ask them whether *maar*, or kinship relations, would not become "nothing" (*thil*) together with *ruaal*—a question invariably answered in the negative. As one middle-aged Gaajok man countered, "We are a social people. How could *maar* ever end?" Nevertheless, it would appear that *ruaal* and *maar* were gradually beginning to take on mutually independent meanings, for some Nuer at least. If it were to continue, this trend could stimulate a more radical rethinking of the nature and limits of kinship ties in the future.

By no means do I wish to suggest that current debates about the nature and logic of incest prohibitions were purely an intellectual exercise, a juggling of "secondary explanations." On the contrary, this was the stuff of which wars were made. Among the eastern Gaajok, for example, there was a situation in which a man impregnated a girl who was "related" to him, and a "cow of incest" was duly sacrificed by an earth priest in the hope of protecting the couple from the negative consequences of their act. The girl, however, died shortly after giving birth, whereupon her family demanded bloodwealth compensation from her lover. The local court, however, ruled against a bloodwealth transfer on the grounds that a "cow of incest" had been sacrificed prior to delivery. The deceased girl's brother, infuriated by this verdict, immediately mustered a war party. In a second case, a young man became involved in a heated argument with a renowned Gaajok earth priest over whether his relations with the girl he wished to marry were incestuous. The priest, unswayed by the young man's arguments, insisted upon and performed a sacrifice of atonement and separation. A few nights later, the young man ambushed and killed the earth priest. Examples of this nature could be multiplied. But it should be clear that the definition of whether a particular relationship was incestuous or not was often a matter of sheer force.

Fundamental to this polemic was a nexus of historical factors discussed in chapters 2, 3, and 4, only the most important of which will be noted again here. The governmental suppression of local warfare and raiding, together with the importation of grain in times of famine, were two factors identified by Howell during the mid-1940s as undermining the importance of extended political alliances in this region (Howell 1954:233). The expansion of cattle markets and the creation of courts likewise increased the viability of smaller, more autonomous communities. The resulting contraction of Nuer communities was especially obvious in parts of contemporary eastern Gaajok country, where those feuds that did erupt during the early 1980s rarely escalated above a single subchieftainship. (Patterns of warfare among the eastern Gaajok were exceptional in this regard due to the presence of a turbulent international frontier running through their territories.) Among the more densely settled western Nuer, in contrast, large-scale battles involving whole "tribal regions" (_rool/door_) were not uncommon during the early 1980s.

Nevertheless, it should not be assumed that a decline in the importance of extended political ties would necessarily lead to the contraction of incest and exogamic prohibitions. The range of persons potentially classified as "kin" (_maar_) vis-à-vis any particular individual was, as we have seen, extraordinarily broad, extending far beyond the number of "relatives" that individual could hope to know during his or her lifetime, let alone those actually appealed to in the give-and-take of daily community life. Ultimately, the perpetuation of this extremely fluid and comprehensive notion of _maar_ depended upon the older generations' success in enforcing conformity to its images of "relationship," its definitions of "incest." And it was precisely in this regard that the older generation had experienced a dramatic loss of power over the previous half century. Not only were parents' decisions and negotiations concerning their children's marriages now subject to government scrutiny, but, more important, they no longer wielded the threat of armed retaliation that formerly held rates of elopement and impregnation in check. The slackening control of the older generation over the selection of its children's mates was especially apparent in the east, where rates of premarital impregnation and the "stealing" of girls were reaching crisis proportions by the early 1980s. Furthermore, the fact that "fertility testing" was increasingly viewed by eastern Nuer youth as the most reliable way of determining the limits of divine tolerance with respect to incest prohibitions also reveals the extent to which the older generation was losing its abilities to assert the ideological dominance of "cattle flows" over "human blood flows" in the selection of their children's mates.

Thus far, in discussing some of the historical processes contributing to a loosening of exogamic bars among the eastern Nuer, I have emphasized the emergence of a public debate about the nature and limits of "incest," which was in turn intimately connected with the experience and interpretation of misfortune; the changing significance of extended political alliances consequent upon the suppression of feuding and the creation of cattle and grain markets; the introduction of government courts, chiefs, and related institutions; and last, the dwindling powers of the older generation to enforce its definitions of "relationship" on contemporary Nuer youths. Yet, if all these factors would seem to have favored a general relaxation of incest and exogamic prohibitions among Nuer over the past half century, then why should one category of *ruaal*, incest with the father's sister's daughter (*nyawac*), have seemingly been isolated for intensification over this same period? Contemporary eastern Nuer attitudes toward FZD incest appear, if anything, all the more anomalous and perplexing. Why should this type of incest, in contrast to all others, have been so strongly banned?

THE GATNA̱AR/GATWAC RELATIONSHIP

Let us look more closely at the structure of this relationship. Evans-Pritchard characterized the bond between "children of the father's sister" (*gaatwac;* sing., *gatwac*) and "children of the mother's brother" (*gaatnaar;* sing., *gatnaar*) as one of "easy companionship," stripped of the reserve that differences of generation fostered in relations with one another's parents (1951b:167).

And this remained the case during the 1980s as well. Yet to my mind one of the most striking aspects of this tie was its "generative asymmetry." By this I mean that one side of this relationship, that of the children (i.e., sons) of the mother's brother, was capable of procreating on behalf of the other side, that of the children of the father's sister, while the reverse situation was not possible.

In figure 5, X stands as *gatnaar* (son of the mother's brother) to Y; and Y stands as *gatwac* (son of the father's sister) to X. This relationship originates, of course, in the tie of siblingship between X's father and Y's mother. Consequently, the patrilineal children of this apical brother-sister pair are bound together by relations of affinity—with X's side being the wife-givers and Y's side being the wife-takers. As the wife-takers, Y's side (*gaatwac*) continues to be indebted to X's family (*gaatnaar*) for having provided them with a woman in marriage (namely, the original sister, or Y's mother). And this asymmetrical linkage strongly colors relations between X and Y. Whereas Y might affectionately refer to his "mother's brother's son" (X) as "our mother's brother" (*nääran*), thereby elevating him by a generation, as it were, X would never "aggrandize" Y, his "father's sister's son," by using a kinship term that implied the latter was a generation older than himself—even in situations where the age disparity between the pair suggested that this was, in fact, the case. This reticence was not simply due to the fact that such a compliment would require crossing a gender divide (that is, X would have to elevate his "father's sister's son" to the category "father's sister"). X would never address his "father's sister's daughter" (*nyawac*) as "my father's sister" (*waidä*) either.

But what I wish to emphasize here is that X could never legitimately procreate for his "father's sister's son" or for any of the latter's patrilineal descendants. X could not marry a wife in the name of his father's sister if she proved barren, nor could he marry a wife in Y's name or inherit any of Y's wives in the levirate. These rules were absolute in all parts of Nuerland, and any transgression would have been considered a highly dangerous act of incest. Indirectly, of course, X could assist Y in marrying in his own name by providing Y with cattle. But X could never legitimately procreate in Y's name. It is as though X's line had already contributed so much to the fertility of Y's line through the provision of Y's mother (that is, X's father's sister) that the potential—or, as it must sometimes have appeared, the burden—of reciprocity lay entirely with Y's line. The long-term bridewealth obligations of Y's line as the wife-takers toward X's line as the wife-givers were already discussed with reference to the limits of cognatic kinship (*nyier nyiët*).

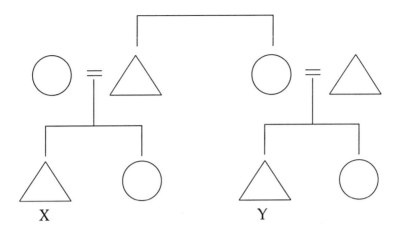

Figure 5.   The *gatn̲a̲ar/gatwac* relationship.

In contrast, Y could legitimately procreate on behalf of his "mother's brother." He could also marry a ghost wife in the name of his "mother's brother" (or X's father) or in the name of his mother's brother's son (or X himself). Y could also cohabit with these men's wives in the levirate. Therefore, if X did not exist, Y could actively and *physically* "generate" him by marrying a wife in the name of X's would-be pater (which is to say Y's "mother's brother"). In brief, one pole of this relationship, that of Y, was capable of assisting the other pole, that of X, by filling gaps in the latter's procreative history or by furthering the latter's procreative goals directly. However, the reverse situation was impossible: X could never legitimately procreate in the name of Y or any of Y's patrilineal kinsmen.

The special "intimacy" of the *gatn̲a̲ar/gatwac* (MBS/FZS) bond originally noted by Evans-Pritchard contrasts sharply with the distance and thinly veiled rivalry characterizing relations among paternal half brothers, *gaatgu̲a̲n.* Whereas the former relationship was profoundly asymmetrical, the latter bond was clearly symmetrical. As I explained in chapter 4, the procreative powers of paternal half brothers were continually being merged and equated through shared rights in the "ancestral herd."

Furthermore, this basic contrast between the closeness and asymmetry of the MBS/FZS relationship as opposed to the competitive symmetry of relations between paternal half brothers radiated outwards to form other important kinship linkages within the broader community. For example, it echoed through the ego-centered opposition between the "children of daughters/girls" (*gaatnyiët*) and fellow agnates or "bulls" (*tut*). From the perspective of the "mother's brother's son" (X) in the MBS/FZS relationship, "children of girls" encompassed not only children of the father's sisters but also all other people related to him as wife-takers (such as the children of married sisters and daughters).

Now, as Evans-Pritchard (1940a:211–236) pointed out many years ago, it was primarily through the cultivation of strong, stable relations with "children of girls" that individual men and women were able to assert greater authority and autonomy in their relations with fellow agnates or "bulls," *tut*—which is to say in their relations with paternal half brothers, paternal uncles, and paternal cousins of every degree.[13] It was upon the shoulders of "children of girls" (*gaatnyiët*) that a man and, in some cases, a woman could rise to positions of community leadership. "What is the great big [man] held up by the children of daughters?" asks a popular Nuer riddle—the answer being the "cattle byre," the symbol of masculine independence par excellence. Significantly, the poles upholding the byre are identified in this riddle not with the man's own sons but with the "sons of girls/daughters."

Viewed from a slightly different perspective, the "children of girls" were all those people capable of extending ego's procreative powers but not of threatening them. In this they were clearly opposed to agnatic kinsmen (*gaatguan/tut*) who were capable of undermining as well as bolstering ego's procreative powers. One of the principal fears in this respect was that a paternal half brother or cousin, if called upon to raise up ego's children, would ignore or abuse their cattle rights in the "ancestral herd" in favor of his own sons. And for this reason most people preferred to entrust the responsibility of marrying a wife in the name of a deceased relative to a sister's son rather than to a paternal half brother (cf. Evans-Pritchard 1951b:158).

This image of "children of girls" as nonthreatening with regard to the fertility of their mother's brother's people was also evident in the symbolism of many contemporary Nuer rituals. Consider the following two examples.

The sacrifice of a bull (as opposed to an ox) was perhaps the most sacred and solemn of Nuer rites (see plate 23). It was usually performed to restore an atmosphere of peace and harmony within the extended community through the airing of hidden grievances. This sacrifice was often as-

13. Ladislav Holy reexamines Evans-Pritchard's observations on the *gatnaar/gatnyiët* relationship in very interesting ways in a later piece (1979a).

Plate 23. The sacrificial slaughter of a bull, eastern Gaajok country. As one of the oldest, leading descendants of the "first comers," Diu Gai, the man in the foreground, was "the spokesman of the cattle camp" for cieng Laang.

sociated with the commemoration of an ancestor. The rite always began in the middle of the night with the bull being driven out of the cattle byre. As it ran out, a man related to the owner of the bull as *gatnyal* ("son of a girl") would pierce the bull's hump with a fishing spear (*bidh*, the "feminine" spear). As soon as the wounded bull charged outside the byre, a man related to the byre's owner as a distant paternal cousin (*gaatguanlendɛ*) would pierce the bull's heart with a fighting spear (*mut*, the "masculine" spear). The following morning, sacrificial invocations over the dead bull would begin. When I asked why only "a son of a girl" could make the initial stab with a fishing spear and why this stab had to be in the bull's hump, I was told, "Have you ever seen a bull die by being pierced in the hump?" The symbolism was clear: "children of girls" as distinct from fellow agnates are "harmless" with respect to the vitality of "bulls" (*tut*).

The *buɔr*, or mud windscreen, built to shelter a woman's cooking fire was a sacred place associated with the divinities and ancestral spirits of her husband's family and, consequently, with the procreative potential of her household as well. When it began to crumble from the rains and needed to be rebuilt, the woman would call someone who stood as *gatnyal*, "the son of a girl/daughter," to her husband's lineage in order to remove the old broken pieces. (An agnatic kinsmen of the husband would never be asked to perform this task.) Here again there appears to be some notion that it is "safer" for "children of girls" to handle one's fertility. When I asked why only a "son of a girl" would be called upon to perform this service, I was told, "It is the same as [the role of the son of a girl] at the sacrifice of a bull."

Yet another way to conceptualize this contrast between the asymmetry of the MBS/FZS relationship and the symmetry of relations between paternal half brothers and by extension all paternal kinsmen (*tut*) is in terms of an opposition between wife-givers/wife-takers, on the one hand, and wife-sharers, on the other. In his analysis of Nuer incest categories, Evans-Pritchard pointed out that agnates were in a very real sense "wife-sharers":

> In view of the importance attached to children by Nuer in determining what is incest, or the degree of it, it may readily be understood why sexual relations with the wives of half-brothers, paternal uncles, and patrilineal cousins of every degree are regarded as being either incestuous peccadillos or not incestuous at all. The wife of a "bull" is, in a general social sense, the wife of all "bulls," of the paternal kin, and of the lineage. She is "our" wife and the "wife of our cattle." Likewise her children are the children of the lineage, of the agnatic group, and of its cattle. Hence sexual relations with the wives of these agnates, if not approved, are condoned, for they are the wives of all. (1951b:45)

The relationship between *diel* and *jaaŋ* ("assimilators" and "assimilated") discussed earlier may be understood as yet another variant of the asymmetry binding "children of the mother's brother" and "children of the father's sister" (MBS/FZS). As Evans-Pritchard explained, individual *dil* endeavored to assert their autonomy vis-à-vis other *diel* during their nineteenth-century advance by attracting and assimilating as large a personal following of "Dinka" (*jaaŋ*) as possible (1940a:220–248; cf. Holy 1979a). Or, in the words of an older Gaajok *dil*: "[At that time] everyone wanted to gather as many *jaaŋ* around himself as possible in order to fight against his paternal cousins [*gaatguanlendɛ*]."

There were two main modes for *diel* to assimilate *jaaŋ*: adoption and marriage. In the case of young male immigrants or captives, the adoption process was formalized through the sacrifice of an ox (or goat) and the ritual conferral of the pater's agnatic spear-call (*mut*). The cattle rights of adopted sons were no different from those of biological sons: Ideally, all of them drew in turn on their pater's herd in order to marry, bear heirs, and extend the patriline. In the case of young female captives and immigrants, the adoption process did not usually require a formal sacrifice but only the rubbing-on of cattle dung ash. Following this rite an adopted daughter could either be married out for cattle or be conferred on a resident or immigrant "Dinka" man for few or even no cattle. In the latter case she helped to bind her immigrant husband to her father's community. An unadopted captive girl could also be taken directly as a wife by her *diel* host or by one of his close kinsmen. In the former case the issue of bridewealth cattle did not arise. But if the captive was to be married off to a more distant "relative," it sometimes did—in which case it was often problematic. When the prospective groom and the nominal father of the bride were closely related, the bridewealth obligations of the wife-takers and the bridewealth claims of the wife-givers were likely to overlap in some instances— a situation that would necessitate a good deal of "negotiation," if not kinship "gerrymandering," to pull off. In fact, complexities of interlinked bridewealth claims were cited by several contemporary eastern Jikany as the principal reason that women captives during the nineteenth century were usually married off to or conferred on resident "Dinka" rather than being married off to paternal kinsmen by their *diel* captors.

However, it is possible to understand this alleged preference from a different perspective. Owing to the "generative asymmetry" of the "mother's brother's son/father's sister's daughter" (MBS/FZD) relationship, it was "structurally" and "politically" advantageous for ambitious *diel* to accumulate resident communities of *jaaŋ* men by giving them adopted or even "real" sisters and daughters in marriage rather than by marrying close female relatives of these attached men themselves. From the perspective of male and female "assimilators," it was better to have your sister or daughter marry into an immigrant "Dinka" family that you wished to integrate than to marry into that family yourself. This was because the "Dinka" sons produced by a married sister or daughter could later be given *diel* cattle in order to marry in the name of their *diel* hosts. In this way, "Dinka" that were attached as wife-takers (that is, as children of the father's sister) or, alternately, as children of girls could be used to rapidly expand the patrilineal descent group of their *diel* patrons. Their *diel* sponsors, in contrast, being in the position of children of the mother's brother, could assist assimilated Dinka men to marry in their own names through gifts of cattle, but the former could never legally engender heirs for these attached *jaaŋ*. Because of the exogamic bar to intermarriage among "first comers," eastern *diel* men had to marry female descendants of latecomers, but it was politically more advantageous for them to seek wives from the communities of latecomers gathered around other, more distant *diel*.

In a provocative essay Gough (1971) suggests that one of the consequences of the nineteenth-century migrations of the Nuer across the White Nile was that it placed *diel* women as well as *diel* men at a substantial advantage when it came to building up resident communities of *jaaŋ*. Owing to high mortality rates among men, as well as to the rapid increase in herd size and pasturage that accompanied these invasions, barren *diel* women were often able to marry wives in their own right and to be assimilated as "honorary" brothers in order to help solidify their father's line.[14] Gough's analysis of the critical importance of *diel* sisters in the emergence of a more marked status differential between the descendants of "assimilators" and "assimilated" in the east finds added support in the structural analysis offered here of the "generative asymmetry" at the heart of the "children of the mother's brother/children of the father's sister" bond.

Now, once one realizes the organizational significance of the "generative asymmetry" characterizing the *gatnaar/gatwac* (MBS/FZS) relationship, the relative "seriousness" of incest with the father's sister's daughter (*nyawac*) becomes more understandable. For a man to lie with his father's sister or with his father's sister's daughter would be to negate this principle of asymmetry directly—and thus to deny the integrative and procreative potential of this bond. Furthermore, since the "generative asymmetry" of this relationship radiated outwards to sustain broader power differentials within the extended community, it is, perhaps, readily understandable that some contemporary Nuer men and women, at least, would define sexual relations with the "father's sister's daughter" as more "dangerous"—more socially disruptive—than incest with a full daughter or a full sister. There was simply much more depending upon the procreative asymmetry of the MBS/FZD relationship since it lay at the heart of Nuer notions of transgenerational alliance as well as of established power networks within the extended community.

But having understood all this, are we really any closer to resolving this puzzlingly regional variation in contemporary Nuer attitudes toward incest with the father's sister's daughter? Everything I have said thus far about the "generative asymmetry" of the *gatnaar/gatwac* relationship was

---

14. What I mean by "honorary" brother here is that, often, after the passage of a few generations, the descendants of a female *dil* were assimilated as full *diel* by treating their apical ancestress as if she had been a man (cf. Evans-Pritchard 1951b and Gough 1971).

valid in all Nuer regions, both west and east. Moreover, it was "true" when Evans-Pritchard carried out his research in the early 1930s, just as it was "true" during the 1980s. And thus, we are left with the same tantalizing questions: Why should the "seriousness" of incest with the "father's sister's daughter" have been "recognized," so to speak, only by easterners? And why only sometime during the last fifty or so years? For answers to these questions, we must turn now from a discussion of the circulation of human blood to that of cattle.

CONTEMPORARY PATTERNS OF BRIDEWEALTH
DISTRIBUTION: REGIONAL VARIATIONS

One of the most striking regional differences in contemporary patterns of bridewealth distribution revolved around the relative negotiating powers of the bride's mother's brothers. Among contemporary westerners the mother's brother usually negotiated directly with the groom's party for his family's portion of the bridewealth cattle—generally some eight or ten head out of a total of twenty-five or thirty. Without his full satisfaction and approval, the marriage could not take place. Moreover, it was quite common for the mother's brother to host an additional wedding feast after the successful conclusion of these bridewealth negotiations. Among the eastern Jikany, in contrast, the mother's brother did not exercise the same degree of autonomy in bridewealth negotiations. It was, rather, the father and paternal uncles of the bride who took responsibility for negotiating the mother's brother's share of the bridewealth cattle as well as their own. Indeed, if relations between the bride's father and mother's brother were especially strained, the latter might not be summoned to participate in the negotiations with the groom's kinsmen at all. Moreover, the mother's brother's family's portion—which rarely exceeded four or five head of cattle out of a total of twenty-five or thirty in this region—was sometimes not handed over until the bride's father and brothers decided to do so. For this reason it was not uncommon among eastern Nuer during the early 1980s for "impatient" mother's brothers to pursue their bridewealth claims through the courts. Some eastern Nuer had even begun to take the attitude that the mother's brother had little or no claim in his sister's daughter's bridewealth. For instance, Nyatang Biel, a middle-aged eastern Gaajok woman who had lived for several years among the western Bul Nuer, was openly critical of the prominent negotiating role played by the mother's brother in that region: "What right does the mother's brother have? Did he not receive cattle on the marriage of his sister? She was purchased and that was that!" (*Caa ɛ kɔk, cɛ thuk!*)[15]

The mother's brother was not the only relative to have suffered losses of wealth and influence due to the increasingly accepted image of marriage as a kind of "purchase" or "contract" in the east. In general contemporary eastern Jikany Nuer had begun to take a very low-key attitude toward the redistribution of bridewealth cattle to distant relatives (*jicuŋni raar*)—as opposed to the immediate family of the bride. Eastern courts were frequently inundated with disgruntled relatives seeking an official rupture of bridewealth claims in each other's daughters (*dak maarä*), whereas such cases were comparatively rare among contemporary westerners.[16] As one eastern woman put it: "People have become 'wise' [*Ci naath ŋɔani ŋac*]; that person now has his things and this person, his."

One of the factors eastern Nuer commonly cited as having contributed to this well-recognized contraction of patterns of bridewealth distribution was the increasing penetration of guns (and to a lesser extent radios, currency, and other items) into the bridewealth system. Although in principle a rifle received in bridewealth was to be bartered for cattle in the event that the bridewealth cattle proper fell short of satisfying all outstanding claims, in practice eastern Nuer acknowledged that guns received in bridewealth were almost invariably "eaten" whole by the bride's immediate family at the expense of outlying kin. Furthermore, the devastating impact of the first civil-war era on eastern Nuer patterns of bridewealth distribution should not be underestimated in this regard. Entire communities were destroyed, herds annihilated, and a significant percentage of the older generation brutally slain. It was primarily during these years that guns began to eclipse cattle as the most coveted bridewealth gift in the east. Guns, still rare in the west during the early 1980s, were not standard items of local

15. See Evans-Pritchard (1956:223–235) for the meaning of *kok* during the 1930s (here translated as "to purchase").

16. In the west, *dak maarä* cases usually revolved around the severing of "friendship relations" as opposed to kinship relations. The former were considered individual pacts in which the two men involved vowed to provide one cow upon the marriage of their daughters. Unlike the transgenerational bridewealth claims of "relatives," the cattle obligations of "friendship" bonds did not extend to the calves of the cows received. In other words, these voluntaristic relationships could be severed by the courts once it was established that the same number of cattle had been offered by both sides. It did not matter if one of the cows offered had died shortly after being received while another had generated five calves. Unlike blood-based bonds of "kinship," social relations between "friends" (*maathni*) had no transgenerational significance. Being entirely volitional, friendship ties did not extend to encompass either one's calves or one's children.

warfare or bridewealth exchange before the eruption of the second Sudanese civil war.

As a result of these and undoubtedly many other historical circumstances, the cattle ties formerly binding children of the father's sister and children of the mother's brother had become frayed and loose among the eastern Jikany. And thus, to reflect back on the apparent "hardening" of eastern Nuer attitudes toward FZD incest, might not this refurbished incest prohibition be seen as means by which the "intimacy" of the *gaatnaar*/*gaatwac* bond was being reinforced in spite of dwindling cattle connections? It is as though the "seriousness" of incest with the "father's sister's daughter" (*nyawac*) became apparent only when the bridewealth claims of the mother's brother's children (*gaatnaar*) began to be taken less seriously.

But why so much concern over an act of casual sexual intercourse? Would it not have been sufficient for contemporary eastern Nuer to prevent intermarriage between cross-cousins in order to maintain their community structures? Here I think it important to consider once again contemporary controversies over the limits of incest. The strong "death-threatening" ban on sexual intercourse with the father's sister's daughter had the effect of shielding this relationship from the pragmatic "fertility testing" of incest limits going on in so many other contemporary spheres of Nuer kinship. Moreover, the strongly shared conviction that "no sacrifice" was powerful enough to counter the negative consequences of FZD incest removed the primary motivation for confession. Consequently, were a case of FZD incest to occur on occasion, it was highly unlikely that it would be publicly "recognized." "The cow of [incest with] the father's sister's daughter can't be rushed to [the place of sacrifice] fast enough [to save lives]." In this way, the structural asymmetry of this tie was further insulated from the public rethinking and questioning of incest limits going on with respect to other kinship relations. In fact, though I documented several cases of incest between brothers and sisters and between fathers and daughters in the east, I have never heard of a case of incest with the father's sister's daughter.

Yet was it merely a matter of substituting a strengthened incest prohibition for weakening cattle ties? Looking at this evolving relationship more closely, it would appear to reflect a fundamental change in the commitment of the two sides to their mutual relationship. It was as though the children of the father's sister were pulling away from their mother's brother's children with the argument that the latter's claims to bridewealth cattle were exorbitant and unjustified. At the same time, the "children of the mother's brother" appeared to be clinging to their "father's sister's children" with an intensified concept of incest. When one considers that the asymmetry of this relationship (both in terms of cattle rights and in terms of its regenerative potential) favored the "children of the mother's brother" (or wife-givers') side, this is scarcely surprising.

But it does raise the question of whether this recently intensified incest prohibition benefited some segments of the contemporary eastern Nuer population more than others. Of course, in theory this prohibition applied to everyone: Everyone had some people who stood in a relationship of "children of the father's sister" and, by extension, *gaatnyiët* (wife-takers). The likelihood that individual wife-givers would actually be able to capitalize upon this structural asymmetry, however, varied significantly across community populations. Nuer men and women who lived together with their "father's sister's children" were obviously in a better position to call upon them in times of hardship, whether this be to support them in disputes with fellow wife-sharers or simply to help out with the harvest. Such support could be reciprocated in many ways, not the least of which was through gifts of cattle.

Evans-Pritchard described how ambitious individuals who had managed to collect a personal following of "children of girls" often struck off to found new communities, thereby achieving greater autonomy in their relations with fellow "bulls." In the first generation this attached following consisted primarily of the husbands and children of married sisters and married daughters. In subsequent generations the descendants of these women were collectively known as "children of the father's sister" (or simply "children of girls") by resident "bulls." They, too, were free to build up personal followings of co-resident wife-takers and thus could perhaps branch off at some point to found their own communities. (Due to the increasing viability of smaller Nuer community groupings, it is probable that co-resident "children of girls" were splitting off more rapidly and more effectively since the 1940s than was possible prior to British colonial conquest.) These "children of girls" were prohibited, however, from marrying back into the lineage of their apical ancestress for at least six generations, in accordance with the cognatic exogamic principle of "daughters of daughters" (*nyier nyiët*) discussed earlier. But, as I emphasized, there was very little consensus among contemporary eastern Nuer about the exact generational limit of this prohibition. And some marriages had begun to take place after a lapse of only four or five generations.

Now it was clearly in the interests of local "bulls" to delay the point at which co-resident "children of girls" could potentially reverse their status as dependent wife-takers by becoming wife-givers to the bulls. From this perspective, the reinforced incest taboo pertaining to the "father's sister's daughter" could be seen as a stern warning by older "bulls" to their *own* sons not to threaten their privileged position within the community by seeking lovers among their father's sister's daughters. Considering that the older generation as a whole was quickly losing control over the selection of its children's mates, it would be difficult to imagine a more effective means of ensuring the younger generation's compliance with such an aim. The transgenerational scope of FZD incest thus became less a matter of public debate and definition than one of how willing the would-be lovers were to risk possible death by *ruaal*. And in assessing the potential dangers involved, the fact of co-residence would be heavily weighed by Nuer.[17]

To the extent that contemporary eastern Nuer beliefs surrounding FZD incest helped delay possible status reversals between wife-givers and wife-takers within the extended community, they served to bolster old power networks: They favored those Nuer whose parents and grandparents had succeeded in creating a co-resident following of "children of the father's sister." And to the extent that these long-standing "bulls" of the community continued to identify themselves as *diel* ("first comers/assimilators"), this incest prohibition may be related to the exogamic concept of *maar diilä*, "relationship of the *diel*," described earlier. It will be remembered that most contemporary easterners maintained that the agnatic descendants of *diel* should never intermarry, even after a lapse of ten or twelve generations. This prohibition, like that surrounding incest with the "father's sister's daughter," could thus also be seen as an injunction directed primarily at the sons of the influential not to weaken their position within the wider community by challenging the asymmetrical status of their relations with co-resident "Dinka."

Eastern *diel* had good reasons to worry about a possible collapse of their dominant status and position vis-à-vis co-resident latecomers following colonial conquest. Among the early acts of the British colonial regime in that region was the elimination of the *dil*/non-*dil* distinction in the determination of bloodwealth payments. By the late 1940s the British administration had also begun to appoint assimilated "Dinka" as high-ranking government chiefs, abandoning an earlier policy in which every effort was

17. The reason that co-residence would be such an important consideration relates to some of the general patterns and concepts of food sharing (*nyuak*) set forth in chapter 4. Incestuous liaisons that crosscut bonds of food sharing as well as those of blood or cattle were considered especially grievous. For a more thorough explication of this cultural premise, see Hutchinson 1992b.

made to select only *diel*. It would seem that the descendants of eastern Nuer *diel* responded to these setbacks by creating a new title and office of their own, called *ruic dää wec* (literally, "spokesman [located] in the midst of the cattle camp"). Selected by informal consensus from among the oldest *diel* of a particular region, the "cattle camp spokesman" was called upon during the early 1980s primarily to perform special sacrifices, especially those connected with the killing of bulls and other rites intended to enhance the well-being of the community as a whole.[18] Among western Nuer, in contrast, where the status distinction between "assimilators" and "assimilated" was much less pronounced during the early 1930s, there were no cattle camp spokesmen of this nature recognized during the 1980s. Yet, with the noteworthy exception of the *ruic dää wec*, the prestige of eastern *diel*, so marked at the inception of colonial rule, had declined markedly by the early 1980s. Many eastern Jikany men and women were, in fact, beginning to argue at that time that the *jaaŋ/diel* dichotomy had little political relevance any more and, therefore, could easily be disregarded entirely. It remains to be seen whether the exogamic concept of *maar diilä*, which many contemporary easterners found difficult to explain, will yield to growing political and economic pressures toward a greater democratization, as it were, of community power relations in the near future.

CONCLUSIONS

Recapitulating my argument, I have suggested that acts of incest between a man and his "father's sister's daughter" directly challenged the "generative asymmetry" of the MBS/FZS relationship lying at the heart of Nuer notions of transgenerational alliance. And as such, acts of FZD incest threatened wider power differentials within the extended community, including those inherent in the "fellow bulls"/"children of girls" and "assimilators"/ "assimilated" relationships. It is therefore reasonable, at least in the abstract, that some contemporary Nuer might have defined FZD incest as more "dangerous" than incest with a sister or a daughter. Nevertheless, since the socially disruptive potential of this type of incest remained, in principle, constant in all Nuer regions over this fifty-year period, I invoked a number of regionally specific historical factors to explain why it was that contemporary easterners alone had come to recognize, so to speak, the "seriousness" of this offense.

18. The region in which a particular *ruic dää wec* was recognized during the 1980s was not fixed but usually did not extend beyond that of a "tertiary tribal section," in Evans-Pritchard's terminology—or a contemporary subchieftainship.

I pointed out, for example, that the asymmetry of status and power implicit in the *diel/jaaŋ* relationship was much more pronounced among eastern Nuer at the advent of colonial rule. Moreover, due to the relatively rapid incorporation of eastern Nuer communities into the wider political economy of Sudan in the years that followed, these three interrelated sets of alliances were eroded faster there than they were in the west. The extent of this erosion was especially evident in the historical tendency toward a contraction in the east of both exogamic prohibitions and bridewealth claims. The dynamism of these trends—inseparable from the governmental suppression of feuding and the introduction of chiefs, courts, markets, guns, currency, and so forth—was also generated, I argued, by the interplay of life experiences and cultural categories developing out of the pragmatic "fertility testing" of specific incest prohibitions increasingly adopted by eastern Nuer youths. And this was in turn intimately bound up with contemporary Nuer controversies over the nature and limits of incest more generally.

In other words, those segments of eastern Nuer communities that had previously enjoyed an exceptionally advantageous position within the asymmetrical structure of local alliance patterns experienced the greatest loss of power and privilege during the colonial and postcolonial periods. The "hardening" of eastern Nuer attitudes toward incest with the "father's sister's daughter" (*nyawac*) could be viewed, therefore, as a means by which those segments of the population had endeavored to check the corrosive influence of a wide variety of historical factors upon local alliance patterns and thereby reinforce inherited positions of power and leadership within the extended community. The structural significance of the bar on intermarriage among eastern *diel* was similarly interpreted.

Yet one of the most striking aspects of contemporary eastern Nuer beliefs about the severity of FZD incest and about the impossibility of intermarriage among *diel* was that they did not really fit into current debates over the nature and limits of incest. Beliefs about the former were effectively insulated from the "fertility testing" so central to this debate, while beliefs about the latter could not be easily explained in terms of either shared blood or shared cattle. That this radical Nuer discourse should have hesitated at precisely these points need not surprise us, however. In many ways, it was only a scavenger prowling around for dead and rotting "truths." The live "truths," those still breathing power and privilege, were not in danger.

6 The Emergence of Bull-Boys
Political Leadership, Legitimacy, and
Male Initiation

Initiation, what does it bring you? A person who hasn't been
initiated marries and lies with girls. There is nothing that initiation
brings.

A scarified western Nuer youth

During the early 1980s there was a tremendous debate brewing among
Nuer deep within the countryside as well as among the urban literate elite
concerning the ultimate significance of male initiation, the historical conditions that gave rise to this rite, and its contemporary sociopolitical relevance. The questions this controversy addressed were profound: Is manhood
something that must be proven to self and others through the ordeal of
scarification at initiation? Or is *gaar* ("scarification") primarily a means
of ethnic identification developed during a period of intense inter-"tribal"
warfare that is now no longer necessary? What is a man and what is a
boy? What distinguishes the Nuer as a people—indeed, as "the people of the
people"? Is scarification an indispensable element of this distinction or
not?

Interestingly, this controversy appears to have developed among the
western Nuer a full generation before it spread to the eastern Jikany. Yet
everywhere it was associated with the emergence of a small but growing
class of school-educated youths who had rejected the rite of initiation entirely in an effort to identify themselves more broadly with other "black
peoples" of southern Sudan and elsewhere in Africa. Although sexually
mature and thus equated in some respects with other "bulls of the herd,"
these uninitiated adults were not fully assimilated into the category of
"men" (*wuuni*; sing., *wut*): A *wut* was he who bore the six parallel marks
of *gaar* across his brow. Rather, these individuals straddled the categories
of "boyhood" and "manhood," being dubbed by the scarified and unscarified alike as "bull-boys" (*tut dhɔali*; sing., *tuut dhɔal*)—a marvelous oxy-
moron that clearly conveyed their liminal status.

The appearance of this new breed of "boy-men" provoked a society-

270

wide reassessment and clarification of the role of initiation in the transferal of *mut* (agnatic spear-calls), *ric* (named age-sets), *böth* (sacrificial meat) rights, and other kin- or age-related privileges and obligations across the generations. Suddenly, the older generation was compelled to specify exactly what initiation conferred. Hence, for many years now Nuer men and women have been grappling with questions such as: Are full bloodwealth compensation claims of fifty head of cattle applicable to bull-boys slain in battle? To what extent are kinsmen morally obliged, if at all, to "kindle a fire" in the name of bull-boys who die heirless? Are *tut dhɔali*, like their scarified brothers, subject to the milking prohibition? Should a bull-boy who lies with another man's wife be held liable for adultery compensation in the form of six head of cattle? Should bull-boys be elected as government chiefs? Do their words carry the same weight as those of initiated men? What social handicaps, if any, do these boy-men share?

This chapter traces the development of this debate from, roughly, the late 1940s, when the first bull-boys appeared among the western Nuer, through the extremely controversial proclamation issued by the (unscarified) SPLA commander of the Western Upper Nile in 1988 outlawing initiation for western Nuer youth. These themes will draw us into a more general discussion of points of cooperation and contention between the small but powerful literate elite, many of whom were incorporated into regional and national governmental institutions, and local government chiefs and other rural community leaders, few of whom had benefited directly from the meager educational resources intermittently extended to this region over the previous sixty years. For the latter group, as we shall see, "paper" (*waragak*, from the Arabic *waraqa*) and the mysterious powers of literacy it embodied were becoming increasingly powerful symbols of their deepening dependence on expanding national and regional state power networks as well as of their growing vulnerability to the arbitrary intervention of such powers.

THE ELECTION OF AN EXECUTIVE CHIEF
AMONG THE EASTERN JIKANY NUER: 1981

The election of a high-ranking government chief was always a spectacular affair.[1] Hours before the official proceedings began, the candidates and their

---

1. Unfortunately, the security situation had deteriorated to such an extent by 1982 that no chiefly elections were held during my stay among the western Nuer. I was thus unable to find out whether or not there were significant regional contrasts in this regard at that time.

supporters would assemble by community (*ciëŋ*) to chant war songs and charge about in battle formation displaying their strength and determination before all rivals. Depending on the type of government "cloth" (*biiy*) at stake, sometimes as many as five hundred men would appear on the scene. Women, in contrast, rarely attended. The raucous blare of poorly played bugles and shrill war cries added to the cacophony. And as the din and dust rose, the parading "fighting lines" (*dep/tuɔŋ*) would begin to fracture as inspired warriors armed with sticks would spin off in different directions to challenge invisible foes. Usually they veered off as dueling couples who, after jousting with each other for a few moments, would suddenly wheel around together and lunge into a one-kneed stance. At that point their imaginary spears would turn into rifles to be cocked, aimed, and then fired simultaneously at a common enemy before each pair of dancers fused again into the main battle line. Amidst the extraordinary hubbub of the charging, chanting crowds, uniformed policemen would dart nervously this way and that, waving whips and shouting at the top of their lungs, in an effort to maintain a margin of order. And should they lose control, a lorry of government soldiers stood by ready to intercede at that first sign of violence.

Eventually, it would be announced that the visiting local government inspector (*mabetaic*, before 1971 called the assistant district commissioner) and his entourage were ready to begin, whereupon the policemen, barking and swinging their whips all the while, would gradually corral the crowd, seating everyone on the ground before a long row of empty chairs. Next, one by one, the uniformed district officers would parade in, ranking themselves spontaneously from center to periphery in the selection of seats. At times there was considerable reshuffling of positions before all were satisfied. In the eyes of the seated masses it was as though the government (*kume*) suddenly flashed into visibility (see plate 24).

Depending on who was in attendance, short speeches were then delivered by the district heads of the police force, the army, the prison system, the "Sudanese Socialist Union," and the like, after which the *mabetaic* offered a major address. Typically, these speeches mixed appeals for cattle contributions for government-sponsored "self-help" projects with stern warnings "to stop fighting" and "to keep your clothes on." When the number of chiefly candidates appeared inordinately large—as was not uncommon, since any taxpaying male over thirty could nominate himself for chiefly office—the local government inspector would sometimes attempt to persuade some of them to withdraw voluntarily so as to reduce the possibility that a larger, internally divided *ciëŋ* would be forced to surrender

Plate 24. The candidates, chiefly elections, eastern Gaaguang country.

the "cloth" to a smaller, more unified one. Such upsets were widely regarded as fertile grounds for violence. All candidates holding positions within the local chiefly hierarchy were also reminded that they must renounce, immediately and definitively, all claims on their present offices in order to contest in the election.

Following these preliminaries, the candidates were usually given an opportunity to make brief, last-minute election appeals before the voting began. In my experience these speeches were either terse affirmations of the candidates' sincerity and ability to represent their constituency among the "foreigners" (*turuɔk*) or strident calls for the provision of additional governmental services. A few examples jotted down during the election preliminaries of the "court president" of the eastern Gaajak Nuer in 1981 convey their general tenor: "I am a man of your cattle camp and together we can win this cloth!" (Thunderous applause.) "I have a gun and I have two wives. There is nothing I have to purchase—not even a chicken!" (The candidate immediately burst into a well-known song of the late prophet, Ngundεng Bong.) "I am a fearful man in that I don't desire that people should kill one another. I like *ciëŋ* [in the sense of harmonious living] very much. Together we can make this cattle camp work. We are going to stand among the *turuɔk!*" "Our country is impoverished and confused. We have no fishing nets—we need schools and doctors. The people of the town are eating well, but our hunger is killing us. Our country is divided/

destroyed!" "I am a soldier, I don't know kinship (*maar*), I have neither a mother nor a brother [read: 'I will be an impartial court president']. But the person who does wrong, I am going to kill!"

In the case of the selection of "subchiefs," the voting that followed was straightforward: The candidates jumped to their feet, whereupon their supporters scrambled in behind them to form long, waving queues. As the crowd thus sorted itself out, individuals would often twist and strain to see how far rival lines stretched. Eventually, all "votes" were counted and the official winner announced. At that point the victorious community usually burst into song, and, as the emotions of the crowd surged, it was not unusual to see disillusioned candidates dragged off by the police, kicking and screaming threats of violent revenge.

The voting procedure for "court presidents" and "executive chiefs" was more complicated and less dramatic. For though any taxpaying male from the community could stand for such posts, only headmen, subchiefs, local policemen, court clerks, and other persons actively holding local administrative positions were eligible to vote. The voting, moreover, was carried out by secret ballot—a fact that was bitterly resented by some because, as one eastern Nuer explained, it made it impossible to know whether someone had "crossed over" community lines. Because literate Nuer were few and far between, each candidate was asked to hold a piece of paper, on which was drawn a boat, tree, house, or other easily identifiable object, and to stand in a row just outside the building where the voting was to take place (see plate 25). The voters would then file by, one by one, in order to deposit their ballots (consisting of a blank piece of paper) into one of a similarly labeled set of election bags inside the building. While the votes were then tallied, the result was never immediately announced. Rather, the local government inspector was required to forward his election report directly to the commissioner's office in Malakal, where it was "evaluated," together with relevant police records and other undisclosed considerations, before the official proclamation of the victor. Hence, in contrast to the climactic "stand-up-and-be-counted" finale of "subchief" selections, the initial fanfare of higher-ranking chiefly elections tended to fizzle into a state of suspended animation that often extended over a period of weeks, if not months.

Such was the case in the election I witnessed at Malual, a small market center on the banks of the Baro River, in January 1981, in which ten eastern Jikany (Gaaguang) men presented themselves for the office of "executive chief." Just as the candidates were about to be granted time to make their election speeches, the youngest of them—a bull-boy by the name

Plate 25. The election of an executive chief: Blank papers in hand, official voters file past the candidates (each of whom is holding a paper with a particular icon) to deposit their ballots inside the house.

of Burciere Dup—rose and explained to the local government inspector that he had something important to say. The youth, who was literate in Arabic, was working as a government police officer at the time. Pulling a piece of paper from the pocket of his green khaki uniform, Burciere Dup turned his back to the crowd and, while facing the inspector, explained that his principal motive for seeking election was to get "people who have knowledge of government ways" into chiefly offices. "I do not speak with trickery," he claimed, "but because I know that many serious errors have been committed by some of the men here."[2] Reading from his prepared notes, he proceeded to accuse two of his fellow candidates of having killed persons, two of "crimes" relating to women, and a fifth of "cattle theft." He concluded his moralizing speech, which was peppered with phrases such as "yours is a very bad crime indeed" and "no one who has committed a crime like yours should be allowed to stand for the chieftaincy," with sycophantic thanks to the local government inspector and other visiting officials for having heard him out.[3] By that time, however, his words could

2. The local government inspector, I should note, had previously announced that any candidate who had committed a criminal offense would be ineligible to run—and he included in this category the offenses of adultery, homicide, and theft (even the theft of government property, he stressed).

3. These and other quotations cited below were gleaned from a tape recording I made of the interchange, the translations being mine as well.

scarcely be heard above the rage of the crowd shouting out comments like: Ɛ *jin ŋa?* ("Who [the hell do you think] you are?") and *Gat ɛmɔ ɛ dɔar!* ("This boy is a fool/idiot!"). In the heated rebuttals that followed, Burcierɛ's rivals either denied the allegations or justified their actions by calling attention to the fact that, during the first civil-war era, when most of these "errors" (*dueri*) supposedly took place, there was no government active in their region. They also bitterly attacked the presumptuousness and inflated claims to "knowledge" of the unscarified "boy."

The first accused man responded: "What this boy says, some of it may be true and some of it may not. We cannot know what this boy is doing. During the war, every man had to depend on himself—this person went his way and that person his. But, now, if the government agrees [to what this boy says], where are we? Who are we? There is no crime that I have committed. There was a feud and people were living in the bush. Boy, who [the hell] do you think you are? Are you a man? Who are you? There are no thieves among us—walk/go away!" This condemnation of the youth's arrogance was roundly seconded by irate calls from the crowd: "Yes, you tell him! You tell him!" The second accused man then rose and said: "Does this boy think he can 'eat' me? Who is he, anyway? Is he a man or . . . a woman?" At that point, the local government inspector, David Deng Athorbei, who was himself an unscarified Dinka (Atuot), interrupted the speaker, saying: "There is to be no further talk about 'boys': Some of the highest-ranking people in the government are not scarified!" The third respondent began: "You claim to know, but you know nothing! But you are not going to confuse everyone. I have a gun, and in a gun fight I can't know [for sure] whether or not I have killed someone—no one can know that! All you can know is that a son of such and such a community has died. It is death—but the rest is a lie! That paper [alluding to the one from which Burcierɛ read] will mislead people today. But I am happy with what you have said because the people you are now confusing with that paper are the same ones who will go [to vote] with paper today!"

"I know this boy," claimed the fourth respondent, ostentatiously spicing his speech with Arabic words. "We spent three days together at the school of the Arabs. But when the war broke out, I joined the Anyanya [the implication being that Burcierɛ was not so brave]. At that time, there was a girl who stole herself to me. She later went back and was married by her [current] husband. Many years ago, my case was heard. I was not jailed and I was not fined. And now, eleven years later, this man says, 'You cannot stand [for office] because you once feuded for a girl!' Well, then, I will sit and study. For now the *turuɔk* [foreigners] know people by a way that we cannot know. Perhaps there are people who have killed others but have not confessed. Perhaps such a person will stand [for government office]. But it is my word that there was no girl that I stole who could be called a 'wife.' " The fifth and final rebuttal carried a veiled threat: "You say that I have committed a crime, but that is not true! You are like a little boy who has sat down in a cattle byre full of men—people who know themselves to be men. There is no girl talk [here]. Why are you walking around with nothing—not even a spear? You could be killed! What can you ask [of a group of men]? No matter, this is nothing because, today, we are going to know your name. Is there any [other] man here who is not scarified? Who do you think you are? Perhaps you have misled people [with that paper] and perhaps people have not been misled. This boy is an idiot! There is no one who can sit on the head of the drum! Now, we are all going to vote. We are going to select the chief and we are going to go with a man who greets others [and brings them peace]. You are alone. This boy is an idiot!" Lots of laughter followed.

The local government inspector then rose and announced: "Everyone has the right to stand for office. This man has said that some of you have killed people and that others of you have committed adultery. I will look into these charges, but [for now] no one is disqualified. However, I strongly object to the idea that nonscarification should be used as a reason to exclude someone [from chiefly office]. Even I, the assistant district commissioner, am not scarified: There are people who are capable who are not scarified. No one is disqualified." It was thus widely agreed that Burcierε Dup lost this searing debate—a fact that he himself appeared to recognize. For shortly after he failed in this election, he submitted to scarification.

This incident raises fundamental questions about the nature of chiefly authority and legitimate leadership among contemporary Nuer. Consensus regarding the ultimate locus of such powers was clearly lacking. In attempting to manipulate the election process as he did, Burcierε Dup was calling attention to the fact that the "real" power—the power to disqualify and appoint candidates for chiefly office—lay not in the popular support of any particular candidate, nor in the inherent strength and cohesion of community groups, but in the provincial capital, in police records, and, ultimately, in the inscrutable political priorities of distant government officials. This radical definition of the situation, though accurate in many ways, nevertheless proved insufficient. For Burcierε, too, could be accused of worldly ignorance by his indignant opponents. Moreover, his speech, directed as it was more to presiding officials than to the other candidates, transgressed a whole set of ethical principles bound up with Nuer notions of a "fair fight." In the eyes of the crowd, the "boy" was a "plotter," a "politician," who lacked the courage to issue a direct challenge. His rivals, in contrast, clobbered him with "straight talk" (*ruai ε jöc*), thereby claiming a kind of moral superiority over him. And in the end, Burciere Dup was compelled to defer to his opponent's definitions of manhood, to their assessments of chiefly powers, by having the marks of *gaar* cut across his forehead.

This incident also brings out important aspects of emerging struggles between the Nuer literate elite and their nonliterate countrymen for positions of community leadership. On the one hand, this rivalry could be defined as "systemic," that is, as built into the bureaucratic constraints and organizational structure of regional governmental hierarchies. On the other hand, it extended far beyond the realm of institutionalized authority. The contrasting images of "power" and "knowledge" that emerged in this election debate were rooted in the different effects that *gɔar*, or "writing," had on the lives of various age and educational groupings. People's assessments of the powers of "paper" to lead or mislead, to report or distort, varied directly with their access to such powers. Finally, this incident reveals the extent to which contemporary Nuer attitudes toward initiation were being actively challenged and changed from within.

CHIEFS AND POLITICIANS

During the early 1980s the political ambitions of leading Nuer politicians, career administrators, and local government chiefs were frequently at odds. Serendipitous appointments and arbitrary removals plagued all levels of regional and national governmental hierarchies at that time. From the perspective of high-ranking government chiefs, the man to be watched above all others was the commissioner in the provincial capital of Malakal, since he alone had the power to install or remove them from office. During the 1950s and 1960s, the commissioner's office was normally filled by "career administrators," who, by definition, rose through the ranks independent of all election formats. Following the Local Government Act of 1971 and the Addis Ababa Agreement of 1972, however, this post was redefined as a "political" appointment to be conferred on an elected member of the Southern Regional Assembly or any other qualified person by the president of the High Executive Council in Juba.[4] However, it was normally an elected assembly member

4. This somewhat arbitrary distinction between "career administrators" and "politicians" was bequeathed by the British colonial administration. As part of their belated attempt to ensure greater southern representation in the central government, the British hastily arranged for parliamentary elections to be held in the south in 1953. The key political issue being debated at the time was whether

rather than an independent "outsider" who was selected for the post. Because the president of the High Executive Council was himself elected by the Southern Regional Assembly, it was normally in his interests to reward key supporters within the assembly with this and other coveted provincial posts at his command. Similarly, it was not uncommon for his appointees to use their administrative authority to depose local government chiefs who had failed to support them in regional elections. During the early 1980s a number of prominent Nuer chiefs were summarily dismissed by then-reigning commissioner of the Upper Nile, Joshua Dei Wal, a Nuer from Nasir District. Luot Riek, the "court president" of cieng Laang (eastern Gaajok), for example, was abruptly "de-sashed" in 1981 without any official justification for his removal. His immediate predecessor, Daniel Lɛau, was allegedly appointed against the will of the community (*Nöŋɛ jɛ ke buɔm, ɛn kume*), only to be removed two years later. Similarly, the two popular court presidents before him, Peter Lam and Gaar Gaai, were both "de-sashed"—for "political" motives, it was alleged—after serving only a year in office. Although the provincial commissioner was far less likely to interfere in regions that fell outside his home constituency, many contemporary Nuer chiefs nevertheless felt vulnerable to what they (and their supporters) defined as a relatively new phenomenon of "being removed for nothing" (*baa wɔc lɔrä baŋ*). One well-respected Gaajok elder, who had occupied the chieftaincy of cieng Laang for more than thirty-five years before being forcibly retired in the mid-1970s, summed up the new forces of "destabilization" emanating from top government offices in Malakal and Juba with the remark, "Chiefs' bottoms today have red hot pepper, for no sooner does a man sit down than he jumps right back up again!" And since the appointment of replacement chiefs was also controlled from Malakal, it was not difficult for the commissioner to manipulate chiefly election results in his own interests if he so desired. Indeed, two months after the above-mentioned elections for the executive chief of the eastern Gaaguang and the court president of the eastern Gaajak were held, one of the officials responsible for counting the ballots expressed in a private conversation with me his pro-

---

the Sudan should seek a future union with Egypt or strive for total independence. During these elections the British administration declared that all persons currently holding government offices in the regional hierarchy would first have to resign from their posts in order to compete in these elections. In this way the British administration sought to force current government officers to make a clear choice between a future career in the "administration" and one in "politics." This bureaucratic stipulation had the effect, of course, of further reducing the small pool of literate candidates that could represent the south on the national parliament.

found disappointment with the fact that, in one case, the (eastern Nuer) commissioner in Malakal had skipped over both the first and second most-popular candidates to award the "cloth" to the third man, who was, presumably, more willing to support him in regional elections.

The "paper" barrier separating nonliterate candidates for chiefly offices from aspiring Nuer "politicians" and "career administrators" was rarely breached in the opposite direction. This was partly a consequence of the fact that successful secondary-school and university graduates were, quite understandably, less attracted to such offices than to more powerful administrative posts in the national and regional governments. Moreover, whenever a secondary-school graduate did seek and obtain an important chiefly office, he was likely to be viewed by at least some of his "political" superiors as potentially threatening—the fear being that he would use his popular support to the detriment of his superiors' election ambitions or otherwise prove less amenable to their directives.[5] From this perspective, Burciere Dup's assessment of the "real" source of chiefly authority and his concomitant claims to "knowledge of government ways" would appear eminently valid.[6]

Nevertheless, rural Nuer constituencies were not in themselves adverse to the election of highly educated chiefs. During the early 1980s the western Nuer boasted two high-ranking government chiefs who had acquired basic literacy skills in English. However, these chiefs were exceptional in that they had acquired their educations locally and had continued to live and work in their rural homelands. For instance, the highly respected head chief of the western Bul Nuer, Luk Gatluak, had acquired his literacy skills

---

5. For example, when Peter Lam, a secondary-school graduate, successfully contested for the court presidency of cieng Laang (eastern Gaajok) during the late 1970s, he was swiftly dismissed by a "political" archrival in Malakal who feared that Peter was becoming "too strong"—or so many contemporary Gaajok Nuer alleged. The official reason cited, however, was Peter Lam's unprecedented insistence that the chiefs of his district be allowed to deduct back government salaries owed them from the taxation money they had collected before forwarding the remaining revenues on to the provincial capital of Malakal.

6. Many contemporary Nuer chiefs also felt extremely vulnerable to the machinations of rebellious "court scribes," who could potentially use their literacy skills to secretly denounce them to officials in Malakal. These attempted "coups," or *inkilaab* (from the Arabic, *inqilāb*), as Nuer referred to them, were sometimes instigated by lower-ranking chiefs who wished to assume the denounced chief's office. I uncovered a number of references to the "beating up of court scribes" by enraged chiefs in the archival record and witnessed one case among the western Leek Nuer in which the court president publicly humiliated and fired his principal scribe after discovering that he had secretly written to the district commissioner accusing the chief of corruption and other power abuses.

in Bentiu. Upon graduation he served as court scribe for many years before being elected as a government chief. During these years he gradually acquired a reputation for defending the rights of ordinary villagers in their confrontations with the regional administration. Consequently, he won his post in an electoral landslide—even though he himself was never scarified.[7] What villagers resisted were the election bids of urbanized Nuer who were not fully engaged with rural community life.

Although many prominent Nuer "politicians" had, through their own vision and determination, won the respect and loyalty of a wide following of rural Nuer, it was my impression that the literate elite was, on the whole, physically and ideologically isolated from the bulk of the Nuer population *rɛi ciëŋ* ("in the rural homelands"). Whereas during the colonial era most Nuer began their educational training at mission- or government-affiliated schools located in their home areas, subsequent generations of students were often forced by war or other pressing circumstances to pursue their educational careers in distant urban environments, if not in neighboring nations. These students were further estranged from their cultural and linguistic heritage following the 1957–58 elimination of Nuer literacy programs previously offered during the first years of primary school. The simultaneous imposition of Arabic as the principal medium of instruction in government schools also crippled an entire generation of Nuer (and other southern) students, who had already begun advanced studies in English. In addition, scores of educated Nuer and other southerners were systematically hunted down and killed by government troops during the first civil war in an unsuccessful attempt to suppress southern resistance. With the resumption of peace in 1972, those university and secondary-school graduates who survived the war were soon drawn en masse to newly created governmental posts in Juba, Malakal, and Khartoum—an exodus that further distanced many of them from the everyday realities and concerns of their rural counterparts. (Nevertheless, by the early 1990s there was reason to hope that the wartime return of a large proportion of the Nuer literate elite to the Upper Nile Province in support of the SPLA would help to reduce this experiential divide and thereby ensure greater understanding and support between them and the bulk of the rural population in the future.)

However, as things stood during the early 1980s, I was discouraged to see the extent to which some aspiring Nuer "politicians" openly exploited

7. Tragically, Luk Gatluak was reportedly murdered by government security forces in 1992 while visiting relatives in Kadugli.

local concepts of hospitality and of spirituality in order to garner support during regional and national elections. Following the abrupt—and, arguably, unconstitutional—dismissal of the Southern Regional Assembly by Gaafar Nimeiri in 1981, I had many opportunities to witness touring "politicians" attempt to convince their rural constituencies of their worthiness for election or reelection. Among the western Nuer it was not uncommon for competing "politicians," some of whom had not been seen in the region for years, to host a rapid series of beer parties throughout the district, during which very little in the way of explicit platforms was offered. When I asked one of these roving candidates whether there was more to these elections than beer, he smiled and said that, regrettably, "politics [in his area] is still conducted on a very low level." Among the eastern Nuer there was one particularly controversial "politician" who succeeded in enhancing his election bid by staging one of the most sacred of all Nuer sacrificial rites—the killing of a bull. Gathering prominent eastern Nuer chiefs and other rural community leaders all the way from Jekau to Ulang to his family's homestead near Nasir, he provided them with a religious context in which they were divinely compelled to reveal any hidden animosities they held toward him (or others in attendance) through what turned out to be hours and hours of sacrificial invocations. The religious objective of this ceremony—as with all "bull killings"—was to restore an atmosphere of communal peace and harmony by transferring any lingering anger associated with previously undisclosed grievances onto the back of the sacrificial victim. These grievances would then be absorbed, together with the bull's blood, into the earth. The host also bestowed several oxen of "hospitality" on the administrative and spiritual leaders of the various sociopolitical divisions represented so that they could distribute the meat to other attending members of their communities. Although I could not help but view this sacrificial ceremony and related acts of hospitality as politically motivated manipulations of local religious practices, I do not think my opinion was widely shared by others in attendance. When I pointedly asked one prominent ex-court president, whom I knew well, whether this ceremony was about "divinity" or "politics," he look surprised and said: Ɛ *duŋ kuɔth* ("It is about Divinity").[8]

The Nuer political elite, of course, had its own battles to fight—particu-

8. While I do not wish to suggest that contemporary members of the Nuer literate elite seeking public offices were, as a group, insincere in their desires to faithfully represent their constituencies' interests, I was nevertheless discouraged at times by the frequency with which allegations of corruption surfaced about them.

larly in Juba—during the years leading up to the renewal of full-scale civil war in 1983. Although they represented the second-largest "ethnic" group in the south after the Dinka, they rarely succeeded in obtaining more than one of the twelve or so cabinet positions in the southern regional government. This was partly a consequence of the fact that educational opportunities for Nuer were developed relatively late. However, it was also due to the incredible openness of Nuer to outsiders as well as to the scarcity of means by which they could attempt to control one another's behavior. As one prominent Juba "politician" explained in 1983:

> We Nuer do not segregate people. Our attitude toward [ethnically based] "politics" is: "It's a lie" (ε *kac*). We think that everyone should be equal. If someone tries to lead, others will not give him a chance. They will ask [in contempt]: *Lenyɛ nath kɛ ŋu?* ("He exceeds people in what?") or *Guan bɛ ni?* ("Where does his father come from?"). And it is always those closest to him who will pull him down. We will listen to prophets. Or if there is a declared fight, we will select a [temporary] leader. But when there is no fighting, there are no leaders. We quarrel to the point of letting ourselves be divided. [Moreover,] our openness is easily exploited by others because we don't keep our secrets. This is well known by southerners—and even northerners.

Although these enduring attitudes greatly enriched the spontaneity and resilience of Nuer communities as a whole, problems of political leadership and social cohesion will undoubtedly continue to prove especially challenging for them in the foreseeable future.

THE SYMBOLISM OF PAPER

Nonliterate Nuer chiefs often felt profoundly vulnerable to the arbitrary intrusion of "political" forces beyond their control through the medium of writing (*gɔar*). As one of the candidates accused by Burcierɛ Dup observed, "now the *turuɔk* know people by a way we cannot know." Moreover, Burcierɛ Dup's claims to superior "knowledge of government ways" were ultimately rooted in his literacy skills, in his mastery of "paper," as it were. And because the vast majority of contemporary Nuer men and women remained totally uninitiated into the mysteries of "writing," "paper" was becoming an increasingly powerful—if not "fetishized"—symbol of their simultaneous dependence on and estrangement from the powers of the government. Movements of "paper" now marked the conclusion of each new court case and the passing of each taxation season. More interesting, where one sent one's tax papers—that is, to which chiefs and which courts— was increasingly viewed by many Nuer as a political commitment about where one's loyalties would and should lie in the event of an eruption of intercommunity fighting. This was partly because membership in any particular "community" was defined on a voluntary social basis rather than a territorially circumscribed one. During tax time, local headmen were often forced to travel considerable distances—and, indeed, sometimes, deep into Dinka country—in order to collect annual tribute payments from dispersed community members. Furthermore, there were several cases I witnessed among the western Nuer in which local government chiefs arrested and publicly reprimanded individuals who had "crossed over" community lines (*caa rɔ wel/caa kai kuic*) in order to support relatives on the opposing side during major intercommunity battles. As far as the arresting chiefs were concerned, the key question was, "Where does he send his papers?" (*Waragaanikɛ, baa kɛ jak nikä?*).[9] Moreover, when attempting to enlist the support of higher-ranking government officials, most contemporary Nuer, whether literate or not, operated under the assumption that the written word was far more potent than the spoken. "It is better to talk to the *turuɔk* in his own language," one woman explained, "which means you must speak to him through paper (*rɛi waragak*)." Wherever they went, touring local government inspectors and other prominent state officials were normally pursued by a steady swarm of little white "papers," each carrying a personal plea for attention and assistance. Court clerks and other literate members of the community were constantly being asked by their nonliterate associates to inscribe their requests for assistance on "paper."

In brief, "paper" was the principal medium through which contemporary Nuer men and women sought to tap the powers of the government. Through their mastery of "paper," the literate elite had the capability not only of speaking to the *turuɔk* in their own language but of potentially helping people transcend their "second class" status within the profoundly "racialized" structure of the contemporary Sudanese state. By the close of

---

9. I have purposely avoided embarking on a major reanalysis of transformations in patterns of feuding alignment among Nuer over the last sixty years. This is not because I have insufficient information to attempt such an analysis: I carefully and patiently reconstructed the community alignment patterns of seven major feuds that erupted during my fieldstay. Rather, my reasons for reserving this topic for future publications is that it would necessitate a major review of the scores of "secondary reanalyses" of Evans-Pritchard's earlier materials that have already been attempted; thus, it would prove unnecessarily burdensome in the context of this book. Nevertheless, I should perhaps stress that any attempt to use more contemporary data on feud-alignment patterns to reevaluate, say, Evans-Pritchard's "fission/fusion" model would have to take into account the revolutionary impact of government chiefs' courts on Nuer concepts of "community" (*ciëŋ*). And this impact, as I have suggested, was deeply entwined with the emerging symbolism of "paper" as well as that of "guns" and numerous other factors.

the first civil war in 1972 everyone had come to realize the urgency of developing a large Nuer literate elite for these purposes. Indeed, of all the hardships generated by the current Sudanese civil war, it was the total collapse of local educational opportunities—the absence of schools, teachers, books, paper, and pens—that was most distressing to many of the rural eastern Nuer with whom I spoke in 1992.

For without access to the hidden powers of "paper," Nuer women and men remained extremely vulnerable to arbitrary manipulations by the regional and national governments. As Philip Machar, a self-educated Gaajok Nuer, explained in 1982:

> You could be presenting your case before the district commissioner when all of a sudden he reaches into his breast pocket and pulls out a piece of paper and announces: "It says here you are lying!" What can you do? You didn't see the paper written. How can you argue with a piece of paper? Your case is finished!

Not surprisingly, these feelings of vulnerability were often accompanied by more general sentiments of inherent "inferiority" and "ignorance" with respect to other "ethnic" and "racial" groups with greater literacy skills. As was noted in chapter 1, many contemporary Nuer characterized themselves as "an ignorant people" owing in large part to their inabilities to read and write. Having heard numerous self-deprecatory assertions of this nature throughout the early 1980s, I was heartened to learn on my return to the Sobat valley in 1992 that at least one contemporary Nuer prophet by the name of Wutnyang Gatakɛk (Wutnyaŋ Gatäkɛk) had begun to challenge these feelings of inferiority directly in some of his public addresses. In a major speech delivered to an assembly of several thousand eastern Gaajok Nuer in May 1992, Wutnyang pointedly remarked:

> To be intellectual does not mean to be white. Black is very important. The white man does not write in a white color: He writes in a black color, which means that black is very important. [Therefore,] do not be at a loss because you are not white. You will never be white.[10]

The spiritual and military activities of Wutnyang Gatakɛk will be explored more fully in chapter 7.

Interestingly, before the Arabic-derived term *waragak* gained currency among Nuer, "paper" was categorized as a type of *wal* or "herbal medicine." This was in part because "paper" was initially introduced in many

10. This quotation is taken from a public address delivered by Wutnyang at Ketbek, near Nasir, on 27 May 1992.

areas in the form of medical prescriptions dispensed by touring British district commissioners and missionary personnel. Their recipients were instructed to guard such papers carefully until such time as they could be redeemed at medical dispensaries then operating in various district towns. According to James Mabor Gatkuoth, these "papers" were commonly stored at that time on the end of a split sorghum stalk or other reed and placed, together with other protective "medicines," above the inner doorway of the cattle byre until such time as a trip to the dispensary could be organized. Hence, "paper" was initially perceived, like other indigenous "medicines," as a source of secret healing powers. Indeed, during the early 1980s I often heard nonliterate Nuer compare the hidden forms of knowledge conveyed through "paper" with the powers of "Divinity." I recall, for instance, a particularly ironic incident in which a prominent western Nuer prophet attempted to verify whether my literacy skills were as extensive as they were reputed to be. Handing me an identity card bearing the picture of its owner, he asked me to whom it belonged. When I correctly read the owner's name, the prophet gasped and said, *Ɛ kuɔth* ("It is divinity"). Similarly, I often heard rural men and women equate "school boys" (literally, "boys of the house of writing" [*dhooli duël gɔarä*]) with *gok*, or "prophets," in that they, too, "know things [that others do not]" (*ŋackɛ ŋɔani*) and they, too, "reject bloodshed" (*lokɛ riɛm*). In much the same way that people looked to prophets as agents of peace, so they regarded "school boys" as persons who valued the pen above the spear. Indeed, one of the first songs taught to the hundred or so Nuer boys who were forcibly rounded up in 1946 to open the newly created government school at Atar declared that their pens *were* the spears that would enable them to change the world for the better.[11] This imagery was also apparent in the principal metaphor used at that time for the act of writing itself: *Gɔar* was the act of "spearing" (*yiethɛ*) one's words onto paper, as in the expression *Caa ciödɛ yieth wal/waragak* ("His name was speared onto [the] paper"). Armed with these powerful yet peaceful "spears," "school boys" were regarded by the wider community as potential agents for the mediation of armed disputes: *Reikɛ naadh* ("[School boys] separate [fighting] people"). And indeed, during my first year of fieldwork among the eastern Gaajok Nuer, a group of secondary-school students, who were on leave visiting their families, successfully banded together in order to mediate and eventually defuse a major feud that erupted between two adjacent communities.

---

11. These boys became known as the "blue-boys" because of the identical blue cloths issued them just prior to their arrival at the school.

In some ways the emerging symbolism of "paper" mirrored that of "blood." For people experienced both these social media as "substances" that bound their individual and communal welfare to distant—and largely inscrutable—suprahuman powers. Like blood, "paper" was also a deceptive medium in that it conveyed hidden inner distinctions despite its outward uniformity. What's more, many men and women were beginning to develop this analogy quite explicitly during the early 1980s. I recall, for instance, a situation in which a young, nonliterate, western Nuer man attempted to explain to me how a man could have many "loves" while still favoring one above all the rest. "Why, it's like paper," he remarked: "A person can have many pieces of paper and still have one piece that s/he likes very much." On another occasion, I was discussing the relationship between menstrual blood and the human fetus with a nonliterate Gaajok mother, who firmly maintained that "the woman's blood is the child." When I then asked her about what role sperm (*dieth*) played, she laughed and said: "Oh, it's like [that of] paper." I interpreted her enigmatic comment to mean that sperm, like "paper," was *puạlɛ*, or "light"—that is, insignificant in comparison with the mother's contribution of blood. On yet another occasion an older eastern Gaajok man invoked a "paper" metaphor to explain to me how so many thousands of Dinka men could have been absorbed by the Nuer as "Nuer" during the nineteenth century. "It's like this, Nyarial," he began: "If you have a piece of paper and it is a 'real person' (*raam mi raan*) and you place it down here on the ground, then tomorrow, when you come back, you will find a whole stack of papers and the top piece would look exactly like the bottom one." I found the implicit "reproductive" imagery of these metaphors especially intriguing. Although Nuer defined paper money as "bloodless" and hence as lacking the procreative capabilities of cattle, their images of "paper" as the medium of literacy's powers appeared more ambiguous in this regard.

Significantly, some people were even developing metaphorical linkages between "paper" and "cattle" during the 1980s. For example, a person who had succeeded in acquiring cattle as a direct result of his or her literacy skills could refer to such cattle as *yɔk waragak* ("the cattle of paper")—this being a subcategory, as it were, of the more general category "cattle of money." Furthermore, when significant numbers of such cattle were used by their owner to marry a wife, it was not uncommon in the west for the first child born to the union to be named *Waragak*, if a boy, or *Nyawaragak*, if a girl. This was done in recognition of the fact that, had it not been for the father's knowledge of "paper," that child would never have been born. Clearly, "paper" holds the promise of becoming an increasingly important symbol of interpersonal relations for Nuer in the years ahead. For like "blood," "paper" is capable of spanning, whether as metaphor or medium, the experiential extremes between social intimacy and social distance as well as between human vitality and human vulnerability.

REGIONAL VARIATIONS IN CONTEMPORARY
NUER ATTITUDES TOWARD BULL-BOYS

Bull-boys were not accepted equally in all Nuer regions during the early 1980s. Whereas significant numbers of eastern Nuer school boys only began to resist public pressure to scarify during the 1970s, the abandonment of initiation among the western educated elite began in the late 1940s. Consequently, I met a considerable number of unscarified western Nuer fathers and grandfathers, some of whom occupied prominent positions within the local chiefly hierarchy. For example, both the head chief of the western Bul Nuer (historically one of the most isolated and economically "underdeveloped" Nuer regions) and the executive chief of the western Jagei bore no marks of *gaar*. Among the eastern Jikany, in contrast, there were no bull-boys occupying positions of chiefly authority during the early 1980s. Indeed, to the best of my knowledge there was only one case in the history of the eastern Jikany Nuer in which a bull-boy managed to acquire a position as a chief. That case was unusual in that the *tuut dhɔ̱al* concerned, Gatkuoth Puor, was the eldest son of an extremely popular eastern Gaajok court president, Purdet Buop, who had died suddenly while holding office. Gatkuoth was employed as a medical officer in Nasir at the time of his father's death. And his succession to his father's office was facilitated—or so several contemporary Gaajok Nuer alleged—by the provincial commissioner of the time, a Lou Nuer who was said to be a close personal friend and affinal relative. Although Gatkuoth Puor proved a capable court president, his appointment was, nevertheless, bitterly resented in some quarters owing to the fact that he was raised as a "town boy" (*Malakiya*, from the provincial capital) and was unscarified. That same year Gatkuoth died of a fluke injury incurred during a recreational match of football (soccer). Although his death was mourned by many, some people claimed that he was really killed by the collective anger of community "ghosts" (*jɔɔk*) and "divinities" (*kuuth*) who were offended by the idea that "a community still possessing men could be ruled by a boy" (*Nakɛ wec, /kɛn jɔɔk kɛnɛ kuuth wec ɛ nhɔk kɛ ɣöö ca wec dee ruac ɛ dhol a te wuuni thi̱n*). And, according to them, this tragic event continued to discourage bull-boys from competing for chiefly offices in the east through the early 1980s.

It is difficult to know why some western Nuer youths began rejecting scarification a full generation before their eastern brothers. Certainly, their historical lead in this respect was not attributable to regional advantages in the development of schools, churches, towns, markets, or the like. In general these institutions evolved earlier and more rapidly among the eastern Jikany. Rather, I suspect that emerging disparities in regional attitudes toward initiation derived from ideological differences developed during the nineteenth-century advance of the eastern Jikany across the White Nile. For the advancing eastern Nuer, the significance of scarification was undoubtedly intensified during that period by their mass assimilation of Dinka and Anyuak captives and immigrants. We know, for example, that it was not uncommon during the early 1900s for absorbed Dinka captives and immigrants to be rescarified in the Nuer fashion (Evans-Pritchard 1940a:221–222). And in relation to the nonscarifying Anyuak, it would not be surprising if the eastern "first comers" began to view initiation rites as powerful means of recruiting and definitively affiliating new community members. These thoughts were prompted initially by Dr. Gabriel Giet Jal, who argued that the continuing resistance to the emergence of bull-boys in the east was rooted in the fear that wide-scale abandonment of the rite of scarification would permit recently absorbed Anyuak communities to reassert their cultural and ethnic independence.

Nevertheless, I was struck by the fact that these fears, if widely shared by the eastern Jikany, were not uttered in their public discussions of the contemporary relevance of scarification. Rather, their arguments for and against the importance of initiation tended to pivot around the issue of "manhood" itself. Indeed, the eastern Jikany Nuer had by that time developed an elaborate ideology of male superiority centering on the concept of "a real man" (*wut pany*)—meaning in such contexts someone who was "majestic," "virtuous," and "glorious." A *wut pany* was someone who was bold yet not unreasoned in his reactions, was generous and capable of uniting others, and, most important, was "cool" or incisive in his speech. According to many eastern men and women, sons who were especially truculent or troublesome in their youth were the most likely to mature into "real men." They argued that a boy who fully explored the negative consequences of a quick temper and violent reactions while young would soon "find his head" and thus develop into a more stable and reasoned adult.[12]

---

12. As I suggested in my discussion of food sharing in chapter 4, the support of Nuer mothers appeared to be especially important in stimulating this gradual process of self-discovery.

Interestingly, the expression *wut pany* was also occasionally applied by eastern men to women and girls, as in the expression *ε nyal me wut pany* ("She is a 'real man' girl"). However, the criteria for conferring this compliment on women, eastern men stressed, were quite different from those used in the case of men. A "real man" girl, I was told, was someone who was "respectful" or "reticent" in her relations with others (*ε nyal me dual dual*), who knew shame (*pöc*), and thus deferred readily to her husband's and parents' wills. Interestingly, the expression "She is a 'real girl' girl" (*ε nya mi nyal pany*) was never used.[13] Although contemporary western Nuer who had visited the eastern Jikany or had otherwise interacted with them were often aware of the central role the concept of *wut pany* played in that region, they themselves did not invoke it. In fact, this ideological development was nowhere found among the western Nuer at that time. Indeed, many westerners characterized the eastern Jikany as "obsessed with their manhood" and would cite as additional evidence the latter's reluctance to abandon initiation even in the case of educated youths. The application of the expression *wut pany* to women or girls was likewise viewed by western Nuer as yet another indication of the bizarre idiosyncrasies that had developed in the eastern Nuer dialect.

THE SOCIAL DEFINITION OF BULL-BOYS

What, then, did contemporary eastern and western Nuer speak of as being lost to bull-boys? During the early 1980s the general consensus appeared to be that bull-boys were socially deficient vis-à-vis the scarified in three respects: They were said to lack *wuut* (the generalized status of "manhood" itself), *mut* ("agnatic spear-calls"), and *ric* (formal membership in a named "age-set").

Significantly, the meaning of *wuut* had evolved independently of this controversy in one very important respect. Whereas the typical age of initiates ranged during the early 1980s from between nine and thirteen years, this was far lower than the fourteen- to sixteen-year age-range characteristic of initiates during the early 1930s and the sixteen- to eighteen-year age-range thought common at the turn of the century (Evans-Pritchard 1940a:249). A multitude of factors contributed to this lowering of the typical age at which boys were initiated, the most important of which included: (a) the colonial suppression of raiding and feuding, which

---

13. The term *tuut juɔt* (literally, "bull-girl") was used, however, to indicate a fully mature unmarried girl who had reached an age at which most of her contemporaries were already married and bearing children.

greatly reduced the likelihood that newly *gaar*ed youths would be immediately overwhelmed in battle; (b) the desire of local communities to meet certain minimum tax-roll standards in order to acquire and maintain rights to specific government "cloths" or chiefly offices (in Nuerland, only scarified men were listed and taxed); (c) a significant increase in the number of women who, having lost their husbands during the first civil war, sought to initiate their sons as soon as possible in order to strengthen the latters' inheritance rights; and (d) the desire of the boys themselves to attain the privileges of manhood earlier than their forefathers.[14] Due to this decline in age of the average initiate, it was not uncommon during the early 1980s for boys to be scarified before reaching "puberty" (*juel*). The fact that many newly scarified "men" had to wait for years before enjoying the sexual privileges ritually conferred upon them at initiation while more and more bull-boys were actively engaging in courtship and marriage further complicated this situation. "Manhood" was increasingly considered a matter of degree rather than a definitive status. There were numerous occasions, for instance, in which I heard older men publicly ridicule and belittle these pubescent *wuuni* as no better than "boys" since they "still know nothing of girls." I also heard such "men" derogatorily referred to by older men as *wuuni gaari* (sing., *wut gaari*), an expression that suggested that they were men only in the sense of bearing the marks of *gaar*. Similarly, a young man could praise himself in song by declaring "I'm not [merely] a *wut gaari*," thereby implying that he was, rather, a fully grown warrior, capable of assuming all the social privileges and responsibilities appropriate to "manhood."

Although scarified members of the younger generation had developed a counterideology in which they claimed to be stronger and braver than previous generations of men (for had they not withstood the pain of initiation at an earlier age?), members of the senior generation sometimes voiced concerns that this well-recognized drop in the typical age of initiates would ultimately result in an inferior, not superior, breed of warriors. They reasoned that, since boys were now being initiated at a younger age, they were engaging in sexual relations earlier as well. And a man who engaged in sexual relations before becoming fully mature—"before his bones had completely hardened"—risked being permanently weakened in the process: "His knees will grow weak/soft (*kɔc*)"; "he will be unable to run well in battle."

14. Reportedly, there were many boys who wished to be scarified during the first civil war in order to join the Anyanya movement.

Interestingly, somewhat similar "scare tactics" were used by the older generation during the 1940s and 1950s to discourage their sons from abandoning the rite of initiation entirely. At that time it was not uncommon for senior men to argue that bull-boys were bound to prove sterile: "Even if one marries, his wife will not give birth" (*Cäŋɔ wɛ kuen ɔ, /ci cieɣdɛ bi dap*). During this same period many Nuer courts adopted a short-lived policy of whipping bull-boys convicted of adulterous liaisons or other sexual offenses instead of fining them in cattle as was standard for scarified men. As time passed, however, and the first bull-boys began to marry and produce offspring, this interpretation of the fecundating force of scarification was no longer tenable. Many senior men, nevertheless, went on to argue—albeit briefly—that the children of bull-boys would not survive. However, it is extremely significant that the right of bull-boys to marry and thus draw on their families' herds for bridewealth cattle was never questioned.

Far more effective in discouraging the abandonment of initiation during this and subsequent periods were the conservative opinions of marriageable girls. According to Peter Gatkuoth Gual, there were two well-known cases among the Lou Nuer during the late 1960s in which highly educated men were eventually forced to scarify in order to marry. David Nyang Dak was a graduate of the University of Khartoum at the time he returned to his home area in search of a wife. Finding himself completely rejected by the marriageable girls of his area, he lay down and was scarified in 1969. Similarly, Dak Tut, a sergeant major in the Sudanese army stationed in Akobo during the mid-1960s, was belatedly marked in 1967 after being shunned by the woman he wished to marry. By the early 1980s, however, most western and eastern Nuer girls had come to accept the idea that school boys might legitimately refuse initiation. They nevertheless expected boys raised in the cattle camps—who, of course, formed the vast majority—to demonstrate their courage and strength through the ordeal of scarification. It was thus very difficult at that time for an unscarified youth who did not fall cleanly in the category of *dhooli duël gɔ̱ärä* to be accepted by village girls. Mature school boys, in contrast, were classified together with government officials, teachers, bureaucrats, medical personnel, and all others who had knowledge of reading and writing as *turuɔk*—which by that time was a status that could be claimed with pride. However, the underlying implication was, as James Mabor Gatkuoth explained, that they were "not fully 100 percent Nuer." Consequently, school boys were excused by local girls if their knowledge, say, of singing and dancing was not on a par with their scarified brothers. But one had to be fully literate in either English or Arabic to lay effective claim to this status during the early 1980s.

The conservative opinions of marriageable girls, of course, had to be weighed by past and current generations of school boys against other social pressures emanating from the distant, urban, educational environments in which so many of them found themselves during much of their adolescence. In these social environments the marks of *gaar* could easily be twisted by other (nonscarifying) peoples into evidence of inherent "backwardness" and "ignorance." And indeed, in the cultural discourse that developed around initiation, bull-boys commonly stressed the physical effects of *gaar* on the "body" and the negative gaze of cultural "outsiders" in justifying their rejection of this rite. The scarified, in contrast, tended to emphasize the courage and self-control required to withstand the ordeal of initiation itself, the transformative impact this experience had on the "person" as a whole, and the permanent social obligations this transformation entailed (cf. chapter 4). Consequently, much of this contemporary debate revolved around the relative significance of these two visions of *gaar*. However, there were some indications during the early 1980s that even fully scarified *wuuni* were beginning to view the marks of *gaar* with increasing ambivalence. As one western *wut* commented: "No one today tries to make his scars stand out a lot [by rubbing cattle dung ash in the open wounds] like in the past. It's just the fact of having been initiated that matters. If it were somehow possible to remove the marks afterwards, everyone would like it."

In addition to *wut*, bull-boys were said to lack membership in a formal *ric*, or age-set. By the early 1980s this social deficiency was not problematic since their relative position within the age-hierarchy could be easily estimated. *Tut dhɔali* were no freer than their scarified brothers to breach "incest taboos" with respect to the daughters of age-mates or to transgress *ric*-related prohibitions surrounding cooking and eating.[15] Indeed, un-

---

15. The only noteworthy difference in this regard was a tendency for Nuer residing in local market centers or regional towns, a larger percentage of whom were unscarified, to adopt a more age-egalitarian attitude toward commensality among themselves. Whereas in the villages it was occasionally expected that younger men (*ŋuɛani;* sing., *ŋuɛat*) would demonstrate greater self-control by refraining from participating in collective meals when the meal was sparse so as to allow older men to satisfy their hunger, in urban centers older and younger men alike were expected at least to taste what was offered so that "a man's stomach would know that he had eaten."

scarified men were, if anything, under greater pressure to conform to masculine ideals of self-control in matters of food and drink in order to assert their social equality with scarified "men." Although I occasionally heard bull-boys teased about the fact that they were, in principle, still capable of milking, they would refuse this task as well as all others that might identify them with "women."

Because bull-boys were not formally integrated into the age-set system, their social personalities were more individualized in the sense that they had no named *ric* in which they could take collective pride.[16] Their lack of *ric* also left them vulnerable to unflattering comparisons with women: *Duŋ thilɛ ji ric, luɔtdɛ ɣöö ciaa ric ciëk* ("If you don't have a *ric*, it means that yours is the *ric* of women"). Fully scarified "men," in contrast, often took tremendous pride in the heroic accomplishments of fellow *ric*-mates as well as in any innovations in singing and dancing techniques, courting practices, fighting tactics, dress, or the like which they as a set introduced. Among the contemporary eastern Jikany Nuer, initiation in the junior age-sets normally spanned a period of three or four years, although some sets were subcategorized by additional names conferred in particular years. Moreover, it was not always clear in that region whether any particular named *ric* was a subcategory of a senior set or a fully differentiated set on its own. This was because the ritual "hanging up of the knife," which formerly separated the closing of one age-set and the opening up of another by a gap of a few years, had by that time long been abandoned in this and, indeed, all other Nuer regions. Whereas in 1981 the eastern Gaajok boasted between thirteen and fifteen named age-sets—depending on with whom one spoke—containing living members, the western Leek Nuer had only six, on which everyone fully agreed.

Lack of a *mut*, or an ancestral "spear-call," also left bull-boys vulnerable to degrading comparisons with women. Several scarified men remarked that the funeral of a bull-boy resembled that of a woman in that neither one required the ceremonial invocation of an agnatic spear-call. At marriage, too, the spear-calling rite was normally modified or skipped over entirely in the case of bull-boys. Among the western Leek Nuer, for example, I was told that the *guan böthni* of a bull-boy would normally substitute a reed of grass for a real spear when calling out the *mut* of the "boy's" father. Yet, once again, these ritual adjustments were not in themselves socially handicapping. And they were never used as a rationale by

16. Bull-boys did not conceive of themselves as forming a separate *ric* of their own in which they could take collective pride.

the scarified to exclude bull-boys from the distribution (*böth*) of sacrificial meat or to deprive them of inherited rights in the "ancestral herd."

Whereas a half century earlier the ritual conferral of a common agnatic spear-call (*baa mat mut*) and of *böth* rights (*lath böthni*) were inseparable aspects of—and, indeed, interchangeable expressions for—the rite of adoption, it would seem that the relationship between these two aspects of kinship had become less clear-cut by the early 1980s. It was as though people had sought to overcome some of the social ambiguities created by the appearance of bull-boys by letting the concepts of *mut* and *böth* quietly drift apart.

By far the greatest right lost to bull-boys during the early 1980s related to bloodwealth compensation claims: Bull-boys slain in battle were normally compensated, like other "boys," at half the indemnity rate of that established for scarified men—which is to say, at the rate of twenty-five head of cattle (Howell 1954:57). More important, the families of bull-boys who died heirless were not under the same spiritual obligations to marry ghost-wives in their names as those governing the death of fully scarified young men. My inquiry into this issue was complicated, however, by several important factors. First, I found people reluctant to admit that any males born into their families might be abandoned to the "complete" death. Consequently, it was difficult to elicit clear statements as to when in a person's life ghost marriage becomes a feasible option for surviving kinsmen and when (or the conditions under which) it becomes a moral imperative. (The former point was commonly identified at that time with the eruption of a child's lower incisors.) Second, most bull-boys at that time were self-professed Christians, and most Christians, as I will explain in chapter 7, objected to the provision of ghost wives as a matter of principle. Nevertheless, it appeared that the cattle rights of bull-boys, unlike those of the scarified, did not extend beyond their death. For it was the rite of initiation that marked the formal entrance of a young man into the patrilineage of his father. Consequently, bull-boys, like other uninitiated youth, were not fully ratified members of their father's descent group. Consequently, they lacked the right to invoke the father's ancestral "spear-call."

In addition to having prompted a radical reassessment of the meaning and contemporary sociopolitical relevance of such concepts and statuses as *wut, mut, ric, böth, dhool,* and *gaar,* the emergence of bull-boys seriously undermined the ideological prominence of the "cattle over blood" value principle in the creation of enduring social ties—and along with it the former powers of senior, cattle-wealthy men. In the eyes of the unscarified, manhood was neither a gift ritually conferred by the older generation nor an achievement realized through a courageous act of self-control. It was simply a status that came gradually together with the social respectability acquired through age. Moreover, the former centrality of human/cattle relations in the structuring of contemporary age and gender relations was similarly displaced: In the eyes of bull-boys the coming of manhood was no longer defined in terms of a radical transformation in their relations with cattle. Finally, the powerful blood bonds forged between fellow initiates at scarification, so important in reinforcing the hierarchical structure and internal unity of named *ric*, were increasingly irrelevant to this new breed of "boy-men."

RECENT SPLA CHALLENGES TO INITIATION

In early 1987 (or perhaps late 1986) the SPLA zonal commander of the Western Upper Nile attempted to outlaw initiation for western Nuer youth by decree. He simultaneously sought to prohibit the extraction of the lower incisors, an operation that was commonly performed on young children of both sexes around the age of seven or eight. Government fines of one heifer were to be imposed on the family of the child or initiate concerned as well as on the person who had performed the operation. This startling administrative move provoked immediate and considerable public resistance. "We had to do a lot of propaganda among the women," the commander explained in a 1990 interview, "because, for the mother, the initiation of a son is like a promotion." "But the greatest trouble we faced was from the prophets," he remarked. The commander went on to explain how, not long after this decree was issued, he had been approached by a group of prophets who offered numerous arguments why initiation should be allowed to continue and asked, in turn, for the reasons the SPLA was attempting to stop it. According to the commander, one prophet raised the objection "How will we [know ourselves when we go to] fight the Dinka?"—a question firmly answered with the statement, "That is not the way of prophets now!" In justifying this decree, Commander Machar said that he stressed three main points: first, that initiation was physically detrimental in that it severed the nerves near the eyes, thereby increasing the likeliness of blindness in old age; second, that "the Dinka are leaving [scarification]"; and finally, "that our children are now going abroad to places that are too distant [for scarification to be relevant]." The prophets, however, remained unconvinced, warning the commander that "our gods will reject this law." "I told them," the commander said, "that I am part of the gods since I am one of their descendants and that is my word!"—a reference to the fact that the commander is an immediate descendant of a renowned prophet of the air divinity Tɛny (hence his full name, Riäk Machar Tɛny). After this turbulent exchange, some people continued to evade this decree by scarifying their sons in distant rural areas. However, according to the commander, one of those initiated died, whereupon his family came running to the courts in order to sue for "bloodwealth" compensation from the man who cut him—a suit that was upheld by the courts. After a second death occurred, the commander stated, people's attitudes began to change. "Now the prophets are saying that I was right: *kume ɛ kuɔth* [The government is divinity]!" "So, for three years now there have been no initiations [in the Western Upper Nile]," he concluded.

Once again, I am unable to offer any independent assessment of the efficacy—or inefficacy—of this remarkable SPLA decree, since I was unable to revisit the Western Upper Nile in 1992. Nevertheless, I am skeptical that a rite that was implicated in so many dimensions of Nuer concepts of sociality could be definitively suppressed in this way. The commander himself remarked that some westerners were now going as far as Khartoum in order to be scarified. And indeed, displaced Nuer communities in the Khartoum were continuing to perform initiations when I visited that area in 1990. It was my impression that this decree was designed in part to shield future generations of Nuer men from the negative gaze of cultural "outsiders" and partly to undercut narrow "tribal" identifications in the political interests and unity of the southerners as a whole. However, these motives, if present, were not explicitly expressed. Furthermore, I doubt whether the commander was fully cognizant of the "secondary" impact the governmental suppression of initiation would have on the age-set system or on bonds of agnation connected with the concept of *mut* at the time he issued this decree. And significantly, this law was not reiterated when the commander later assumed control of the central and eastern regions of the Upper Nile. It remains to be seen, therefore, whether the decree will have a lasting impact on the western Nuer or die a quiet death. Be that as it may, it would certainly seem to mark a potentially critical turning point in western, if not eastern, Nuer attitudes toward scarification, *wut*, *mut*, *ric*, and related issues explored in this chapter.

Looking to the future, the long-range impact of the current civil war on Nuer attitudes toward scarification is likely to prove mixed. Although scarcities of food and cattle—as well as outstanding SPLA decrees—had significantly reduced the scale and frequency of male initiation rites in both the west and the east, it is highly significant, I think, that scarifications continued to be performed on "displaced" Nuer boys living on the outskirts of Khartoum and other northern cities during the early 1990s. And in light of the rapid escalation of hostilities between the eastern Jikany Nuer and their Anyuak neighbors during this same period, I suspect that the rite of *gaar* will retain a special importance in that region for many years to come.

7 "Cattle Aren't Killed for Nothing"

Christianity, Conversion, and the Enduring Importance of Prophets

One of the more ironic twists to have developed in the Nuer language in recent years concerns the meaning of the expression /Caa yaŋ na̱k ba̱ŋ lɔrä ("A cow is not killed just for nothing"). During the 1930s this expression was universally invoked by Nuer to affirm their rejection of the nonsacrificial slaughtering of cattle and other livestock for purposes of meat consumption. "Except on those rare occasions when dire necessity or custom compels them to do so, Nuer do not kill cattle except in sacrifice; and it is regarded as a fault to kill them 'bang lora,' 'just for nothing,' the Nuer way of saying that they ought not to be killed for meat. . . . There is indeed a very strong feeling, amounting to a moral injunction, that domestic animals—sheep and goats as well as cattle—must not be slaughtered except in sacrifice. . . . This injunction explains why Nuer are not expected to, and do not, provide meat for guests, and also why I was unable to buy beasts from them for food for my own household" (Evans-Pritchard 1956:265, 263). According to Evans-Pritchard this injunction was not simply "negative": "It is not that they must only kill for sacrifice but that they must sacrifice to kill" (1956:269). "It is the role and destiny of cattle to be slaughtered in sacrifice. Sacrificial slaughter thus stands at the very center of the idea of killing, and sacrificial flesh at the very center of the idea of feasting" (1956:269). And in the sense that all cattle were "set apart or reserved for sacrifice" at that time, Evans-Pritchard considered them to be "sacred" in the eyes of Nuer (1956:266). Indeed, he was told that "an ox slain simply from desire for meat may cien, take ghostly vengeance on, its slayer, for it has cuɔŋ, right, in the matter" (1956:265).

By the early 1980s, however, the expression /Caa yaŋ na̱k ba̱ŋ lɔrä had been redeployed by burgeoning Nuer Christian communities in the east to mean "A sacrificed cow is a wasted cow." Cattle, in other words, should be slaughtered only for purposes of meat consumption. For as far as rural Nuer converts were concerned, the first article of the Christian faith was a negative one: "Thou shalt not kill cattle in sacrifice." As John Kang, a prominent Nuer pastor, remarked in 1983, "If Jesus Christ (Yeçu Kritho) died for you, what need, then, is there to kill a cow?"

The impact of this sweeping Christian rejection of cattle sacrifice on both the cattle/human equation and the cattle over blood value principle was profound. By seeking to strip cattle of their mediating role with divinity, local Christian leaders were indirectly threatening to dismantle the elaborate age, gender, and descent distinctions around which these cultural tenets revolved. This ban also made it far more difficult for Christian converts to seek the spiritual counsel of local prophets, earth priests, diviners, and healers of all sorts. Prayer, like "salvation," was increasingly deemed an individual affair in which men and women, old and young, rich and poor were presumed equally capable or incapable.

Intensifying controversies between Christian and non-Christian Nuer over the efficacy of rites of cattle sacrifice formed only one dimension, however, of a far more complex process whereby cattle were gradually being stripped of their "sacred" character—in Evans-Pritchard's sense of this term. Growing Nuer confidence in the efficacy of imported Western medicines and related etiologies of disease had also provoked widespread reassessments of the role of Divinity—and hence the relevance of cattle sacrifice—in the creation, treatment, and prevention of sickness and death. Whereas occurrences of serious illness and death during the 1930s were invariably attributed to manifestations of divine anger over some fault (duer) or wrongful action on the part of the affected person or someone closely related to him or her (Evans-Pritchard 1956:188–196), during the 1980s the question "Why is s/he ill?" was rapidly being overshadowed in some contexts by the question "Of what is s/he ill?" In much the same way that the introduction of currency undermined the socially augmented sense of self that people cultivated in and through their relations with cattle, so, too, increased Nuer appreciation of the potency of imported biomedicines (wal tuɔ̯ruɔ̯k) significantly secularized and individualized people's understandings and experiences of instances of serious illness and death.

The sacrificial significance of cattle was further undercut by people's acceptance of a more open identification between cattle and meat—an identification fostered in part by the development of regional cattle markets and partly by evolving Nuer practices and principles of hospitality. By the early 1980s most Nuer men and women were well aware that the vast majority of cattle exported from their territories was destined for meat markets in northern Sudan and Egypt. Consequently, when local prices for whole beasts were driven down by political upheavals or by interruptions in long-distance transport, some Nuer sought to obtain more cash for their oxen and other livestock by butchering them and selling their meat in local district centers. The shame formerly attached to the slaughtering of cattle for meat was thus gradually reduced by the mediating influences of money and markets. Moreover, because of deepening social contacts with British administrative officials and northern Arab merchants, many Nuer had begun to accept the premise that important "guests" (*jaal*) should be honored with an abundance of freshly killed meat. The nonsacrificial slaughter of "the cattle of guests" (*yɔk jaali*) thus became an important means by which ambitious individuals could attempt to forge stronger, more personal bonds of solidarity with prominent "outsiders" in the endless game of personal network building. But the fact that these changing hospitality practices required a contraction, if not complete denial, of the rights of extended kin to share in the meat of the beasts so slain was a major source of social contention during the early 1980s.

Along with these developments the massive cattle losses caused by recurrent wars and famines and coercive government programs to promote Islamic conversion caused many contemporary Nuer men and women to question the centrality of cattle sacrifice in their lives. This chapter traces regional variations in the relative tempo and thrust of these developments and explores their more subtle impact on people's interpretations of the boundary separating what lies within and beyond human control. It also attempts to capture some of the social and emotional turmoil generated by Nuer encounters with the rival forces of Christianity and Islam while simultaneously demonstrating the enduring resilience and transcendent creativity of local prophetic traditions.

BLOOD AND FOOD: THE CULTURAL DIVISION OF THE COW

If human blood was what bound the greatest of human aspirations—the desires for life, health, fertility, and communal peace—with the transcendental powers of divinity, then cattle as objects of spiritual dedication and sacrifice were the principal medium through which these bonds were negotiated and affirmed (see plate 26). In fact, cattle were the means by which people entered into communication with divinity in all its mysterious manifestations during the early 1930s. For Nuer they were "the link between the perceptible and the transcendental" (Crazzolara, quoted in Evans-Pritchard 1956:271). Although not all animal sacrifices at that time were in-

Plate 26. A western Nuer prophet sacrifices an ox to ensure the swift recovery of a number of newly marked initiants.

tended to promote favorable blood flows within or between persons, all revolved around an implicit, if not explicit, "identification" of human and cattle "vitality" (cf. Evans-Pritchard 1956:248–271)—an identification that, we have seen, was thoroughly imbued with metaphors of shared blood. Indeed, the salience of this blood-based interpretation of the unique bonds uniting people and cattle appears to have been extended and reinforced by the introduction of currency and the resulting expansion of regional cattle and labor markets.

During the 1930s Nuer dedicated and sacrificed cattle (or their symbolic substitutes) on a wide variety of occasions. Examples include:

> when a man is sick, when sin has been committed, when a wife is barren, sometimes on the birth of a first child, at the birth of twins, at initiation of sons, at marriages, at funerals and mortuary ceremonies, after homicides and at settlements of feuds, at periodic ceremonies in honour of one or other of their many spirits or of a dead father, before war, when person or property are struck by lightning, when threatened or overcome by plague or famine, sometimes before large-scale fishing enterprises, when a ghost is troublesome, &c. (Evans-Pritchard 1956:197–198)

Evans-Pritchard distinguished two broad types of offerings. "Collective sacrifices" were intended to sacralize and confirm "a change of social status— boy to man, maiden to wife, living man to ghost—or a new relationship between social groups—the coming into being of a new age-set, the uniting of kin groups by ties of affinity, the ending of a blood feud—by making God and the ghosts, who are directly concerned with the change taking place, witnesses of it" (1956:199). "Piacular sacrifices," in contrast, were "performed in situations of danger arising from the intervention of Spirit in human affairs, often thought of as being brought about by some [human] fault" (1956:272). Sometimes the human error (*duer*) committed was considered so grave that sacrifices of purification and atonement required the ritual participation of a divinely inspired prophet, earth priest, healer, or other spiritually endowed specialist. Otherwise expressed, "piacular sacrifices" enabled individuals to deflect or assuage the legitimate moral wrath of divinity by offering a substitute victim whose life and blood would be finished together with the human offense (Evans-Pritchard 1956:220–221). As Lienhardt (1961:24) pointed out in a discussion of comparable sacrificial principles among the Dinka, "Relationships between human beings and the divine are regulated by the transfer of cattle in dedication and sacrifice, [just] as conflicts between different human groups are resolved by the simple transfer of cattle from the offending to the offended group." In their role as sacrificial surrogates, cattle greatly enhanced men's powers to deflect dangerous intrusions of divinity, thereby reinforcing men's claims of physical and moral superiority over women and children—a theme developed at length in chapter 4.

What merits special emphasis here, however, is that the transformative potency of this symbolic identification between human and bovine vitality depended directly on the contextual suppression of the idea that cattle were a source of food. This is not to deny the fact that the sacrificial slaughter of cattle (and other livestock) was normally followed by a collective feast in which the social relations of the sacrificing group were represented and reaffirmed through the distribution (*böth*) of specific portions of meat on the basis of a system of inherited rights (cf. Evans-Pritchard 1956:112, 214–215, 218–220, and Lienhardt 1961:23–24). Nevertheless, I mean to emphasize the fact that the act of consuming the victim's flesh for the satisfaction of human bodily needs was always divorced in concept, if not also in context, from preceding acts of spiritual dedication (*buk*), invocation (*lam*), and sacrifice/slaughter (*nak*).[1] During my first year of field research, there was, in fact, one occasion in which I manipulated this ideological divide in my own interests. Not having eaten anything other than porridge and milk for weeks, I perked up my ears one day in court when I heard that a sacrifice to sever an incestuous relationship was about to take place. For I knew that the man who produced the sacrificial ox was not allowed to partake of its meat. I thus joined the shouting, jostling crowd of people who had gathered to beg a bit of meat from the court policemen entrusted with carving up the carcass. Having gratefully received a small handful, I immediately retired to a friend's house in the hope of grilling and eating it with her. As we were cooking the meat, however, six more people arrived—all of whom watched silently as I later carved the meat into six small tidbits. Not wishing to offend these people by directly exclud-

---

1. Except in situations where sacrificial offerings were directed against a generalized community threat, such as an epidemic, or where part or all of the victim's carcass was symbolically identified with "the badness to be removed," the victim's flesh was always consumed by some segment of the extended community. Specific individuals were sometimes barred from participating in the feast of certain types of piacular sacrifices, owing to their close relationship with either the immediate cause or sponsor of the sacrifice concerned. Moreover, it was not uncommon for individuals who held or aspired to positions of religious leadership within the community to refrain from eating the meat of cattle and other domestic livestock in all contexts. For by so doing they proclaimed in a manner beyond question the "purity" of their sacrificial motives. Their offerings, in other words, could never be interpreted as prompted by gastronomic interests. My principal host in western Nuerland, for example, was one such individual.

ing them from our would-be feast and yet knowing full well that if all of them partook there would be nothing left for my friend and me, I held out the bowl of cooked meat to each of them in turn and said, "Here, would you like a piece of 'incest meat' (*riŋ ruali*)?" The first poor woman, clearly stunned by this unabashed equation of the meat with its sacrificial context, fumbled and dropped it back into the bowl—whereupon her neighbor immediately chimed in, "You see, your hand refuses it." Although several of the other women did accept a piece, my friend and I were left with more meat than we would otherwise have had. Whether these women saw the hunger that motivated my ruse or attributed my peculiar turn of phrase to gross cultural ignorance, I cannot say. However, this interchange—which now strikes me as both humorous and shameful—erased any lingering doubts I might have had concerning the existence of a sharp conceptual divide between the "blood" and "food" dimensions of sacrificial offering. Indeed, any weakening or blurring of this ideological divide would have had important implications not only for people's interactions with divinity and cattle but also for relations of autonomy and dependence between the sexes and between senior and junior age groups. And it was precisely this symbolic division that was being vigorously challenged during the 1980s by the expanding Nuer Christian community in the east. I will return to this issue following a brief discussion of the declining importance of cattle sacrifice in Nuer responses to outbreaks of illness and death.

CHANGING INTERPRETATIONS OF ILLNESS AND DEATH: THE IMPACT OF WESTERN BIOMEDICINES AND CHRISTIAN CONVERSION

I was once drawn into a discussion between two elderly Leek Nuer women who were earnestly wondering whether it was possible for a child to die "without having been killed by Divinity." The philosophical issues with which they were grappling were profound: "Is there such a thing as a 'meaningless' death—a death that bears no moral message from God?" I suspect that this question would have been unthinkable half a century earlier. For all deaths at that time were interpreted as manifestations of divine anger, even those attributed more directly to spear wounds, poisoning, the curse of the dead (*cien*), the impact of evil medicines (*wal*), or the malicious powers of "red-eyed" *pɛth* or other lethal forces. As the ultimate guardian of human morality, Divinity was believed either to punish individual wrongdoers directly or to allow other death-bearing forces to become active (Evans-

Pritchard 1956:191ff.). One Gaajok man captured this idea well when he said, "Divinity is always the second spear"—that is, the one that lends lethal impact to the first.

Consequently, whenever death, severe illness, or other misfortune struck during the early 1930s, those affected would "search their consciences to discover what fault might have brought it about" (Evans-Pritchard 1956:21). Sacrifices of expiation and atonement were likely to follow. For such sacrifices to be effective, however, it was first necessary for people to discover through acts of confession, possession, or prophetic divination the specific cause or divinity that had taken offense. As the late Peter Gatkuoth Gual remarked during one of our extended discussions of Evans-Pritchard's interpretation of Nuer religion, "Ours is a very pragmatic religion—either the sacrifice is judged successful and the person cured or it is not, in which case further reflections and sacrifices will take place."

Furthermore, as I soon discovered, most people attributed instances of sustained illness and death to the activities of lesser "divinities of the earth" (*kuuth piny*), which are distinct from "divinities of the air/cool breezes" or "of the above" (*kuuth duɔŋä/kuuth nhial*). Evans-Pritchard portrayed these opposed refractions of "Spirit" as forming part of a spiritual spectrum that ranged from an overarching image of social encompassment, associated with a "high God" (*kuɔth nhial*), through progressively narrower social and genealogical divisions to what were essentially individual relations with the divine (1956:117–122). But it was my impression that people conceptualized divinities of the air and earth as locked in a perpetual struggle for spiritual preeminence in the world of human beings. "*Kuuth nhial* and *kuuth piny*," I was repeatedly told, "are not related to one another" (*thilkɛ maar*): "There is no peace between them." Rather, it was the role of "divinities of the air," through the auspices of their earthly representatives, the prophets (sing., *gok/guan kuɔdh*), to suppress troublesome divinities of the earth and thereby shield people from the illnesses and misfortunes they so often brought.

Although divinities of the earth could sometimes be tamed and used for good, they were characterized as essentially evil and destructive. Once they attached themselves to particular families or persons, they fully expected to share in the material wealth of the families so possessed. Should their periodic demands for fresh beer, goats, cattle, and other sacrificial offerings not be fully satisfied, they could swiftly turn on their human hosts, causing them illness and other afflictions. Significantly, the malicious powers of evil medicines (*wal*) and "sorcerers" (*jiwal*) were equated directly with the activities of specific and individually named divinities of the earth. One older Leek woman summed up people's basic attitudes toward these unpredictable and ever-demanding spiritual beings with the words "Divinities of the earth are the owners [literally, 'the fathers'] of confusion and affliction" (*kɛ guan nyɔɔn*).

Divinities of the air, in contrast, were considered to be both less numerous and more powerful than lower divinities of the earth. As free-floating agents of that single, overarching, and distant force of creation "Divinity of the sky" (*kuɔth nhial*), divinities of the air offered more direct (and hence potentially more effective and beneficial) channels of spiritual communication and supplication. Divinities of the air were also known from time to time to select extraordinary individuals to serve as their earthly agents by descending upon them ("like a shooting star") and possessing them. The heart, body, and tongue of a person thus possessed were said to be profoundly "cooled" by the air divinity's presence—a metaphor that suggested, among other things, an increased capacity for the promotion of states of generosity, health, fertility, unity, and peace in both self and others. Although the historical emergence of powerful prophets remained as unpredictable and individualized as the divinities of the air that inspired them, their abilities to offer fresh visions of the world continued to be appreciated across the generations.

In an excellent account of evolving Nuer idioms and practices of prophecy, the social historian Douglas Johnson (1994) provides detailed biographical sketches of some of the most important Nuer prophets to have emerged over the past 100 years or more. His carefully reconstructed personal histories show how important the early spiritual activities and revelations of Ngundɛng Bong, the first major Nuer prophet, have remained as sources of inspiration and guidance for many indigenous prophets. His study also shows how aspiring Nuer prophets were continually called upon to demonstrate their unique ties with divinity through the curing of illness, the restoration of fertility, and the prevention of death. For example, Ngundɛng Bong became renowned for having suppressed a devastating combination of smallpox and rinderpest epidemics that erupted during the late 1880s by symbolically burying them beneath a massive, conical, earth and ash mound (*biɛ*) constructed with the help of thousands of Nuer and Dinka volunteers (Johnson 1994:117–124). Or, to take a more recent example, Kun Thoän, a contemporary Gaaguang prophet I knew well, was alleged to have "burned" the "evil medicines" of the entire region during the late 1970s, thereby temporarily neutralizing the specific divinities of the earth associated with them.[2] Moreover, as will be explained shortly, one of the principal reasons that increasing numbers of eastern Nuer were turning to Christianity during the early 1980s was their hope that conversion would afford them some immunity from those tedious and oppressive agents of illness and death—divinities of the earth.

Nevertheless, the two elderly Leek Nuer women mentioned above were debating the meaning of death not with explicit reference to Christian doctrines but, rather, to a distinction increasingly being drawn at that time between "illnesses of divinity," or, simply, "divinity" (*juath kuɔdh* or *kuɔth*), and "sickness" (*juei;* pl., *juath*). Significantly, many people identified more serious eruptions of the latter as *juath tuɔruɔk* ("foreign illnesses"). Though the term *turuɔk* was originally adopted during the 1800s from the Arabic word for Ottoman "Turk" (*turki*) and subsequently extended to all other foreign invaders, including the British, it is perhaps more accurately translated in contemporary contexts as "those sharing in or exercising foreign powers." During the 1980s this term was commonly applied to—and proudly claimed by—Nuer holding local administrative positions as well as by members of the literate elite and those aspiring to it. "Foreign illnesses" were thus those that could be potentially cured with the aid of imported pharmaceuticals, whereas "illnesses of divinity" could not.

By that time, everyone was aware that some of the most deadly and pervasive diseases they suffered were conveyed by insects or local water supplies. *Malëëria*, for instance, had become a household word that was routinely invoked to explain sudden fevers and chills and just about any form of erratic behavior, including more enduring states of nonprophetic "madness" (*yoŋ*), which would almost certainly have been attributed a half century earlier to divine possession. In fact, several older men and women chuckled openly at the naiveté of their forefathers when recounting how the latter had sought to cool malarial fevers (formerly known as *lerɛkɔɔn*)

---

2. This much-praised spiritual intervention was said to be wearing off by the early 1980s. I should also stress that many contemporary men and women felt threatened by what they perceived to be an alarming increase over the previous half century in the importation of lethal "medicines" from Dinka, Baggara Arab, Fellata, and other neighboring communities. Individuals frustrated by negative court verdicts or by their inabilities to avenge slain kinsmen directly would often travel to distant regions to purchase evil medicines to "hurl" upon their enemies. These medicines could also prove dangerous to their owners: They could easily turn and attack their host if improperly handled.

prior to the introduction of quinine and chloroquine by ritually shattering a molded clay elephant with a spear. Indeed, I found that children as young as five and six were often familiar with the terms, if not medicinal effects as well, of *kɔlɔrɛkuin* (chloroquine), *pɛnɛthilin* (penicillin) and *tɛptɔmaithin* (streptomycin). In fact, collective faith in the curative powers of imported biomedicines (*wal tuɔruɔk*) had grown so strong that nearly every rural community had some member allegedly skilled in the "art of injection" (*raam me ŋac tuɔm*)—claims that were frequently belied by the abscess-scarred bodies of young children and, more tragically, by the withered limbs of otherwise strapping adolescents. One middle-aged western Nuer conveyed the awe with which many people had come to view the curative powers of Western medicines—and the "white people" (*nei ti boor*) who were presumed to have created them—when he jokingly remarked that "the only thing left for white people to do is to bring back the dead to life." During the extended "self-help" programs (*kum rɔɔdu ke rɔa*) launched immediately after the close of the first civil war, scores of rural Nuer communities banded together to collect cattle in order to build local dispensaries in the hope—long since dashed—that the central government would fulfill its promise of supplying them with the requisite equipment and personnel. By the early 1980s, however, the only medical supplies that trickled down from the north were hand carried by returning Nuer migrants. There were still no doctors operating in the extended region—only a handful of medical assistants, many of whom had been neither paid nor supplied by the central government for years. Consequently, easily preventable and curable illnesses such as measles, cholera, tetanus, amoebic dysentery, malaria, yaws, syphilis, and hepatitis remained virulent killers. And everyone complained bitterly about the seemingly willful indifference of the central government to their health needs.[3]

3. Collective faith in the efficacy of *wal tuɔruɔk*, however, was not always so strong. Because the number of Nuer who received government or missionary medical attention during the 1920s, 1930s, and 1940s was relatively small, many people were first introduced to the powers of imported biomedicines through government-sponsored cattle inoculation campaigns. During the 1940s and 1950s the government vaccinated many thousands of Nuer cattle against rinderpest, contagious bovine pleuropneumonia (CBPP), trypanosomiasis, and haemorrhagic septicaemia (HS). The initial benefits of these inoculation programs, however, were marred on several occasions by the eruption of additional cattle plagues, some of which were previously unknown in this region. For example, when the British administration sought to counter a devastating outbreak of trypanosomiasis in the Upper Nile Province in 1946–47 by vaccinating more than 400,000 Nuer and Dinka

People were also highly cognizant of the fact that the lives of many of their cattle could be saved each year if they had access to appropriate vaccines. Whereas Nuer confronted with severe cattle plagues during the 1930s apparently took heart in the idea that their cattle, in dying, had shielded them from death (Evans-Pritchard 1956:271), individuals no longer interpreted such cattle losses during the 1980s in these quasi-sacrificial terms. Rather, many Nuer had begun to adopt a "Christian-like" attitude toward the prevention of cattle disease: *Luäk rɔɔdu ke yöö bi kuɔth ji luäk* ("Help yourself so that God may help you").

For these reasons, people's interpretations of the boundary separating what lay within and beyond human control was gradually shifting. With respect to foreign illnesses, the question "Why is s/he ill?" was being replaced by more pressing struggles to obtain the specific foreign medicines needed to achieve an effective cure. Although most people continued to maintain that both death and birth were "things of Divinity," some contemporary Nuer—such as the two elderly Leek women cited above—were becoming more skeptical of Divinity's role in the generation of certain illnesses and deaths.

This trend was most apparent among Christian converts, many of whom had begun to invoke Western concepts of "disease" rather than "divinity" as the ultimate cause of death. During the extended literacy classes that so often preceded conversion, local evangelists frequently introduced Western notions of hygiene as well as "germ-based" etiologies of disease. Converts were urged to boil water provided to infants during the first few years

---

cattle against the disease in 1948 and 1949, the immediate results were far from positive. Owing to the forced clustering of local herds, this vaccination program was accompanied by serious outbreaks in some areas of HS, a "comparatively unknown disease" at that time (UNPMD, Aug. 1948), and of cattle plague in others (UNPMD, June 1949). As the presiding British assistant district commissioner wrote at the time: "This [turn of events] was unfortunate, not so much from the point of view of the tryps [trypanosomiasis] medicine, which, it is hoped, will not be required again for many years, but because it makes the Lau [Nuer] reluctant to have, let alone to buy, vaccine for H.S.—'if one medicine gives the cattle such a violent disease, it is obviously madness to have another to cure the first one' " (UNPMD, Aug. 1948). Indeed, some Nuer and Dinka groups apparently continued to refuse government-supplied vaccines against HS well into the 1960s (UNPMD, Mar. 1962). A bad lot of CBPP vaccine disseminated in 1950 resulted in a similar drop in Nuer confidence in government cattle inoculation campaigns (UNPMD, Apr. 1951). Nevertheless, demands for rinderpest and trypanosomiasis medicines continued to grow, especially after the administration attempted to reduce risks of contagion by instituting schedules, under the auspices of local chiefs, in which individual herds could be inoculated on specific days.

of life. The agency of mosquitoes in the generation of malaria and of contaminated water in the spread of cholera were commonly explained and stressed. These fundamentally "amoral" explanations of illness, which highlighted the physical vectors of contamination rather than the social and spiritual ramifications of individuals' faults (*dueri*), had also started to influence non-Christians in the east to some extent by the early 1980s. Although cattle remained closely associated with an individual's abilities to cope with eruptions of human and bovine illnesses, they were being increasingly treated by Christians and non-Christians alike as sources of capital for the purchase of foreign medicines or for the funding of distant trips to hospitals in Malakal or Khartoum. And the fact that money for the purchase of such medicines could effectively be raised through other means (such as through the sale of grain, wage labor, or beer brewing) meant that the religious authority formerly enjoyed by senior, cattle-wealthy men was contracting together with the scope of illnesses of divinity. Furthermore, it was my experience that many Christian evangelists stressed the evil agency of the devil—viewed as an inherently irrational and pernicious force—rather than that of God in attempting to explain specific instances of death. Although Christians sought to invoke the shielding powers of God through collective and individual prayer, experiences of severe illness and death were increasingly divorced from the moral introspection and sacrificial offerings of atonement characterizing non-Christian responses to these threats. The evangelical forms of Presbyterian Protestantism that were rapidly gaining acceptance among the eastern Jikany during the 1970s and early 1980s had thus contributed to a radical "secularization" and "individualization" of this domain of Nuer social life.

What's more, the emerging Christian leadership in the east was increasingly arguing that the converts must suspend all interactions with local prophets and diviners—even those not involving cattle sacrifice. On several occasions I was approached by worried Gaajok children with some version of the question, "Is it true that a [baptized] Christian will die if s/he goes to a prophet for treatment?" Although I sought to allay such fears, their poignant question revealed the deep wedge local evangelists were attempting to drive between Christian converts and the rest of the community. I was also struck by the fact that, in seeking to sever all ties with indigenous healers and prophets, local Christian evangelists glossed over the creative tension between divinities of the air and the earth by lumping them all together under the imported category of "devils" (*guan jiäkni* or *caitaani*, from the Arabic *shayṭān*, devil). The Christian leadership sought, it would seem, to prevent people from developing creative fusions of the protective work of prominent prophets with the moral teachings of Christ. However, this spiritual and moral divide did not go unchallenged.

REGIONAL VARIATIONS IN THE IMPACT OF CHRISTIANITY: 1980–90

The Eastern Jikany Nuer

These shifts in Nuer interpretations of the causes of illness and death appeared minor compared to the tremendous ideological controversies generated in other aspects of Nuer social life by the efflorescence of Christianity in the east. Between 1970 and 1983, fifty-six separate (American) Presbyterian congregations sprang up among the eastern Gaajok of Nasir District alone. Conversion rates among the eastern Gaajak and Lou Nuer were apparently equally astounding during these years. Significantly, this dramatic wave of Christian conversion in the east did not extend at that time to the western Nuer. Nor was it directly attributable to the proselytizing efforts of foreign missionaries. All foreign church workers were expelled from southern Sudan by 1964, and at the time Christianity had made little impact on rural Nuer communities either east or west of the Nile—its influence having been largely confined to a small, school-educated elite. Rather, the confluence of historical factors that eventually propelled Christianity forward in this region was infinitely more complex. Perhaps the most important of these was a highly insensitive government program of forced "Islamization" and "Arabization" (originally imposed on southerners during the 1950s and 1960s, and then expanded after 1983). This coercive government program (that was designed to suppress southern Sudanese calls for greater political autonomy) unwittingly transformed the act of Christian conversion into a powerful political statement of rejection and independence. The post–first-civil-war rise of Christian conversion in the east must therefore be seen as part of a more generalized political quest by Nuer to resist a coercive national state structure increasingly inspired by Islamic fundamentalist ideals.

In the eyes of northern Muslim Arabs, Nuer (and other politically marginalized peoples of the Sudan) had neither an indigenous language nor a religion. According to the official propaganda disseminated by government schools, Arabic was the only language (Arabic, *lūgha*) spoken in the Sudan. All other Sudanese languages were proclaimed "dialects" of Arabic (colloquial Sudanese Arabic sing., *ruṭānā*). Now, *ruṭānā* is an extremely derogatory term that implies unintelligibility, being more or less synonymous with "jabbering" or "gibberish." And much to my initial astonishment and dismay, this government-propagated definition of the "linguistic tree" of

Sudan was accepted wholly and uncritically by nearly all the school children and the vast majority of school-educated adults I came to know during the early 1980s. Consequently, there were numerous occasions when I pointed out to friends and acquaintances what I considered to be the inherent irrationality and unacceptability of this definition of their language (*thok*, literally, "mouth" in Nuer). "Don't you realize that this is an insult [*kuith*]?" I would argue. "It's as if the government is saying that yours is not a 'mouth' but only a 'tongue' [*lep*]!"

Similarly, most contemporary northern Muslims rejected the idea that the religious heritage of Nuer and other southern Sudanese peoples constituted a religion (Arabic, *dīn*), equating it, rather, with the worship of devils, an opinion that was increasingly echoed, as we have seen, by Nuer Christian evangelists themselves. Since the central government had repeatedly rejected indigenous religious traditions in the south as legitimate alternatives to the Muslim faith, it concentrated increasingly on forcibly converting southerners to Islam. Because Christianity was one of the three "religions of the book" recognized by Islam, the government-backed *jihad* was more difficult to justify, theologically and politically, with respect to southern Christian converts. In brief, the gradual efflorescence of Christian conversion among Nuer was attributable in large part to the politicization of religious identities that gained momentum throughout Sudan during the first and second civil wars.

Despite the government's concerted efforts to foster Islamic conversion among southerners, I met only one rural Nuer during the early 1980s who was a practicing Muslim—and he happened to be employed as the caretaker of the local mosque in Bentiu. Although I was told that there were Muslim Nuer living in Malakal and Khartoum at that time, there was absolutely no evidence that Islam was gaining converts among rural Nuer. Traces of previous government programs of coercion were still evident in the Arabic names imposed during the late 1950s and early 1960s on an entire generation of Nuer students, following the abrupt 1957–58 shift from English to Arabic as the principal medium of instruction in government schools. But for the vast majority of contemporary Nuer, Islam continued to be associated during the 1980s with the governmental suppression of their political and economic aspirations—an association greatly strengthened by President Nimeiri's surprise declaration of a particularly narrow and brutal version of Islamic shari'a laws as the law of the nation in 1983.

When I occasionally asked individual Nuer why Islam had won so few converts among them, my question was usually dismissed with some disparaging comment rather than with a reasoned theological argument. One

Lou man, for example, expressed open contempt for the crouched prayer position favored by Muslims as opposed to the upright kneeling position with outstretched arms and upturned palms and eyes favored by Nuer: "How can God listen to the prayers of someone who has his anus wagging up in the air at Him?"[4] Other people expressed repugnance at the idea of mass circumcision the men and, especially, the women of their home communities. Although Nuer occasionally performed circumcision on men who were suffering from venereal infections, such men, degradingly referred to as *thony*, were vulnerable to insulting allusions to the event for the rest of their lives. (I reserve a discussion of more recent governmental attempts to overcome these cultural prejudices among "displaced" Nuer in the north for a later section.)

Christianity's appeal was further enhanced by growing Nuer appreciation of the importance of literacy and of formal education in combating their second-class status within an otherwise northern-dominated government administration. Owing to what many contemporary Nuer viewed as the unforgivable failure of the British colonial regime to open any government schools in their area before 1946–47, the early linkage established between literacy and Christianity during the 1920s and 1930s by the American Presbyterians at Nasir, the Verona Fathers at Yoinyang, and the Church Missionary Society at Ler remained firm in people's minds even in the early 1980s.[5] This linkage was in many ways reinforced by the boom following the first civil war in Nuer labor migration to northern cities. These migrations transformed many northern churches into the social and educational hubs of what was otherwise experienced as an extremely dispersed and alienating urban environment—one in which cattle, of course, played no direct part. Consequently, many young men and women continued to view Christian conversion during the early 1980s as the indispensable first step toward mastering the mysterious powers of the written word. As one poorly paid Nuer construction worker put it in 1983: "It would be better for me to hear God's word, be baptized, go to school and [thereby] find a better job." Outside of a few short literacy primers, the only book published in the Nuer language in 1983 was a translation of the New Testament, together with a highly selective summary of early sections of the Old Testament (which, not surprisingly, contained no refer-

4. This particular religious slur dates back well into the nineteenth century, as will be evident from a passage of one of Ngundeng Bong's prophetic songs quoted at the end of this chapter.

5. For an extended account of the establishment of missionary education in this region, see Passmore-Sanderson and Sanderson (1981).

ences to animal sacrifice or polygyny). This book, which was selling at the rate of some 500 copies a month in 1982 at the main Khartoum Bookshop, formed the core of the informal literacy classes then operating under the auspices of a handful of Khartoum churches. Classes were normally held during evening and weekend hours by scores of unpaid Nuer volunteers, who magnanimously shared their literacy skills with hundreds of highly motivated Nuer students, who, in turn, were asked only for a few piasters for chalk supplies. During a series of visits to these overflowing, bustling church centers during 1981, 1982, and 1990, I was deeply impressed by both the scale and remarkable success of this bootstrap literacy operation. Moreover, many of the young men and women who acquired their initial literacy skills in the Nuer language in this way later returned to their home communities extolling the benefits of the Christian faith as well as of literacy. They thus joined the swelling ranks of the religious revolution then gaining momentum throughout eastern Nuerland.[6]

The desire of many people to rid the world of evil medicines and of troublesome divinities of the earth was another prime motive for conversion to Christianity during the 1970s and early 1980s. I recall, for instance, a dramatic divorce suit among the eastern Gaajak in 1982 in which an older woman with four living children unsuccessfully attempted to leave her husband's home. During the trial she explained that she was a medium and a diviner who feared that her divinity was turning on her and would kill her and her children if she did not find some way of definitively ridding herself of it. However, her husband, who had apparently gained considerable cattle wealth through his wife's religious powers, adamantly refused to let her burn her divinity's objects and convert to Christianity. She also accused him of repeatedly beating her and of bribing her older brother with a new set of clothes to oppose the divorce—an allegation that was immediately confirmed, much to the amusement of the court, by a supercilious grin on the part of her embarrassed older brother. In the end the woman was forced to return to her husband's home under a police escort. She left the court screaming at the court president that his decision was tantamount to a death sentence and that she would only run away again at the first opportunity.

The increasing importance of Christian conversion in the neutralization

---

6. The subsequent suspension of all government schools operating in the Upper Nile (outside of the provincial capital of Malakal) following upon the renewal of civil war in 1983 further accentuated this association between literacy and Christianity. What little education took place in rural regions during the first decade of the current war was largely confined to Nuer churches.

of dangerous divinities of the earth was also revealed in a second court case I attended in this same region in 1982. A man accused his neighbor of resorting to sorcery shortly after he fell seriously ill following a bitter dispute over the disappearance of a grass boundary marker separating their adjoining maize fields. The presiding court president, hoping to elicit a clear confession, ordered the man's neighbor to receive twenty-five lashes. After only ten lashes, however, the man confessed and produced the offending medicine. The court president then presented the confessed sorcerer with a stark choice: three months' imprisonment or conversion to Christianity. The man, of course, opted for the latter.

Although the degree of immunity that Christian conversion provided against oppressive earth divinities and against the vindictive practices of sorcerers (jiwal) was still being discovered and assessed on a case-by-case basis by individual families, this new religion certainly offered fresh hope to many who had failed to transcend recurrent bouts of infertility, severe illness, infant mortality, and cattle plagues through cattle sacrifices and appeals to local prophets.[7] Furthermore, the strong, continuing association in people's minds between Christianity and education ensured that, by the early 1980s, leading members of some of the most politically powerful Nuer families had also endorsed conversion.

Although it remains to be seen whether the post–first-civil-war efflorescence of evangelical Protestantism in the east will prove enduring, one contemporary eastern Nuer evangelist had begun to invoke the "dour prophecy of Isaiah" (Scroggins 1991) as a persuasive argument for further conversions. In an extended 1991 interview with the journalist Deborah Scroggins, the Presbyterian minister at Nasir, James Mut Kueth, argued that the future of Sudan was foretold in Isaiah 18. "Woe to the land shadowing with wings, which is beyond the rivers of Ethiopia . . . and here, 'swift messengers' will come to 'a nation scattered and peeled.' " James Mut Kueth went on to explain that Isaiah's messengers "were the missionaries who came to teach the Nuer about the Gospel. But, just as Isaiah predicted,

---

7. In fact, when I discussed this issue with some of the earliest and most devout eastern Nuer converts I met, I frequently uncovered personal histories of recurrent infant mortality, early parental loss, and similar hardships. Indeed, one eastern Gaajok woman I met in 1982 went so far as to claim that *Ji luäy kuɔdh labkε caan* ("The people of the church are inherently poor/unfortunate"). "People who come from large families with lots of cattle and children," she continued, "are not the ones converting." Although her comment did not strike me as particularly accurate at that time, it certainly represented her determination to resist rising pressures from her neighbors and kin to convert to Christianity. Moreover, it may have reflected an earlier historical reality.

the Nuer did not convert fast enough or well enough. So God doomed them to war and famine" (Scroggins, ibid).

> "Here he [Isaiah] is saying there should be great hunger and the birds and animals of the forest should feed on the bodies of the people," Rev. Kueth says, his eyes fixed on the [Sobat] river. "All this I have seen. Even the dead bodies were floating on this river (when the rebels captured a nearby town in 1989), the bodies were just floating. You would see the body of a big man, and you would see that it is eaten by vultures. Even you are almost to cry. But Isaiah says it is not the end of the world. It is not Doomsday." The Nuer just need to be better Christians, and peace and the trappings of Western civilization will return. "Jesus is our doctor from God," he explains. . . . "If all of us, we had faith in God, we couldn't get diseases, we would have clothes. Now we have all these problems. If we had faith in God, we would have no problems on Earth." (Scroggins, ibid.)

The future, I fear, holds many profound disappointments for the Reverend Mut Kueth and his followers. It remains to be seen whether such disappointments will eventually provoke increased disillusionment with Christian doctrines or, alternatively, further elaborations and intensification of them.

The Western Nuer

The impact of Christianity on rural Nuer communities west of the White Nile, in contrast, appeared negligible before the outbreak of the second civil war. This was due in part, I suspect, to the fact that western Nuer territories were initially set aside by British colonial agents as a Roman Catholic "sphere of influence." The Verona Fathers, an Italian sect, established the first Catholic mission in the region at Yoinynang during the early 1920s. Headed by an exceptionally talented linguist and social historian, Father J. P. Crazzolara, this mission soon produced an excellent Nuer grammar (Crazzolara 1933) and gathered most of the materials necessary for a Nuer dictionary. Following the outbreak of World War II, however, the Verona Fathers were abruptly expelled by the British for "security reasons" and replaced by a British sect, the Mill House Fathers, headed by Father J. Kiggen. This latter group, it seems, faced considerable difficulty in mastering the Nuer language—judging, that is, from the lamentable quality of the Nuer dictionary it eventually produced (Kiggen 1948).[8] Furthermore, unlike Protestant mis-

---

8. Apparently, Father Crazzolara generously handed over all the Nuer materials he had gathered for his dictionary project to Father Kiggen upon expulsion. Unfortunately, Father Kiggen then decided that the Nuer language required far fewer vowels than Father Crazzolara indicated. He never seems to have realized the importance of aspiration and nonaspiration in differentiating Nuer vowels. Conse-

sionaries working among the eastern Nuer during this same period, the Catholic church neither produced nor used a Nuer version of the New Testament. Consequently, the spread of the Catholic faith was not associated in Nuer experience with the grass-roots literacy campaigns that later played such an important role in gaining Protestant converts in the east. Last, I should stress once again that western Nuer regions were spared some of the worst effects of the first civil-war era by unusually high floods that severely restricted troop movements. Consequently, the concentration of early Nuer converts along the Ethiopian frontier during the first civil-war era—an extremely important factor in uniting and galvanizing their subsequent proselytizing efforts among the eastern Jikany Nuer throughout the 1970s and 1980s—did not encompass the western Nuer. And thus, despite the presence of small Christian congregations in local market centers and the nominal conversion of the educated elite, cattle sacrifice remained, in my experience, the central rite of western Nuer religious practices through the early 1980s. The general attitude of western Nuer villagers toward Christianity at that time was aptly summed up by one Leek man who said, "The British left together with their God."

By the mid-1980s, however, this situation had changed dramatically. Western Nuer communities were being swept up in a wave of Christian conversion that appeared to equal, if not exceed, that experienced by the eastern Jikany during the late 1970s and early 1980s. These same regions were, of course, heavily devastated by that time by recurrent cattle and slave raids carried out by northern Misseriya and Rizeiqat Arab militias sponsored by the government. In many ways these Nuer groups were some of the least prepared, militarily and psychologically, for these orchestrated attacks. Whereas the eastern Nuer had already gained considerable military skills and weaponry during the first civil war, the western Nuer were noticeably deficient in both these respects at the start of the second. I suspect that the sheer magnitude of devastations experienced by western Nuer communities by the mid-1980s was a significant factor in their growing

---

quently, Kiggen proceeded to merge a set of different a-like, e-like, and o-like sounds, without any indications of aspiration, in order to produce a dictionary based largely on Crazzolara's notes that contained line after line of seeming homonyms. Fortunately, Father Kiggen did not stray from Crazzolara's sensitivity to consonant changes at the ends of words. However, the exceptionally helpful tonal notations Crazzolara used in his Nuer grammar were also dropped by Kiggen. For me and many other Nuer or would-be Nuer speakers, Father Kiggen's decisions to simplify Crazzolara's notational system have proven nothing short of tragic.

willingness to experiment, as it were, with "new" sources of spiritual inspiration and protection.

My impressions of this stunning about-face in western Nuer attitudes toward Christianity were gleaned primarily from a series of interviews conducted with the SPLA commander of the Western Upper Nile in 1990. "Christianity is the *only* thing that has been growing in the Western Upper Nile during this war!" Commander Machar jokingly began. He went on to describe how he had been approached at his headquarters one Sunday morning in 1987 by a group of some 600 hymn-singing, drum-thudding civilians with the complaint that all of them wished to convert to Christianity but that there was no one in the entire region capable of baptizing them. Considering it his responsibility to "look after the spiritual needs" of the local population, the commander immediately summoned a Nuer-speaking Dinka pastor from Yirol by "military order" and furnished him with a car and driver for the express purpose of baptizing would-be converts throughout the Western Upper Nile. The pastor was initially sent southwards to Adok in the hope that he would eventually make his way northwards, covering the entire district. However, after a full month of baptizing day in and day out, the beleaguered pastor returned to the commander's headquarters and requested permission to return to Yirol in order to plant for his family. The commander countered by offering to have SPLA officers in Yirol assume responsibility for planting for his family and urged the pastor to complete his religious duties. Following another month of full-time baptizing, the pastor returned utterly exhausted with a second plea for release. After a meeting with the local Christian leadership, the commander agreed to this request but suggested that the pastor ordain someone else to carry on in his place. For there were still many congregations among the Leek and Bul Nuer clamoring for his services. But the pastor firmly rejected this possibility on the grounds that he was Anglican whereas the people of the immediate region were predominantly Presbyterians. "But that didn't stop you from baptizing them!" the commander pointed out. In subsequent meetings with local Nuer evangelists, the commander emphasized that he would make every effort to attend to their spiritual needs by creating, if necessary, an All-African Council of Churches to take the place of the Sudan Council of Churches, which had thus far failed to respond to his urgent requests for additional pastors. In discussions with Father Zachariah, the Nuer leader of the local Catholic congregation, the commander laughed and said: "If the church doesn't send you help soon, I will use my powers to make you a bishop if necessary!"

The commander further explained that he had begun to enlist the help of local evangelists in an effort to curb homicidal attacks on individuals suspected of being sorcerers or possessors of the evil eye. After government chiefs' courts collapsed in 1984 and before the SPLA established administrative control of the region in 1987, hundreds of suspected sorcerers were killed and their properties confiscated. One ruthless prophet of the divinity Jiaar, who emerged among the western Jikany Nuer in 1984, was alleged to have executed more than fifty individuals brought before him on suspicions of sorcery before dying himself of kala-azar in December 1985.[9] "He found being a prophet very profitable," laughed the commander, "and he didn't want any competition." As part of the SPLA's initial efforts to suppress "extra-judicial executions" and to reestablish a viable administrative network of local chiefs and courts, many of these sorcery cases were reexamined. According to the commander, more than fifty families that had lost members in this way were compensated with bloodwealth cattle by the end of 1989. The commander further decreed that persons who either confessed to or were convicted of the use of harmful medicines by the courts would be subject to a term of imprisonment of between six and twelve months, during which time their properties were not to be destroyed or confiscated. The commander stressed that this policy was initially opposed by many people on the grounds that it would only result in the subsequent release from prison of even more vindictive and dangerous personalities than went in. But the commander was firm and suggested that local chiefs withhold judgment pending a trial period. He further explained that, as soon as anyone was convicted and imprisoned for sorcery, he would quietly notify local church leaders saying, "Here is someone rejected by society": "For I knew that after six months of continual indoctrination, the prisoner would come out saying something quite different from when he went in." This "rehabilitation strategy" was apparently quite novel at that time in the west, but it had been foreshadowed, as we have seen, by recourse to Christian conversion in the sentencing of convicted sorcerers by some eastern Nuer chiefs during the early 1980s.

In supporting the growth of the Christian church in this region, the commander was aware of the galvanizing potential of religious oppositions in the continuing military struggles between the SPLA and the central

---

9. This prophet, whose given name was Duoth, claimed the divinity Jiaar Wan, who, in the cosmology of the western Nuer, was reputed to be one of the most brutal "younger brothers" of the divinity Deng (or the most powerful of all air divinities).

government. Although Commander Machar assiduously protected the right of local prophets and non-Christian Nuer to pursue their own routes to divine inspiration, he pointed out that many Nuer Christian songs had begun to sound like SPLA war songs. "If the Spirit can't move you," he laughed, "you can move the Spirit!" And thus, the religious "schismogenesis" set in motion by government programs of forced Islamic conversion continued to escalate during the second civil war.

Because I was prevented for security reasons from traveling to the Western Upper Nile during my visit to the Sobat valley in June 1992, I have no firsthand information about the scale or the regional intricacies of this post-1983 flood of Christian conversion in the west. Consequently, I will restrict myself to observations about the religious beliefs and practices of the western Nuer as I knew them during the early 1980s, contrasting them with comparable materials gathered among the eastern Jikany during this same period.

CATTLE AND THE TRANSCENDENCE OF DEATH: A CASE FROM WESTERN NUERLAND

The continuing centrality of cattle sacrifice and exchange in Nuer interpretations and experiences of illness and death was everywhere evident among the western Leek during the early 1980s. Within a half hour's walk of my principal residence at Tharlual, there lived two regionally renowned prophets, whose healing powers were identified with divinities of the air, as well as several more minor prophets and healers—all of whom spent many hours each day or week attending to families afflicted with serious illnesses, infertility, cattle deaths, and the like. The main homesteads of the better-known prophets were often swollen by individuals seeking longer-term protection and care and by others who, having received effective assistance in the past, were returning with generous bowls of beer and grateful offerings of cattle for the divinities concerned. In addition, the extended community of Tharlual had a resident "man of cattle" (*wut yɔɔk*) who was widely consulted by people seeking protection from cattle epidemics. There was also the prominent family of earth priests with whom I lived and whose head, the late Kelual Nyinyar Rik, was also head chief of the Leek Nuer. I thus had numerous opportunities to attend cattle sacrifices for both collective and piacular purposes—as Evans-Pritchard defined these.

Yet, of all the cases of illness and affliction that I followed in this region, there was one that impressed upon me more than any other the transformative potential of cattle sacrifice and exchange in the transcendence of death. The case revolved around the emergence of a relatively minor prophet—even by his own accounts—called Mawiyah, a humorous and amicable man in his mid-thirties. I first met this prophet through a young woman friend who was bringing his principal divinity a large bowl of beer together with the request that she be allowed to wean her young child. She explained that she had had great difficulty in conceiving before the spiritual intervention of Mawiyah. She thus considered her young daughter the child of his divinity—*mun ɛ kuɔth*. Hence, before weaning her child, she had to ask the divinity's permission. It was thus a comparatively joyful occasion that first brought me to the home of Mawiyah.

Following an extended seance session for the benefit of my friend and other visiting supplicants in Mawiyah's byre and house, I began to ask him about how his principal divinity had fallen upon him. He and others in attendance explained that some ten years earlier his younger brother, Kam, had slain a Leek man from the community of Cier during a major spear battle with the community of Padang. Kam immediately submitted himself to purification rites performed by an earth priest, and bloodwealth compensation was duly paid. However, the brothers of the deceased remained embittered and were alleged to have traveled south to Adok in order to purchase a powerful medicine (*wal*) in the hope of obtaining vengeance. Within a period of a year, all three of Mawiyah's brothers and his mother were struck by sudden illness and death. Bereft of his closest relatives, Mawiyah proceeded to hold a special seance and sacrificial session, in which the divinity of the evil medicine that had been "hurled" upon his family was eventually summoned and spoke through him. The divinity announced that it had decided to abandon its killing ways and would cause no more harm to Mawiyah's family. In other words, this special seance session enabled Mawiyah to transform this divinity from a spiritual enemy into a spiritual ally whose powers could now be tapped for the preservation of life rather than for evil. This divinity, moreover, proved true to its word. For gradually, Mawiyah acquired a reputation for effective spiritual intervention in curing the sick and the barren. More significant still, Mawiyah proceeded to use the cattle resources obtained from grateful recipients of his divinity's blessings to arrange ghost marriages for two of his deceased older brothers as well as for his father. By 1983 he had thus married three ghost wives—though he had yet to marry a wife in his own name.

Before meeting Mawiyah, I had no idea that lower divinities of the earth could be transformed in this way. It is also important to realize that cattle, as objects of spiritual dedication and sacrifice, were the indispensable medium through which Mawiyah managed to capture and convert, as it were, this highly vindictive and lethal manifestation of divinity into a force for the betterment of the human condition. As objects of bridewealth exchange, cattle were also essential for the revitalization and continuity of Mawiyah's extended family and lineage. Nevertheless, it was precisely the possibility of resorting to possession, cattle sacrifice, and ghost marriage in order to transcend devastating experiences of personal loss, that was being increasingly challenged by Nuer Christian evangelists in the east.

FEELINGS OF POWERLESSNESS CREATED UPON CONVERSION

Because Christianity, as interpreted by eastern Nuer converts during the early 1980s, addressed a far narrower range of life's crises and human misfortunes than those formerly associated with cattle sacrifice, there was what might be called a human power vacuum inevitably created upon conversion. The depth of this contrast was first impressed upon me by an incident that occurred at a Christian naming celebration for a newborn child in the remote Gaajok village of Görwal in 1981.[10] As the festivities were drawing to a close, a man in his late thirties entered the host's homestead, sat down, and announced that he had something he wished to say to the gathering of some thirty Christian neighbors and friends. In the discussion that followed it became clear that he was one of a minority of younger men in the immediate community who had not been attracted by Christianity. Planting a delicately twisted "stick of divinity" before him, he complained about the increasing pressure he felt from his neighbors to convert. "I've come here today," he announced, "to find out what your divinity can do for me." "I have three big problems," he explained, "sorghum—the birds are eating my crops; dysentery—my children are dying; and cattle—they're being wasted on [ineffective] prophets." A leading member of the local congregation responded with the admission that Yeçu Kritho could do little for him as far as the birds and his dying children were concerned: "The children of Christians also die of *weath* [dysentery and other rapidly debilitating childhood illnesses], and our crops are also eaten by the birds." "The only real difference," she concluded, "is that *jiluäy kuɔdh* [the people of the church] don't kill cattle for nothing." "So, if you were to become a Christian," she continued, "no more cattle would be lost on [ineffective] prophets." "But even if I converted," the man countered, "my father, who is still alive, would con-

10. The name of this village means "in need of medicine"—a legacy of the tremendous hardships experienced by this region during the first civil war.

tinue sacrificing cattle all the same." Convinced that the new religion of his neighbors had nothing to offer, the man rose and reiterated that he was not going to be pressured into conversion—whereupon several people reassured him that he was not to worry because his message had been heard.

My initial impressions of the relative narrowness of Christian religious explanations and practices were later reaffirmed during numerous discussions with eastern Nuer Christians and non-Christians alike. One prominent eastern Gaajok evangelist confessed openly to being troubled by the fact that Christianity offered no real explanation for instances of infertility and infant mortality. I also recall a poignant interchange between a man named Thomas Tut Thoan and several fellow converts that took place a few days after Tut's five-year-old son fell into a submerged well dug into the base of a nearby stream and drowned. "My heart wants to sacrifice a cow," he confessed: "I keep asking myself, Why did my little son die?" "You cannot know the will of God," his companions responded: "It is better to forget this death. There is no reason for it. You cannot know the meaning of death."

The complete absence of specifically Christian mortuary practices and ceremonies was especially disorienting for individuals like Thomas Tut and for the expanding eastern Nuer Christian community. Grieving converts were expected to refrain not only from cattle sacrifice but also from all other traditional mourning practices such as the donning of a mourning cord, the abandonment of bodily care, and so forth. Although local church leaders had sought to institute several differences in the burial position of the corpse, recommending a horizontally extended body turned toward the east rather than a curled and folded position with the face pointing west, they offered absolutely nothing in the way of replacement rites. As a result, during the early 1980s many eastern Nuer Christians were adapting the northern Islamic practice of holding a special mortuary feast (*kärama*), in place of the more traditional mourning practices, in an attempt to find a suitable means of expressing their loss and coping with their grief.[11] Although local evangelists openly lamented this turn toward Islamic mourning practices, they devoted surprisingly little thought or energy to the development of Christian alternatives. Consequently, many eastern Nuer Christians appeared to be at a loss about how to handle social and spiritual crises formerly resolved through cattle sacrifice. During an informal gath-

---

11. For detailed descriptions of indigenous mourning practices, see Evans-Pritchard (1949a; 1956:146–153).

ering of leading church women on Christmas morning in Ulang in 1981, for instance, one older eastern Gaajok woman spontaneously confessed to having committed incest with her husband's brother several years earlier. Deeply troubled by the recent death of two of his children, she was uncertain whether she should turn to the assistance of an earth priest and thus sought the advice of the other women present. Her companions flatly rejected this option, which everyone realized would necessitate the sacrificial splitting of an ox, and suggested instead that the woman's confession before them was sufficient in itself to right the wrong she had committed in the eyes of God: Ɛn *täämɛ ɛ duer cuɲä* ("It is [now] a wrong 'righted' ").

Faced with these obvious ritual and explanatory lacunae, many professed Christians continued to resort on occasion to cattle sacrifice. I could not help but smile, for instance, when an older eastern Gaajak man, who happened to mention carrying out a major sacrifice the day before while in the company of a local government chief, was promptly teased: "But I thought *caa wiidu läk* ['you were baptized,' literally, 'had your head washed']." "That's true," the man responded, "but the only thing is that it wasn't a big washing." One prominent eastern Nuer politician with whom I discussed these issues was frankly skeptical of the wave of Christian conversion following the first civil war in the east: "When people discover that Christianity offers no real solutions to their problems, they will grow disillusioned and turn again to the old Nuer gods!"

A MOTHER'S ACT OF DESPERATION

During my first year of fieldwork among the eastern Gaajok Nuer, I became aware of the personal anguish and social turmoil caused by the failure of Christianity to deal with the full range of life's crises addressed by cattle sacrifice through my friendship with a prominent female evangelist named Sarah Nyadak Toäng (Nyadäk Tɔäŋ). Sarah Nyadak was a multitalented mother in her late thirties who, in addition to being a skilled mid-wife and elected leader of the local women's union, was *kiit diin* (literally, "song singer") of the rapidly expanding Christian community of cieng Laang. This honorary title, Sarah explained, indicated that she "had been baptized twice" and "could only die on a Sunday." Sarah's semiofficial evangelical position within an otherwise totally male-orchestrated church organization assured her frequent involvement in the spiritual crises of women members—and aspiring members—of the local Presbyterian congregation. And it was through accompanying Sarah on many of her impromptu visits to troubled families that I first began to understand the magnitude of the religious revolution then gaining momentum throughout eastern Nuerland.[12]

From the beginning of our relationship, Sarah simply assumed on the basis of my education and national origin that I shared her beliefs in Christ and the devil, in heaven and hell, and in original sin—a misconception that I did little directly to dislodge. Preferring to swallow from time to time the lump of hypocrisy than to threaten my rapidly deepening friendship with Sarah, I kept my doubts to myself. Since I usually said little or nothing during Sarah's extended counseling sessions, this mask was not difficult to bear. Moreover, it lightened considerably once I discovered that Sarah sincerely placed the unity and harmony of the families she counseled above her own Christian zeal. On several occasions I heard her advise prospective Christians against conversion on the grounds that it would hopelessly divide their families.

One afternoon, as Sarah and I were on our way to attend the conversion ceremony of a prominent local family, we stopped off to see Nyapuka. Sarah explained that Nyapuka and her husband, self-professed Christians both, had recently requested that a special prayer be said for their measlestricken child. Upon entering the homestead, we found a profoundly depressed Nyapuka cradling a heavily pocked three-year-old girl. After an exchange of greetings, Nyapuka's husband, who was clearly angry and upset, turned to Sarah and said: "What is this God that sends us so much evil? We buried this child's older brother just a few days ago and now she, too, is dying!" "It's not God that has killed your child but the devil [*guan jiäkni*, literally, 'the possessor/father of badness/evil']," Sarah answered. I cringed. "Wah!" retorted the man. "That's nonsense! There's no devil— life and death are both things of God!" An awkward silence fell. Then Sarah changed course: "I know many Christians who have faced far greater hardships than yours without losing their faith! Gai Tut and his wife lost four children and Nyawic Buol lost five." I cringed again. Sarah went on listing the personal tragedies of various church members. What she failed to mention, however, was that she had lost five children with her first husband before turning to the church and finding a Christian husband who gave her a surviving son. "We've come here to pray for the child," she con-

12. Sarah received no regular income from her community services, besides the occasional gifts offered after exceptionally difficult deliveries. Rather, she supported herself and her sole surviving child, a boy of ten, by brewing of local beer for sale. Her (second) unofficial husband, who was off working and studying in Khartoum, also sent small remittances from time to time.

cluded, "so, let's pray." "Nyarial," she announced, "will lead our prayer." This pronouncement took me totally by surprise. Never before had Sarah asked me to participate directly in her counseling sessions. Embarrassed and flustered, I tried to wiggle out of her request: "But, Sarah, I really don't know how to pray well in Nuer." "It doesn't matter," she countered, "you can pray in English." Trapped in my own webs of hypocrisy, I hesitantly began a short English prayer in which I stressed the heartfelt wishes of everyone present for the swift and complete recovery of the child. I knew full well that neither Sarah nor the parents of the child understood a word of what I was saying. Although I expected Sarah to round out my statement with a long Nuer prayer of her own, she rose and announced instead that we had to leave. While our abrupt departure came somewhat as a personal relief, it seemed to magnify the awkwardness and incompleteness I sensed in my own prayer.

By the time we reached the homestead of the three middle-aged brothers who wished to convert along with their wives and dependents, the local choir had already assembled. Under the direction of the homestead owners, Sarah and others went about plucking sacrificial mementos, healing medicines, and other religious paraphernalia from above the byre doorway, from around the sacrificial post, and from inside the surrounding houses. These were then set alight a short distance away in the bush, while the choir—a coterie of drum-beating teenage men and girls—circled the fire singing their favorite Nuer hymns. The local evangelist, a wiry man in his forties, gave the family's dome palm a few swift hacks with an ax to indicate that no further libations of beer need be poured at its base (see plate 27). Gradually everyone regrouped around the family's main hearth, whereupon the evangelist, waving a Nuer translation of the New Testament in one hand, began to preach. His sermon was short and to the point: "You're not getting this God for nothing! You must work hard and show yourselves to be Christians." "Christians," he stated emphatically, "reject bloodshed and help to break up fights whenever they occur. And remember, no adultery—and no more cattle sacrifices or brewing of beer for prophets!" After elaborating briefly on each of these themes, he concluded his spirited speech with a reference to original sin: "You're all bad, you were born bad." When he had finished, the women of the homestead began serving bowls of freshly brewed beer, whereupon conversations drifted to merrier topics and the flirtations between the girls and young men in the choir intensified.

On our way back home, Sarah decided to drop in again on Nyapuka's family. We arrived, however, to discover five men squatting near a fresh

Plate 27. Conversion ceremony, eastern Gaajok country. Household medicines and other traditional religious items are burned as the family's dome palm is "desanctified" with a few swift strokes of an ax.

pile of chyme, or *wau*. Sarah took one look at the scene and immediately dove into the house where, we were told, Nyapuka and her husband were. During Sarah's absence I gently asked the men waiting outside what was going on. "Nothing really," one of them replied. "It's just that there was a goat that died." "How did it die?" I asked naively. "Of illness," responded another. "Oh, that's too bad," I said, "what illness was it?" The men exchanged a rapid series of glances. Finally, one of them, pointing to the pile of chyme, proposed, "The goat ate so much grass that its stomach split open." At that point I let our conversation drop—for it was obvious to all that this lie was intended to cover up the awkward fact that the goat had been sacrificed and that these men had come to claim their *both* rights in the distribution of its meat. Meanwhile, discussions inside the house grew louder and louder. "Why have you split your home so?" Sarah's voice rang out. At one point she emerged to tell me that Nyapuka's husband had offered to a kill a different goat for us in hospitality. "But knowing them," she added derisively, "they're sure to invoke [*lam*] it—so, I think we should just go." After further discussions inside the house, Sarah reemerged carrying a peace offering of two legs taken from the original sacrificial goat. Handing one to me, Sarah said, "Come on, let's go."

It was only after our departure that Sarah revealed, much to my astonishment, that Nyapuka, not her husband, had boldly sacrificed the goat for her child's well-being. Her husband only learned of the sacrifice upon his return from a neighboring homestead, and shortly thereafter his relatives got wind of the deed and appeared to claim their meat rights. Significantly, Sarah seemed far less upset that a sacrifice had occurred in a nominally Christian household than about the fact that Nyapuka had brazenly transgressed a major gender boundary—for only men were supposed to kill animals in sacrifice. Under the circumstances I viewed Nyapuka's usurpation of this masculine prerogative as not only understandable but admirable. Sarah, however, was less sympathetic: "They have split their home. There's nothing to be done. Their children will surely continue to die."

THE CATTLE OF DIVINITY AND THE CATTLE OF GUESTS

Although it is readily understandable why many Christian converts continued to resort to cattle sacrifice on occasion, I was surprised to discover the extent to which Christian preferences for silent, individualized prayer had begun to infiltrate the sacrificial rites of non-Christians in the east by the 1980s. The long, rambling invocations (*lam*), which Evans-Pritchard regarded as so central to sacrificial occasions during the 1930s and which continued to dominate western Nuer religious practices through the early 1980s, were now frequently dispensed with by many non-Christian Nuer in the east. In their place stood a new notion of collective prayer, *lam lɔic* ("invocations of the heart")—a concept clearly shaped by Christian preferences for silent, individualized prayer. Immediately prior to the sacrificial slaying of the cow, the person responsible for the offering would announce a moment's silence, during which time all those assembled would "pray in their hearts" for divine intervention and support for whatever spiritual danger or celebratory act motivated the sacrifice—a practice that, as far as I am aware, did not extend to the western Nuer at that time. By avoiding explicit references to divinity, non-Christians certainly made it easier for Christian kin and neighbors to attend their ceremonies if they so desired. And in general I was impressed by the mutual tact and tolerance demonstrated during this period by eastern Nuer Christians and non-Christians alike. Whenever seemingly unresolvable devotional differences surfaced, they would be made light of with the phrase *kuɔth ɛ kɛl* ("Divinity is one").

Yet just how long this mutual respect would last appeared increasingly uncertain. A vigorous debate was developing among the eastern Jikany Nuer during the early 1980s over whether Christians should eat the meat of cattle sacrificed by non-Christians. This debate was undoubtedly influenced by Islamic notions of purity: The eastern Nuer were fully aware that devout Muslims would reject the meat of cows speared through the heart in the traditional Nuer manner. However, the real tensions flowed from growing resentment on the part of nonconverts toward Christian kin and neighbors. While publicly disdaining the rite of cattle sacrifice itself, the Christians still expected to share in the feast that followed.

The emergence of this public debate was complicated and reinforced by two other historical developments. The first was a more general tendency among Nuer, both east and west of the Nile, to accept the nonsacrificial slaughter of cattle for meat consumption. As early as 1954 some easterners, I explained earlier, had started to butcher their oxen in district market centers in order to sell their meat for cash—a trend first documented in Nasir (UNPMD, March 1954). This trend, however, did not spread as far or as rapidly as might be supposed. During the early 1980s fresh meat was rarely available outside of major town centers such as Nasir and Bentiu. And to the best of my knowledge, meat was never exchanged for cash in Nuer villages. Yet even so, there were many older men and women who spoke deploringly of the seeming readiness of the younger generation to kill cattle for food. "In the old days our grandfathers would have had to be starving before they would have considered killing a cow [for meat]," one western Leek elder claimed. "But today, people don't wait so long."

Extended periods of famine and losses experienced during the first civil war also drove many men and women, especially in the east, to identify cattle more openly with meat. Planting became increasingly difficult as thousands of families were driven from their homes by rebel-seeking army battalions. Roving bands of southern rebels vigorously scoured the countryside in an increasingly desperate search for food. Toward the end of that war, food shortages in some areas were so severe that southern rebels reportedly butchered pregnant heifers for food. Sacrifice, of course, was not an issue in this wartime scramble for food.

Changing notions of hospitality was the second factor contributing to increased Nuer acceptance of the nonsacrificial slaughtering of cattle and other domestic animals. Although Nuer had long been masters of hospitality,[13] it was only during the colonial period that some of them began to adopt the premise that especially important "guests" (*jaal;* sing., *jal*) should be received with an abundance of freshly killed meat. Newly appointed government chiefs wishing to ingratiate themselves with touring British colonial officials were probably among the first Nuer to slaughter cattle in honor of distinguished guests. Increased social contacts with northern Arab merchants, many of whom established semipermanent residences in the region, may also have contributed to the dissemination and legitimation of the concept "the cow of the guests" (*yaŋ jaali*).

By the early 1980s, moreover, some Nuer—particularly easterners—had adopted this practice among themselves. A cow of the guest was often slaughtered, say, to mark the safe return of a highly educated or otherwise politically prominent relative who had spent a year or more away working in distant cities. Gatwic Lul, a prominent Nuer judge whose duties rarely enabled him to travel to his home area, remarked that if his rural relatives were unable for some reason to slaughter a cow for him upon his arrival home, he would purchase one himself for this purpose rather than rupture what he considered to be a long-standing honorific tradition in his family. I have also seen leading members of a younger age-set in the east invoke

13. If it had not been the case that Nuer were masters of hospitality, it would be difficult to imagine how they could have successfully assimilated so many thousands of Dinka and Anyuak during their nineteenth-century expansions. Relations with these immigrants and captives were solidified through the generous bestowal of wives, cattle, meat rights (*böth*), and leadership opportunities.

this hospitality concept in order to hold a special feast for their closest comrades—although in this case, as in many others, a *thäy deel* (male sheep or goat) was used in place of an ox.

Unlike cattle offered in sacrifice, a cow slaughtered in hospitality was not invoked (*lam*) prior to slaughter. Nor was it pierced through the heart with a spear (an operation known as *nak*) like a "sacrificial cow" or *yaŋ kuɔdh* (literally, "cow of divinity").[14] Rather, a cow of the guest, people stressed, was always slain at the throat (in an operation known as *ŋuɔt*). When the "cow" concerned was, in reality, a sheep or a goat, there was no difference in the mode of slaughter between sacrificial and hospitality victims: Smaller livestock were invariably killed at the throat (cf. Evans-Pritchard 1956:211). Nevertheless, because cattle remained the quintessential sacrificial victims in Nuer eyes, this *nak/ŋuɔt* distinction in slaughtering practices was important particularly since it was increasingly associated with two very different patterns of meat distribution, each with its own set of rules.

In essence cattle slain at the throat were considered to be less subject to the transgenerational claims of extended kinsmen and kinswomen to specific portions of meat. In the attempt to reserve as much meat as possible for the honored guests, many eastern Nuer hosts did not feel obliged to notify relatives of their intent to slaughter a cow of the guests at all. Should their kinsfolk and neighbors nevertheless appear and controversies over the distribution of meat develop—a pattern that appeared to be common at this time—the owner of the beast would usually attempt to defend his behavior by arguing that *both* rights apply only to cattle offered to divinity. I witnessed one situation in which the meat of a bull-calf slain on the occasion of a *nööŋ* ("the bringing [of a new bride to her husband's

14. The term "cow of divinity" could also be applied to any cow that had been set aside for future sacrifice. As Evans-Pritchard explained (1956:40), individual cows were sometimes dedicated to specific divinities during the 1930s by rubbing their backs with dung ash or by adorning them with special wooden beads, metal rings, or other ritual objects. Such were also referred to as "cattle of divinity." Special restrictions on consumption were often placed on the milk of such cows. Moreover, it was expected that her first male calf, when mature, would also be sacrificed to the same divinity. To dispose of a cow of divinity by means other than sacrifice was to risk the wrath of the divinity concerned. And for this reason, such cattle were rarely parted with in bridewealth or bloodwealth exchange at that time (Evans-Pritchard 1956:40–41). Although these practices remained firm among the western Leek Nuer through the early 1980s and, to a lesser extent, among non-Christian Nuer families in the east as well, people's concepts of cattle of divinity had been reshaped somewhat by the increasing prominence of the concept of cattle of guests in their everyday social life.

Plate 28. Four of the seven girls returning home after delivering a new bride to her husband's home.

home]") became the subject of two successive quarrels. No sooner had the eastern Gaajok host of the wedding party fended off the meat demands of a vocal gathering of kinsmen with the assertion that the bull-calf had been slain as a cow of the guests, not as a cow of divinity, than a parallel argument erupted between one of the seven visiting girls being honored and a kinswoman who happened to live in the host's immediate community. In both cases it was the meaning and relevance of *both* claims that was being disputed. As things turned out, the owner of the bull-calf retained only its head and loins, distributing some of the viscera to attending kin, while the group of seven visiting girls—one of whom was me—proceeded to consume all four legs and most of the rest of the ox over the next four days (see plate 28).[15]

15. It could be argued that animals slaughtered in connection with marriage festivities were never subject to the extended *both* rights governing those sacrificed for piacular purposes, since the *juak* (loins), *kau* (chest), *leat* (lower back), and *jiac* (stomach) of the victim were normally shared collectively and respectively by all older men, younger men, girls, and women attending the wedding celebration. Nevertheless, there was always some degree of extended *both* claims honored in the distribution of the animal's legs on such occasions during the 1930s.

Although Evans-Pritchard also witnessed major arguments over the distribution of meat at weddings and other sacrificial events during the early 1930s, I suspect that these arguments were framed in quite different terms from those I witnessed during the early 1980s. In much the same way as "people of the government" (*jikume*) seized upon the bull-calf sacrificed during bloodwealth cattle transfers as an opportunity to affirm their mutual solidarity, some Nuer were beginning to invoke the concept of cow of the guest however they wished, in the attempt to create more powerful personal networks within the broader community. It was not the concept of *both* that was becoming obsolete. Rather, this concept was being redirected toward the affirmation of "new" social linkages and identities, some of which were in direct tension with the long-standing rights of distant agnates and close cognates to share in the meat of one another's cattle.

The post–first-civil-war wave of Christian conversion in the east added further impetus to this trend. Since Nuer converts rejected the very concept of cattle of divinity, all livestock slain by them fell, at least in principle, into the residual category of cattle of the guests. Consequently, many eastern Nuer converts during the early 1980s felt freer to distribute the meat of such cattle, as this suited their immediate purposes. There simply were no fixed rules in such cases at that time—a fact that added considerable bitterness to emerging debates over whether Christians should share in the meat of cattle sacrificed by non-Christians. During the extensive Christmas celebrations in Ulang in 1981, for instance, local evangelists, pastors, "song leaders," and other attending church officials spent much of their meeting time negotiating a mutually acceptable system of *both* rights among themselves with respect to the division of the three oxen slain collectively by their congregations (see plate 29). In brief, Christian converts challenged not only the sacrificial significance of cattle but also the transgenerational *both* obligations binding extended agnatic and cognatic kin.

THE EVOLUTION OF CHRISTIAN DOCTRINES IN THE EAST: 1990–93

Perhaps it was the relative youth and puritanical strains of evangelical Protestantism spreading throughout eastern Jikany communities during the early 1980s that accounted for its striking orthodoxy. As late as 1992, eastern Nuer church leaders still appeared to be more concerned with stamping out all vestiges of cattle sacrifice than with developing substitute religious practices.[16] I was also discouraged to learn on my return visit to the eastern Jikany in 1992 that all forms of dancing, the drinking of home-brewed beer,

Plate 29. Christmas morning in Ulang: the nonsacrificial slaughter of cattle for purposes of hospitality by Christian converts outside the boundaries of a specially constructed churchyard fence.

and the smoking of tobacco had been redefined by local church leaders as fundamentally "un-Christian" forms of sociality. No ideas of this sort were espoused during the early 1980s. The church was also becoming much more vehement in its condemnations of polygyny. Whereas local evangelists and laypersons took the attitude during the early 1980s that, as long as Nuer pastors had only one wife, the rest of the congregation could marry as it pleased, church leaders were pushing during the early 1990s for monogamy to be imposed on lay elders as well. After failing to win support for a generalized Christian ban on polygyny during a series of church meetings in early 1992, several leading Nuer pastors and evangelists began to deny the rite of communion (*riɛm* Yeçu, literally, "Christ's blood") to women converts who had been married as junior wives by their husbands. Polygynously married men, however, remained free to receive communion—which was normally offered twice a year—as were their first wives. In other words, these church leaders were seeking, as one put it, to impose monogamy "indirectly" through the stigmatizing exclusion of secondarily married wives.

I was nevertheless surprised that local church leaders would have embarked on such a campaign at a time when the sex ratio of the general population was becoming increasingly skewed through the loss of so many fighting men and when polygyny was generally perceived to be on the increase.[17] One prominent Nuer pastor justified granting communion to polygynously married men on the grounds that the church was finding it very difficult to attract older men: "They refer to the church as a place of play (*guääth ŋar*) more appropriate to children (*ɛ duŋ gaan*) than to grown men, and thus we didn't want to risk alienating them further." Considering that the act of conversion by senior men was tantamount to a voluntary renunciation of their religious authority as the sacrificers of cattle and hence as the principal defenders of their wives and children against dangerous intrusions of divinity, it is not surprising that local church leaders

16. The Reverend Paul Bol, a major leader of the Presbyterian church in the east, remarked in 1992 something to the effect that his "first priority was to educate the local population in the basic tenets of Christianity." For only after this was accomplished could the development of alternative Christian responses to the social and emotional crises formerly handled through cattle sacrifice begin.

17. On a lighter note, I recall an early conversation with Kelual Nyinyar Rik in 1982 in which he asked me whether men's taking of only one wife in America was "something of the heart" (that is, voluntary) or was based on "the word of God." When I replied that it was neither of these two things but rather "a law of the government," he laughed and said, "It must have been the women who made that law."

were finding them more difficult to recruit than younger men and women of all ages.

Local church leaders also appeared to be adopting an increasingly intolerant attitude toward ghost wives. This term encompassed both women who were originally married by a pro-husband for the purpose of revitalizing the name and line of one of his deceased relatives and leviratic widows who continued to procreate in the name of their late husbands by having selected a pro-husband from among their immediate affines or a lover of their own choice.[18] Of course, by seeking to restrict these forms of marriage, local Christian evangelists were indirectly undermining some of the most fundamental kinship values, including the premise that the passage of cattle, not semen, established patrilineal lines of descent and the premise that close agnates and cognates were morally bound to ensure the "procreative immortality" of relatives who died heirless.

Hardening church attitudes in these regards were attributable in large part to increased contacts during the second civil war between local Nuer evangelists and expatriate church officials who, from their offices in Kenya and elsewhere, were trying to put their stamp on what was becoming one of the fastest-growing movements of Christian conversion in the world. And yet, as late as 1992, local Nuer evangelists and pastors had still not succeeded in passing an official policy condemning polygyny, ghost marriage, or widow inheritance for converts. In fact, many eastern Nuer converts I met in 1992 argued that leviratic unions and ghost marriages could still be arranged—without transgressing church doctrines—so long as the women concerned were allowed to conceive their children with men other than their Christian pro-husbands.

Nevertheless, when I suggested to one leading Nuer pastor that, as far as I was aware, nothing in the New or Old Testaments expressly forbade the marrying of wives in the name of deceased kinsmen, the Reverend Paul Bol countered my statement with the question "Is there ghost marriage where you come from?" I rejected this question on the grounds that it implied that whatever marriage customs were currently prevalent in the United States and Europe were somehow the "correct" ones and thus that there was nothing unique to Nuer marriage practices that could be deemed worthy in itself. Discussions such as these—in which I found myself in the

---

18. For ethnographic details, see Evans-Pritchard's discussions of ghost marriage, widow inheritance, and widow concubinage in *Kinship and Marriage among the Nuer* (1951b).

highly ironic position of advocating Nuer marriage practices to local Christian evangelists who assumed, more often than not, that Euro-American practices were inherently superior—usually depressed me. For it seemed that the eastern Nuer Christian leadership was at that time in the process of destroying far more than it was creating.

THE ENDURING IMPORTANCE OF INDIGENOUS PROPHETS: THE CASE OF WUTNYANG GATAKƐK

Although Christianity had proven a potent force of social and ideological transformation among Nuer in recent decades, people's confidence in the efficacy of cattle sacrifice and the spiritual powers of prophets was by no means on the point of imminent collapse in 1992. The prophetic songs of the late Ngundɛng Bong, for example, remained crucial points of reference in people's attempts to comprehend the devastating course and future outcome of the second Sudanese civil war (cf. Johnson 1985, 1994). The fact that sections of his sacred songs allegedly foretold both the inevitability and ultimate success of the present war of southern liberation enabled Nuer Christians and non-Christians alike to believe that the tremendous human sacrifices involved were purposeful and ordained by Divinity. As one eastern Gaajok fighter commented in 1992, "We know that all these deaths are not meaningless because they were foreseen by Ngundɛng and will ultimately result in our freedom."

Moreover, because contemporary Nuer evangelists had demonstrated little interest in filling the ritual lacunae created by their sweeping ban on cattle sacrifice, several contemporary Nuer prophets were beginning to step into this spiritual void to develop powerful syncretic blends of their own. By the early 1990s the most powerful of these by far was a young Lak Nuer prophet named Wutnyang Gatakɛk, who leaned heavily on the earlier revelations and spiritual activities of Ngundɛng Bong in developing his reputation. Wutnyang Gatakɛk translates literally "Man of Crocodile, Son of Reputation"—a name meant to suggest, I was told, that, when crossed, Wutnyang could react as viciously as a crocodile. By 1992 he had, in fact, raised his own personal army—known as the "white army"—consisting of several thousand loyal Nuer recruits. Indeed, it was Wutnyang's personal forces (together with SPLA-affiliated remnants of the former Anyanya II army) that delivered the single, most powerful blow to the national army during the early 1990s: the surprise attack and temporary capture of the government-held town of Malakal in mid-October 1992.

Yet Wutnyang was also a renowned peacemaker who had repeatedly sought to defuse intensifying intra- and interethnic conflicts that had been developing during the first decade of the second civil war between various Nuer communities and between them and their Dinka, Anyuak, and Uduk neighbors (cf. Johnson 1994:348–351). As an unswerving advocate of political independence for the south, Wutnyang had played an especially crucial role in uniting and galvanizing continued Nuer military resistance against the Islamic zeal and oppressive political and economic policies of the Khartoum government. During the early months of 1992, for example, he successfully negotiated the complete and seemingly definitive unification of all outstanding forces of the Anyanya II army with the Nasir faction of the SPLA, under the current command of Riäk Machar.[19] This was a much-heralded accomplishment. Long before the SPLA split in 1991 over whether it should fight for a "united, democratic, secular Sudan" or for "the right of self-determination" for the south, there were numerous smaller rebel bands operating in the Upper Nile Province that were openly advocating southern secession and who were loosely united under the title Anyanya II. Although the bulk of Anyanya II forces—which were overwhelmingly composed of Nuer—merged with the SPLA during the mid-1980s, some units remained distant and distrustful of the SPLA's aims. And many of these units were subsequently drawn into an unholy alliance with the Sudanese army, from which they received arms and immunity from attack as part of the central government's policy of aggravating southern political divisions in order to develop a proxy war against the SPLA. Wutnyang, however, eventually succeeded in rupturing this alliance between the government army and remnant forces of the Anyanya II through a combination of persuasion and direct military action (for details, see Johnson 1994:350–351).

When I first met Wutnyang in Nasir in June 1992, he appeared to be a remarkably young man in his mid-to-late twenties (see plate 30). Bedecked in knee-length blue jallabiya, a white rosary necklace complete with a cross, and a white beaded anklet (similar to that worn by the divine king of the Shilluk), he maintained that there was no real tension or contradiction between his divinity's powers and those of the Christian church. In fact, he publicly encouraged people to continue praying in their churches at the same time as he stressed the strength of his spiritual powers, to-

---

19. This SPLA group subsequently adopted the title of SPLA-United—and later the Southern Sudan Independence Army (SSIA)—to distinguish itself from "mainstream" SPLA forces that have remained under the command of John Garang.

Plate 30.   The contemporary Lak Nuer prophet Wutnyang Gatakɛk.

gether with the prophetic truth of Ngundeng's songs. Although some people identified Wutnyang's principal divinity as Deng, the most powerful air divinity and the one claimed previously by Ngundeng Bong, Wutnyang himself spoke only of *kuɔth*—"Divinity" in the abstract or "God." By so doing, he implicitly reinforced the idea that the ultimate source of his spirituality was the same as that of Christian converts since *"kuɔth ɛ kɛl"* ("Divinity is one"). Unlike many other renowned Nuer prophets, Wutnyang did not lapse into frenzied states of possession. Nor had he revealed any divinely inspired songs of his own by that time. He appeared, rather, to be a remarkably calm and mild-mannered man whose divinely sanctioned powers of cursing nevertheless inspired widespread fear and respect.

While in Nasir, Wutnyang delivered three major public addresses between 27 May and 1 June 1992. Although I arrived a few days too late to attend these events the community was still buzzing about them. Consequently, it was not difficult to piece together extensive eye-witness accounts and thereby gain a vivid picture of what these meetings entailed. I also obtained full recordings of all three of Wutnyang's public addresses as well as rough English translations of them, made by Simon Kun at the request of the commander. On the basis of this information and on that of several conversations I had with Wutnyang himself, it is possible to identify some of his principal aims and to illustrate them with brief excerpts from his speeches.[20]

Among the most important of these was a divinely sanctioned call for greater peace and cooperation among Nuer and their Dinka, Anyuak, and Uduk neighbors. The local population, he urged, should take pride in themselves as southerners (*jinubni*) and as black people (*nei ti caar*) who were capable of "progressing"/"arriving"(*wä nhiam/cop*) by dint of their own resources and efforts. In his words:

> If we want ourselves to be independent and respected by other people then we had better work hard so that we feel our independence. Our work should not be fighting alone—it should go hand in hand with the work we can do in our home areas. . . . Let us cease all accusations that this is done by Dinka and that by Shilluk. We had better work together as southerners in the south. . . . Do not join the policy of tribalism that is being carried out by some people who are interested in forming tribal lines. You had better live together in

20. Limitations of space preclude a full presentation and analysis of Wutnyang's speeches here. I hope to make these available to interested readers in subsequent publications.

peace, and anybody can be a leader if he is a southerner, no matter where he comes from.

In attempting to heal some of the intra- and interethnic wounds that had developed during the first decade of the current war, Wutnyang was especially critical of people's deepening dependence on UN food relief.[21] He viewed this physical dependence as something that was both disgraceful in itself and socially destructive. He thus urged the local population to reject "the shameful status of being refugees in your own land" by cultivating and working harder to lift themselves out of poverty.

> All people of the world do not respect you—not because we do not fight but because we depend on what we receive from others. We are not respected because we are not rich. But if this disregard comes because we are not rich then we must work [harder]. . . . [Now] we simply move to the place that we hear has relief food. But when are we going to receive people who are looking for food in our place? I think we can help other people if we work hard and get rich since everything that can be grown can be grown on this land. . . .
>
> Any area that receives relief food from the UN automatically becomes a starving area. Because relief food does not bring riches to the local population but starvation to the place. The idea that you have put in your mind is to cultivate [only] a small area of a few inches with cash crops in the hope that you will obtain additional relief food. But how can we really live on that food? If you think the UN is helping you to get rich, then you are blind and underdeveloped! The white man is helping a little and he is doing something beneficial to him. He can take something from your ground here that can help you for centuries [a reference to the rich oil reserves of the region]. . . .
>
> This relief has destroyed our relationship with the Dinka and other groups. People are saying that the relatives of John Garang [i.e., the Dinka] are the ones who received a lot of food over the last nine years. And now that it is also coming to you, it will divide you. The Lou Nuer are saying, "The [eastern] Jikany are the people who consume this food," and the Jikany are saying, "This relief operation started in our area and it is ours," and "Why should this food be collected by other people?" This [attitude] is very bad indeed.[22]

21. Dependence on UN food relief was minimal in Nasir District prior to June 1991. However, that month witnessed a sudden, massive influx of some 370,000 southern Sudanese refugees from southwestern Ethiopia immediately following the collapse of Mengistu's Dergue government in late May 1991.

22. Tensions between the eastern Jikany and Lou Nuer, which initially began over the question of wheat, soon escalated into major intercommunity battles over land and cattle rights. Prior to the outbreak of the second civil war and the subsequent introduction of food relief in this region, relations between the eastern Jikany and Lou Nuer were exceptionally harmonious. The two groups shared many dry-season grazing grounds, and intermarriage between them was common. Consequently, the rapid escalation of violence between these two groups during 1992 was truly alarming. Although the SPLA intervened militarily in early 1992,

The person who says these things is not an old man but a young man. Why should you be assisted when you can work and assist other people? . . . This relief should not create hatred between related peoples because it is an issue of small importance. What has killed us [in the sense of destroying our social relations] is this wheat! . . .

But ninety sacks of grain that are cultivated and harvested by one person and brought to us by boat [and plane] will never help us—we, these suffering people. This grain can only be meant for the elderly and the children, not for the youth. If we had our independence, for instance, could we not help those who cannot help themselves? If so, why not establish ourselves so that we can help those who cannot help themselves in our society and elsewhere?

Wutnyang's shaming strategy was apparently effective. His audience was reportedly stunned by the suggestion that they should work not only to reduce but to reverse the flow of food aid into their home areas. A major public drive to prepare fields for planting immediately followed. Unfortunately, late rains and serious shortages of seed and other agricultural inputs meant that this drive was not as successful in 1992 as people had hoped.

In addition to advocating greater economic self-sufficiency and political unity, Wutnyang endeavored to improve the moral state, as it were, of people's everyday social relations. Operating as a one-man peripatetic court, he freely offered his divinely backed services as a counselor and arbitrator to any and all persons who might desire assistance in resolving especially intractable disputes, personal mysteries, or other social problems. Most of his waking hours were, in fact, devoted to resolving the personal problems of the scores of supplicants who came to him for spiritual guidance each day. Furthermore, Wutnyang claimed to be a powerful seer who could recognize "thieves" (*cueer/kuëël*) and cause their deaths if they refused to confess their misdeeds publicly and return all stolen goods.[23] His reputation for sniffing out thieves was greatly enhanced by a bizarre incident that occurred during his first public address in Nasir. Immediately before beginning his speech, Wutnyang sacrificed twenty-three oxen that were presented to him by the extended community, by puncturing them one after the other through the heart with his sacred spear. Toward the end of his lengthy address, however, two of these oxen recovered consciousness and rose to their feet. Wutnyang spontaneously told the assembled

---

these conflicts continued to gain momentum through late 1994—at which time concerted efforts to reestablish a state of peace were initiated by the SPLA leadership.

23. Theft was, in my experience, practically unknown among rural Nuer prior to the outbreak of the second civil war in 1983. And thus, in focusing his spiritual powers on the issue of theft, Wutnyang was creatively grappling with a social problem that everyone perceived to be both novel and disturbing.

crowd of some 6,000 people that these blood-oozing, head-bobbing beasts were scanning the crowd for thieves. If all thieves did not step forward immediately, Wutnyang warned, they would surely die before the night was through. This brilliant improvisation soon brought forth three self-confessed thieves—and, as a consequence, Wutnyang's reputation for protecting the moral standards of the community soared.

Although Wutnyang may have analyzed the spiritual causes of many instances of illnesses and infertility brought to his attention by specific supplicants, I was struck by the fact that none of his public addresses contained any direct or even indirect references to the antisocial activities of sorcerers or to troublesome divinities of the earth. By concentrating his visionary powers on the social problem of theft—as opposed, say, to the malicious powers of sorcerers and the ravages of disease—Wutnyang certainly succeeded in differentiating his divinity's powers from those of both the church and foreign medicines. Did Wutnyang's silences cloak a recognition of—or conscious compromise with—the rising importance of Christian conversion in the "rehabilitation" of sorcerers and in the neutralization of troublesome divinities of the earth? This was not a question I could—or should—have asked Wutnyang Gatakek. However, he was the only person who could have answered it.

In discussing Wutnyang's activities with local Presbyterian church leaders, all of whom attended his public meetings, I sensed a profound ambivalence. While most of them flatly dismissed Wutnyang's claims of divine inspiration, they often acknowledged the inherent importance and beneficial potential of his strident mobilization and peacemaking efforts. "We tell our people," one pastor commented, "that it is alright to attend his speeches but that they must not take any cases to him."

Significantly, local church leaders, in conjunction with expatriate missionaries in Nairobi, hastily arranged to hold a long-awaited ordination ceremony for three Nuer pastors just three days after Wutnyang's first address to the Nasir citizenry. After many years of pleading for the ordination of additional pastors, the Nairobi office finally complied. The timing of this event may have been purely coincidental. But many attending Nuer as well as several expatriate relief workers with whom I spoke interpreted it as a conscious attempt by the church hierarchy in Nairobi and beyond[24] to counter Wutnyang's rising popularity with a major rally of their own—

24. One of the church dignitaries who flew into Nasir for the occasion reportedly introduced himself to some local evangelists with whom I spoke as the "Presbyterian equivalent" of the Pope of the Catholic church.

a rally that was by no means as well attended as those of Wutnyang. According to the Reverend Paul Bol, Wutnyang was specially invited to attend this ceremony by local church leaders, most of whom had respectfully attended his public addresses. Although Wutnyang allegedly accepted this invitation, he failed to appear—much to the embarrassment and disappointment of the internationally assembled Presbyterian leadership. Wutnyang then sent a letter of congratulations and apology the following day. In it he stated that he had very much wished to attend the ordination but had been prevented from doing so by the large number of people who had come to him seeking spiritual guidance that day. "Wutnyang is a very clever man"—was the reluctant admission of the checkmated pastor.

Wutnyang Gatakek clearly remains a fascinating historical figure whose spiritual and military activities deserve far greater attention than can be devoted to them here. For the moment I simply wish to stress the ideological gulf separating his vision of the future from that promoted, directly and indirectly, by Nuer church leaders during the early 1990s. With respect to the latter, we have seen how large numbers of contemporary men and women had turned to Christian conversion partly in the hope that it would help to bolster them against an increasingly intrusive and coercive Islamic state. And yet, this religious movement also implicitly validated the external world and promoted a continuing ideological and material dependence on it. Wutnyang, in contrast, stressed the values of economic self-sufficiency and political independence above all else. He believed that a united southern Sudan was inherently capable of achieving whatever military or developmental goals it set for itself. And this divinely inspired call for local empowerment, as it were, had proven inspirational to many war-ravaged Nuer communities during the early 1990s.

FUTURE PROSPECTS: CHRISTIANITY, ISLAM, AND PROPHETS

We have seen how the "sacred" status of cattle—in Evans-Pritchard's definition of this term—was seriously challenged by the spread of Christian conversion among Nuer communities both east and west of the White Nile. Although small pockets of Roman Catholicism were established among the western Nuer during the early colonial period, their historical impact appeared negligible in 1992 when compared with the waves of Presbyterianism lapping in from the east. Having aligned itself with the powers of literacy and of Western medical practices, the Protestant church succeeded to a large extent in banishing rites of cattle sacrifice to the margins of people's interpretations and experiences of illness, infertility, and death. In so doing,

it contributed to the secularization of large areas of contemporary Nuer social and moral life formerly associated with the activities of Divinity in its
myriad manifestations.

On the one hand, Christianity came to symbolize for many Nuer the
possibilities of political equality, community development, and self-en-
hancement in the context of an increasingly coercive and stratified nation-
state inspired by Islamic fundamentalist ideals. On the other hand, new
converts were often uncertain how to respond to the vast sweep of moral
dilemmas and existential crises formerly requiring sacrificial offerings of
purification and atonement. The central obligation of kinsmen to help one
another achieve personal immortality through the birth of children was
also undercut by the increasing intolerance demonstrated by local church
leaders toward polygyny, ghost marriage, and widow inheritance. Before
the introduction of Christianity, Nuer religious practices were not directed
toward a world yet to come but, rather, toward a secure and valid life in
this world and continued participation in it after death. Modifications in
gender and age hierarchies among Christian converts inevitably followed
as the former religious authority of household heads coalesced around
emerging church leaders. The significance of cattle was very different in a
world where neither war nor prayer knew age or gender boundaries.

The sacrificial importance of cattle was also weakened, as we have seen,
by the introduction of imported pharmaceuticals,[25] by the expansion of
meat markets in the south, and by changes in Nuer hospitality practices—

---

25. With respect to growing Nuer confidence in and desires for Western
pharmaceuticals, I would like to suggest that there may be ways for them to reduce
their dependence on expensive and unreliable imports in the future while
simultaneously taking advantage of the medical knowledge and technological
advances on which some biomedicines are based. Three examples spring to mind.
The first concerns the possibility of reducing the debilitating and often lethal
effects of anemia in pregnant and birthing women by substituting dietary
supplements of cooked cattle blood for imported supplies of iron syrup. Anemia
is always a risk in pregnancy, but in the southern Sudan where recurrent bouts
of malaria result in the repeated breakup of red blood cells, it is endemic. Having
been earlier introduced to iron syrup, many contemporary men and women were
well aware of its beneficial effects but were unable to obtain it. What they did not
seem to realize, however, was that rich supplies of iron could be obtained from
their cattle—without endangering the health of the latter. Cooked cattle blood was
not a standard item of Nuer diets during the 1980s, being used only in times of
hardship. However, considering the fact that blood played such a central role in
their understandings of conception, pregnancy, and birth, it would not be difficult,
I think, to convince them that these processes could be facilitated in women
through the increased consumption of cattle blood.

all of which blurred the conceptual dividing line formerly separating cattle's roles as symbols of blood and sources of food. These developments in turn contributed to controversy over the rights of extended kinsfolk to share in the meat of one another's cattle. These rights were increasingly marginalized by individuals who sought to use their cattle wealth to consolidate "new" social collectivities and to create more personal bonds of hospitality with powerful "outsiders."

It seems likely that current associations in Nuer thought between community advancement and Christian conversion will continue to develop in the context of the ongoing second Sudanese civil war. One reason is purely material: Much of the humanitarian assistance entering Nuer regions during the early 1990s was both donated and distributed by Christian-affiliated aid organizations. Although the vast majority of humanitarian aid (and, especially, bulk items such as wheat and seed) were still being distributed in 1992 by UNICEF, the World Food Program, and other secular organizations, the proportion of this aid was quickly dropping while that of church-affiliated contributions was rising. Moreover, judging from comments made by several expatriate aid workers I met in Nasir in June 1992, these Christian-affiliated organizations were consciously seeking to strengthen local Presbyterian congregations by directly channeling specific

---

The second example concerns the future health of their cattle. There is a new vaccina-virus rinderpest vaccine, developed through recombination gene technology, that holds considerable promise. Once a single cow is injected with it, the owner can then use that cow to create additional vaccine for the rest of his herd (Yilma 1989, 1990). This can be done by making small cuts on the vaccinated cow, removing the scabs that form, and, after drying and pounding these, adding them to small cuts made in other cattle. Although this technological advance may create certain health risks (most notably, for persons in direct contact with the live vaccine), it would seem worthy of further exploration in this region. The carefully controlled introduction of this new vaccine could potentially obviate the difficulties of maintaining extensive "cold chains" (that is, refrigeration) for anti-rinderpest campaigns and reduce the risks of spreading secondary cattle infections through the forced congregation of herds for vaccination (McCorkle and Mathias-Mundy 1991:74–75). Moreover, the cost of imported needles and syringes would likewise be reduced. Although these particular suggestions would do nothing to curb the most serious health threat Nuer currently face—namely, the lethal kala-azar epidemic that has been raging in Western Upper Nile since the mid-1980s—the donation of several tons of dumhurriya (a kind of course, opaque, cotton cloth) and a score of treadle sewing machines for the making of mosquito nets certainly would. Doubtless there are many other means by which concerned humanitarian relief organizations could potentially reduce these people's long-term dependence on imported biomedicines. But, in my opinion, these three ways would be a good way to begin.

disbursements, educational opportunities, and training programs through them.

Material inducements were also playing a crucial role at that time in the central government's efforts to promote Islamic conversion among the hundreds of thousands of "displaced" southerners that had fled northwards. In fact, the government-backed relief organization known as the Islamic Call made conversion a prerequisite for access to grain allotments and educational institutions. At the same time, the central government was making it difficult, if not impossible, for other humanitarian organizations to work among the "displaced." But what remains to be seen is how deep and lasting these relief-induced conversions among Nuer and other displaced southerners will prove in decades ahead. Will it remain purely "self-interested" and "nominal"? Or will it develop into the self-perpetuating wave of southern conversion that the current Khartoum regime desires? Although this will undoubtedly depend in part on how long the current war lasts, I suspect the real answer to this question will lie with the thousands of southern children who are currently attending Islamic schools in the north because there are no other educational opportunities available to them.

Yet, however strong the rival forces of Islam and Christianity may prove in the decades ahead, it should not be assumed that they will necessarily succeed in displacing the importance of prophets in Nuer social life. Wutnyang's strategy of denying the existence of any inherent contradiction between his divinely inspired messages and those of the Christian church would seem eminently recyclable. Moreover, the prophetic songs of Ngundeng Bong are likely to remain a source of collective inspiration for Nuer and other southern Sudanese for many generations. I thus offer here, by way of conclusion, an inevitably partial and transient reading of a particularly valued and relevant song passage from these sacred oral traditions.[26]

Rool me caa bɛrɛ bi yiath piny.
A country in which a flag will be planted.

26. Although I cannot be certain, I presume that this song was composed sometime during the 1880s or 1890s—long before the firm establishment of British colonial rule in this region. I openly apologize to my Nuer readers for any misunderstanding or inaccuracies I may have developed in attempting to "hear" this song.

(Currently read by many Nuer as an allusion to the future political independence of the south.)

ɛ ɣän i guɛcä jɛ /ci ŋɔakɛ bi gɔu.

I foresee that things will not go well.

Thok jak bɛ dhoŋ wuɔc.

The "union jack" will soon be wiped out.

Baa rɛk dhɔali waŋ.

The town of the unscarified boys (Arabs) will burn.

Biɛ a lac kä ji paam.

You will shit [with fear] from the people of the mountains.
(Often read as an allusion to the military might of southern rebel forces, whose principal headquarters were established during both civil wars at "Bilpaam" in southwestern Ethiopia.)

Kɛl me cä guic kä naadh
ɛ bi thul kɛ jiek kam nä tɔ.

One thing I see is that people will be caught up in a windy maelstrom in the meantime.

/Caa lɛ bɛn kuic kä /caa lɛ ränh.

They will not jump across and they will not run towards.
(Currently read as an allusion to government spies and other forces of political indecision.)

Bä laad nööŋ kä dhool nyälä
Bä ruacdä jiec runɛ me doŋ.

My words will be brought by the son of Nyala;
[but] the meaning of my words will [only] become clear in another year.

Ci cäŋɔ bak, ciɛ a guut
Lathker yienɛ ŋuɛani, ciɛ a wiidä ŋɔaŋ kɛ lep ciɛaŋ.

When the sun rises, your [faces] become gloomy.
Soldiers and youth, your faces will be exhausted with the dawning of [each new] day.
(Read as a warning of the hardships people will suffer in war.)

Kɔaŋ Car yieth bil, baa wadh kɛ rom ɛ bi röt
tɛarä koor me te cuɔŋ.

Koaŋ Car [a divinely inspired person], [other people] will hold back and you will cry out [because you want to fight]: "A war that has the right."

Kiɛ cuɔŋdä yiɛ biɛ ku ŋac kam dɔar.

Or is it my right [that is being fought]? You will know before long.

Kɛn gat kuɔl ɛ caa mutdu ku guath
kam dan ciɛ thil reei

Those sons of Kuol ["blackness"], your spear has been taken out. [But] there is no separating/mediating [our fight].
(Sometimes interpreted as a declaration of war by the "black peoples" of the south.)

Dei yiom kuɔdhɛ
ɛ yiou yɔɔk kulaŋ ma.

Spiritual assistant, [where are] the sacred spears [to guide your cattle]?

Dhool Ker, ba wadh Ker,

Son of Ker, brave Ker [translation tentative],
(Interpreted as a war cry to encourage fighting.)

Palɛ bär cai.

Spare the Anyuak and the Burun [peoples].

Bä yaŋ tiac kä dɛŋ guarɛ
Bia jämbiɛli ruay.

I will sacrifice for Deng our fathers.
You will "shiny colored stones" [money] "discuss" [pay over].
(Sometimes interpreted as an allusion to the subsequent development of the cattle trade.)

Nath palɛ Dɛŋ ke tharuun
biɛ a te kɛ guaath me tɔt.

You people who pray to God with your asses, your time is limited!
(The period of Arab/Muslim domination will be short!)

Afterword

Because there are no immediate prospects of a reconciliation between warring factions of the SPLA or of serious peace negotiations between the SPLA and the Khartoum government, this book must remain open-ended. To give it a false sense of closure would do injustice to the continuing hardships and uncertainties with which Nuer and other "black peoples" (*nei ti c̱a̱a̱r*) of Sudan are grappling. I shall nevertheless attempt to bring together a few themes developed in earlier chapters with an eye to what the future may hold.

First, people's confidence in the inherent "security" of their cattle wealth will undoubtedly continue to decline in the context of the second civil war. This war has already reduced many Nuer families and communities to an unprecedented state of poverty. It has also provoked a tremendous redispersion of the Nuer population both within and beyond their prewar territorial borders. At the risk of oversimplification, it is possible to divide contemporary Nuer communities into three main groups: those that have established themselves on the outskirts of northern cities, those that have taken refuge inside Kenya and other neighboring nations, and those that have remained deep within the southern war zone itself. (At the time of this writing, the last of these three groups forms the vast majority.) Each of these three sets of communities is now wrestling with very different problems and circumstances. Those Nuer men, women, and children who fled northwards have no direct access to cattle at present, although many of them retain rights in the surviving herds of relatives in the south. These people, as I explained earlier, have responded to their current predicament by extending and elaborating the role of money cattle in the creation and affirmation of enduring bonds of *maar* among themselves. Similarly, most Nuer and other southerners who have taken refuge in neighboring countries currently have little or no direct access to cattle. Many of them have limited access to money as well, having been reduced to complete dependence on UN food distributions in official refugee camps along the Kenyan and Ethiopian borders. The same is true, moreover, of increasing numbers of displaced Nuer men and women within the southern war zone itself. Yet how each of these various Nuer groups will evaluate the relative significance of cattle and money in their daily lives—and how far apart their evaluations will drift—will depend in large part on how long this war lasts.

Significantly, there are mounting indications that the tide of displaced Nuer and other southerners flowing into the north has begun to reverse itself. During 1992 and 1993 many thousands of Nuer men, women, and children reportedly returned to the Western Upper Nile under pressure from government bulldozers. Similarly, the number of Nuer refugees residing in neighboring countries has contracted significantly since 1991, this being primarily a consequence of the mass evacuation/expulsion of some 370,000 southern Sudanese (mainly Dinka and Nuer) from southwestern Ethiopia immediately following the collapse of Mengistu's Dergue government in late May of that year. Many thousands of Nuer who were permanent residents of Ethiopia were also driven back into the Sudan at that time. This mass exodus was followed by limited disbursements of UN-affiliated humanitarian relief. Even though this influx of food aid has relieved mounting pressures on the cattle and grain resources of those Nuer and other southern communities that have remained within their home territories, it has also had serious negative repercussions on intercommunity relations within the extended Sobat valley region.[1]

Although the present civil war represents by far the greatest challenge that Nuer and other southern Sudanese communities have faced during the twentieth century, there is reason to believe that the future holds even more daunting challenges ahead. For whatever forms of government or governments eventually emerge from the ashes of this war, one thing is certain: The issues of oil and water will rise together with them. Since the bulk of these coveted resources lie within Dinka and Nuer territories, these peoples are likely to suffer the economic and environmental repercussions of their large-scale exploitation most intensely.

The Egyptian government is already growing impatient with the forced delay of the Jonglei Canal Project. It stands to gain half of whatever annual increase in the Nile's flow the canal creates. Although it is by no means certain that the first phase, let alone second and third phases, of the Jonglei Canal Project will ever be completed, if they are, the critical dry-season

1. Some of the most serious intercommunity fighting over food resources during the early 1990s has been between the Lou and eastern Gaajok Nuer. Significantly, these heavily intermarried sections were among the most tension free of all neighboring Nuer groups I knew prior to the outbreak of the second civil war. Indeed, all indications are that the wartime explosion of this social divide has no known precedents.

grazing capacity of surrounding Dinka and Nuer populations will be decreased dramatically (for details see Howell, Lock, and Cobb 1988). Moreover, it is becoming increasingly obvious that, even in its unfinished state, the Jonglei Canal has seriously disrupted both the water regime and migration patterns along the 262 kilometers that were dug before construction on the 360-kilometer length canal was suspended in 1984.[2] Because the excavated earth was simply piled up in a massive mound running along the eastern side of the canal without any provision for bridges or tunnels, the seasonal floodwaters to the east have reportedly been expanding in range and intensity. Surrounding Nuer and Dinka communities have thus been forced to concentrate their cattle on reduced grazing grounds, where they remain vulnerable to the rapid spread of cattle epidemics as well as to wartime attacks (Douglas Johnson, personal communication).[3] And thus, whether or not the Jonglei Canal Project is ever resurrected when this war ends, these and other environmental consequences of its partial construction will require immediate government attention if the economic viability and self-sufficiency of Nuer and Dinka populations in the extended region are to be ensured.

As for the future exploitation of southern oil deposits, the balancing of "regional," "national," and "international" interests—however these may be conceptualized at the conclusion of this war—are likely to prove even more difficult to achieve and maintain in the years ahead.[4] Because the

2. Operations were abruptly halted after an SPLA attack on the headquarters of construction operations near the mouth of the Sobat River resulted in four ex-patriot workers killed. The gigantic digging machine used in the canal's construction was also blown up by the SPLA. The destruction of this machine, which was capable of moving more than 2,000 tons of earth an hour under ideal conditions, has made the postwar completion of the Jonglei Canal a far more expensive proposition.

3. The migrations of domestic and wild animals across the canal's axis has also resulted in a considerable loss of life. According to Douglas Johnson (personal communication), the shifting water regime has increased the incidence of certain cattle diseases that were previously rare or unknown in the region. Dinka populations around Bor reportedly experienced the ravages of trypanosomiasis for the first time in 1991, and the infiltration of snails has caused a serious increase in the occurrence of liver flukes in cattle throughout the region (Douglas Johnson, personal communication).

4. Although the southern regional government in Juba never attempted to assert exclusive claims over the oil deposits within its territories, having sought only an an equitable revenue-sharing agreement with the Khartoum government, the same cannot be said of the national regime. One of the more inflammatory moves made by President Nimeiri before his popular overthrow in 1985 was the creation of a "new" province in the Western Upper Nile that was to be administered directly from

richest oil deposits thus far discovered lie just south of the administrative line established between northern and southern Sudan at independence, the possibility of continuing border disputes cannot be dismissed even if the SPLA and the Sudan government come to a mutually agreeable peace settlement in the near future.[5] And because surrounding rural communities are likely to have little say in any future governmental decisions regarding the oil or the Jonglei Canal Project, their long-term economic well-being will depend directly on whatever political forces come to represent them when this war ends.

Yet of all the social disruptions this war has caused during its first decade, the complete collapse of educational opportunities in the south—and hence the loss of yet another generation of southern school children—is likely to have some of the most serious, long-range, negative effects on the abilities of Nuer and other southern communities to achieve a greater degree of political and economic equality in the future. Unless this issue is given immediate priority by UN-affiliated relief organizations, southern vulnerabilities to the arbitrary intervention of government guns and the mysterious powers of "paper" are likely to grow over the decades ahead.

Viewed from another perspective, all of these pending political, economic, and environmental issues would appear to be rooted in a long-standing "crisis" of governmental legitimacy that has dogged the Sudanese state—and its political and military opponents—throughout the twentieth century. Like so many other arbitrarily created, economically strapped, and ethnically diverse postcolonial states in Africa and beyond, the process of "nation-building" has proven anything but inevitable in Sudan. Current attempts by the Sudanese government to acquire a "new" aura of national unity through the invocation of Islamic fundamentalist ideals represents only the most recent in a long series of ideological oscillations between secular (and/or "racial") and religious bids for political authority. Simi-

---

Khartoum. Designed to encompass the richest known oil deposits in the south as well as lesser deposits immediately to their north, this newly dubbed Unity Province came complete with a flag sporting the image of an oil rig.

5. The main exploratory efforts of both Chevron and Total Corporations concentrated during the 1978–84 period in the Bentiu and Adok regions of the Western Upper Nile Province and in the Machar Marshes within the Melut-Malakal-Nasir triangle in the eastern Upper Nile—all in southern Sudan.

Peter Nyot Kok (1992) has written an excellent historical synopsis of the past and present state of play among the various regional, national, and international forces implicated in the simmering oil politics of Sudan. I recommend it to all interested readers.

larly, attempts by the SPLA to convince Nuer recruits and ordinary villagers that the overarching political context of a "government war" should
take precedence over the personal identities and kinship affiliations of the
combatants must be understood in part as an implicit bid for political legitimacy. But the fact remains that no bid for political authority—whether
asserted on the basis of religious or secular ideals—has thus far succeeded
in forging a firm and enduring sense of nationhood among the diverse
peoples of Sudan.

On the contrary, it would appear that the recurrent failure of "nation-
building" in the midst of the success of elements of "secularization" has
gradually led more and more ordinary Sudanese citizens to conclude that
the only power of any real value is that of the gun. The full ramifications
of this deepening "culture of violence" on the social organization of Nuer
communities and of Sudanese peoples as a whole are not yet known. However, it seems likely that people's confidence in the efficacy of persuasion
and compromise—as opposed to aggressive acts of forceful expediency—
will continue to decline during the course of the second civil war. As
Wutnyang Gatakek pointedly remarked in one of his June 1992 public addresses, "the smoke and sound of the gun has caused the youth to become
crazy and to behave very badly toward you elders." However, it is not only
the social powers of senior Nuer men that are directly threatened by the
raw power of the gun but also those of women and girls of all ages. I worry
that there may well come a time when Nuer men and women will "forget"
the fact that the force of the gun says nothing definitive about the moral
quality or physical strength of the human being behind it. On this score
I was particularly disturbed to learn of the formal "graduation song" allegedly taught to all SPLA recruits prior to the movement's split in 1991.
The song, which was composed in Arabic and reportedly sung by successful trainees upon the formal conferral of their guns, runs as follows:

> Even your mother, give her a bullet!
> Even your father, give him a bullet!
> Your gun is your food; your gun is your wife.

Clearly, it will not be easy for future political leaders to reverse such
glorifications of naked violence—especially since the very existence of "government rule" has been so closely associated in the thought and experience
of ordinary citizens with the demonstrated power to kill with impunity.

Furthermore, current controversies over the limits of moral accountability in times of war are likely to resurface in powerful ways immediately following the restoration of peace—however and whenever that may

be achieved (cf. Nyong'o 1992). This war has already created many deep wounds and intensified many inter- and intraethnic divisions among southern and northern groups. If a lasting peace is to be achieved, every effort must be made to restore a sense of generalized social morality among ordinary citizens by confronting these sharpening social and ethnic divisions directly. In the case of Nuer, their relations with the Dinka and the Anyuak have deteriorated to such an extent that separate peace negotiations will be required—as will major public rituals of purification and atonement—if the security of the extended region is to be assured at the conclusion of this war.[6] Ideally, these negotiations could be complemented by a realistic program of disarmament that would offer material compensation and take into account the fact that, in many areas, guns are collectively owned by families and have penetrated the bridewealth system.[7] On this score I am not optimistic. Few records on past weapons disbursements have been kept by either the SPLA or government officials. Moreover, there is every reason to believe that the eastern Jikany Nuer will continue to exploit the Ethiopian border running through their territories to evade future governmental attempts at arms control.

Finally, there is the question of whether of not future political leaders will take responsibility for rectifying past atrocities. Although I assume that some form of amnesty will have to be declared, the important question is whether it will be defined in such a way as to preclude future government leaders from taking direct actions to "free" the thousands of Dinka, Nuer, and Nuba women and children who have been kidnapped and enslaved during this war by northern Rizeigat and Misseriya Arab militias. And what will become of all the children who have been forcefully conscripted into the fighting ranks of rebel and national armies? It is around questions such as these—as well as the issues of oil, water, and political power sharing—that prospects of achieving a lasting peace in this region will revolve.

6. The "invention" of public rituals of purification and atonement could, ideally, be used to heal sharpening "religious" divisions by enlisting, say, prominent Nuer prophets, earth priests, cattle-camp spokesmen, Christian pastors, Muslims, and so forth in support of a lasting peace settlement.

7. By far the most effective means of collecting guns among the Nuer would be to offer in exchange some form of livestock—cattle or goats—as part of a more general postwar aid program of "restocking" their herds.

APPENDIX

Comparative Divorce Rates among the Nuer, 1936–83

In support of my claim that jural divorce rates surged among the Nuer between 1936 and 1983, I shall present four marital surveys, all tabulated according to Barnes's now standard techniques (1949). The first set of data was gleaned from Evans-Pritchard's oft-cited 1936 survey of the western Leek community of Nyueny (1945), in which he recorded the marital histories of thirty-two adult women (plus a female husband). It was primarily on the basis of this marital survey—the most detailed and extensive undertaken—that Evans-Pritchard inferred that "divorce" was rare among Nuer, particularly after the birth of a child to the union. Of the thirty-two adult women he sampled, only two had ever experienced "divorce." One was barren and "divorced" once because of it, while the other, apparently fertile, was "divorced" twice—with only the first of these unions producing a child (Evans-Pritchard 1945:34, 36). Thus, of the three "divorces" recorded by Evans-Pritchard as such, two were childless. Fortunately, it was possible for me to compensate methodologically for inconsistencies in Evans-Pritchard's usage of the terms "marriage" and "divorce" by calculating key divorce ratios twice. At times Evans-Pritchard equated the completion of a "marriage" with the completion of all ceremonial phases, including the consummation rite (muɔd nyal). At other times he identified a completed "marriage" with the birth of the first child to the union (cf. Hutchinson 1990). In order to compensate for these vacillations in Evans-Pritchard's writings, I calculated "divorce" ratio C twice, according to Evans-Pritchard's more inclusive and exclusive definitions of marriage—and hence divorce—respectively.

The second survey compiles the marital histories of 122 Leek Nuer women living in the extended community of Tharlual in 1983. Because I conducted this survey after having become acquainted with many of these women over nearly eleven months of residence, I am confident of its accuracy and completeness. Like Evans-Pritchard's 1936 survey, it, too, provides information on the fecundity of unions dissolved, thereby making it possible to tabulate alternative ratios accordingly. Although the bulk of my argument about rising divorce rates rests on comparisons between these

357

1936 and 1983 female-based surveys, I also include two male-based surveys for the unique perspectives they might offer. Survey 3, which complements the second, provides the marital histories of 41 male household heads residing in Tharlual in 1983. The final survey is compiled from a very rough census carried out in 1981 among the Gaawär Nuer, under the auspices of a research team investigating the possible impact of the Jonglei Canal Project (cf. Howell, Lock, & Cobb 1988). Since this information was collected by mobile teams of assistants, about which I know little, I can speak neither for the conditions under which it was conducted nor for its accuracy or completeness. I include it, nonetheless, as a quasi-check on the "reasonableness" of my own male-based survey and as an index of divorce rates in more eastern Nuer regions. Finally, I should stress that my sole purpose in presenting these admittedly nonrandom, narrowly based surveys is to show that "divorce" rates—however broadly or narrowly defined—were rising among the Leek Nuer and that this rise was significant enough to be relevant to the arguments set forth in chapters 2 and 4.

When reviewing tables 1–6, the first thing to be noted is the striking, across-the-board rise in divorce rates. The proportion of women divorced in the region nearly doubled between 1936 (6.25 percent) and 1983 (12.29 percent); and the mean number of divorces per female sampled rose from .09 to .45 (see tables 1 and 2 respectively). Furthermore, divorce ratio C, which Barnes considered the most revealing figure for comparative purposes, jumped from 13.0 in 1936 to 38.2 in 1983 in the female-based surveys (see table 3).

The sharp decline in the percentage of widow concubines revealed in table 1 is also noteworthy and attributable, I suspect, to factors such as (1) declining mortality rates among men—the western Leek being one of the few Nuer groups to have escaped the first Sudanese civil war (1955–72) relatively unscathed; (2) a possible drop in the average age of the women sampled—in which case the true rise in the percentage of women divorced over the years may be underestimated; and (3) increasing reluctance among court officials to protect and enforce widows' rights to select their lovers— a trend I documented in chapter 4. Significant as well is the emergence of a new category of women—"independent divorcees"—many of whom maintained themselves during the 1980s through the brewing of beer for local sale (see table 1).

The conspicuous gender disparity in the average number of "divorces" reported, evident in tables 2 and 3, should also be noted. Whereas 36 percent of the Leek women sampled in 1983 claimed to have experienced "divorce," only 27 percent of the Leek men interviewed responded likewise.

Table 1. Present marital status

	Western Leek, 1936*		Nuer Women, 1983	
Simple legal marriage	6	(19%)	68	(56%)
Ghost marriage	5	(16%)	14	(11%)
Leviratic marriage	2	(6%)	3	(3%)
Widow concubines	6	(19%)	3	(3%)
Wives living in adultery	1	(3%)	1	(1%)
Unmarried concubines	3	(9%)	14	(11%)
Independent divorcees	0		4	(3%)
Divorcees at natal home	0		1	(1%)
Old women without mates	9	(28%)	14	(11%)
TOTAL	32	(100%)	122	(100%)
Number of women divorced	2	(6.25%)	15	(12.29%)

*SOURCE: Evans-Pritchard (1945:38).

Table 2. Cumulative marital experience

	Women		Men	
	Leek, 1936	Leek, 1983	Leek, 1983	Gaawär, 1981*
Number in sample	32	122	41	426
Number divorced at least once	2	44	11	122
Total divorces	3	55	18	158
Mean number of divorces per head	.09	.45	.44	.37
Percentage ever divorced	(6%)	(36%)	(27%)	(28%)

*SOURCE: Unpublished preliminary findings of the 1981 Jonglei Canal area survey. It includes the demographic survey samples of Ayod, Mogogh, Wau, Pieri and Kuac Deng areas.

Divorce ratio C is thus considerably lower when calculated on the basis of men's as opposed to women's reports in the 1983 surveys—though there is remarkable statistical consistency in this regard between the 1981 and 1983 male-based surveys. A gender difference is also evident in tables 4 and 5, with Leek women reporting far more divorces involving dead children than Leek men. These intriguing discrepancies stem in part from

Table 3. Divorce ratio C

	Women		Men	
	Leek, 1936	Leek, 1983	Leek, 1983	Gaawär, 1981*
Number of divorces	3	55	18	158
Number of divorces plus number of extant marriages	23	144	78	748*
Divorce ratio C	13.0	38.2	23.0	21.1

*Jonglei Canal survey data for extant marriages is based on number of wives reported by informants.

Table 4. Number of children born to wife before divorce

	Leek Women, 1983			Leek Men, 1983		
None born	23		(42%)	7		(39%)
1 born	24		(43%)	6		(33%)
0 living		9			1	
1 living		15			5	
2 born	6		(11%)	4		(22%)
0 living		3			0	
1 living		1			2	
2 living		2			2	
3 born	2		(4%)	1		(6%)
0 living		1			1	
1 living		1			0	
2 living		0			0	
TOTAL	55		(100%)	18		(100%)

the fact that "divorce" was, linguistically, a more marked experience for women. A "divorced woman" was a *ciek me kɛaɣ*—a term encompassing unmarried mothers as well. No parallel term existed for men. Therefore, unions dissolved shortly before or after completion of the ceremonial phase were far more likely to stigmatize the divorced woman than the divorcing

Table 5. Number of children living at time of divorce

	Leek Women, 1983		Leek Men, 1983	
None born to union	23	(42%)	7	(39%)
0 living	13	(23%)	2	(11%)
1 living	17	(31%)	7	(39%)
2 living	2	(4%)	2	(11%)
TOTAL	55	(100%)	18	(100%)

Table 6. Recalculated divorce ratio C

	Leek Women, 1936		Leek Women, 1983	
Number of divorces*	1	(3 − 2)	32	(55 − 23)
Number of divorces plus number of extant marriages	21	(20 + 1)	121	(89 + 32)
Divorce ratio C	4.76		26.4	

*Includes only divorces of marriages "completed" with the birth of a child. This definition of divorce ignores the possibility that some childless unions may endure.

man—particularly if co-residence had occurred. Whereas the man would probably find it advantageous to dismiss the whole affair as an insignificant "nonmarriage," the woman would find it more difficult to shed the label "divorcee." The tendency for women to report greater numbers of divorces involving dead children is also understandable in these terms. From the husband's perspective a marriage cursed with infant mortality could be severed without any lingering affinal ties and without any permanent change in his social status. From the wife's perspective, in contrast, a dead child as much as a live child confirmed her status as an adult—as a *ciek* or "woman/wife."

Finally, I should stress that "divorce" after the birth of the first child was not very unusual in the 1980s. Indeed, only 42 percent, and 39 percent of the divorces presented in tables 4 and 5, occurred before the birth of a child. Moreover, if we count only "divorces" involving the dissolution of marriages "completed" with the birth of a child, the surge in divorce ratio

C between 1936 and 1983 appears even more striking (see table 6). Of course, the complex issue of infant mortality must be considered. But even if we discount for the moment deceased children, the mean number of divorces involving a living child experienced by the Leek men and women sampled in 1983 was .22 (9/41) and .16 (19/122), respectively, as compared with only .03 (1/32) in 1936. Furthermore, divorces with two living children were recorded in table 5—and examples of others involving as many as four living children were provided in chapter 4. In sum, the option of jural divorce no longer lapsed in the 1980s with the birth of a second child.

Bibliography

ARCHIVES AND MANUSCRIPT COLLECTIONS

Civsec   Civil Secretary's Files, National Records Office, Khartoum, Sudan

DAK   Dakhlia (Interior) Files, National Records Office, Khartoum, Sudan

END   Eastern Nuer District Files, Nasir, Upper Nile Province, Sudan

SAD   Sudan Archive, Oriental Library, University of Durham, England

SIR   Sudan Intelligence Reports, University of Khartoum Library, Khartoum, Sudan

UNP   Upper Nile Province Files, National Records Office, Khartoum, Sudan

UNPAR   Upper Nile Province Annual Reports, Western Nuer District Files, Bentiu, Upper Nile Province, Sudan

UNPMD   Upper Nile Province Monthly Diary, University of Khartoum Library, Khartoum, Sudan

PERIODICALS COVERING THE CURRENT CIVIL WAR

Southern Sudan Vision, 77 Levita House, Charlton St., London NW1 ILS.
Sudan Democratic Gazette, P.O. Box 2295, London W14 OND.
Sudan Monitor, 7 Bury Place, London WC1A 2LA.
Sudan Update, Box 'CPRS', London WC1N 3XX.

FILM

1994   The Price of Survival: A Journey to the War Zone of Southern Sudan. John Ryle and Bapiny Tim Chol. London: Bright Star Productions.

BOOKS, DISSERTATIONS, AND ARTICLES

Abdel-Rahim, M.
    1968   The Development of British Policy in the Southern Sudan, 1899–1947. Khartoum: University of Khartoum.
Africa Watch
    1990   Denying the Honor of Living: Sudan—A Human Rights Disaster. London: Africa Watch Committee.
Ahmed, Abdel Ghaffar M.
    1973   Some Remarks from the Third World on Anthropology and Co-

lonialism: The Sudan. *In* Anthropology and the Colonial Encounter. T. Asad, ed. Pp. 259–270. London: Ithaca Press.

1979   "Tribal" Elite: A Base for Social Stratification in the Sudan. *In* Toward a Marxist Anthropology: Problems and Perspectives. S. Diamond, ed. Pp. 321–335. The Hague: Mouton.

Ahmed, Abdel Ghaffar M., and Mustafa Abdel Rahman

1979   Small Urban Centers: Vanguards of Exploitation—Two Cases from Sudan. Africa 49(3):258–271.

Ajawin, L. A., and J. Y. Arop

1987   [Interview with] Lam Akol Ajawin and Justin Yaac Arop. Africa Report 32(3):53–60.

Akol, Joshua Otor

1986   Refugee Migration and Repatriation: Case Studies of Some Affected Rural Communities in Southern Sudan. Ph.D. dissertation, Anthropology Department, University of Manitoba, Canada.

Alban, A. H.

1940   Gwek's Pipe and Pyramid. Sudan Notes and Records 23:200–201.

Alier, A.

1990   Southern Sudan: Too Many Disagreements Dishonoured. Exeter, England: Ithaca Press.

Al-Moghraby, A. I., and M. O. As-Sammani

1985   On the Environmental and Socio-economic Impact of the Jonglei Canal Project—Southern Sudan. Environmental Conservation 12(1):41–48.

Al-Rahim, M. A., R. Badal, A. Pardallo, and P. Woodward, eds.

1986   Sudan since Independence. London: Gower.

Amnesty International

1989   Sudan: Human Rights Violations in the Context of Civil War. London: Amnesty International.

Appadurai, Arjun

1986   Introduction: Commodities and the Politics of Value. *In* The Social Life of Things: Commodities in Cultural Perspective. A. Appadurai, ed. Pp. 3–36. Cambridge: Cambridge University Press.

Arens, W.

1983   Evans-Pritchard and the Prophets: Comments on an Ethnographic Enigma. Anthropos 78:1–16.

Asad, Talal

1986   The Concept of Cultural Translation in British Social Anthropology. *In* Writing Culture. James Clifford and George Marcus, eds. Pp. 141–156. Berkeley: University of California Press.

Asad, Talal, ed.

1973   Anthropology and the Colonial Encounter. London: Ithaca Press.

Barnes, J. A.

1949   Measures of Divorce Frequency in Simple Societies. Journal of the Royal Anthropological Institute 79:37–61.

Beidelman, T. O.

1966   The Ox and Nuer Sacrifice: Some Freudian Hypotheses about Nuer Symbolism. Man (n.s.) 1:453–467.

1968 Some Nuer Notions of Nakedness, Nudity, and Sexuality. Africa 38:113–131.

1969 The Ox and Nuer Sacrifice. Man (n.s.) 4:290–291.

1971 Nuer Priests and Prophets: Charisma, Authority, and Power among the Nuer. *In* The Translation of Culture. T. O. Beidelman, ed. Pp. 375–415. London: Tavistock Press.

1974 Bibliography of the Writings of E. E. Evans-Pritchard. London: Tavistock Press.

1981 The Nuer Concept of *Thek* and the Meaning of Sin: Explanation, Translation, and Social Structure. History of Religions 21:126–155.

Beshir, Mohammed Omar

1968 The Southern Sudan: Background to Conflict. London: Hurst and Co.

Biowel, P. C.

1984 The Christian Church in the Southern Sudan before 1900. *In* Southern Sudan: Regionalism and Religion. M. O. Beshir, ed. Pp. 205–223. Khartoum: University of Khartoum, Graduate College.

Bohannan, Paul

1955 Some Principles of Exchange and Investment among the Tiv. American Anthropologist 57:60–70.

1959 The Impact of Money on an African Subsistence Economy. Journal of Economic History 19:491–503.

Bonte, Pierre

1975 Cattle for God: An Attempt at a Marxist Analysis of the Religion of East African Herdsmen. Social Compass 22:381–396.

1979 Pastoral Production, Territorial Organisation, and Kinship in Segmentary Lineage Societies. *In* Social and Ecological Systems. P. C. Burnham and R. F. Ellen, eds. Pp. 203–234. London: Academic Press.

Bourdieu, Pierre

1977 Outline of a Theory of Practice. R. Nice, trans. Cambridge: Cambridge University Press.

1979 Algeria 1960. R. Nice, trans. Cambridge: Cambridge University Press.

Buchler, I. R.

1963 A Note on Nuer Residence. American Anthropologist 65:652–655.

Burr, J. M., and R. O. Collins

1995 Requiem for the Sudan: War, Drought, and Disaster Relief on the Nile. Boulder, CO: Westview Press.

Burr, Millard

1990 Khartoum's Displaced Persons: A Decade of Despair. Washington, DC: U.S. Committee for Refugees.

Burton, John W.

1974 Some Nuer Notions of Purity and Danger. Anthropos 69:517–536.

1975 A Note on Nuer Prophets. Sudan Notes and Records 46:95–107.

1978 Living with the Dead: Aspects of the Afterlife in Nuer and Dinka Cosmology. Cambridge Anthropology 3:38–60.

1981a	Ethnicity on the Hoof: On the Economics of Nuer Identity. Ethnology 20:157–162.
1981b	God's Ants: A Study of Atuot Religion. St. Augustin, Germany: Anthropos Institute.
1981c	Independence and the Status of Nilotic Women. Africa Today 28:54–60.
1981d	The Wave Is My Mother's Husband: A Piscatorial Theme in Pastoral Nilotic Ethnology. Cahiers d'études africaines 21:459–477.
1982	Nilotic Women: A Diachronic Perspective. Journal of Modern African Studies 20:467–491.
1983a	Answers and Questions: Evans-Pritchard on Nuer Religion. Journal of Religion in Africa 14:167–186.
1983b	Same Time, Same Space: Observations on the Morality of Kinship in Pastoral Nilotic Societies. Ethnology 22:109–119.
1984	Christians, Colonists, and Conversion: A View from the Nilotic Sudan. Ethnology 23:349–369.
1987	A Nilotic World: The Atuot-Speaking Peoples of the Southern Sudan. New York: Greenwood Press.

Butt, A.

1952	The Nilotes of the Anglo-Egyptian Sudan and Uganda. London: Oxford University Press (for the International African Institute).

Buxton, J.

1958	The Significance of Bridewealth and the Levirate among the Nilotic and Nilo-Hamitic Peoples of Southern Sudan. The Anti-Slavery Reporter (ser. 6) 11(3):66–75.

Clifford, James

1988	The Predicament of Culture: Twentieth-century Ethnography, Literature, and Art. Cambridge, MA: Harvard University Press.

Clifford, James, and George Marcus, eds.

1986	Writing Culture: The Poetics and Politics of Ethnography. Berkeley: University of California Press.

Collins, Robert O.

1971	Land beyond the Rivers: The Southern Sudan, 1898–1918. New Haven: Yale University Press.
1983a	Pounds and Piasters: The Beginning of Economic Development in the Southern Sudan. Northeast African Studies 5:39–65.
1983b	Shadows in the Grass: Britain in the Southern Sudan, 1918–1956. New Haven: Yale University Press.
1990	The Waters of the Nile: Hydropolitics and the Jonglei Canal, 1900–1988. Oxford: Clarendon Press.

Collins, Robert O., and Francis Mading Deng, eds.

1984	The British in the Sudan, 1898–1956: The Sweetness and the Sorrow. London: Macmillan.

Comaroff, J.

1985	Body of Power, Spirit of Resistance: The Culture and History of a South African People. Chicago: University of Chicago Press.

Comaroff, J., and J. L. Comaroff
1990   Goodly Beasts, Beastly Goods: Cattle and Commodities in a South African Context. American Ethnologist 17:195–216.
1991   Of Revelation and Revolution: Christianity, Colonialism, and Consciousness in South Africa. Volume 1. Chicago: University of Chicago Press.

Coriat, P.
1993   Governing the Nuer: Documents by Percy Coriat on Nuer History and Ethnography, 1922–1931. Edited and introduced by D. Johnson. Journal of the Anthropological Society of Oxford: Occasional Papers 9. Oxford: JASO.

Crazzolara, J. P.
1932   Die Gar-Zeremonie bie den Nuer. Africa 5:28–39.
1933   Outlines of a Nuer Grammar. Modling bei Wein: Studia Instituti Anthropos.
1934   Die Bedeutung des Rindes bei den Nuer. Africa 7:300–321.
1953   Zur Gesellschaft und Religion der Nuer. (Unpublished translation available at Oxford University.) Modling bei Wein: Studia Instituti Anthropos.

Daly, M. W.
1986   Empire on the Nile: The Anglo-Egyptian Sudan, 1898–1934. Cambridge: Cambridge University Press.
1991   Imperial Sudan: The Anglo-Egyptian Condominium, 1934–1956. Cambridge: Cambridge University Press.

Daly, M. W., and Ahmad Alawad Sikainga, eds.
1993   Civil War in the Sudan. London: British Academic Press.

Deng, Francis Mading
1971   Tradition and Modernization: A Challenge for Law among the Dinka of Sudan. New Haven: Yale University Press.
1984[1972]   The Dinka of the Sudan. Prospect Heights, IL: Waveland.
1986   The Man Called Deng Majok: A Biography of Power, Polygyny, and Change. New Haven: Yale University Press.
1988   Dinka Response to Christianity: The Pursuit of Well-Being in a Developing Society. In Vernacular Christianity: Essays in the Social Anthropology of Religion. W. James and D. Johnson, eds. Pp. 157–169. Oxford: Journal of the Anthropological Society of Oxford.

Deng, Francis Mading, and M. W. Daly
1989   Bonds of Silk: The Human Factor in the British Administration of Sudan. East Lansing, MI: Michigan State University Press.

Deng, Francis Mading, and Larry Minear, eds.
1992   The Challenges of Famine Relief: Emergency Operations in Sudan. Washington, DC: Brookings Institute.

De Waal, Alex
1989   Famine That Kills: Darfur, Sudan, 1984–1985. Oxford: Clarendon Press.
1993a   Some Comments on Militias in Contemporary Sudan. In Civil War

in the Sudan. M. W. Daly and Ahmed Alawad Sikainga, eds. Pp. 142–156. London: British Academic Press.

1993b   Starving out the South, 1984–89. *In* Civil War in the Sudan. M. W. Daly and Ahmad Alawad Sikainga, eds. Pp. 157–186. London: British Academic Press.

Digerness, Olav

1978   Appearance and Reality in the Southern Sudan: A Study of the British Administration of the Nuer, 1900–1930. Major Thesis in History for the Higher Degree, University of Bergen, Norway.

Donham, Donald, and Wendy James, eds.

1986   The Southern Marshes of Imperial Ethiopia: Essays on History and Social Anthropology. New York: Cambridge University Press.

Doornbos, Martin, Lionel Cliffe, Abdel Ghaffar M. Ahmed, and John Markakis, eds.

1992   Beyond Conflict in the Horn: The Prospects for Peace, Recovery and Development in Ethiopia, Somalia and the Sudan. The Hague: Institute of Social Studies.

Duany, Wal

1992   Neither Palaces nor Prisons: The Constitution of Order among the Nuer. Ph.D. dissertation, Department of Political Science and School of Public and Environmental Affairs, Indiana University.

Evans, T. M. S.

1978   Leopard Skins and Paper Tigers: "Choice" and "Social Structure" in *The Nuer*. Man (n.s.) 13:100–115.

1982   Two Concepts of "Society as a Moral System": Evans-Pritchard's Heterodoxy. Man (n.s.) 17:205–218.

1983   Mind, Logic, and the Efficacy of the Nuer Incest Prohibition. Man (n.s.) 18:111–133.

1984   The Paradox of Nuer Feud and the Leopard-skin Chief: A "Creative" Solution to the Prisoner's Dilemma. American Ethnologist 12:84–102.

Evans-Pritchard, Edward E.

1933   The Nuer: Tribe and Clan (Part I). Sudan Notes and Records 16:1–53.

1934   The Nuer: Tribe and Clan (Part II). Sudan Notes and Records 17:1–57.

1935   The Nuer Tribe and Clan (Part III). Sudan Notes and Records 18:37–87.

1936a   Customs and Beliefs Relating to Twins among the Nilotic Nuer. Uganda Journal 3(3):230–238.

1936b   Daily Life of the Nuer in Dry Season Camps. *In* Custom in King: Essays Presented to R. R. Marett. L. H. D. Buxton, ed. Pp. 291–302. London: Hutchinson.

1936c   The Nuer: Age-Sets. Sudan Notes and Records 19:233–271.

1937   Economic Life of the Nuer (Part I). Sudan Notes and Records 20:209–245.

1938a   Economic Life of the Nuer (Part II). Sudan Notes and Records 21:31–77.

1938b   Some Aspects of Marriage and the Family among the Nuer. Zeitschrift für vergleichend Rechtswissenschaft 42:306–392.

1939	Nuer Time-Reckoning. Africa 12:189–216.
1940a	The Nuer: A Description of the Modes of Livelihood and Political Institutions of a Nilotic People. Oxford: Clarendon Press.
1940b	The Nuer of the Southern Sudan. *In* African Political Systems. M. Fortes and E. E. Evans-Pritchard, eds. Pp. 272–296. London: Oxford University Press.
1945	Some Aspects of Marriage and the Family among the Nuer. Lusaka: Rhodes-Livingston Institute.
1946	Nuer Bridewealth. Africa 16:247–257.
1947a	Bridewealth among the Nuer. African Studies 6:181–188.
1947b	A Note on Courtship among the Nuer. Sudan Notes and Records 28:115–126.
1948a	A Note on Affinity Relations among the Nuer. Man 48:3–5.
1948b	Nuer Marriage Ceremonies. Africa 18:29–40.
1948c	Nuer Modes of Address. Uganda Journal 12:166–171.
1949a	Burial and Mortuary Rites of the Nuer. African Affairs 48:56–63.
1949b	The Nuer *Col Wic*. Man 49:7–9.
1949c	Nuer Curses and Ghostly Vengeance. Africa 19:288–292.
1949d	Nuer Rules of Exogamy and Incest. *In* Social Structure. M. Fortes, ed. Pp. 85–103. Cambridge: Cambridge University Press.
1949e	Nuer Totemism. Annali Lateranensi 13:225–248.
1949f	Two Nuer Ritual Concepts. Man 49:74–76.
1950	The Nuer Family. Sudan Notes and Records 31:21–42.
1951a	Kinship and Local Community among the Nuer. *In* African Systems of Kinship and Marriage. A. R. Radcliffe-Brown and D. Forde, eds. Pp. 360–391. London: Oxford University Press.
1951b	Kinship and Marriage among the Nuer. Oxford: Clarendon Press.
1951c	Some Features and Forms of Nuer Sacrifice. Africa 21:112–121.
1952a	A Note on Nuer Prayers. Man 52:99–102.
1952b	Some Features of Nuer Religion. Journal of the Royal Anthropological Institute 81(1–2):1–13.
1953a	Bridewealth and the Stability of Marriage. Man 53:80.
1953b	The Nuer Conception of Spirit and Its Relation to the Social Order. American Anthropologist 55:201–214.
1953c	Nuer Spear Symbolism. Anthropological Quarterly 26:1–19.
1953d	The Nuer Spirits of the Air. Annali Lateranensi 17:55–82.
1953e	The Sacrificial Role of Cattle among the Nuer. Africa 22:181–198.
1954a	The Meaning of Sacrifice among the Nuer. Journal of the Royal Anthropological Institute 84:21–33.
1954b	A Problem of Nuer Religious Thought. Sociologus 4:23–41.
1956	Nuer Religion. Oxford: Clarendon Press.
1966	Twins, Birds, and Vegetables. Man (n.s.) 1:398.
1970	Comment on Littlejohn. Bijdragen tot de Taal-, Land- en Volkenkunde 126:109–113.
1976	Some Reminiscences and Reflections on Fieldwork. *In* Witchcraft, Oracles, and Magic among the Azande. Abridged with an introduction by Eva Gillies. Pp. 240–254. Oxford: Clarendon Press.

Fabian, Johannes
    1983   Time and the Other: How Anthropology Makes Its Object. New York: Columbia University Press.

Fardon, Richard, ed.
    1990   Localizing Strategies: Regional Traditions of Ethnographic Writing. Edinburgh: Scottish Academic Press.

Feierman, Steven
    1990   Peasant Intellectuals: Anthropology and History in Tanzania. Madison: University of Wisconsin Press.

Ferguson, James
    1985   The Bovine Mystique. Man (n.s.) 20:647–674.

Fergusson, V. H.
    1921   The Nuong Nuer. Sudan Notes and Records 4:146–155.
    1923   Mattiang Gok Witchcraft. Sudan Notes and Records 26:319–328.
    1924   Nuer Beast Tales. Sudan Notes and Records 7:106–112.
    1930   The Story of Fergie Bey. London: Macmillan.

Firth, Raymond
    1966   Twins, Birds, and Vegetables: Problems of Identification in Primitive Religious Thought. Man (n.s.) 1:1–17.

Forbes, Lesley
    1985   The Sudan Archive of the University of Durham. In Modernization in the Sudan. M. W. Daly, ed. Pp. 161–170. New York: Lilian Barber Press.

Foucault, Michel
    1978   The History of Sexuality, Vol. 1. R. Hurley, trans. New York: Vintage Books.
    1985a   The Care of the Self. The History of Sexuality, Vol. 3. R. Hurley, trans. New York: Vintage Books.
    1985b   The Use of Pleasure. The History of Sexuality, Vol. 2. R. Hurley, trans. New York: Vintage Books.

Galaty, J., and P. Bonte, eds.
    1991   Herders, Warriors, and Traders: Pastoralism in Africa. Boulder: Westview Press.

Garang, John
    1987   John Garang Speaks. M. Khalid, ed. London: Kegan Paul International.

Geertz, Clifford
    1988   Works and Lives: The Anthropologist as Author. Stanford: Stanford University Press.

Glickman, Maurice
    1971   Kinship and Credit among the Nuer. Africa 41:306–319.
    1972   The Nuer and the Dinka: A Further Note. Man (n.s.) 7:586–594.
    1974   The Dinka and the Nuer. Man (n.s.) 9:141–142.
    1977   Nuer and Dinka. Man (n.s.) 12:342.

Gluckman, Max
    1955   The Peace in the Feud. In Custom and Conflict in Africa. Pp. 1–26. Oxford: Blackwell.

Goodfriend, Douglas
    1982   Cybernetics of Nuer Society. Eastern Anthropologist (Lucknow) 35:1–24.

Gough, Kathleen
    1971   Nuer Kinship: A Re-examination. *In* The Translation of Culture: Essays to E. E. Evans-Pritchard. T. O. Beidelman, ed. Pp. 79–121. London: Tavistock Publications.

Gourlay, K. A.
    1972   The Ox and Nuer Identification. Man (n.s.) 7:244–253.

Grandin, Nicole
    1982   Le Soudan nilotique et l'administration britannique (1898–1956). Leiden: Brill.

Greuel, P. J.
    1971   The Leopard-Skin Chief: An Examination of Political Power among the Nuer. American Anthropologist 73:1,115–1,120.

Haight, B.
    1972   A Note on the Leopard-Skin Chief. American Anthropologist 74:1,313–1,318.

Hayley, Audrey
    1968   Symbolic Equations: The Ox and the Cucumber. Man (n.s.) 3:262–271.

Heusch, Luc de
    1985   Sacrifice in Africa: A Structuralist Approach. Linda O'Brien and Alice Morton, trans. Bloomington: Indiana University Press.

Holy, Ladislav
    1979a   Nuer Politics. *In* Segmentary Lineage Systems Reconsidered. L. Holy, ed. Pp. 23–48. The Queen's University Papers in Social Anthropology 4. Belfast: Department of Social Anthropology, the Queen's University.
    1979b   The Segmentary Lineage Structure and Its Existential Status. *In* Segmentary Lineage Systems Reconsidered. L. Holy, ed. Pp. 1–22. The Queen's University Papers in Social Anthropology 4. Belfast: Department of Social Anthropology, the Queen's University.
    1987   Comparative Anthropology. Oxford: Basil Blackwell.

Howell, Paul P.
    1945a   A Note on Elephants and Elephant Hunting among the Nuer. Sudan Notes and Records 26:95–104.
    1945b   The Zeraf Hills. Sudan Notes and Records 26:319–328.
    1947   On the Value of Iron among the Nuer. Man 47:131–134.
    1948a   The Age-set System and the Institution of the "Nak" among the Nuer. Sudan Notes and Records 29:173–181.
    1948b   Pyramids in the Upper Nile Region. Man 48:52–53.
    1952   Some Observations on the Distribution of Bloodwealth among the Nuer. Man (n.s.) 52:19–21.
    1953a   Some Observations on Divorce among the Nuer. Journal of the Royal Anthropological Institute 83:136–146.

1953b Some Observations on "Earthly Spirits" among the Nuer. Man 53 (n.s.):85–88.

1954 A Manual of Nuer Law. London: Oxford University Press.

1983 The Impact of the Jonglei Canal in the Sudan. Geographical Journal 149(3):286–300.

1988 Conclusions. In The Jonglei Canal Project: Impact and Local Opportunity. P. P. Howell et al., eds. Pp. 449–469. Cambridge: Cambridge University Press.

Howell, Paul P., and B. A. Lewis

1947 Nuer Ghouls: A Form of Witchcraft. Sudan Notes and Records 28:157–168.

Howell, Paul P., M. Lock, and S. Cobb, eds.

1988 The Jonglei Canal Project: Impact and Local Opportunity. Cambridge: Cambridge University Press.

Huffman, Ray

1929 Nuer-English Dictionary. Berlin: Dietrich Reimer.

1931a English-Nuer Dictionary. London: Oxford University Press.

1931b Nuer Customs and Folklore. London: Oxford University Press.

Hutchinson, Sharon

1980 Relations between the Sexes among the Nuer: 1930. Africa 50:371–387.

1985 Changing Concepts of Incest among the Nuer. American Ethnologist 12:625–641.

1990 Rising Divorce among the Nuer, 1936–1983. Man (n.s.) 25:393–411.

1991 War through the Eyes of the Dispossessed: Three Stories of Survival. Disasters 15:166–171.

1992a The Cattle of Money and the Cattle of Girls among the Nuer, 1930–1983. American Ethnologist 19:294–316.

1992b "Dangerous to Eat": Rethinking Pollution States among the Nuer of Sudan. Africa 62:490–504.

1994 On The Nuer Conquest. Current Anthropology 35:643–651.

Ibrahim, A. M.

1984 The Environmental Impact of the Jonglei Canal in the Sudan. In The Nile Valley Countries: Continuity and Change. Vol. 2. M. O. Beshir, ed. Pp. 18–30. Khartoum: University of Khartoum, Institute of African and Asian Studies.

Jackson, H. C.

1923 The Nuer of the Upper Nile Province. Sudan Notes and Records 6(1):59–107; 6(2):123–189.

Jal, Gabriel Giet

1987 The History of the Jikany Nuer before 1920. Ph.D. dissertation, History Department, School of Oriental and African Studies, University of London.

James, Wendy

1979 'Kwanim Pa: The Making of the Uduk People: An Ethnographic Study of Survival on the Sudan-Ethiopian Borderlands. Oxford: Clarendon Press.

1988 The Listening Ebony: Moral Knowledge, Religion, and Power among the Uduk of Sudan. Oxford: Oxford University Press.

1990a Introduction to paperback edition of E. E. Evans-Pritchard, *Kinship and Marriage among the Nuer*. Oxford: Clarendon Press.

1990b Kings and Commoners: The Ethnographic Imagination in Sudan and Ethiopia. *In* Localizing Strategies: Regional Traditions of Ethnographic Writing. R. Fardon, ed. Pp. 96–136. Washington, DC: Smithsonian Institution Press.

1994 War and "Ethnic Visibility": The Uduk on the Sudan-Ethiopian Border. *In* Ethnicity and Conflict in the Horn of Africa. Katsuyoshi Fukui and John Markakis, eds. Pp. 140–164. London: James Currey.

James, Wendy, and Douglas Johnson, eds.

1988 Vernacular Christianity: Essays in Social Anthropology of Religion. Oxford: Journal of the Anthropological Society of Oxford.

Johnson, Douglas

1979 Colonial Policy and Prophets: The "Nuer-Settlement," 1929–30. Journal of the Anthropological Society of Oxford 10:1–20.

1980 History and Prophecy among the Nuer of Southern Sudan. Ph.D. dissertation, Department of History, University of California, Los Angeles.

1981a The Fighting Nuer: Primary Sources and the Origin of a Stereotype. Africa 51:508–527.

1981b Percy Coriat on the Nuer. Journal of the Anthropological Society of Oxford 12:199–206.

1982a Evans-Pritchard, the Nuer, and the Sudan Political Service. African Affairs 81:231–246.

1982b Ngundeng and the "Turuk": Two Narratives Compared. History in Africa 9:119–139.

1982c Tribal Boundaries and Border Wars: Nuer-Dinka Relations in the Sobat and Zaraf Valleys. Journal of African History 9:183–203.

1985 Foretelling Peace and War: Modern Interpretations of Ngundeng's Prophecies in the Southern Sudan. *In* Modernization in the Sudan. M. W. Daly, ed. Pp. 121–134. New York: Lilian Barber Press.

1986a The Historical Approach to the Study of Societies and Their Environment in the Eastern Upper Nile Plains. Cahiers d'études africaines 26(1–2):131–144.

1986b Judicial Regulations and Administrative Control: Customary Law and the Nuer, 1898–1954. Journal of African History 27:59–78.

1986c On the Nilotic Frontier: Imperial Ethiopia in the Southern Sudan, 1898–1936. *In* The Southern Marshes of Imperial Ethiopia: Essays in History and Social Anthropology. D. Donham and W. James, eds. Pp. 215–245. Cambridge: Cambridge University Press.

1988a Adaptation to Floods in the Jonglei Area: An Historical Analysis. *In* The Ecology of Survival: Case Studies from Northeast African History. D. Johnson and D. M. Anderson, eds. Pp. 173–192. Boulder, CO: Westview Press.

1988b	The Southern Sudan. Minority Rights Group Report 78. London: London Minority Rights Group.
1989	Enforcing Separate Identities in the Southern Sudan: The Case of the Nilotes of the Upper Nile. *In* Les Ethnies ont une histoire. J.-P. Chrétien and G. Prunier, eds. Pp. 234–245. Paris: Karthala.
1992	On Disciples and Magicians: Diversification of Spiritual Power among the Nuer during the Colonial Era. Journal of Religion in Africa 22(1):2–22.
1994	Nuer Prophets: A History of Prophecy from the Upper Nile. Oxford: Oxford University Press.

Johnson, Douglas, and Gerard Prunier

1993	The Foundation and Expansion of the Sudan People's Liberation Army. *In* Civil War in the Sudan. M. W. Daly and Ahmad Alawad Sikainga, eds. Pp. 117–141. London: British Academic Press.

Jonglei Investigation Team

1954	The Equatorial Nile Project and Its Effects in the Anglo-Egyptian Sudan. 4 vol. London: Sudan Government Printer.

Kahlid, Mansour

1985	Nimeiri and the Revolution of Dis-May. London: Kegan Paul International.
1990	The Government They Deserve: The Role of the Elite in Sudan's Political Evolution. London: Kegan Paul International.

Kameir, El Wathig

1980	Workers in an Urban Situation: A Comparative Study of Factory Workers and Building Site Labourers in Khartoum. Ph.D. dissertation, Anthropology Department, University of Hull.

Kameir, El Wathig, and Z. B. El-Bakri

1985	Unequal Participation of Migrant Labour in Wage Employment. *In* Population and Development Projects in Africa. J. I. Clarke et al., eds. Pp. 53–67. Cambridge: Cambridge University Press.

Karp, I., and K. Maynard

1983	Reading *The Nuer*. Current Anthropology 24:481–503.

Keen, David

1994	The Benefits of Famine: A Political Economy of Famine and Relief in Southwestern Sudan, 1983–1989. Princeton: Princeton University Press.

Kelly, Raymond C.

1983	A Note on Nuer Segmentary Organization. American Anthropologist 85:905–906.
1985	The Nuer Conquest: The Structure and Development of an Expansionist System. Ann Arbor: University of Michigan Press.

Kiggen, J.

1948	Nuer-English Dictionary. London: St. Joseph's Society for Foreign Missions, Mill Hill.

Kingdon, F. D.

1945	The Western Nuer Patrol, 1927–1928. Sudan Notes and Records 26:171–178.

Kok, Peter Nyot

1992   Adding Fuel to the Conflict: Oil, War, and Peace in Sudan: Pros-
            pects for Peace, Recovery, and Development in Ethiopia and the Su-
            dan. *In* Beyond Conflict in the Horn. M. Doornbos, L. Cliffe, Abdel
            Ghaffar M. Ahmed, and J. Markakis, eds. Pp. 104–112. The Hague:
            Institute of Social Studies.

Kurimoto, Eisei

1992a   An Ethnography of "Bitterness": Cucumber and Sacrifice Recon-
            sidered. Journal of Religions in Africa 22(1):47–65.

1992b   Natives and Outsiders: The Historical Experience of the Anywaa of
            Western Ethiopia. Journal of Asian and African Studies (Tokyo)
            43:1–43.

1993   "The Dergue Brought the Dinka and Nuer on Us": Effects of the
            Sudanese Civil War on the Ethiopian Anywaa (Anuak). Paper pre-
            sented at the Workshop on the Sudanese Civil War, Oxford Uni-
            versity.

1994a   Civil War and Regional Conflicts: The Pari and Their Neighbours
            in South-eastern Sudan. *In* Ethnicity and Conflict in the Horn of
            Africa. Katsuyoshi Fukui and John Markakis, eds. Pp. 95–111. Lon-
            don: John Currey.

1994b   Inter-Ethnic Relations of the Anywaa (Anuak) in Western Ethiopia:
            With Special Reference to the Majangir. *In* New Trends in Ethiopian
            Studies. Papers of the Twelfth International Conference of Ethio-
            pian Studies, Vol. 2. Pp. 899–911. Lawrenceville, NJ: Red Sea Press.

Lako, G. T.

1985   The Impact of the Jonglei Scheme on the Economy of the Dinka.
            African Affairs 84(334):15–38.

Lan, David

1985   Guns and Rain: Guerrillas and Spirit Mediums in Zimbabwe.
            Berkeley: University of California Press.

Lewis, B. A.

1951   Nuer Spokesmen: A Note on the Institution of Ruic. Sudan Notes
            and Records 32:77–84.

Lienhardt, R. Godfrey

1961   Divinity and Experience: The Religion of the Dinka. Oxford:
            Clarendon Press.

1963   Dinka Representations of the Relations between the Sexes. *In* Stud-
            ies of Kinship and Marriage. Royal Anthropological Institute Oc-
            casional Paper No. 16. I. Shapera, ed. Pp. 79–92. London: Royal An-
            thropological Institute.

1975   Getting Your Own Back: Themes in Nilotic Myth. *In* Studies in
            Social Anthropology: Essays in Memory of Evans-Pritchard by His
            Former Oxford Colleagues. J. Beattie and R. G. Lienhardt, eds. Ox-
            ford: Clarendon Press.

1981   The Sudan—Aspects of the South: Government among Some of the
            Nilotic Peoples, 1947–1952. Journal of the Anthropological Society
            of Oxford 12(3):185–198.

1982   The Dinka and Catholicism. *In* Religious Organization and Religious Experience. J. Davis, ed. Pp. 81–95. London: Academic Press.

1985   Self: Public and Private: Some African Representations. *In* The Category of the Person: Anthropology, Philosophy, History. M. Carrithers et al., eds. Pp. 141–155. Cambridge: Cambridge University Press.

Littlejohn, J.

1970   Twins, Birds, etc. Bijdragen tot de Taal-, Land- en Volkenkunde 126:91–114.

McCorkle, C. M., and E. Mathias-Mundy

1991   Ethnoveterinary Medicine in Africa. Africa 62(1):59–93.

MacDermott, B. H.

1972   The Cult of the Sacred Spear: The Story of the Nuer Tribe in Ethiopia. London: Robert Hale.

Mack, John, and Peter Robertshaw

1982   Culture History in the Southern Sudan: Archaeology, Linguistics, and Ethnohistory. Nairobi: British Institute in Eastern Africa.

Majok, D. D.

1984   British Religious and Educational Policy: The Case of Bahr-al-Ghazal. *In* Southern Sudan: Regionalism and Religion. M. O. Beshir, ed. Pp. 224–240. Khartoum: University of Khartoum, Graduate College.

Makec, John Wuol

1988   The Customary Law of the Dinka People of Sudan in Comparison with Aspects of Western and Islamic Laws. London: Afroworld.

Malwal, Bona

1981   People and Power in Sudan: The Struggle for National Stability. London: Ithaca Press.

1985   The Sudan: A Second Challenge to Nationhood. New York: Thornton Books.

Marcus, George, and D. Cushman

1982   Ethnographies as Texts. Annual Review of Anthropology 11:25–69.

Marcus, George, and M. Fischer

1986   Anthropology as Cultural Critique: An Experimental Moment in the Human Sciences. Chicago: University of Chicago Press.

Marx, Karl

1967[1867]   Capital: A Critique of Political Economy. Vol. 1. New York: International Publishers.

Mawson, Andrew

1984   Southern Sudan: A Growing Conflict. World Today 40(12):520–527.

1989   The Triumph of Life: Political Dispute and Religious Ceremonial among the Agar Dinka of the Southern Sudan. Ph.D. dissertation, Anthropology Department, Cambridge University.

Mawut, L. L.

1986   The Southern Sudan: Why Back to Arms? Khartoum: St. George Press.

Middle East Report and Information Project
    1985   Report from the South: Khartoum's Greatest Challenge. MERIP
              Reports 135:11–18.
Middleton, John, and David Tait, eds.
    1958   Tribes without Rulers: Studies in African Segmentary Systems.
              New York: Humanities Press.
Milner, G. B.
    1969   Siamese Twins, Birds, and the Double Helix. Man (n.s.) 4:5–23.
Minear, Larry
    1991   Humanitarianism under Siege: A Critical Review of Operation
              Lifeline Sudan. Trenton, NJ: Red Sea Press.
Moore, Sally Falk
    1972   Legal Liability and Evolutionary Interpretation: Some Aspects of
              Strict Liability, Self-help, and Collective Responsibility. *In* The Al-
              location of Responsibility. M. Gluckman, ed. Pp. 51–108. Manches-
              ter: University of Manchester Press.
    1986   Social Facts and Fabrications: "Customary" Law on Kilimanjaro,
              1880–1980. Cambridge: Cambridge University Press.
Murray, Colin
    1981   Families Divided: The Impact of Migrant Labour in Lesotho. New
              York: Cambridge University Press.
Newcomer, P. J.
    1972   The Nuer Are Dinka: An Essay on Origins and Environmental De-
              terminism. Man (n.s.) 7:5–11.
    1973   The Nuer and the Dinka. Man (n.s.) 8:109–110.
Niblock, T.
    1987   Class and Power in the Sudan: The Dynamics of Sudanese Politics,
              1898–1985. London: Macmillan.
Nyong'o, Peter Anyang'
    1992   Accountability and Civil Society. *In* Beyond Conflict in the Horn:
              Prospects for Peace, Recovery, and Development in Ethiopia and
              the Sudan. M. Doornbor et al., eds. The Hague: Institute of Social
              Studies.
Okamura, J. Y.
    1972   Kinship and Credit among the Nuer: A Comment. (With Rejoinder
              by M. Glickman.) Africa 42:338–341.
Osman, Abdelwahab A. M.
    1989   The Political and Ideological Development of the Muslim Brother-
              hood in Sudan, 1945–1986. Ph.D. dissertation, Political Science De-
              partment, University of Reading, England.
Parkin, David
    1980   Kind Bridewealth and Hard Cash: Eventing a Structure. *In* The
              Meaning of Marriage Payments. J. L. Comaroff, ed. Pp. 197–220.
              New York: Academic Press.
Parry, J., and M. Block, eds.
    1989   Money and the Morality of Exchange. Cambridge: Cambridge Uni-
              versity Press.

Passmore-Sanderson, L. M.
1962   Educational Development in the Southern Sudan: 1900–1948. Su-
            dan Notes and Records 43:105–117.
1980   Education in the Southern Sudan: The Impact of Government-
            Missionary-Southern Sudanese Relationships upon the Develop-
            ment of Education during the Condominium Period, 1898–1956.
            African Affairs 79:157–169.
Passmore-Sanderson, L. M., and G. N. Sanderson
1981   Education, Religion, and Politics in Southern Sudan, 1899–1964.
            London: Ithaca Press.
Peace in Sudan Group
1990   War in Sudan: An Analysis of Conflict. London: Peace in Sudan
            Group.
Pocock, David
1974   Nuer Religion: A Supplemental View. Journal of the Anthropologi-
            cal Society of Oxford 5:69–79.
Pojo do Rego, Antonio Carlos
1980   Nuer e Burundi: Autoridade e poder em duer sociedades africanas.
            Africa (Sao Paulo) 3:56–72.
Prunier, G.
1989   Le sud-Soudan depuis l'indépendance (1956–1989). In Le Soudan
            Contemporain. M. Lavergne, ed. Paris: Karthala.
Ranger, Terence
1985   Peasant Consciousness and Guerrilla War in Zimbabwe: A Com-
            parative Study. London: James Currey.
Richards, A. I.
1941   A Problem of Anthropological Approach. Bantu Studies 15:45–52.
Riches, D.
1973   The Nuer and the Dinka. Man (n.s.) 8:307–308.
Riesman, Paul
1977   Freedom in Fulani Social Life: An Introspective Ethnography. Chi-
            cago: University of Chicago Press.
Rosaldo, Renato
1986   From the Door of His Tent: The Fieldworker and the Inquistor. In
            Writing Culture. J. Clifford and G. Marcus, eds. Pp. 77–97. Berkeley:
            University of California Press.
Roussel, P. J.
n.d.   Some of the Difficulties Facing the Establishment of Local Govern-
            ment among the Nuer People of the Sudan, with Special Reference
            to the Zeraf Island Rual District Council. Manuscript (author's
            files).
Ryle, John
1989a   Displaced Southern Sudanese in Northern Sudan, with Special Ref-
            erence to Southern Kordofan and Darfur. London: Save the Chil-
            dren Fund.
1989b   The Road to Abyei. Granta 26:41–104.
1991   The Meaning of Survival for the Dinka of Sudan. Manuscript.

1992 The "Paired Settlements" in Southern Darfur, Sudan, 1988–1990. Manuscript.

Sacks, Karen
1979 Causality and Chance on the Upper Nile. American Ethnologist 6:437–448.

Sahlins, Marshall
1961 The Segmentary Lineage: An Organization of Predatory Expansion. American Anthropologist 63:322–345.

Salzman, P. C.
1978 Does Complementary Opposition Exist? American Anthropologist 80:53–70.

Sansom, Basil
1976 A Signal Transaction and Its Currency. *In* Transaction and Meaning. B. Kapferer, ed. Pp. 143–161. Philadelphia: Institute for the Study of Human Issues.

Schneider, David
1953 A Note on Bridewealth and the Stability of Marriage. Man 53:55–57.

Sconyers, David J.
1978 British Policy and Mission Education in the Southern Sudan: 1928–1946. Ph.D. dissertation, History Department, University of Pennsylvania.

Scott, Phillipa
1985 The Sudan People's Liberation Movement (SPLM) and Liberation Army (SPLA). Review of African Political Economy 33:69–82.

Scroggins, Deborah
 The Sunday Journal of the Atlantic Constitution, March 10, 1991.

Seligman, C. G., and B. Z. Seligman
1932 Pagan Tribes of the Nilotic Sudan. London: G. Routledge and Sons.

Shipton, Parker
1989 Bitter Money: Cultural Economy and Some African Meanings of Forbidden Commodities. Washington, DC: American Anthropological Association.

Simmel, Georg
1978[1900] The Philosophy of Money. T. Bottomore and D. Frisby, trans. London: Routledge and Kegan Paul.

Singer, Alice
1973 Marriage Payments and the Exchange of People. Man (n.s.) 8:80–92.

Soule, M.
1931 Some Nuer Terms in Relation to the Human Body. Nasir, Sudan: American Mission.

1932 Some Nuer Diseases and Their Remedies. Nasir, Sudan: American Mission.

Southall, A.
1976 Nuer and Dinka Are People: Ecology, Ethnicity, and Logical Possibility. Man (n.s.) 11:463–491.

1986 The Illusion of *Nath* Agnation. Ethnology 25:1–20.

Southern Development Investigation Team

    1955   Natural Resources and Development Potential in the Southern Provinces of the Sudan: A Preliminary Report. London: Sudan Government Printer.

Svoboda, Terese

    1985   Cleaned the Crocodile's Teeth: Nuer Song. Greenfield Center, NY: Greenfield Press.

Taussig, Michael

    1980   The Devil and Commodity Fetishism in South America. Chapel Hill: University of North Carolina Press.

    1987   Shamanism, Colonialism, and the Wild Man: A Study in Terror and Healing. Chicago: University of Chicago Press.

Turner, Terence

    1986   Production, Exploitation, and Social Consciousness in the "Peripheral Situation." Social Analysis 19:91–115.

Twose, N., and B. Pogrund, eds.

    1988   War Wounds: Development Costs of Conflict in Southern Sudan. London: Panos Institute.

Vandevort, Eleanor

    1968   A Leopard Tamed: The Story of an African Pastor, His People, and His Problems. London: Hodder and Stoughton.

Verdon, Michel

    1982   Where Have All the Lineages Gone? Cattle and Descent among the Nuer. American Anthropologist 84:566–579.

Voll, J. O., and S. Potts Voll

    1985   The Sudan: Unity and Diversity in a Multicultural State. Boulder, CO: Westview Press.

Vossen, Rainer, and Marianne Bechhaus-Gerst, eds.

    1983   Nilotic Studies: Proceedings of the International Symposium on Language and History of the Nilotic Peoples, Cologne, January 2–6, 1982. Berlin: Dietrich Reimer.

Wakoson, Elias Nyamlell

    1984   The Origin and Development of the Anya-Nya Movement, 1955–1972. In Southern Sudan: Regionalism and Religion. M. O. Beshir, ed. Pp. 127–204. Khartoum: University of Khartoum, Graduate College.

Waterbury, John

    1979   Hydropolitics of the Nile Valley. Syracuse, NY: Syracuse University Press.

Westermann, D.

    1912   The Nuer Language. Mitteilungen des Seminars für Orientalische Sprache 15:85–141.

Woodward, Peter

    1990   Sudan, 1898–1989: The Unstable State. Boulder, CO: Lynne Rienner Publishers.

    1991   Sudan after Nimeiri. New York: Routledge.

Yar, Manasseh A.
  1988   Social and Economic Change in Western Nuer. M.A. thesis, Institute of African and Asian Studies, University of Khartoum.
Yilma, T.
  1989   Prospects for the Total Eradication of Rinderpest. Vaccine 7:484–485.
  1990   A Modern Vaccine for an Ancient Plague: Rinderpest. Biotechnology 8:1,007–1,009.

Index

Abith, Sudan, 13
Abu Gigra rifles, 111
Adam (first man), 252
Addis Ababa, Ethiopia, 113
Addis Ababa Agreement (1972), 4n, 70, 135, 146, 278
Administrative centers, 33
Adok, Sudan, 15, 228, 319, 322, 354n
Adoption, assimilation through, 260–61
Adultery, 40n, 77; and barrenness, 172; children of, 173, 178, 198, 217–18, 219, 221–22; compensation for, 218, 219, 221–22; definition of, 217n; as disqualification for chieftaincy, 275, 276–77; and divorce, 218, 219, 220, 221–22, 225–26, 227; indifference to, 217–18; litigation over, 219n, 220–22; penalization of, 217–22, 292; as religious offense, 220
Affinal kinship: exogamic limits of, 247; overlapping blood-cattle bonds of, 250–51
Africa Watch, 8n
Age: of marriage, 204; and procreative rights, 174–75; and sharing of food, 200
Age-mates, blood bonds of, 185
Age-set (ric): initiation into, 185; lack of membership in, by bull-boys, 290, 293–94, 295–96; overlapping blood-cattle bonds of, 250–51; sexual transgressions within, 242, 249n, 293; sharing of meat within, 294–95; transferral of, 53, 270–71
Agnatic kinship, 32; autonomy within, 258, 266–67; blood bonds of, 185, 188; exogamic limits of, 242–45, 267; opposition of chil-

dren of girls to fellow agnates, 257–58; overlapping blood-cattle bonds of, 250–51; procreative symmetry of, 257, 260; recognition of, with sacrificial meat, 251n; reinforcement of alliances through cattle, 174–75; tracing descent of, 170, 172–75, 232–35
Agriculture, settlement of land claims, 114
Air divinities, 306, 307, 311, 321
American Presbyterian mission school, 121 & n, 314
American University of Cairo, 32
Ancestral herd, 62 & n, 85, 257, 258, 295
Anemia, 346n
Anglo-Egyptian Condominium Government of Sudan, 3n, 21–22, 30–31 & n, 63–68, 110, 112
Anyanya I, 6n, 111n; confrontation with government, 135; incorporation into regional administration, 135–36; initiation requirement for, 291n; mobilization of Nuer by, 134; tactics of, 141 & n
Anyanya II: confrontation with government, 338; kidnapping of civilians, 13; political objectives of, 6; and unification of rebel forces, 339
Anyuak, the: defusing of ethnic tension with, 339, 341–42; expansion of Nuer against, 31, 32; gun trading by, 111; hostilities with Nuer, 298; methods of warfare with, 124, 147; Nuer assimilation of, 37, 241, 289, 331n; peace negotiations with, 356; protection by blood-wealth compensation, 129; recruitment of plantation labor among,

Photo by Glenn Reynolds

Sharon Hutchinson is currently an Associate Professor in the Department of Anthropology at the University of Wisconsin—Madison. She received her doctorate in anthropology from the University of Chicago in 1988, after which she was an Assistant Professor of Anthropology at Yale University for two years before joining the faculty at Wisconsin.

Text: 10/13 Aldus
Display: Aldus
Index: Paul Spragens
Composition: J. Jarrett Engineering
Printing and binding: Maple-Vail Manufacturing Group